Craft Capitalism

Craftsworkers and Early Industrialization in Hamilton, Ontario, 1840–1872

Many studies have concluded that the effects of early industrialization on traditional craftsworkers were largely negative. Robert B. Kristofferson demonstrates, however, that in at least one area this was not the case. *Craft Capitalism* focuses on Hamilton, Ontario, and demonstrates how the preservation of traditional work arrangements, craft mobility networks, and other aspects of craft culture ensured that craftsworkers in that city enjoyed an essentially positive introduction to industrial capitalism.

Kristofferson argues that, as former craftsworkers themselves, the majority of the city's industrial proprietors helped their younger counterparts achieve independence. Conflict rooted in capitalist class experience, while present, was not yet dominant. Furthermore, he argues, while craftsworkers' experience of the change was more informed by the residual cultures of craft than by the emergent logic of capitalism, craft culture in Hamilton was not retrogressive. Rather, this situation served as a centre of social creation in ways that built on the positive aspects of both systems.

Based on extensive archival research, this controversial and engaging study offers unique insight to the process of industrialization and class formation in Canada.

(The Canadian Social History Series)

ROBERT B. KRISTOFFERSON is an assistant professor of Contemporary Studies and History at Wilfrid Laurier University, Brantford.

Craft Capitalism

Craftsworkers and Early Industrialization in Hamilton, Ontario, 1840–1872

Robert B. Kristofferson

UNIVERSITY OF TORONTO PRESS
Toronto Buffalo London

Toronto Buffalo London
utorontopress.com

ISBN 978-0-8020-9127-7 (cloth)
ISBN 978-0-8020-9408-7 (paper)

Library and Archives Canada Cataloguing in Publication

Kristofferson, Robert, 1965–
Craft capitalism : craftworkers and early industrialization in Hamilton, Ontario, 1840–1872 / Robert B. Kristofferson.

(The Canadian social history series)
Includes bibliographical references and index.
ISBN 978-0-8020-9127-7 (bound)
ISBN 978-0-8020-9408-7 (pbk.)

1. Artisans – Ontario – Hamilton – Social conditions – 19th century.
2. Industrial revolution – Ontario – Hamilton – History – 19th century.
3. Hamilton (Ont.) – Social conditions – 19th century. I. Title.
II. Series: Canadian social history series

HD2346.C22H35 2007 338.7′20971352 C2007-900474-1

University of Toronto Press acknowledges the financial assistance to its publishing program of the Canada Council for the Arts and the Ontario Arts Council.

University of Toronto Press acknowledges the financial support for its publishing activities of the Government of Canada through the Book Publishing Industry Development Program (BPIDP).

This book has been published with the help of a grant from the Canadian Federation for the Humanities and Social Sciences, through the Aid to Scholarly Publications Programme, using funds provided by the Social Sciences and Humanities Research Council of Canada.

Contents

List of Tables

Acknowledgments

This book began as a doctoral dissertation in the Department of History at York University. I would like to thank Craig Heron, Bettina Bradbury, Susan Houston, Gordon Darroch, Gregory Kealey, Paul Craven, and Stephen Brooke for the valuable roles they played in shaping that project. In particular, Bettina Bradbury pulled me out of the clouds and onto firmer ground with her reminder that a dissertation without a title really isn't one, then casually asking if 'craft capitalism' might best describe the craftsworkers I was studying. Craig Heron's excellent supervision is surpassed only by his valued friendship. His timely, comprehensive and insightful comments helped thicken the roots of the project while also encouraging confidence to go where my own reasoning suggested. That, I believe, is the height of the supervisory art.

Archivists and librarians in Hamilton and Toronto provided important support for this project. I would especially like to thank Margaret Houghton, Brian Henley, and the numerous other staff members of the Special Collections Department of the Hamilton Public Library for their cheerful help.

Thanks are also due to the measures of friendship and intellectual stimulation provided by Lisa Chilton, Magda Fahrni, Kathryn McPherson, James Moran, Adele Perry, Steve Penfold, Gillian Poulter, and Melissa Turkstra as I grappled over time with the ideas that became this book. Special thanks to James Muir for reading sections of this book and offering important advice.

In addition to his valuable feedback, I would like to thank Gregory Kealey for his interest in making this part of the Canadian Social History Series. The publication process was made smooth by a number of people at the University of Toronto Press who helped minimize the pain of my errors, especially Charles Stuart and Frances Mundy. Len Husband has provided excellent, cheerful, and positive editorial support throughout.

At Wilfrid Laurier University I would like to thank Dean Bruce Arai for his help in providing a research term in the final stages of manuscript preparation.

My parents, Alfred B. Kristofferson and Marianne Walters have provided copious measures of encouragement and support throughout the years during which this project has taken shape. And, most of all, this project was nurtured in the environment of love, patience, and support proved by Megan Hobson and my sons Henry and Edwin.

Craft Capitalism

Introduction: Artisans, Craftsworkers, and Social Relations of Craft-Based Industrialization

In studies written over the past two or three decades, dispossession has been the story of the artisan / craftsworker / skilled worker during industrialization. Articles and monographs, mainly by practitioners of the 'new' labour history, have woven Marxist theory into a heavy empirical cloak from myriad accounts of the despoliation of the means of production from craftsworkers throughout Western industrialization.[1] Related fields of research, such as a gender history concerned with mapping the masculine contours of male craftsworkers' experience of nineteenth-century industrialization, have also by and large adopted the dispossession model as a base upon which to elaborate their own studies.[2] In Canada, the proletarianization of the craftsworker has become the received view in the historiography.[3]

Referred to variously as 'proletarianization,' the 'declension model,' the 'shop-breakdown model,' and the 'decline of the traditional small producer,' dispossession accounts outline the various and overwhelming ways traditional artisan-craftsworkers became increasingly proletarianized over the nineteenth century. They provide a collective portrait of the varied ways master artisans along with their journeymen and apprentices working in households or handicrafts workshops lost their ability to compete with more modern forms of industrial production and were forced into the ranks of an ever-expanding, increasingly urban and propertyless wage-earning workforce.

As such, the dispossession model has itself taken shape in an overall interpretation of industrialization that has greatly emphasized the general triumph of industrial capitalism. Whether concentrating on large capital outlays, elaborate managerial systems, or inherent competitive advantage, or presenting individual industrial sectors as representative of industrial development as a whole (such as textiles or primary iron and steel), these accounts typically describe the obliteration of traditional forms of production and present the rise of modern industry and the move towards mass production methods as inevitable.[4] Whether made consciously or not, this connection has led to overarching assertions that present the rise of modern industry and the decline of the craftsworker as two sides of the same equation. Witness Charles Seller's recent conclusion that the market revolution in Jacksonian America 'inaugurated an irreversible proletarianization of the mechanic class.'[5]

Challenging this orthodoxy over the past two decades has been an alternative, but somewhat fragmented, view of both industrialization and artisan-craftsworkers' place within it. The view that there was some variability to industrialization underlies this newer interpretation. Raphael Samuel was among the first to effectively challenge the received view by exposing the 'combined and uneven' nature of Great Britain's industrialization. The process of mechanization, he demonstrated, was 'neither linear nor smooth.' He found that modern industry often 'incorporated older systems of production rather than superseding them' and frequently led to both the creation of new labour-intensive jobs and a proliferation of small producers. In his view 'steam power and hand technology ... were two sides of the same coin.' Since their initial presentation to members of the British-based History Workshop, Samuel's findings have had a profound influence on accounts of industrialization in Europe, Great Britain, and North America.[6]

However, while these accounts provide a more variable and textured view of industrialization, they are still often ultimately rooted in the same teleology and determinism as the scholarship they revise. For example, in his recent survey of European work on industrialization, James Farr has noted that while many historians have opted for a more 'evolutionary' view of industrialization in recent years, 'few disagree on its eventual magnitude.' In a similar vein, Patrick O'Brien and Caglar Keydar masterfully outline a skill-intensive variety of industrialization in France that achieved levels of productivity comparable to Britain's through most of the nineteenth century. They still conclude, however, that the sublimation of the workshop by the factory was an inevitability. Even while arguing that mechanization was neither linear nor smooth, Samuel himself agrees that it was a 'process' all the same.[7] The effect of this teleology on treatments of craftsworkers is evident in the Canadian historiography, where historians have either acknowledged combined and uneven development before proceeding on to accounts of dispossession or presented it as an economic feature that forestalled but did not prevent craftsworkers' inevitable decline.[8]

Another promising line of enquiry, which escapes the determinism still evident within the combined and uneven development paradigm in crucial respects, began around the mid-1980s in the pioneering works of Michael Piore, Charles Sabel, and Jonathan Zeitlin. In an effort to inspire contemporary industrial strategies, Sabel and Zeitlin set out in a seminal article to show that there were – and indeed, are – historical alternatives to mass production. In contrast to dominant accounts, which concentrate on productive systems characterized by high throughput, specialized machines, unskilled labour, and tight administrative structures oriented towards mass markets, the authors held up to scrutiny a viable alternative of industrial production. As the flip side of mass production, they revealed the historical importance of 'flexible specialization' – a productive system characterized by a highly skilled workforce employing general-purpose (flexible) machinery to produce a diverse range of products for fragmented and unsteady markets. The authors showed ample historical (and contemporary) precedent for this system's 'possibilities for prosperity.'[9]

The 'historical alternatives' approach holds that various national and regional economies took shape differently depending on the decisions and opportunities of historical actors. These 'strategic choices' aggregated to set particular economies on differing roads to industrialization. Sabel and Zeitlin note that 'Economic agents ... do not maximize so much as they strategize. By this cryptic locution, we mean that they are at least as concerned with determining, in all senses, the context they are in as they are in pursuing what they take to be their advantage within any context.'[10] The result of this was a veritable 'mix' in national and regional forms of industrial development. In their original formulation, Sabel and Zeitlin contrasted the ubiquity of flexible industrialization in nineteenth-century France with its pervasive rigidity in North America. They presented Great Britain as something of a counterbalance between the two.[11] However, subsequent research has shown strong currents of flexible specialization existing up through much of the second wave of industrialization in the United States.[12] Philip Scranton, for example, has shown that by 1909 up to a third of that nation's total industrial output could be attributed to firms specializing in custom and batch production.[13] In light of this mounting empirical research building on their original hypothesis, Sabel and Zeitlin have modified their original proposition to account for the co-functioning of mass production and flexible specialization in changing proportions throughout Western industrialization.[14]

The historical-alternatives approach has opened up cracks in the received view of the structural dimensions of industrialization, but it also begs for a problematization of the particular social relations of production experienced by craftsworkers along these alternative paths. The dispossession model, rooted as it has been in 'narrow track' views of industrialization, clearly makes less sense as the only narrative of craftsworker experience of industrialization. However, an appreciation of the fundamentally different social relations of production that must have taken shape in such economies has not made the research agenda.

A good deal of research has attempted to wed these exceptional social actors to the familiar logic of the mass production route. In their attempts to address this issue some historians have entered into the breach by providing accounts of how these craftsworkers and artisanal small producers simply underwent a specific kind of proletarianization or experience of alienation from capitalism in this industrializing context. A number of wide-ranging studies of British and European cities and towns have pointed towards increasing power differentials rooted in such factors as a developing experience of capitalist class relations as a function of a progressive 'squeeze' put on small producers and journeymen through dependency-inducing credit and marketing arrangements, the increasing power of merchant-capitalists, the propensity of small producers to act as 'nascent capitalist masters,' and a variety of other developing arrangements. Needless to say, all these factors are presented as leading ultimately to heightened general levels of conflict rooted in these varieties of dispossession.[15] Echoes of this in the Canadian historiography are seen most particularly in examinations of independent commodity producers in dependent staple economies, many of whom while not directly proletarianized were nonetheless subjected to the contradictions of capitalism.[16]

Other historians have viewed social situations that do not fit the mass-production model as somehow allowing pre-industrial social relations to live on, almost artificially, before ultimately succumbing to capitalism's logic. For some, the sharp edge of class was blunted by such practices as paternalism, which allowed important elements of pre-industrial social relations to extend into the industrial age to serve as temporary but effective tools of class quiescence.[17] Paternalism *was* a key element of craft culture well into industrialization, but its contours must be seen in a broader view than that provided through the lens of capitalist inevitability. Similarly, Raymond Williams's insights into the functioning of base and superstructure in Marxist theory has compelled some historians to view 'residual' cultural elements as artificially living on into the industrial age before inevitably becoming 'emergent' by its logic.[18] By and large, historians have failed to recognize that a 'residual' culture (like craft) could be modified and adapted to the new circumstances of industrialization without being simply replaced by 'emergent' (capitalist) culture.

Another ultimately limited attempt to unravel the social behaviour of actors within flexible economies has been made in recent years in an edited collection of conference papers by practitioners of the historical-alternatives approach. While the editors assert in their introduction that this type of productive system 'came to impart a distinctive hue to the local society as a whole,' the collection really only considers how the realities of flexible economies influenced the actions of entrepreneurs and managers in cultivating and monitoring markets, encouraging various forms of government to adopt favourable legislative frameworks, or in building and shaping institutions of marketing, finance regulation, and employment. The influence of these economies on the shaping of collective bargaining institutions and collective regulation of the labour market receives some mention, but a keen eye is not firmly cast on the actual social relations of production. As such, the latest manifestation of the historical-alternatives approach does not meaningfully consider the implications this type of industrialization might have held for either class formation or the social experience of class.[19]

The need to recognize alternative paths of economic development and the social relations they spawned has also been urged as a research direction within the 'transition to capitalism' debate in the U.S. historiography. Much of the debate in the 1980s and 1990s was concerned more with the relative weightings of use and exchange value or related degrees of market integration than with close attention to the mode of production.[20] In a survey of this debate in 1995, however, Michael Merrill suggested that conflating markets with capitalism has increasingly confounded historians in this field. Merrill lauds the work of such authors as James Henretta and Allan Kulikoff for outlining the existence of non-capitalist social structures in the United States during the eighteenth and nineteenth centuries. But the 'foregone conclusion' of capitalism's triumph, he argues, has blinded even these authors from seriously examining what he calls variously the 'alternate paths' or 'anticapitalist alternatives' that were likely followed in the 'many different market economies' that developed alongside capitalism.[21] As in the historiographic schools cited above, however, a research direction that addresses social relations within these alternative productive systems has yet to take shape. The notable exception to this are the various studies exploring the social dimensions of the non-capitalist planter South in the United States.[22]

To move most effectively in this direction, it is fruitful to consider the relation of the historical-alternatives approach and its related historiographies to another somewhat muted body of historical enquiry, one rooted not just in Marx's *stages* of economic development but also in his *paths* to industrialization. Implicit in the historical-alternatives approach is the argument that flexible industrialization was achieved in large part by craft-based industry led by artisanal small producers. That artisans led much of this industrialization needs to be made more explicit and problematized for its social consequences. The fact that small producers (some of them, in fact, quite large) came from the same ranks as those whom they employed would have had a profound effect on the social relations of production in those workplaces and communities. While Marx and subsequent writers recognized this path of industrialization, it did little to alter their understanding of the linear inevitability of decline. More importantly, it has prevented any serious or sustained consideration of the stage of craft dominance.[23]

Some research has been undertaken to determine the extent of artisan-led industrialization in various locations. In the United States, for example, studies of Paterson, Newark, Cincinnati, and other centres have determined that initial industrial growth in those towns was achieved in large part by artisan-entrepreneurs. However, the social consequences of this growth have generally been interpreted along the familiar lines of helping either to sustain pre-industrial (residual) social relationships in the industrial age and/or leading to a perhaps forestalled but nonetheless deterministic proletarianization – the inevitable pulling apart of masters and men.[24] In the main, however, the artisan-entrepreneur is still an agenda awaiting research.

This situation has been greatly exacerbated by discrete bodies of historiography that on balance treat workers and those for whom they worked as separate categories. Labour historians have generally presented histories of vibrant, multifaceted, and colourful workers in opposition to a static and uniformly oppositional group of employers – the ubiquitous capitalistic class. The artisan-entrepreneur has yet to find his place in accounts of middle-class formation or business history.

The journeyman (and apprentice) craftsworker is the other social actor to be considered in the context of artisan-led, flexible industrialization. It must be asked, more specifically, just how applicable the dispossession model was to journeyman craftsworkers in this industrialization context. In determining the answer it is crucial to pay close attention to journeyman craftsworkers' ownership or loss of control of the means of production. Some studies have shown that, given time, journeymen and their artisan-employers did indeed grow far enough apart and lifetime wage earning did become enough of a predominant social experience that a real dispossession of the means of production was effected.[25] In other cases journeyman immiseration was achieved more indirectly through a 'squeeze' put on their small-producer bosses by chains of dependency on larger capital.[26] This view that all roads to industrialization led in short order to the working class will be challenged by this study.

The historical alternatives and related historiography suggest that at least some (and, in fact, many) small artisan-producers were not only successful enough to stay in business, but also that in order for flexible industrialization to sustain itself and grow over time it also had to have some means of *reproducing* itself. This likely had a twofold meaning for a large number of journeyman craftsworkers. Not only did they maintain substantial control over the means of production in their day-to-day work routines, but they also laboured under the hope – indeed, precedent – that they would obtain ownership of it in their lifetimes. The unique class position and consequent social behaviour this situation would engender will be a central point of examination in this study.

All of this is not to say that flexible industrialization must, by its nature, follow a path forever divergent from the mass-production route. The historical-alternatives approach is at its most useful with the suggestion that there is no single route to industrialization. But one cannot simply assume all flexible growth was enduring. It is easy to understand the flexible-specialization model, for instance, as broadly characteristic of earlier stages of industrial development identified by Marx and elaborated to limited effect by historians of combined and uneven development. The Marxist stage of 'manufacture,' in particular, is generally characterized by expanding artisan-led enterprise that, while having undergone significant change, still carries with it important continuities in craft and craft culture.[27]

In some cases alternative paths may never converge with the mass-production route. But in other cases they may lead towards – indeed, feed into – it. It is the task of the historian to avoid reading into the evidence the direction that development ultimately did take and to appreciate that the historical actors of any type of industrialization behaved without this foreknowledge. The concentration on the mass-production route and its teleological treatment by many historians has generally resulted in a historiography that considers earlier stages of craft production more as the first steps towards the elimination of craft than periods with particular dynamics and social relations. This book will consider how craftsworkers lived through such a stage of economic development – 'manufacture' – and did so along a particular path of industrialization. It will explain how they came to 'make sense' of this convergence of historical circumstance and created a society distinctive to it. It will show how they came to terms with living through a period of industrialization where much had changed, but much remained the same.

Consideration of the above historiography ultimately begs the question why mid-nineteenth-century Hamilton, Ontario, provides a suitable locale for examining these issues. To best provide an answer, it is first necessary to examine interpretations of Canada's and, in particular, Ontario's industrialization. Older accounts, concentrating single-mindedly on staple development, all but ignored the role of industry in the economy of nineteenth-century Canada.[28] This view was bolstered in the early 1970s by a new scholarship that also discounted the significance of the country's manufacturing base before its domination in the first decades of the twentieth century by U.S. branch plants. Tom Naylor, one of this school's leading voices, argued that indigenous industrial development was intentionally stifled by the failure of the country's mercantile and financial elite to invest in industry.[29] New generations of scholars have since challenged both these views, uncovering the impressive degree of manufacturing activity that went on across the country during the nineteenth century. This critique took shape most forcefully in the Ontario historiography in powerful studies of working-class development in the context of industrialization in Toronto and Hamilton. Gregory Kealey and Bryan Palmer, the authors of these studies, demonstrated that there had been significant industrial growth in these cities beginning in the mid-nineteenth century. As a rejoinder to Naylor, both authors pointed to an appreciable degree of merchant involvement in industrialization in their respective locales. In a joint study of the Ontario labour movement in the 1880s, Kealey and Palmer extended this analysis to Ontario as a whole.[30] Yet, whether industrialization was ignored, downplayed, or touted as an event that occurred with considerable mercantile involvement in the nineteenth century, little room was devoted anywhere to serious consideration of industrialization's alternative paths.

Indeed, some historians have more recently begun to question how representative these locales were of the province's overall industrialization. Craig Heron, for example, has noted that the new labour history has 'presented the Ontario evidence within a universal paradigm of industrial capitalist development ... The formation and struggles of the working class seemed to unfold in a pattern roughly similar to those in most other industrializing areas of the world in the period, particularly Britain and the United States. By extension, readers might also easily assume that the wider experience in Ontario was simply Toronto and Hamilton writ large.'[31] The view that the capital-intensive, specialized industries visible in such cities as Toronto or (even more so) Montreal typified industrial development has been challenged in recent years by a growing body of research on Ontario that suggests that an impressive degree of industrial growth was achieved in the middle decades of the nineteenth century by the astute and highly selective efforts of small producers to service the growing staple economy and, perhaps more importantly, to supply the niche markets generated by its many linkages. In Ontario, the ability of industrialists to expand and specialize their production facilities remained constrained by limited domestic markets up through the latter decades of the nineteenth century. Elizabeth Bloomfield and Gerald Bloomfield have shown that in 1871 the aggregation of these small producers accounted for the lion's share of industrial output in the province. The mean size of industrial establishments that year was still less than five workers. The result, it appears, was a type of industrialization characterized by flexible specialized enterprise functioning in limited markets and tooled for the necessity of product diversification. Modern industry, found in larger centres such as Toronto or Montreal by this point, was still the exception and not the rule in overall industrial development. While it has been suggested by a number of scholars that artisan-entrepreneurs achieved significant industrial growth in the province, this assertion has itself not been the subject of methodical examination.[32]

Chapter 1 will show that Hamilton emerged as one the leading centres of Ontario's and Canada's first industrial revolution by the early 1870s by following this flexible specialized path of industrial growth.

Hamilton was the leading national example of this more typical kind of industrialization in nineteenth-century Canada, an industrialization likely typical of many other cities but left largely unexplored by historians more eager to explain what came after it. Industry in Hamilton was much freer of the economies of scale, integrated markets, capital concentration, strong impetus towards mechanization, and relentless searches for increasing divisions of labour than were many industries in U.S. or European cities and towns by later in the mid-nineteenth century. As a result Hamilton's industrial entrepreneurs were able to follow a more classical path to industrial development characterized by flexible enterprise that, in relative terms at least, remained somewhat free from direct competition with the mass-production model of modern industry elsewhere. While industry was flexible, however, the degree of industrialization in the city was appreciable. It was the enlarged manufactory operating in generally peaceful coexistence with an expanded number of traditional handicraft enterprises that accounted for this significant degree of industrial growth. The net result of this was an economic situation in which craft production had undergone appreciable change, but still generally created few of the immiserating effects brought by highly capitalized, mass-production-oriented high competition environments typical of some other major segments of the Western industrial world by this time. Rather, an industrialization took shape that was flexible, adaptable, and remarkably advanced; an industrialization, by the early 1870s, that had reached the crest of the wave of 'manufacture.' It is the effect this economic situation had on class formation and the social relations that flowed therefrom, particularly among and between journeymen and master craftsworkers, with which this study is primarily concerned.

Chapter 2 will examine the origins of the craftsworkers at work in these numerous plants. It will show that while some craftsworkers were born in Ontario or the United States, most were newcomers from the British Isles. A survey of the literature on labour migration suggests – and later chapters confirm – that such craftsworkers typically came to North America in hopes of finding less degraded forms of craft employment than they had experienced back home, greater chances for social mobility, and a generally more positive experience of the emerging economic system. This chapter will also show that in addition to working in a preserved craft work environment, these craftsworkers found much in common with those for whom they worked. As such, the chapter outlines the overwhelmingly artisanal origins of the city's industrialists by 1871.

In light of these findings, chapter 3 will consider the impact of artisan-led industrialization on craftsworkers. It will show that the material and social experience of class rooted in capitalism was not the predominant experience of most craftsworkers in Hamilton workplaces by the early 1870s. Rather, artisan-led industrialization overwhelmingly provided a social context within which traditional patterns of craft mobility – particularly the progression of apprentice to journeyman to master – were preserved and even expanded. It will demonstrate that the widespread success of the city's many artisan-industrial proprietors, both large and small, provided a strong cultural symbol of opportunity to local journeymen and apprentices. It will further examine how this perception of opportunity was also based on continued practices of craft mobility in many Hamilton workplaces up through the early 1870s. Throughout early industrialization it remained common for local craftsworkers to rise through the ranks to become their own masters. As aspiring young craftsworkers, their own masters often mentored them in that process. The opportunities to achieve this masculine independence were also significantly opened up in these years with the creation of numerous superintendent and foreman positions that often carried with them some measurable ownership in the means of production, often through part-ownership or anticipated future ownership of the enterprise. It will also be shown that these practices were not just typical of the shops of local artisan-industrial proprietors, but were also well-ensconced in the Great Western Railway's car and locomotive shops, where traditional craft production had been significantly revised and lifetime wage-earning had become the standard for the city's largest industrial workforce.

It will be demonstrated how the buoyant, flexible and adaptable character of the city's industrialization enabled social practices that had a profound effect on the class experience of local craftsworkers by allowing them continued ownership – or anticipation of ownership – of the means of production. Most local craftsworkers actively participated in capitalist institutions but without the alienating aspects of capitalism's material arrangements. With a foot in each of the capitalist and non-capitalist (or craft) worlds, the line between the two was blurred and local craftsworkers' class position was what I have chosen to call 'transmodal.' Dispossessed craftsworkers operating within unambiguously capitalist class relations these were not.

As the use of the term 'transmodal' indicates, as an examination of a previously unexplored economic and social phenomenon, this study requires something of a new vocabulary. This is a study of craftsworker's social experience of industrialization in a particular economic context. While the flexible-specialized character of Hamilton's industrialization was consistent with the nature of industrialization in numerous other urban centres, this similarity is only applicable at the structural level, not at the level of social relations. As the above discussion of the historical-alternatives literature outlines, there was abundant room within flexible economies for the 'squeeze' of capitalism to be felt. This process was forestalled in Hamilton – and likely many other local, regional and (perhaps) national economies – at least before the early 1870s. For the quarter century or so before this, economic circumstance resulted in a more hopeful experience of industrialization among craftsworkers. This experience, which has not previously received consideration in the literature, requires its own name.

Subsequent chapters will explore the social dimensions of craftsworkers' transmodal class position. Chapter 4 will delve deeper into the practice of social relations between masters and men to outline the continuities of craftsworkers' pre-existing culture. It will build on the portrait in chapter 3 of the uninterrupted practice of craft mobility – the cultural keystone of the craft world – to show that other major components of the residual culture of the craft world remained intact in city shops into the industrial age. These continuities included the preservation of a masculine-exclusive workplace in which masters and men maintained a vibrant mutualistic work-based masculine culture both on and off the job. It was also reflected in the maintenance of residential patterns in which both masters and men lived and worked as members of the same organic community. In all, it will suggest that masters and men successfully brought forward many traditional cultural elements to function as serviceable bases for social relations into the industrial age.

However, while craftsworker culture still contained strong residual elements, it was not simply backward looking. The local context of industrialism and the particular class experience it engendered also allowed craftsworkers to forge a culture with strong emergent elements, a transmodal culture. The remaining chapters will explore this culture's emergent aspects in some of its dimensions. Chapter 5 will show how the material experience of Hamilton's early industrialization – a burgeoning capitalism on the one hand and a preserved system of occupational advancement on the other – enabled the formulation by local craftsworkers of a new subject position congruent with its realities: the self-made craftsworker. In its formulations, area craftsworkers explained self-made status as a function of their adherence to certain crucial masculine qualities – independence, perseverance, industry, energy, honesty, hard toil, sobriety, and others – and the rejection of other masculine models, particularly the aristocrat. This masculine typology was built from craftsworkers' social experience of their particular material situation within Hamilton's industrialization.

Chapter 6 will show that the self-made craftsworker also served as a primary identity upon which craftsworkers constructed another emergent cultural form, the self-improving craftsworker. It will show that within the possibilities of industrialization, craftsworkers came to view the simple acquisition of the various traditional manual 'mysteries' of a craft as only part of the requisite 'journey' towards a self-made competence. Many craftsworkers came to understand self-improvement, the continuous updating of skill sets and craft knowledge through applied self-education, as an equally important ingredient to success. The penchant for self-improvement was articulated on an ideological level in numerous speeches and exhortations to young men both from within and without the local crafts community. It was more importantly, however, a practised construction. The chapter will also show how area craftsworkers actively applied themselves to myriad forms of self-improving activity through an impressive variety of local institutions. Taken together, chapters 5 and 6 will suggest some of the broad outlines of transmodal culture.

Chapter 7 will inject the concept of transmodal culture with some specificity through an examination of its expression in the events of the Nine Hours Movement of 1872. The material experience of local craftsworkers enabled them to develop an optimistic view of industrialization, an understanding of themselves as full-fledged actors in the modern political economy. Their situation within this particular industrialization also set the stage for the rise of a widespread feeling of their 'rights' as actors within it. The Nine Hours Movement will be presented as a contest between what craftsworkers perceived to be obstructions to the healthy functioning of the modern political economy and their rights as free actors within it. While conflict rooted in the contradictions of capitalism was not unknown to some Hamilton craftsworkers, the events of that spring and early summer will be explained here not as demonstrations against the alienating features of capitalism but as resistance against those impediments craftsworkers believed were inhibiting its smooth functioning and general upwards trend towards their prosperity. The voices, activities, and institutions of craftsworkers more familiar with capitalism's alienated features, while present, remained marginal. Rather, the Nine Hours Movement, as it unfolded in Hamilton, was largely played out and contained within the transmodal culture of craft capitalism.

It must be acknowledged at the outset that this study's perspective on this historical process is one seen largely through the eyes of a particular social group – artisans and craftsmen. One trouble confronting the historian is the fact that it is this group's more successful members who are probably best represented in the available evidence. The experience of the number of artisans who failed in self-employment, for instance, would be less likely to make it into the historical record than accounts of those who succeeded. This perspective also does not consider how such other actors as women, children, labourers, the city's commercial elite, and others affected this historical process, how such institutions as the family, the tavern, the church, and others helped shape it, or how it was played out in the political realm. It is hoped these will be among the many new research directions encouraged by this study.

It is also necessary to say a few words about the terminology this study will employ to describe its main actors. Discussions of apprentices, journeymen, and masters large and small have a number of potential terms of reference. Noticeably absent from this study will be the term 'skilled worker' in reference to any of the above, since that term denotes a decided position of dispossession within capitalist class relations. Rather, this study will favour the terms 'artisan' and 'craftsworker' to refer to its main actors. While there is some overlap to these terms, they will not be used interchangeably. 'Artisan' will be used mostly to refer to both large and small industrial proprietors and other craftsworkers such as foremen or superintendents known to have direct control of their means of production. This term is not used to reference the more traditional conceptions of the guild-based artisan with roots deep in medieval Britain and Europe. Rather, it will refer to the model of the modern craft master rooted in the late eighteenth and early nineteenth centuries whose identity had been largely freed of its heavy legal and corporatist trappings and replaced with modern conceptions of liberal independence.[33] 'Craftsworker' will be employed to refer mainly to journeymen during that phase in their working lives when they likely did not have direct ownership of the means of production but nonetheless anticipated such ownership. Since virtually all masters referred to herein were once journeymen (and apprentices) they may be dubbed as either craftsworkers or artisans at appropriate places throughout this study.

This study will utilize a variety of sources to formulate and support its argument. Like other studies of craftsworkers during Canada's early industrialization, this study builds much of its evidentiary base from a close reading of the local press. However, instead of generalizing infrequent reports of conflict as representative of the overarching experience of craftsworkers at work and in working communities, it will consider the broader aspects of reportage relevant to the craft world. Among other things, it will show that intricate descriptions of local industrial establishments provide important information about both the personnel behind them and the social relations within them. This treatment of the local press will also suggest that while it is important to understand newspapers as organs of various political positions or as the financed voice of various bourgeois elements, they were often equally (or even more so) creations of the local craft community. As such they were able to express the voices of craftsworkers as forcefully (though perhaps with a different texture) as the much-vaunted labour newspapers so thoroughly mined by historians. As the following pages will show, editorship and often part or full ownership of the local press was often in the hands of craftsworkers themselves. Contained within their pages, with some qualification, therefore, was often the 'voice' of the local craft community. In this light, for example, a newspaper's seeming preoccupation with the promotion of a local mechanics' institute can be understood as less a bourgeois project for social control than an organic expression of the concerns of local craftsworkers.

This study will also make much use of the Industrial Schedules of the 1871 Census of Canada. Neatly coincident with the terminal date of this study, this source provides a comprehensive portrait of manufacturing activity in Hamilton. This source has been transcribed to an electronic database and will provide a variety of forms of quantitative evidence throughout the study. However, in no place will this quantitative evidence be used in and of itself as base upon which to make pivotal conclusions. As the study itself will argue, previous efforts to do so suffer from some serious shortcomings. Rather, quantitative results will be used to show situations that display clearly significant trends (i.e., display indicators that are so strong that there is little room for debate over 'significance') or will be bolstered with appreciable amounts of qualitative evidence in order to provide better grounding for the conclusion.

A number of other sources are also consulted. Prominent among these are other census materials, city directories, credit records, commissioned biographies, and industrial promotional materials. To a lesser extent this study also employs government and trade union journals, the minute books of one local union and other local organizations in which craftsworkers involved themselves, and the few personal papers and diaries relevant to this topic. Much of the study required the cross-linkage of these qualitative sources with the database assembled from the 1871 Industrial Schedules in order to reconstruct the biographies of as many local masters as possible. These qualitative and quantitative sources were cross-linked in an electronic database. Given the comings and goings of numerous masters, the variations in recorded names, and other factors, it was impossible to establish firm links between all masters listed on the census manuscripts and qualitative biographical information.

All the above sources, of course, have to be approached with caution. The biases of census collection are well known, and in the process of assembling this study I did encounter many inconsistencies. The information collected in city directories is often incomplete. The records left by credit-rating agencies tend to favour some kinds of businesspeople over others. Minute books are seldom representative of the dynamics of the meetings they report. Industrial promotionals and commissioned biographies by their nature offer universally positive views of their subjects. All these sources, however, if read carefully, can yield important information to the historical researcher.

Together these chapters will outline the social dimensions of Hamilton craftsworkers' experience of a particular type of early industrialization. They will offer a profound reconsideration of class formation and the elaboration of craftsworker culture in this context, one starkly different than the dispossession model. While this study will show the unfolding of industrialization in Hamilton and craftsworkers' experience of it as different from received views, its intention is to suggest that this historical convergence of circumstance and experience was not unique to Hamilton but repeated in varied and measured ways throughout Western industrialization.

Craft Capitalism describes both the route this industrialization had taken by the 1870s and the stage to which it had developed. As a *route*, most commentators, perhaps in their haste to reach the familiar ground at its end, have looked down this 'really revolutionizing path' – in Marx's words, whereby 'the producer becomes both merchant and capitalist,' thereby fundamentally altering production[34] –

as simply another linear road to decline. This study suggests that there was another craft-based road to industrialization that was not revolutionary at all. This path had the same beginning and end as the really revolutionizing one, but was nonetheless distinct and sported much better views along the way. Neither was this the road less travelled. It was likely as wide, well worn, and direct as its alternative.

But by this road (or another) it is the *stage* that this industrialization had reached which is of equal significance. For a quarter century or more, local craft producers and workers had participated in an industrialization that reached the high point of manufacture by the early 1870s. This was an industrialization that contained a profound degree of change, including the unprecedented introduction of relatively large enterprise to the craft world. Most notable, however, is the fact that this remarkable industrialization had been largely contained within a massive expansion of craft production, ideology, and culture. While some craft entrepreneurs began to innovate in directions that in hindsight suggested a departure from craft practices, this change was interpreted by most craftsworkers through older lenses and did not escape craft ideologies that survived or had developed in new directions, that were informed more by the residual culture of craft than the emergent culture of capitalism. It was a form of industrialization that allowed the appreciable introduction of the institutions and practices of industrial *capitalism* without losing the fundamental underpinnings of the world of *craft* production.

Craftsworkers and communities of craftsworkers that travelled down this road and reached this stage created an industrialization that was transmodal, bridging the pre-existing crafts world and the world of modern capitalism in ways that they understood built on the positive aspects of both. Among its necessary ingredients was a buoyant and expanding economy that encouraged the widespread foundation of flexible, specialized enterprise. Its social relations were imbued with optimism, with hope, with positive anticipation. It is the containment of this profound industrialization – of change – within the pre-existing craft world that characterizes craft capitalism. This social and material arrangement provided little hint to most craftsworkers at the time that this road *would* lead to proletarianization and the stage of manufacture would be supplanted by that of modern industry in the decades to come. In the meantime, craft capitalism served as a centre of social creation.

1

The Structure of Hamilton's Early Industrialization: Continuity and Change

This study examines the social experience of craftsworkers during early industrialization. But before those depths are plumbed, it is first necessary to gain some understanding of the changing economic and personal structures within which this experience was formulated. To that end, chapters 1 and 2 will assess the degree of continuity and change discernible in Hamilton's first round of industrialization from about the mid-1830s to the early 1870s. By examining the changing context of industry and its personnel in Hamilton during the city's transition from small commercial lakeport to the 'Birmingham of Canada,' these chapters will consider the degree to which industrial growth can actually be assessed as 'revolutionary' by the early 1870s.

This chapter will provide a better understanding of the economic structures within which craftsworkers formed their experience of this process. Its findings will delineate the contours and characteristics – the broad structure – of the city's early industrial growth. More specifically, it will demonstrate that while by the terminal date of this study the work environment of Hamilton craftsworkers had been significantly modified, it had not been fundamentally transformed. It will show that up until at least the early 1870s, artisan-entrepreneurs and craftsworkers in Hamilton achieved an impressive degree of industrialization with profound – almost pervasive – continuity in the pre-existing craft mode of production. These findings suggest that a reinterpretation of the general nature of the first industrial revolution in Hamilton and similar cities and towns throughout North America and beyond should raise important questions about the universal applicability of both the dispossession model and the mass-production model of industrialization upon which it is based.

This chapter is organized into two sections. A short introductory section will outline the nature of industrial growth in Hamilton up to the early 1870s. It will show that the appreciable diversity and scale of the city's industrialization by that point had caused it to emerge as one of the nation's most important industrial centres. A second section will examine the flexible, specialized character of the city's industrial growth by 1871. It will suggest that the city was the leading national example of this more typical kind of industrialization in nineteenth-century Canada, an industrialization likely characteristic of many other cities but left largely unexplored by historians. More importantly, it will show Hamilton's significant industrial growth to have been achieved within a period of uneven industrial development during which an expanded number of small handicraft enterprises stood in generally peaceful coexistence with a considerable number of enlarged manufactories; 'Modern Industry' had yet to make its mark on the city. It will explain how a pronounced industrialization occurred in Hamilton (and likely many similar places through the Western industrializing world) without any necessarily fundamental change in productive relations. This chapter and the next offer a starting point in the reconsideration of early industrialization and the behaviour of its participants. It will provide the contextual footing upon which subsequent chapters will elaborate.

Hamilton's Industrialization by 1871: Local Growth and National Importance

The story of the breadth and depth of Hamilton's industrialization has been told so often that only its general contours warrant repeating here. In the three decades after 1840, Hamilton was transformed from a commercial centre with a sprinkling of small artisan shops into one of Canada's foremost industrial cities. Capitalizing on the booming Ontario wheat economy, the town had already successfully transformed itself from a fledging lakefront settlement into the dominant commercial entrepot at the head of Lake Ontario in the two decades before 1840. Earlier still, the building of a canal through the sand bar separating Burlington Bay from Lake Ontario in 1827 had opened the town up to lake traffic and further ensconced it as a thriving two-way conduit through which agricultural produce and settlers' effects passed each other on their way to their respective markets.[1]

Directing this transformation was a small but growing group of landowners and merchants who profited handsomely from this trade in produce, goods, and land. Operating on the trade frontier, these men were frequently the younger family members or junior partners heading up the satellite operation of larger, typically family-based, metropolitan concerns based in Glasgow or Liverpool, and often administered in the Canadas through intermediate operations in such centres as Montreal, Kingston, or Toronto. Their commercial pursuits allowed them to dominate Hamilton's economy for the following two or three decades and play a guiding hand in the town's social, economic, legal, and political development.[2] The conditions that allowed the establishment of this commercial hegemony also made for slower development but, in the long term, more fertile ground for Hamilton's industrial growth.

The traffic of the thriving lakeport also attracted small artisan manufacturers as early as the 1830s. Seeking to fill one of the numerous modest niches for import substitution in this commercial trade economy, these men also found attractive the town's extensive hinterland markets, stretching from London to Guelph. They also appreciated the town's advantageous position at the head of Lake Ontario, providing them access to raw materials and technology from the larger manufacturing centres to the east along the St Lawrence and Erie Canal systems.[3]

These early enterprises were small artisanal shops employing traditional methods of handicraft production. Most of the earliest of these were oriented towards providing more cost-effective local alternatives to the cumbersome and costly transport of settlers' effects, such as furniture, agricultural implements, or stoves. Others found space in the local economy by setting up in trades such as wagonmaking and blacksmithing where repair and local service could be easily combined with modest manufacture. A number of printing and newspaper establishments also made their first appearance in town by the 1830s. Markets were also sufficient for the tailor, along with the boot and shoe maker, to set up shop in town. These diverse enterprises – and a number of others – made up numerous small islands of manufacture situated opportunistically in the cracks of the local commercial trade and buoyed by the linkages of the staple economy.

Notable from the beginning was the local metal industry. By the 1840s, the city had developed a reputation as a regional metal centre. Its fledgling foundries turned out stoves, farming equipment, and other necessities for settlers on the agricultural frontier. As John Weaver has noted, these early secondary metal producers flourished on Hamilton's unique 'spatial bias' between supplies of raw materials, technology, and labour to the east (especially through the Erie Canal system) and burgeoning markets to the west.[4] By the 1840s these operations, too, were not notable for their size. They were all small operations utilizing the skill of the owner in production and employing the labour of only a few journeymen and an apprentice or two. It is worth noting, however, that the proprietors of a number of these early metal shops – John Fisher, Edward and Charles Gurney, Alexander Carpenter, Edward Jackson, Dennis Moore, among others – were to become major players in the metal industry in later decades.

By the end of this decade, the local industrial economy had achieved an impressive degree of diversification. The Return of Mills and Manufacturers of the 1851 Canada Census, while by no means a complete source,[5] at least gives some hint of this. In primary manufacturing the newly minted city boasted sawmills (4) and breweries (4), cigar factories (3), ropewalks (3), and a potashery and a tannery. In secondary production the list is more impressive. In the clothing sector boot and shoe establishments (4) coexisted with at least one clothing manufacturer and a hat factory. The city's metal industry comprised at least two foundries, an agricultural implements plant, and three sheet iron, tin, and copper establishments. The wood and paper products sector was dominated by carriage and wagon works (6) and planing mills (3), as well as a chair factory, a sash and blind works, a broom manufactory, and a cabinet shop. Miscellaneous industries also included a mustard and spice mill, a soap and candle factory, and two brickyards. This imperfect source likely significantly underestimates the true diversity of industrial undertaking, failing to account, for instance, for any of the city's blacksmiths, and vastly underenumerating the number of tailoring establishments. While already having grown somewhat diverse, however, the census also reveals the almost universally limited nature of this enterprise. Michael Katz has shown in his study of the size of business enterprise in the city in 1851 that the small establishment was almost universal in the city that year.[6] While the roots of a fledgling, diversified manufacturing sector had been laid by this time, this collection of small enterprises hardly amounted to what could be characterized as a thriving industrial community.

Nothing did more to change this state of affairs than the opening of the Great Western Railway (GWR) in 1854. The construction of the company's own car and locomotive shops in the mid-1850s brought one of the country's largest industries to the city. By 1857 the GWR's Hamilton shops employed upwards of six hundred tradesmen and labourers.[7]

The building of the railway itself stimulated industrial activity in Hamilton. Local foundrymen and others contracted space in the GWR's large new shops and recruited teams of craftsworkers to turn out railway rolling stock. Spin-off enterprises also flourished. Scottish immigrant Alexander Main, for example, founded a rope works to fill orders for ship's rigging, harnesses and hemp items, and later bell cord, twine, and string for railway car tuffeting. The increased local transport and haulage requirements of railway also stimulated the growth of local carriage and wagon industries.[8] Carriage maker James Williams took the opportunity to considerably expand his decade-old enterprise during the early 1850s, finding it necessary to promote his former foreman Henry Cooper to junior partner. This made good sense, since Williams himself was likely absent from the works much of the time, busily overseeing the operations of the new railway cars works he had opened in league with local foundryman John Fisher in spring 1852. As an enterprise founded separately from the GWR shops, the size of William and Fisher's Hamilton Car Factory and Foundry – by 1853 employing eighty men and having turned out more than two hundred cars 'of all descriptions' within its first year of operations – gives some idea of how abruptly the railway changed the city's industrial landscape.[9]

The GWR helped bring further substance to the city's diversity of industry through the numerous economic linkages it occasioned via the opening of new markets and provision of cheaper access to primary production goods. The city became home during the early to mid-1850s to an impressive number of industrial enterprises that would themselves grow and flourish in subsequent decades. The primary products sector saw the addition of Leopold Bauer's brewery and the marble works of both Hurd & Roberts and Thomas McCoombs. Isaac Chilman, who would become the proprietor of the city's largest bakery by the end of the decade, set up shop in the city sometime around 1850. Furniture maker Charles Meakins established his business interest in the city in the early 1850s before transforming this enterprise into a substantial brush factory some years later. Charles Thomas and Thomas White, manufacturers of pianos and melodeons, respectively, also set down their business roots in this decade. Shoemaker Robert Nisbet opened what would become one of the largest shoe and boot factories in the Dominion by the 1870s in the first half of this decade. In the metal sector, especially, many enduring and successful enterprises were founded in this decade, including the Young Brothers Brass Foundry, Nelson Robbins' grate and railing manufactory, Benjamin Greening's Victoria Wire Works, the Copp Brothers Empire Foundry, F.G. Beckett's Atlas Engine and Boiler Works, Elijah Ware's scale works (later Gurney and Ware), and George Grayson's steel spring shop.[10] This list, while by no means comprehensive, provides some understanding of the increasing variety of industrial undertaking in the city during the early and mid-1850s.

An economic depression fuelled in part by railway speculation kicked the feet out from under much of this new industrial activity beginning in 1857. The most prominent industrial casualty was undoubtedly Daniel C. Gunn, a former wharfinger and GWR freight superintendent, who had purchased the Williams and Fisher Hamilton Car Factory and Foundry for $36 000 shortly before the international financial panic hit Hamilton. After investing at least a further $15 000 in the enterprise, Gunn was in trouble by 1858 and had gone 'all to pieces' by the next year, leaving him publicly disgraced and the 100 to 150 hands he employed looking for work.[11] Many of the city's other industrial establishments did manage to weather this economic storm, but only by scaling back production, reducing wages, or simply letting go sizable sections of their workforces.[12] This shedding of jobs was reflected in the city's substantial population loss, estimated at more than 20 per cent between 1858 and 1862.[13]

When the ashes of this economic distress began to settle in the early 1860s it was evident that the city's industrialization had not been thwarted. Buoyed by this renewed economic optimism, the *Hamilton Times* published a long series of articles profiling the growing diversity, productive capacities, and ever-increasing number of hands employed by local industrial establishments in the early 1860s. Indeed, it is notable that major new industries were founded during the most dismal years of the economic depression. The opening of Richard Wanzer's Canada Sewing Machine Company factory in 1859 portended the development of a new and thriving industrial sector over the next decade. The partnership of future senator William E. Sanford with Alexander McInnes in the manufacture of ready-made clothes in 1862 saw the creation of another major industry, one that would assemble the city's largest workforce and establish a trade from Manitoba to the Maritimes in just a few short years. The tenacity of Hamilton's' fledgling industrialists, as subsequent chapters will show, is also seen in the fact that many of the proprietors of Hamilton's most substantial industrial establishments by the 1870s were men who started more modest concerns in the city before the economic calamity of the late 1850s.

A survey of Hamilton industry in 1871 provides a picture of the considerable size and diversity that Hamilton's flourishing industrial sector had managed to achieve in this short period of time. The database of Hamilton industrial establishments assembled for this study

Table 1.1 Employment and production in manufacturing, Hamilton, 1871

		Employees								
Industry	n	M>16	F>16	M<16	F<16	Wages ($)	Raw mat. ($)	Prod. val. ($)	Val. add. ($)	Val. add. (%)
1. Primary										
A. Agricultural										
Breweries	6	36	0	0	0	9,262	36,627	76,116	39,489	1.44
Cider/wine	3	4	0	0	0	1,132	1,207	3,725	2,518	0.09
Meat curing	10	42	2	5	0	8,644	284,687	333,337		0.00
Rope and twine	2	17	0	6	0	4,430	10,860	17,280	6,420	0.23
Tanneries	2	15	0	1	0	5,900	30,750	41,500	10,750	0.39
Tobacco	7	89	14	44	27	38,729	116,577	184,114	67,537	2.46
Miscellaneous	3	9	0	3	0	3,563	100,900	122,000	21,100	0.77
TOTAL	33	212	16	59	27	71,660	581,608	778,072	196,464	7.15
B. Forest										
Asheries	1	6	0	0	0	1,000	1,000	185	2,185	0.08
TOTAL	1	6	0	0	0	1,000	1,000	3,185	2,185	0.08
C. *Minerals*										
Marble/stone	3	60	0	0	0	24,600	18,700	46,988	28,288	1.03
Miscellaneous	1	1	0	0	0	0	120	625	505	0.02
TOTAL	4	61	0	0	0	24,600	18,820	47,613	28,793	1.05

<u>*2. Secondary*</u>										
A. Beverages/food										
Aerated water	2	7	0	0	2	2,600	8,000	16,000	8,000	0.29
Bakeries	12	41	2	2	0	16,206	96,980	122,039	25,059	0.91
Chocolate/coffee/spice	3	3	0	1	0	800	7,000	13,700	6,700	0.24
Confectionery	10	37	4	11	2	11,629	100,498	144,564	44,066	1.60
TOTAL	27	88	6	14	4	31,235	212,478	296,303	83,825	3.05
B. Chemical										
Patent medicines	5	10	0	5	0	4,100	6,790	22,450	15,660	0.57
Vinegar	3	14	0	3	0	5,816	59,401	118,060	58,659	2.14
Soap and candle	4	28	0	2	0	8,600	60,950	81,170	20,220	0.74
TOTAL	12	52	0	10	0	18,516	127,141	221,680	94,539	3.44
C. *Clothing*										
Boots/shoes	23	248	60	21	0	99,051	196,832	355,230	158,398	5.77
Clothing/tailored goods	28	195	420	46	53	116,938	406,252	602,075	195,823	7.13
Dresses/millinery	14	0	100	1	13	15,132	24,863	54,909	30,046	1.09
Furs/hats	9	56	86	8	16	36,050	53,900	127,025	73,125	2.66
Gloves/mitts	1	1	4	0	0	1,560	750	3,500	2,750	0.10
Shirts/collars/ties	1	1	4	1	0	1,886	1,500	4,200	2,700	0.10
Miscellaneous	1	0	3	0	0	520	706	1,200	494	0.02
TOTAL	77	501	677	77	82	271,137	684,803	1,148,139	463,336	16.87
D. Leather										
Saddle/harness	9	69	1	9	0	20,268	28,304	72,500	44,196	1.61
TOTAL	9	69	1	9	0	20,268	28,304	72,500	44,196	1.61

Table 1.1 Employment and production in manufacturing, Hamilton, 1871—(*continued*)

Industry	n	Employees				Wages ($)	Raw mat. ($)	Prod. val. ($)	Val. add. ($)	Val. add. (%)
		M>16	F>16	M<16	F<16					
E. Metal										
Agricultural implements	1	86	0	4	0	45,000	7,000	125,000	52,000	1.89
Blacksmithing	6	18	0	2	0	4,785	3,263	10,680	7,417	0.27
Boilers/engines	2	117	0	12	0	42,080	47,000	112,260	65,260	2.38
Fittings	3	28	0	5	0	9,416	9,230	28,431	19,201	0.70
Machines	4	38	0	4	0	15,400	9,230	37,700	28,470	1.04
Furnaces/stoves/heaters	7	307	0	6	0	121,900	135,580	377,223	241,643	8.80
Railway locomotives*	1	400	0	0	0	200,000	(See 'Note on GWR' below)			n.d.
Rolling mill products	1	190	0	35	0	80,000	410,000	680,000	270,000	9.83
Sewing machines	4	339	1	138	0	154,800	140,300	511,760	371,460	13.52
Tin/sheet iron products	8	55	0	1	0	20,466	36,540	78,790	42,250	1.54
Tinsmithing	6	10	0	4	0	3,574	5,980	15,100	9,120	0.33
Wire	1	3	0	3	0	1,100	3,500	7,000	3,500	0.13
Castings	2	55	0	3	0	2,1000	26,900	64,200	37,300	1.36
Miscellaneous	3	28	0	3	0	9,624	10,830	36,200	25,370	0.92
TOTAL	49	1674	1	220	0	729,145	911,353	2,084,344	1,172,991	42.71
F. Printing										
Bookbinding	3	9	7	3	2	4,044	3,780	11,000	7,220	0.26
Engraving/lithographing	1	4	0	0	0	2,000	1,500	5,000	3,500	0.13
Printing/publishing	6	88	4	15	0	38,190	34,043	85,000	50,957	1.86
TOTAL	10	101	11	18	2	44,234	39,323	101,000	61,677	2.25

G. Textiles										
H. Wood/paper										
Bags/boxes, paper	2	1	4	2	0	1,100	5,800	7,900	2,100	0.08
Barrels	2	12	0	2	0	6,220	3,750	14,750	11,000	0.40
Baskets	2	3	0	0	0	350	560	1,800	1,240	0.05
Boxes, wood	2	4	0	3	0	2,500	3,100	8,400	5,300	0.19
Brooms/brushes	8	47	21	24	1	22,340	36,766	90,700	53,934	1.96
Cabinets/furniture	11	66	1	6	0	18,942	12,176	53,070	40,894	1.49
Carriages	9	73	0	5	0	21,940	12,029	45,265	33,236	1.21
Musical instruments	5	47	1	2	0	21,848	21,015	65,600	44,585	1.62
Railway cars*	1	600	0	0	0	300,000	(See: 'Note on GWR')		n.d.	n.d.
Planing/moulding	3	43	0	11	0	17,800	12,400	36,950	24,550	0.89
Sashes/doors/blinds	2	20	2	4	0	8,800	19,000	31,000	12,000	0.44
Boats/ships	3	14	1	0	0	5,000	3,400	10,675	7,275	0.26
Coffins	4	9	1	1	0	1,800	2,666	6,100	3,434	0.13
Miscellaneous, paper	1	2	0	1	0	400	1,500	3,500	2,000	0.07
Miscellaneous, wood	2	7	0	4	0	3,000	2,500	8,000	5,500	0.20
TOTAL	57	948	31	65	1	432,040	136,662	383,710	247,048	8.99
I. Construction										
Carpenters and joiners	5	36	0	0	0	15,450	10,050	32,450	22,400	0.82
Painters	5	22	0	0	0	9,540	8,050	23,434	15,384	0.56
Plumbers/gasfitters	3	15	0	5	0	5,800	10,310	21,500	11,190	0.41
Builders	14	357	0	10	0	119,810	63,700	209,750	146,050	5.32
TOTAL	27	430	0	15	0	150,600	92,110	287,134	195,024	7.10

Table 1.1 Employment and production in manufacturing, Hamilton, 1871—(*continued*)

		Employees								
Industry	n	M>16	F>16	M<16	F<16	Wages ($)	Raw mat. ($)	Prod. val. ($)	Val. add. ($)	Val. add. (%)
J. Miscellaneous										
Brick/tile	5	80	0	20	0	14,200	7,223	36,600	29,377	1.07
Gas	1	12	0	0	0	5,300	12,300	33,854	21,554	0.78
Glass	1	58	0	25	0	42,500	20,050	85,000	64,950	2.36
Jewellery/watches	3	3	0	2	0	675	1,580	5,000	3,420	0.12
Photographs	5	6	4	1	0	1,058	613	4,590	3,977	0.14
Pottery	1	16	0	2	0	4,500	4,100	12,000	7,900	0.29
Trunks/boxes/valises	1	3	0	1	0	1,000	1,263	3,000	1,737	0.06
Miscellaneous	6	24	12	2	0	11,280	24,400	48,050	23,650	0.86
TOTAL	23	202	16	53	0	80,513	71,529	228,094	156,565	5.70
TOTALS	329	4,344	759	540	116	1,874,948	2,905,131	5,651,774	2,746,643	100

Source: Manuscript Schedule 6- 'Return of Industrial Establishments'. District No. 24 (Hamilton). 1871 Census of Canada Manuscripts.

*Note on GWR – Output figures for the Great Western Railway do not appear here because they were not reported on the Industrial Census. The GWR's aggregate census information has been broken down here to reflect the different sectoral orientations of its locomotive (metal) and car (wood/paper) shops. The sources do not provide definitive information as to how the railway's total reported shop workers were split between these two shops, so estimations were necessary. Paul Craven's comparative examination of the locomotive and car shop payrolls were particularly useful in making this determination. His findings suggest that by the early 1870s the car shops employed roughly half again as many workers as the locomotive shop. Out of a total workforce of 983, then, such a breakdown would assign 393 to the locomotive shop and 590 to the car Shop. (If 'x' represents the locomotive Shop, then $x + 1.5x = 983$). Of course, such concrete numbers suggest a degree of precision not provided in the sources. One must be able to account for such variables as pay differentials between shopcrafts (and many others) to make this determination more accurate. The census information is also just a momentary 'glimpse' at the GWR workforce. Craven has shown, for example, that there was more fluctuation in car shop workforce size than in the locomotive shop. Given that the present data do not allow for more accurate determinations, these numbers must be understood as gross estimates. To reflect this statistical inexactitude, this study will move away from the above formulaic determinations of workforce size to suggest that the locomotive shop may have employed *as many as* 400 workers and the car shop *as many as* 600 workers. Similarly for wages (the only financial particular provided by the GWR to census-takers), out of an aggregate payroll of $500 000 a rough estimate of the shopcrafts based on the above workplace formula would assign $200 000 in wages to the locomotive shop and $300 000 in wages to the car shop. For the comparative payroll determination, see Paul Craven, "Labour and Management on the Great Western Railway," in *Labouring Lives*, ed. Craven (Toronto: University of Toronto Press, 1995), 377, fig. 7. Many thanks to Paul Craven for advising me on this matter. Paul Craven, personal communication with author, 17–18 March 2003.

from the manuscript schedules of the 1871 Census of Canada provides rich information regarding the city's industrial development.[14] Census takers were able to enumerate 328 industrial establishments in Hamilton by 1871. These enterprises employed 5743 men, women, and children. In exchange for wages totalling $1 874 948 that year, workers in these establishments turned $2 905 131 worth of raw materials into $5 651 774 in product, thereby generating $2 746 643 in value-added production.[15]

A sectoral look at industrial activity in the city provides more insight into the sheer scale and degree of diversification achieved by industry by 1871. Table 1.1 shows that, in line with its reputation established in the 1840s, industrial activity was dominated by the secondary-metal sector, which accounted for about 43 per cent of the city's value-added production that year. The traditional core of the secondary-metal sector, the production of such items as furnaces, stoves, heaters, agricultural implements, castings, tinsmithing and sheet iron products, was itself still quite strong, representing about 14 per cent of manufacturing added value. Many of the old players had become more ensconced in these sectors over recent years and had grown appreciably in size, including the L.D. Sawyer Agricultural Implement Works, the foundries of James Stewart, Anthony and William Copp, Edward and Charles Gurney, and Dennis Moore, as well as Moore's tin, japan, and pressed-ware manufactory. However, the recent internal growth of these subsectors was also evident: the Turnbull Brothers' Mary Street foundry had achieved marked growth since its founding in the late 1850s, the foundries of William Burrow, Charles Stewart, and John Milne, Matthew Howles and Alexander Gartshore, and Thomas Cowie had all been founded during either the mid-1860s or early 1870s, and William Turnbull had recently founded a separate tin and galvanized iron works.

Equally notable was evidence of recent diversification within the secondary-metal sector. The car shops of the Great Western Railway, converted from a subcontracted to a company-run operation in the mid-1850s, were the most striking example of this. Production was given a further boost when locomotive production was added to the GWR's Hamilton facility in 1860. As Paul Craven and Tom Traves have shown, the railways – including the GWR – 'owned and operated some of the largest and most sophisticated manufacturing plants in the Canadian economy ... the railways were Canada's first large-scale integrated industrial corporations.' While the company did not report the value of its industrial operations in 1871, it did report that

983 men were employed in the shops, making it Ontario's largest industrial employer.[16]

The GWR also contributed directly to Hamilton's industrial diversity in one other important way. The erection of a rolling mill near its locomotive and car shops in 1864 increased its reputation as the country's premier iron centre. A little more than half a decade into operation, census-takers reported that the GWR rolling mill employed 190 men and paid $80 000 annually in wages. Rolling mill management also reported aggregate annual production valued at $680 000, though this figure must be questioned since much production value was achieved in rerolling the GWR's own rails, the original value of which was likely not accounted for in this total. With this proviso in mind, the rolling mill itself accounted for somewhere close to 10 per cent of all value-added production in Hamilton by 1871.[17]

The stimulus of market integration and the linkages offered within the metals sector itself also encouraged the commencement of other important varieties of secondary metal production. F.G. Beckett's Atlas Engine and Boiler Works began feeding Hamilton industrialists' growing appetite for steam sometime around 1855. By 1863 it was reported that Beckett steam engines powered twenty-one local plants.[18] By 1871 Beckett boasted $100 000 in annual product value and paid his 120 employees wages totalling $40 000 a year. Similarly, the T. and F. Northey steam engine works had grown from a small operation in the early 1860s to an employer of 31 men whose combined labour turned out $33 000 worth of product in 1871.[19] Elijah Ware's Provincial Scale Works had commenced business in the city around 1856. A few years later Ware had partnered with the Gurneys, and by 1871 the Gurney, Ware Scale Works employed 22 men and boys and turned out $25 000 in annual product.[20] Also of note was Benjamin Greenings's fledgling Victoria Wire Mills, which, while still a relatively small operation in 1871, would expand markedly over the next two decades.

The most notable diversification within secondary-metal production, however, was the forward linkage addition of sewing machine production in the 1860s and early 1870s. Spurred on by the ability to jump U.S. patent protection, sewing machine manufacture accounted for about 14 per cent of all value-added production in Hamilton by 1871, making it the city's leading industrial subsector. Richard Mott Wanzer and John Nathanial Tarbox, proprietors of the city's largest sewing machine plant, were the first to set up shop in town, their half-dozen hands turning out four machines a week beginning in 1860. A few years later the number of sewing machine establishments proliferated – Wilson, Bowman & Company (1868), Gardner Sewing Machine Company (1870), Hespeler Sewing Machine Company (1871), and Appelton Knitting Machine Company (1871) – making Hamilton the capital of sewing machine production in Canada by the early 1870s. When the information for the 1871 census was collected, Wanzer's was the city's largest sewing machine producer, employing 275 men and boys and turning out $210 000 in annual product. The other two sewing machine works, however, were also of impressive size. Two hundred thousand dollars of annual product was turned out by Wilson, Bowman's 130 men and boys, and Frederick Gardner's more modest plant still employed 70 men and boys to create $100 000 in product. Only two years into operation, the Appleton Company gave employment to between 80 and 90 hands. While information regarding the Hespeler Company is scarce, it was reported only a year after commencing operations that this sizable plant was 'worked to its utmost capacity.'[21]

The secondary-metal industry made the most appreciable contribution to the city's value-added production, but other sectors also made significant contributions and contained establishments of notable size. The clothing sector, accounting for 17 per cent of value-added production in 1871, was the most sizable of these. Production in the boot and shoe subsector was lead by John McPherson & Company, a massive operation employing 175 men, women, and children and racking up $200 000 in yearly sales. This was one of the city's first truly large industrial establishments, growing from a small shop in the early 1850s to employing over one hundred hands shortly after its reorganization around 1862. Philo Dayfoot's boot and shoe manufactory also claimed small shop origins in the 1850s. By 1871 this less impressive establishment employed 49 operatives to manufacture $42 000 in annual product. The 25 employees of Robert Hopkins, the city's other sizable boot and shoe manufacturer, created a similar annual product value.[22]

The clothing and tailored goods subsector was home to one of the city's most sizable establishments. After the GWR shops, the 455 hands employed at the Sanford and McInnis ready-made clothing manufactory made it the city's second-largest industrial employer. Founded in 1862, this establishment relied on its mainly female outwork workforce to assemble $350 000 in product just nine years later. This subsector also displayed a strong mid-level component, with six firms producing between $12 500 and $40 000 in annual product and employing between 15 and 30 hands each.

Hats and furs was the other well-developed subsector of the local clothing industry. Glassco & Sons, employing 23 hands, and Turner and Company, employing 37, claimed respective annual products of $25 000 and $12 000. The 74 operatives employed at the much larger Galbraith & Green Felt Hat Works manufactured annual product worth $60 000.

The wood and paper products sector, comprising close to 9 per cent of value-added production in 1871, also contained a diversified number of sizable operations. Among those producing more than $10 000 in annual product or employing more than 20 hands were the piano manufactories of Charles Thomas, William and Joseph Herald and Thomas White, James Thonton's melodeon works, the City Coach Factory and the Hamilton Coach Factory, the cabinet and furniture establishments of James Reid, Joseph Hoodless and Thomas Hill and Graham Murdoch, the brushworks of Alfred Green and of C.W. Meakins & Sons, Allan Easson's broom and brush manufactory and the Mugridge Broom Factory, and George Batcheler's, George Sharpe & Sons', and Michael Brennens's planing mills.

Fitting the same criterion in the construction sector, itself accounting for 7 per cent of value-added production in 1871, were the Young Bros. Plumbers, the carpenter David Edgar, and the carpenters and builders Robert Chisholm, William Clucas, and C. Allan. Especially notable in this sector was the builder C. Kempster, whose workforce of 250 manufactured lumber and erected buildings worth $103 500 in 1871.

A number of larger industrial establishments also flourished in the chemical sector. Vinegar production was especially prominent, with the establishments of Birely and Company, Williamson and Company, and Benjamin Charlton turning out annual product ranging from $25 000 to $61 060. The soap and candle production facilities of David Morton, John & James Judd, and James Walker and Company similarly boasted annual products of between $13 670 and $52 000.

In primary production, the agricultural products sector was itself quite diverse and contained a number of sizable establishments. After undergoing considerable expansion during the 1860s, Peter Grant's Spring Brewery employed 24 hands and turned out an annual product worth $44 000 by 1871.[23] F.W. Fearman's pork-curing establishment, reporting $35 000 of product value, would grow considerably in the next ten years.[24] However, far larger in 1871 was Samuel Nash's pork operation, whose 23 employees processed $220 000 in annual product. Humphery and Newbury, proprietors of the city's largest tannery, and the large grist mill operated by Morgan Brothers boasted $40 000 and $120 000 in annual product respectively. The city's manufactured tobacco and cigar industry was particularly notable, with the firms of Frederick Schwarz, E. Barber & Company, Frederick Schraeder, and Simpson and Stuart varied in size from 12 to 40 hands employed and $15 000 and $40 000 in product value. The largest tobacco producer was the firm of Tuckett and Billings, employing 48 in the smoking and chewing tobacco operation they had founded just five years earlier.

Even in sectors contributing more modestly to total value-added production a number of establishments of appreciable size can be discerned. The brickyards of Alfred Little and Hempler and Company employed 36 and 31 hands respectively. H.A. King engaged 22 hands in the manufacture of whips. Hurd and Roberts Marble Works employed 40 men. Even larger was the Hamilton Glass Company, employing 83 men and boys to turn out $85 000 in product. A small workforce rewarded the shareholders of the Hamilton Gas Light Company with more than $30 000 in sales. The city's baking and confectionery business was dominated by Isaac Chilman, whose 29 hands produced more than $90 000 in product at his two plants. The proprietors of the city's two leading newspapers, the *Spectator* and the *Times*, dominated the local printing and publishing industry, each employing over 40 hands to produce more than $35 000 in product.

Tables 1.2 and 1.3 provide aggregate indicators of the sectoral diversity and sizable number of Hamilton's larger industrial establishments by 1871. For industrial establishments employing 25 or more hands, table 1.2 shows that while the secondary-metal sector made a strong showing, a number of other industrial sectors were also prominent, especially the ready-made and boot and shoe subsectors of the clothing industry. Considered in terms of the number of industrial establishments claiming over $25 000 in product value, table 1.3 shows the secondary-metal industry again to be prominent but not dominant. The combination of the agricultural products and clothing sectors, for instance, overshadows the number of large metal establishments. As the sectoral weightings of value-added production provided in table 1.1 further indicate, this diversification can be discerned in sectoral productivity as well as sheer number of establishments.

In sum, industrial activity had achieved considerable diversity and scale by 1871. The secondary-metal sector – itself significantly internally diversified – led the way. But industrial activity of a notable scale could also be found for an impressive number of individual establishments throughout Hamilton's industrial sectors. It is not

Table 1.2 Industrial establishments claiming 25 or more workers, Hamilton, 1871

Name of establishment	Sector	Subsector	Hands employed
Great Western Railway	Metal/wood	Ry. cars/loco	984
Sanford, McInnis & Co.	Clothing	Clothing	455
R.M. Wanzer & Co.	Metal	Sewing mach.	275
C. Kempster	Construction	Builder	250
GWR Rolling Mills	Metal	Rolling mill	225
John McPherson & Co.	Clothing	Boot/shoe	175
Wilson, Bowman & Co.	Metal	Sewing mach.	131
F.G. Beckett	Metal	Engine/boiler	120
E. & C. Gurney	Metal	Foundry	101
L.D. Sawyer & Co.	Metal	Agri. imp.	90
Rutherford & Company	Misc.	Glass	83
Galbraith & Green	Clothing	Hats, furs	74
Gardner & Co.	Metal	Sewing mach.	70
James Stewart	Metal	Foundry	63
A. & J. Copp	Metal	Foundry	60
P. W. Dayfoot & Co.	Clothing	Boot/shoe	49
Tuckett & Billings	Agri. Prod.	Tobacco	48
C. Stewart & Co.	Printing/pub	Printing/pub.	45
Lawson & McCulloch	Printing/pub.	Printing/pub.	43
Hamilton Malleable Iron Works	Metal	Castings	41
Hurd & Roberts	Minerals	Marble/stone	40
E. Barber & Co.	Agri. prod.	Tobacco	40
Turnbull & Company	Metal	Foundry	40
Turner & Co.	Clothing	Hats, furs	37
Alfred Little	Misc.	Brick/tile	36
C. W. Meakins & Sons	Wood/paper	Broom/brush	36
Frederick Schwarz	Agri. prod.	Tobacco	32
Hempler & Co.	Misc.	Brick/tile	31
T.F. Northey	Metal	Boiler/engine	31
Munro & Henderson	Clothing	Clothing	30
Dennis Moore & Co.	Metal	Foundry	30
Dennis Moore & Co.	Metal	Tin/sheet iron	30
Ernest Kraft	Leather	Harn./saddle	26
Donald Smith	Clothing	Clothing	26
James Reid	Wood/paper	Cabinet/furn.	25
George Batchelder	Wood/paper	Planing/mould.	25
Robert Hopkins & Co.	Clothing	Boot/shoe	25

Source: 1871 Census Manuscripts

Table 1.3 Sectoral weighting, industrial establishments claiming $25,000 or more annual product, Hamilton, 1871

Sector	n	% total
Agricultural products	10	20.41
Minerals	1	2.04
Beverages/food	2	4.08
Chemical	4	8.16
Clothing	8	16.33
Metals	16	32.65
Printing/publishing	2	4.08
Wood/paper	2	4.08
Construction	2	4.08
Miscellaneous	2	4.08
Total	49	100

Source: 1871 Census Manuscripts

coincidental that this same year Hamilton named itself the 'Birmingham of Canada.'[25]

Indeed, by 1871 all this economic activity had enabled Hamilton to emerge as a major industrial centre both provincially and nationally. In Ontario, Hamilton industry ranked second only to Toronto in terms of capital invested, hands employed, wages paid, value of raw material, and annual product value.[26] Nine Hamilton industrial establishments were ranked in the Top 60 industrial establishments in Ontario undertaken by Elizabeth Bloomfield and G.T. Bloomfield based on the combined factors of number of workers employed, gross production value, value of fixed capital investment, and value added in the manufacturing process reflected in the 1871 industrial schedules.[27] The GWR shops topped the list, but a number of other strong indicators can also be deduced. These four measures placed Sanford, McInnis and Company as the province's largest clothing manufacturer. In boot and shoe production, John McPherson & Company was the province's second-largest producer after Toronto's Sessions, Turner, Cooper. The Wanzer plant ranked as Ontario's largest producer of sewing machines, with the Wilson, Bowman plant ranking third after the Guelph Sewing Machine Company. While Edward and Charles Gurney's Hamilton foundry rated fourth provincially, their ownership of the Gurney, Ware Scale Works and Phoenix Foundry in Toronto was not integrated into this measure. Frederick Beckett's Atlas Engine and Boiler Works ranked fourth in Ontario behind

Table 1.4 Ranked comparison of industrial performance, cities and towns having over 5,000 inhabitants, Canada, 1871

City	A. Capital inv. ($)	B. No. hands employed	C. Am. yearly wages ($)	D. Value. raw material ($)	E. Tot. prod. value ($)	F. Value added ($)	G. Pop.	H. V-A/ capita ($)	I.* Rank totals
Montreal	11,101,031	21,187	5,195,668	19,037,962	32,731,966	13,694,004	107,225	127.71	
Rank	[1]	[1]	[1]	[1]	[1]	[1]	[1]	[1]	5 [1]
Quebec	2,870,638	7,250	1,459,279	4,771,459	8,449,752	3,678,293	59,699	61.61	
Rank	[3]	[4]	[4]	[3]	[3]	[4]	[2]	[7]	17 [3]
Toronto	4,036,158	9,400	2,690,993	7,168,993	13,686,093	6,517,100	56,092	116.19	
Rank	[2]	[2]	[2]	[2]	[2]	[2]	[3]	[3]	10 [2]
Halifax	1,492,944	2,167	732,151	1,331,090	2,817,480	1,486,410	29,582	50.24	
Rank	[7]	[8]	[7]	[8]	[8]	[7]	[4]	[9]	38 [8]
Saint John	2,275,337	7,277	1,796,491	4,540,364	8,312,627	3,772,263	28,805	130.96	
Rank	[4]	[3]	[3]	[4]	[4]	[3]	[5]	[2]	18 [4]
Hamilton	1, 541,264	4,456	1,329,712	2,860,399	5,471,494	2,611,075	26,716	97.73	
Rank	[6]	[5]	[5]	[5]	[5]	[5]	[6]	[4]	26 [5]
Ottawa	1,914,287	3,064	843,521	2,536,664	4,152,960	1,616,306	21,545	75.02	
Rank	[5]	[6]	[6]	[6]	[6]	[6]	[7]	[6]	29 [6]
London	1, 001,789	2,261	687,473	1,955,303	3,436,625	1,481,322	15,826	93.6	
Rank	[8]	[7]	[8]	[7]	[7]	[8]	[8]	[5]	37 [7]
Kingston	526,855	1,298	366,669	717,795	1,348,893	631,098	12,407	50.87	
Rank	[9]	[9]	[9]	[9]	[9]	[9]	[9]	[8]	45 [9]

* Rank totals were calculated by averaging rankings in columns A through E.

Source: Census of Canada, 1871, vol. 1, table 6, 'Population of Cities and Towns having over 5,000 inhabitants compared,' and vol. 3, table LIV, 'Aggregate Value of All Industries in each District.'

Table 1.5 Percentage of total population engaged in industry among Canadian cities with over 10,000 population, Canada, 1871

Top 6 cities	Pop. in industry (%)
Hamilton	21.6
Montreal	20.7
Toronto	18.9
Ottawa	14.8
London	14.6
Saint John	14.2

Source: Elizabeth and G.T. Bloomfield, 'Patterns of Canadian Industry in 1871: An Overview Based on the First Census of Canada,' Research Report No. 12 (Guelph, ON: Department of Geography, University of Guelph, 1990), 55.

Toronto's Dickey Neill, Goldie, McCulloch of Galt, and the Waterous Works of Brantford.[28]

The relative weight of Hamilton industry also fared well nationally. Table 1.4 determines Hamilton to be the nation's fifth-largest industrial centre among cities with five thousand or more inhabitants. Rank totals of this measure average Hamilton's ranking relative to other cities' in terms of capital invested, number of hands employed, amounts of yearly wages, raw material value, and total product value.

However, other measures indicate that industrial activity in Hamilton had taken on an even more intensive form. Assessing in terms of value added per capita, Hamilton ranked fourth nationally among larger town and cities (see table 1.4, column H.). The intensity of industrial activity as it most directly relates to social experience – the central concern of this study – is perhaps most appropriately assessed through a comparative determination of its penetration of local communities. Table 1.5 shows that Hamilton led the nation – exceeding even Montreal – in the percentage of its total population engaged in industrial pursuits. By any of the above measures, however, Hamilton's industrial entrepreneurs and its craft workforce were lead participants in Canada's early industrialization.

The Character of Hamilton's Early Industrialization

Historians have begun to question how representative the type of industrialization identified chiefly by the 'new' generation of Canadian labour historians in their studies of large urban areas actually was of the province's or the country's overall industrialization.[29]

Craig Heron, for example, has noted that the new labour history has 'presented the Ontario evidence within a universal paradigm of industrial capitalist development. The formation and struggles of the working class seemed to unfold in a pattern roughly similar to those in most other industrializing areas of the world in the period, particularly Britain and the United States. By extension, readers might also easily assume that the wider experience in Ontario was simply Toronto and Hamilton writ large.'[30] The view that the capital-intensive, specialized industries visible in large urban centres typified industrial development has been challenged in recent years by a growing body of research on Ontario that suggests that an impressive degree of industrial growth was achieved in the middle decades of the nineteenth century by the astute and highly selective efforts of small producers to service the growing staple economy and, perhaps more importantly, to supply the niche markets generated by its many linkages. The result, it appears, was a type of industrialization characterized by flexible, specialized enterprise functioning in limited markets and tooled for the necessity of product diversification. 'Modern Industry,' such as it existed in such centres as Toronto or Montreal by this point, was still the exception and not the rule in overall industrial development.[31]

However, as the description of Hamilton's industrialization above suggests, the size and importance of industry had meaningfully changed the structural context within which local craftsworkers pursued their livelihoods over the fifteen or twenty years before the early 1870s. Disaggregating this impressive portrait provides a more nuanced understanding of just how much 'change' Hamilton's early industrialization actually entailed.

The adoption of uneven and combined development as a limited international research agenda was outlined earlier. In the Canadian context historians have been slow to adequately integrate the insights of this approach into their analyses. One particular feature of the Canadian literature has been the improper consideration of the stages of industrial capitalist development. For example, inspired by the seminal work of Raphael Samuel, both Bryan Palmer and Gregory Kealey lay the groundwork for their respective studies of Hamilton and Toronto by providing accounts of each city's combined and uneven industrialization. This involved, in both cases, the charting of the industrialization process through broad Marxist categories of primitive accumulation/handicraft production, manufacture, and modern industry. Both authors acknowledge the idea that the coexistence of large, medium, and small industry would have had a pronounced effect on social experience in their respective cities, but fail to integrate this observation in any meaningful way into their analysis. Indeed, both authors conceive of these stages of industrial development *sequentially*, treating the stage of modern industry as an endpoint that had been reached in their localities by the initial dates of their studies. Palmer provides the most rigidly sequential interpretation in his study of Hamilton's combined and uneven industrialization. He characterizes the years before 1853 as the period of 'primitive accumulation,' followed closely by a period of 'manufacture proper,' which spanned about the next decade and a half. He continues: 'By the early 1870s, when Hamilton first attained the reputation it would vigorously defend in later years, as 'the Birmingham of Canada,' the transition to the final stage of capitalist development, what Marx referred to as Modern Industry, was completed.'[32] Indeed, both Kealey's and Palmer's studies are predicated on the understanding that craftsworkers' behaviour was informed by a social experience derived from the overwhelming material experience of 'Modern Industry,' a context with such features as 'large concentrations of workers,' 'extensive mechanization,' and 'an elaborate division of labour.' It is at this point that textured analyses of combined and uneven development become confounded in the teleology of the mass-production model, and obscure from theoretical view the social experience of actors in economies developing along alternative roads of industrialization.

A few historians have found ways to see around this trap. As some of the international literature has suggested, stages of industrial development must be considered *concurrently* in both contextual surveys of industrial growth and the social consequences of that growth. This suggestion has been made most forcefully in the Canadian historiography by Ian McKay in his study of the Halifax baking and confectionery industry. McKay takes seriously the need to consider the impact of stratification within the mode of production in examinations of the social experiences of craftsworkers in early industrialization. However, his suggestion that pursuing this line of enquiry might, among other things, 'be the beginning of an explanation of the stability of nineteenth-century Canadian capitalism' is an agenda that has been left largely ignored in subsequent historiography.[33]

In the right combination, concurrent stages of industrial growth can produce an economic context in which much has changed, but within which there can exist an experience of continuity. Profound change can take place in industry without it having to go the route of mass production or into the stage of 'Modern Industry.' The tremendous change discernible in Hamilton industry by the early 1870s occurred as a result of concurrent stages of industrial growth. But instead of 'Modern Industry' coexisting with other stages of production, it was the advanced stage of 'manufacture' juxtaposed with more traditional craft production that characterized the city's combined and uneven development.

One integral component of analyses that presume the dominance of 'Modern Industry' in craftsworkers' social experience is the idea that industrial capitalism brings along with it a smaller number of larger enterprises. As a result of this, one major way craftsworkers have been presented as becoming subject to the proletarianization process is by becoming unable to pursue the traditional end point of apprenticeship and journeywork, the ability to themselves become self-employed. By this measure, therefore, if the logic of industrialism had truly reached the stage of modern industry in Hamilton by the early 1870s, one likely indicator of this would be a drying up of opportunities for self-employment for craftsworkers, expressed in an overall shrinkage (and coincident increase in size) of the number of industrial establishments in the city.

The available evidence does not support this trend. For example, utilizing the data collected by Michael Katz and his associates in their study of the city between 1851 and 1871, table 1.6 shows that the number of masters and manufacturers substantially increased in a wide array of industrial sectors between 1851 and 1871. Only two sectors, cabinet and jewellery-making, show a decline in opportunities for self-employment, and in both cases this decrease was slight. Overall, by 1871 opportunity for self-employment for master/manufacturers had increased 107 per cent from 1851 and (a still significant) 32 per cent from 1861. Even self-employment opportunities in so-called 'declining trades' such as boot and shoe making and tailoring still recorded comfortable increases. Self-employment opportunity was also still expanding in the metal industry, the leading sector of Hamilton's industrializing economy. While some constriction of opportunity had occurred in this sector over the previous ten years, the twenty-year measure still shows expansion. Also, when aggregated with opportunities in blacksmithing and machine production, the city's larger metal sector shows comfortable growth in opportunities for self-employment by both the ten- and twenty-year measures. Many sectors reported quite marked increases in opportunity. The number of master/manufacturer coopers, 'other construction,' printers, broommakers, tailors, musical instrument makers, and 'oth-

Table 1.6 Demographic characteristics of masters and manufacturers, Hamilton, 1851–71

	Number masters/manufacturers			
Trade	1851	1861	1871	% change 1851–71
Bakers	4	16	25	525
Butchers	1	9	14	1300
Blacksmiths	10	12	14	40
Coopers	1	3	3	200
Builders/carpenters	26	25	39	50
Other construction	14	23	36	157
Metal	26	33	29	11
Cabinet	14	11	12	–14
Printers	6	15	13	116
Coach	7	8	8	14
Broom	2	3	6	200
Boot and shoe	17	28	30	77
Tailors	14	26	38	171
Tobacconists	1	5	9	800
Marble	0	1	1	ind.
Harness and saddle	5	5	8	60
Jewellers	8	5	6	–25
Marine	1	3	9	800
Musical instrument	3	9	9	200
Machinery	3	7	13	333
Other	18	37	52	189
Totals	181	284	374	107

Source: Michael B. Katz, Michael J. Doucet, and Mark J. Stern, *The Social Organization of Industrial Capitalism* (Cambridge, MA: Harvard University Press, 1982). Adaptation of table 2.3.B.

ers' in the city, for example, increased between 100 and 500 per cent over these twenty years. The number of bakers, butchers, tobacconists, and marine producers in the city underwent a phenomenal expansion of over 500 per cent each. By 1871 the number of Hamiltonians self-employed in industrial pursuits was still on the increase.

The depth of Hamilton's combined and uneven development is best appreciated by outlining in some detail the coexistence of small, medium, and large enterprise in both aggregate and sectoral terms by 1871. The nature of the sources does not allow us to determine what the relationship was between smaller and larger industrial enterprise

Table 1.7 Number of industrial establishments, by employment and sector, Hamilton, 1871

	Employees, % (n)					
Sectors	1–5	6–10	11–25	26–50	51+	Total
Metal	44.90 (22)	20.24 (9)	6.12 (3)	10.20 (5)	20.41 (10)	100 (49)
Clothing	51.95 (40)	20.78 (16)	18.18 (14)	5.19 (4)	3.90 (3)	100 (77)
Wood/paper	52.73 (29)	18.18 (10)	27.27 (15)	1.82 (1)	0 (0)	100 (55)
Agri prod.	63.33 (19)	13.33 (4)	23.33 (7)	0 (0)	0 (0)	100 (30)
Construction	51.86 (14)	22.20 (6)	22.20 (6)	0 (0)	3.70 (1)	100 (27)
Chemical	66.67 (8)	16.67 (2)	16.67 (2)	0 (0)	0 (0)	100 (12)
Misc	56.52 (13)	13.04 (3)	17.39 (4)	8.70 (2)	4.35 (1)	100 (23)
All sectors	52.45 (171)	20.24 (66)	16.87 (55)	5.83 (19)	4.60 (15)	100 (326)

Source: 1871 Industrial Schedules

in the two decades preceding the 1870s.[34] But scrutiny of the 1871 census manuscripts is more revealing.

Table 1.7 examines the proportional dispersal of industrial establishments by workforce size in 1871. In aggregate it shows the small shop (employing 1–5 hands) still dominant, accounting for more than 50 per cent of all local manufacturing establishments. More than 70 per cent of industrial establishments still employed ten or fewer workers. The small shop was also still dominant in all seven leading industrial sectors. Conversely, large shops (employing over 50 hands), while undoubtedly an industrial form that had become the subject of much comment and speculation by local craftsworkers as to the direction industry might be heading, were still not numerous by 1871, accounting for under 5 per cent of all establishments and conspicuous only in the metal sector, but even there comprising only about 20 per cent of all metal shops.

This is not to argue that large establishments made only a marginal impact on the city's industrial landscape. As table 1.8 demonstrates, in terms of value-added production and number of hands employed, quite the opposite was true. Over half of all industrial employees worked in plants employing more than fifty hands, and these plants accounted for almost half of value-added production in the city. As the discussion below will explain, what was remarkable about the city's larger industrial establishments was that they were much more often than not the small concern writ large, agglomerations of craftsworkers performing ranges of tasks well within the labour

Table 1.8 Industrial establishments, by employment, distribution of workforce, value-added production, and productivity, Hamilton, 1871

Workforce size	n. est.	Emp. (n)	% employ. in industry	Value added [$]	% value add in industry	Productivity v-a/emp.($)
1–5	171	460	8.01	297,795	10.85	647.38
6–10	66	509	8.87	301,208	10.97	591.76
11–25	55	927	16.14	510,713	18.61	550.93
26–50	19	691	12.03	331,017	12.06	479.04
51+	15	3156	54.95	1,303,950	47.51	600.07
Total	326	5743	100.00	2,744,683	100.00	

Note: The productivity calculation for the 51+ category does not include the 893 employees of the GWR as financial particulars for that concern were not reported on the census.
Source: 1871 Industrial Schedules

process typical of the small shop. They represent the appreciable amplitude of Hamilton's combined development, and underscore how a remarkable degree of industrialization can still structurally contain pre-existing social relations of production. It is, however, also important to reiterate that even by the above measures, smaller concerns were not insignificant. A third of all workers were employed in plants employing twenty-five hands or fewer, and through their labours they provided over 40 per cent of all value-added production. Table 1.8 also shows that the larger shop appears to have made little headway in outstripping the productivity of its smaller counterparts.

Consideration of the overall industrialization process loses its complexity, however, if the historian simply notes the great number of hands employed by, or strong economic performance of, larger industry as evidence that an industrial economy was triumphantly nearing the end point of its march towards modern industry. The temptation here – one repeatedly taken up by those eager to locate initial proletarianization – is to take this as evidence of the death knell of the small concern. Indeed, it ultimately would be, but not by the early 1870s. Small concerns were still appreciably important to the local industrial economy in their sheer number, the number of hands they employed, and their output. Proponents of the 'proletarianization thesis' may retort that, while small concerns might have been numerically dominant, the 'squeeze' was on – masters' incomes, journeymen's wages, and general business viability were all on the edge. Consequently, small masters and their former charges alike were

Table 1.9 Occupational growth/decline, craftsworkers, Hamilton, 1851–71

	Number of craftsworkers			
Trade	1851	1861	1871	% change 1851–71
Bakers	61	62	72	18
Butchers	35	25	66	89
Blacksmiths	113	81	147	30
Coopers	14	10	42	200
Builders/carpenters	292	337	504	73
Other construction	162	222	292	80
Metal	135	136	286	112
Cabinet	80	75	138	73
Printers	59	74	109	85
Coach	65	35	44	–32
Broom	8	13	43	438
Boot and shoe	204	143	209	1
Tailors	155	115	183	18
Tobacconists	13	16	75	476
Marble	40	20	42	5
Harness and saddle	29	24	55	90
Jewellers	19	23	28	47
Marine	2	3	12	500
Musical instrument	1	1	11	1000
Machinists	50	123	455	810
Other	63	73	242	284
Totals	1,600	1,611	3,055	91

Source: Michael B. Katz, Michael J. Doucet, and Mark J. Stern, *The Social Organization of Industrial Capitalism* (Cambridge, MA: Harvard University Press, 1982). Adaptation of table 2.3.B.

forced into wage-earning opportunities at larger, more modern enterprises. As chapter 2 will show in more detail, Hamilton's smaller industrial establishments were still economically viable concerns. Neither in reality, nor in public perception, were small concerns feeling the 'pinch' of advancing industrialization that the 'proletarianization thesis' suggests.

The fact that large firms may have become dominant in terms of workforce size and the scale of their productive activity is also not, in itself, evidence of fundamental change in craftsworker experience. To problematize one popular 'measure' of proletarianization one must ask, for instance, whether Hamilton's industrialization

Table 1.10 Metal sector, by employment, Hamilton, 1871

		Employees		Value added		Steam power	
Employees	Estab. (n)	(n)	[%]	[$]	[%]	n	[%]
1–5	22	63	3.32	35,187	3.00	4	18.19
6–10	9	69	3.64	35,339	3.01	5	55.56
11–25	3	56	2.96	49,365	4.21	3	100.00
26–50	5	172	9.08	118,600	10.11	5	100.00
51+	10	1,535	81.00	934,500	79.67	10	100.00
Total	49	1,895	100.00	1,172,991	100.00	27	

Source: 1871 Industrial Schedules. The 51+ category includes the GWR Locomotive Shops.
See table 1.1 'Note on GWR' for this determination.

meant a decline in skilled trades by the early 1870s. Quite the opposite was true (see table 1.9). Coachmaking was the only trade considered by Katz and associates that showed a decline in number of workers employed between 1851 and 1871. Employment in all other trades increased by about 90 per cent overall from both 1851 and 1861 levels. The city's metal industry fared particularly well. Over 80 per cent more blacksmiths found employment in 1871 than ten years earlier. Metal workers experienced well over a 100 per cent increase in their number by both ten- and twenty-year measures. The number of machinists in the city increased a phenomenal 810 per cent over the twenty years since 1851 and a still impressive 270 per cent from 1861. Respectable increases are also evident in a variety of other sectors. That industrialization may have actually increased, or in some cases created, skilled positions has been central to the findings of other historians.[35]

The persistence of skilled trades itself throws into question the extent to which the division of labour progressed by this time. An examination of the leading sectors of Hamilton's industrial economy confirms that the industrialization process had only a marginal impact on the work routines and opportunities for craftsworkers by the 1870s and brings further scrutiny to the nature of Hamilton's combined and uneven development. While aspects of work changed, much remained the same.

These trends can be seen in secondary metals, the leading sector of Hamilton's industrial economy. As table 1.10 demonstrates, by 1871 the large shop dominated both in terms of hands employed and value-added production. Steam power was also well in evidence, universal in larger shops but also employed to a significant extent in shops with ten or fewer workers. However, the agglomeration of large numbers of workers under one roof and the widespread use of steam power belies much continuity in production.

There was, for example, little link between the large concentrations of workers in larger shops and either elaborate divisions of labour or forms of modern machinery that effectively robbed craftsworkers of their skills. The GWR locomotive shops, for example, may have been the largest employer in the secondary-metal sector, utilized some of the country's most modern technology, and employed in abundance such recently created occupational groups as machinists and fitters. But up through the early 1870s, in both newly created and more traditional trades, production there remained centred on the all-round skills of the well-trained craftsman, and the culture of the shop floor was imbued with intricate job hierarchies that both closely approximated and were likely understood in terms of more traditional craft mobility patterns.[36] Similarly, while work at Great Westerns' adjoining rolling mills made use of giant steam-powered hammers, rollers, shears 'and a dozen other mechanical arrangements,' it still also relied heavily on the manual skills of such new trades as puddlers, rollers, heaters, catchers, and roughers.[37] Both the GWR locomotive shops and the rolling mill created new skilled positions and expanded opportunities in craftswork.

The city's foundry operations were another particularly strong component of the metal sector. A number of these concerns, including the McNab Street, Empire and Gurney foundries and the L.D. Sawyer Agricultural Implement Works, employed workforces of well over fifty men. Wherever possible, they also employed the latest technology, powered by steam. A visitor to the Sawyer Works in 1869 boasted, for example, that 'the mechanical contrivances at work in the Factory are in the highest degree ingenious and all the latest improvements and inventions have been taken advantage of.'[38] However, as a number of studies have noted, moulders' skills remained largely intact through this time period. Employers also had very limited success by this point at hiving the less-skilled aspects of moulders' or patternmakers' work off into less-skilled occupations such as stovemounter, coremaker, or fitter.[39]

Part of the reason employers had not done more to whittle away at the work routines of their patternmakers and moulders was the flexible specialization demanded by limited markets. By the early 1870s, product specialization still lay in the future for Hamilton foundry operations. Ostensibly a 'stove foundry,' the Gurney Brothers' 101 men and boys also produced fireplace grates, hot air furnaces, hot air registers, and agricultural furnaces, and the foundry did an appreciable business in custom castings, especially for the R.M. Wanzer Sewing Machine Company. Also producing sewing machine castings was James Stewart's McNab Street foundry, whose product line included stoves and a variety of railway, engine, and other machine castings. Dennis Moore's product line included stoves, tinware, machinery castings, and agricultural implements. The Mary Street foundry turned out stoves, ploughs, cultivators, machine and engine castings, and engine fittings. The Hamilton Malleable Iron Works turned out all types of castings as well as wagon, carriage, and saddlery hardware, and added stove production some years later.[40] Agricultural implement producers such as L.D. Sawyer still turned out an impressive array of agricultural implements and machinery, including reapers, grain-drills, threshing machines, clover boxes, horse hay forks, and a variety of other agricultural implements.[41] These diversified production runs still demanded the flexible skills of the 'all 'round' moulder or patternmaker.

Product specialization was exhibited by Hamilton's thriving sewing machine manufactories. The relatively short life of this industry (induced by a temporary patent loophole and virtually extinct by 1880) speaks to the folly of such specialization before adequate market consolidation. This specialized industry was also a boon for craftsworkers, likely providing the lion's share of the growth in well-paying machinists' positions outlined in table 1.5. The work culture of the machinist was also well preserved in these plants.[42] Even in a work environment of power planers and lathes, high-speed emery wheels, and polishing, finishing, and milling machines, it was still the skilled hand and personal discretion of the machinist that guided production.[43]

Those industries that grew up to provide the industrializing metal industry with its machinery and motive power did not exhibit much foreordained tendency towards mass production. Rather, the flexible skills and manual dexterity of the craftsworker remained central to the production of special-purpose machinery for industry.[44] This was evident in Hamilton's burgeoning engine and boiler industry, dominated by the early 1870s by the Beckett family's Atlas Works, employing 120 men and boys. A large number of the steam engines and boilers that powered the manufactories of Hamilton and the region were produced here from the mid-1850s. This was custom work. The machine shop, for example, contained an impressive variety of steam-powered machinery by 1865, including lathes and planers, drills, screw cutters, shears, and punching and rolling machines. But the firm still reported that 'all varieties of machine work are executed to order.' Boiler construction also relied almost wholly on hand methods up through these years. The Becketts themselves recognized that the efforts to expand their operations were limited 'only by their inability to obtain a sufficient number of skilled workmen.' The craft skills of the Beckett's workforce were also evident in the firm's diversity of output: stationary and portable engines and boilers of various horsepower for a wide array of uses in manufacturing, agriculture, forestry, and oil production. In addition, the firm boasted of its ability to produce 'pile-drivers, hoisting machines, pumps, sawing machinery, cranes, &c, &c. ... smithwork and repairs at shortest notice' as well as engines to drive threshing machines.[45] The motive power of Hamilton's industrialization and the specialized machinery it operated was created by hand.

The coexistence of small and large shops was another notable feature of the local metal industry. As table 1.7 shows, the small concern was still the most common type of metal shop by the 1870s. It outstripped the large shop (employing fifty or more workers) by a factor of nearly four to one. Some traditional metal trades remained more or less unaffected by industrial growth. The chief business of the GWR rolling mills, which was the rerolling of rails, did little to displace the traditional blacksmith from his local markets. Larger industry like the rolling mills or railway shops actually increased local demand for this trade.[46] Dennis Moore's large tin and sheet iron operation also appears not to have precluded the small shop as the almost universal unit of production in that industry. Again, opportunity for the skilled tinsmith could be found at both these levels.[47]

The establishment of large enterprise could also provide opportunity to the small producer. A number of small machine shops serviced the specialized machinery needs of local industry. The machinist John Leitch, for example, turned out 'machinery of various and many kinds.' The Hamilton Iron Works performed custom engine and boiler fabrication and repair. Samuel J. Moore concentrated efforts in his small shop on the production of tinsmiths' tools. A number of other small producers eagerly inserted themselves into the new niche markets of the industrial economy. Alexander Howie geared his small brass foundry to the production of sewing machine attachments for local large producers. The blacksmith Samuel Spears performed ship work as part of the burgeoning boat building and repair industry that grew around the Great Western's port operations after the mid-1850s.

Table 1.11 Clothing sector – boot and shoe subsector, by hands employed, Hamilton, 1871

	Establishments		Employees		Value added	
Employees	(n)	[%]	(n)	[%]	[$]	[%]
1–5	17	73.90	48	14.59	25,885	16.34
6–10	2	8.70	16	4.87	8,000	5.05
11–25	2	8.70	41	12.46	22,513	14.21
26–50	1	4.35	49	14.89	22,000	13.89
51+	1	4.35	175	53.19	80,000	50.51
Total	23	100.00	329	100.00	158,398	100.00

Source: 1871 Industrial Schedules

Similarly, by 1871 Benjamin Greening's modest wire works turned out product for both the GWR and the rigging needs of local lake traffic.[48] One aspect of the industrialization of Hamilton's metal sector was the proliferation of small producers.

Varieties of this type of industrial development were also well in evidence in the two leading sectors of the city's clothing industry, boots and shoes and clothing and tailored goods. Perhaps more than any other industrial subsector, the local boot and shoe industry exemplified the true breadth of combined and uneven development (see table 1.11). At one extreme was the massive manufacturing operation of John McPherson and Company. This plant employed 175 hands by 1871 and was singular in this industry in its use of steam power to run its 'profusion of machinery,' including cutting, heel-pressing, sewing, pegging, and sole-sewing machines. One 1865 visitor remarked with glee that 'the old method of hand work had been completely superseded.' But even in the overwhelmingly mechanized environment of boot and shoe production, the craft skills of the shoemaker were adapted – and, admittedly, narrowed – into such new (but skilled) occupational categories as lasters, which remained embedded in the labour process for some time to come.[49] And, as later chapters in this book will show, the traditional shoemaker could still find opportunity as a foreman or superintendent inside this plant. It also details how practitioners of both 'new skills' and more traditional craft work inhabited the same social universe, which erased the hard-and-fast distinctions between the two. It further demonstrates that operations of this size and utilizing these more advanced divisions of labour did represent a marked change from traditional craft production, but that

Table 1.12. Clothing sector – clothing and tailored goods subsector, by employment, Hamilton, 1871

Workforce Size	Establishments (n)	Establishments [%]	Employees (n)	Employees [%]	Value added [$]	Value added [%]
1–5	11	39.29	37	5.18	14,650	7.48
6–10	7	25.00	54	7.56	20,200	10.32
11–25	7	25.00	112	15.69	40,973	20.92
26–50	2	7.14	56	7.84	20,000	10.21
51+	1	3.57	455	63.73	100,000	51.07
Total	28	100.00	714	100.00	195,823	100.00

Source: 1871 Industrial Schedules

the social relations craftsworkers practised within their walls were still configured to the craft mode of production.

The McPherson operation must also be considered for its solitary existence in a sea of much smaller boot and shoe enterprises (out of which it had itself sprung), all of which relied on manual power to drive their operations. Custom work and repairs were still the core business of the overwhelming majority of establishments in this sector. The large differences that Kealey found existing between Toronto's large and small boot and shoe producers by 1871 in terms of concentration of workers and value-added production also appear to have been less intense in Hamilton by this year.[50]

This disparity between types of industrial development was also well in evidence in the clothing and tailored goods subsector of the local clothing industry (see table 1.12). Production at the city's only large clothing plant, the ready-made clothing operations of Sanford, McInnis and Company, for example, was typified more by division of labour than mechanization. There, an extensive outwork system had developed, utilizing the flexibility and domestic skills of hundreds of female operatives, stitching pre-cut cloth picked up at the factory door or from a local subcontractor into garments in the 'sweated' comfort of their own homes. The Sanford, McInnis operation, however, had done little to diminish the custom work of the traditional tailor, who existed in greater numbers than ever before, plying their trade inside either the small shop or slightly larger establishment of the merchant tailor. The number of tailors in Hamilton increased 180 per cent in the ten years prior to 1871.[51] The ready-made clothing

Table 1.13 Wood/paper sector, by employment, Hamilton, 1871

		Employed		Value added		Steam power	
Employees	Estab. (n)	(n)	[%]	[$]	[%]	n	[%]
1–5	29	74	7.08	31,083	12.60	2	6.89
6–10	10	76	7.27	44,125	17.89	2	20.00
11–25	15	259	24.80	141,125	57.35	8	53.33
26–50	1	36	3.44	30,000	12.16	1	100.00
51+	1	600	57.42	n.a		1	100.00
Total	56	1045	100.00	246,333	100.00	14	100.00

Source: 1871 Industrial Schedules. The 51+ category includes the GWR Car Shops.
See table 1.1 'Note on GWR' for this determination.

industry also helped add to the ranks of skilled clothing workers through the creation of such newly skilled positions as cutter, fourteen of whom were on the Sanford, McInnis payroll by 1871. The combined and uneven development exhibited in Hamilton's clothing and tailored goods sector would remain a feature of sections of the larger national industry for decades to come.[52]

The wood and paper sector was dominated by the car shops of the Great Western Railway (see table 1.13). By the early 1860s these shops already made up the city's largest congregation of workers under its various roofs. Car builders, a 'large and undifferentiated' section of the force at work within its walls, represented one of the city's most pronounced examples of work organized more on the industrial than the artisanal model. But mobility through the ranks, expressed strongly at both the practical and ideological levels in the shops and embedded in the 'complicated supervisory structures' of this employer, closely tracked the craft mobility traditionally familiar to craftsworkers. This was part of a larger paternalism that, while 'transitional,' was still likely more heavily informed – or 'made sense' of – by understandings derived from more decidedly artisanal contexts. As a whole the car shops were also not an undifferentiated operation. Car builders applied their skills to the production of a still wide array of cars, tenders, and other products. But also at work in these shops were large numbers of more traditional craftsworkers – cabinetmakers, carpenters, upholsterers, painters, and more – whose capacity for artistic finish gained these shops their renown. The environment in which these men laboured was a departure from the past, especially in its scale. But the tools and work processes of the past still remained well in evidence. The blanket of paternalism that overlay the whole operation along with its strong ideologies and practices of career mobility did not yet represent a fundamental departure from the personal labour relationship and craft mobility patterns that characterized artisanal production.[53]

Aside from the GWR car shops, the wood and paper products sector represented the appreciable contribution to aggregate output that could be made by a sector of generally modest-sized producers (see table 1.13). The total output of these smaller producers was also spread over a number of subsectors, including broom and brush making, cabinet and furniture making, carriage making, and musical instrument manufacture (see table 1.1). C.W. Meakins and Sons, the city's largest brush manufacturer, employed thirty-six hands, powered their plant with a fifteen-horsepower steam engine, divided labour between numerous departments, and employed 'a large number of girls' to draw hair or fibre through bored wood cut to size and prepared by semi-skilled male operatives on a variety of belt-driven woodworking machinery. The eighteen employees of Alfred Green, the city's second largest brush manufacturer, by contrast, performed their work by foot power. Similarly, Allan Easson's twelve men and boys used their manual skills to prepare and assemble both brushes and brooms. This plant's traditional handicraft operations were evident to one visitor to the Easson plant in 1868 who observed the firm's proprietors labouring away at the bench alongside the other workers, all wearing 'short aprons of leather, and secure a very lively fraternity when at work.' As the largest of Hamilton's several broom manufactories in 1871, the wedding of broomcorn, twine, and wire to maple, beech, or basswood handles was still wholly executed by the hands of the 'craftsman.'[54]

Steam power was in evidence at a couple of the larger cabinet- and furniture-making establishments in the city. Interestingly, James Reid, the proprietor of the largest of these establishments, turned out his line of 'the very best and finest description of furniture' by exclusive reliance on the hand power of his twenty-four skilled cabinetmakers. Hamilton's furniture industry did not approach the scale, divisions of labour, or degree of mechanization of some other Ontario furniture operations by 1871.[55] This situation was repeated in the local musical instrument industry. The hand was again the motive power at Charles Thomas's piano manufactory, the largest such establishment in this subsector. The variety of skills exercised by his fifteen men was reflected in Thomas's boast that 'his instruments are entirely built in his establishment, from the ripping of the lumber to the last finishing touch.' A couple of slightly smaller piano and organ manufacturers did use steam to power their operations by 1871, but this appears to have simply aided the skilled piano maker in his work. While he had installed some steam-driven machinery, for example, Thomas White reported his 'twelve to fourteen skilled craftsmen are converting wood and metal into shapes, and putting pieces together in complex forms, which the uninitiated may well declare to be incomprehensible.'[56]

The local carriage and wagon industry was composed of an assortment of small and medium-sized producers, with no establishment employing more than twenty-five workers. The sizable works of Jean Pronguey and Thomas McCabe, employing twenty and fourteen men respectively, were still both entirely manual operations. The largest of these establishments, Henry Cooper's Hamilton Coach Factory, was capitalized at $30 000, utilized a ten-horsepower steam engine, and organized its operations on a departmental basis. But, like other mid-nineteenth-century Ontario carriageworks, Cooper's operation appears to have been a conglomeration of artisan-based operations – some of which were independent concerns in their own right – which shared resources and worked on each other's jobs. Cooper's own premises were full of carriagemakers, trimmers, and other craftsmen expert in carriage building, but adjoining the plant – and sharing its steam power – were also George Grayson's carriage-spring manufactory and the Aitchison Brother's planing mill and box factory. As David Burley has noted, such arrangements might have consolidated the stages of production, 'but did not change the means of production *per se*.'[57]

A few operations outside of the leading sectors of Hamilton's industrial economy contributed significantly to value-added production in the city. Two of these subsectors – tobacco and glass manufacture – deserve brief examination here. The forty-eight workers employed by George Tuckett and John Billings used the power of a fifteen-horsepower steam engine to press tobacco into plug form inside their plant. But equally large were establishments of Frederick Schwarz and E. Barber and Company, whose plug tobacco was produced in manually operated presses. The traditional hand-rolling skills of the cigar maker were also still practised in the number of cigar manufactories that coexisted in roughly equal numbers to plug and cut tobacco producers during these years. George Tuckett himself oversaw operations in both sections of this industry. The mechanized press did not affect cigar making itself for some years to come.[58]

Eighty-three men and boys turned out a yearly product worth $85 000 from the sizable works of the Hamilton Glass Company, capitalized at $40 000 by 1871. But this concentration of hands under one roof had done little to alter the labour process. It was the skilled glass maker who still intimately mixed together lime, soda, ash, and sand before firing it and handing it over to be blown into moulds for telegraph insulators or bottles of a wide array of shapes, sizes, and colours. Hand-blowing methods remained common in Hamilton glass factories until the early twentieth century, when the first automatic bottle-making machines were introduced.[59]

Conclusion

Hamilton underwent a profound degree of industrialization and became one of Canada's pre-eminent industrial cities in the approximately two decades before the early 1870s. Industry reshaped the physical landscape of the city. It pulled the economic orientation of the city away from a dominance of commercial endeavour. City boosters now proudly touted Hamilton as the 'Birmingham of Canada' – indeed, an apt comparison to a city of diverse small workshops.

What emerges from the above examination is a preliminary appreciation of the structural dimensions of Hamilton's combined and uneven industrial development by the early 1870s. Small and medium-sized concerns were still well in evidence across all sectors. The continued viability of the smaller concern in the context of advancing industrialism was also reflected in a continued expansion of self-employment opportunities. As chapter 3 will show, these remained generally profitable concerns that showed little sign of being 'done in' by the larger players in their sectors. By 1871, the small concern still remained the city's dominant form of industrial proprietorship.

Larger shops did dominate in terms of value-added production and numbers of hands employed. But size appears to have had only a limited connection to the institution of the various elements of 'modern industry.' Large plants could not on average boast superior productivity to their smaller counterparts. In general, the skills of the craftsworker were preserved across all industrial sectors. The decline of skilled trades was not a common feature of Hamilton's industrial landscape. Overall demand for craftsworkers was on the increase both as a result of the expansion of traditional skilled occupations and the creation of various 'new skilled' occupational categories. In some cases production in large shops had been reorganized and modern machinery introduced. But, with rare exceptions, this did little to lower demand for the skilled hand of the craftsworker. In many cases machinery simply aided the mechanic in his more or less traditional labour process, often lessening the physical demands of his work. Even in large firms where the march towards modern industry was most advanced, factory owners still relied on craftsworkers at crucial stages in their plant's production process and in its management. In those few sectors that did approach mass production – most notably boot- and shoemaking – the craftsworker still found a place in larger enterprise. Establishments such as McPherson's also did little to sink the expanding opportunity of the shoemaker, who still found his niche in the custom work of that subsector's smaller establishments.

The impressive expansion of the city's industrial activity by the early 1870s occurred within a larger context of limited markets and variable demand that did not yet signal a large-scale transition to 'modern industry.'[60] The demands of Ontario's modernizing and expanding economy were still most effectively met by enterprise organized more or less along traditional craft lines, with flexible specialization as its hallmark. Weak and variable demand also commonly meant that large enterprise did not preclude the existence of the small shop. In fact, the hindrance of large, integrated operations by limited markets could spell opportunity for smaller firms eager to insert themselves in the production chains of larger operations, such as small shop machinist Alexander Howie's manufacture of attachments for one of the large local producers of sewing machines. Some industries, notably carriage making and the local boat-building industry, increased output by combining the productive capacities of several independent craft-based concerns. In all, Hamilton's impressive degree of industrialization by the early 1870s had been achieved through the essential preservation and adaptation of craft enterprise.

2

Personal Structures: Craftsworkers and Industrial Proprietors by 1871

Craftsworkers and craft modes of production remained a firmly embedded, even expanded, feature of Hamilton's industrialization through the early 1870s. The proprietors of the city's diverse workshops continued to rely on workers in crafts both old and new for profitable production. The previous chapter outlined the *economic structures* of craft-based industrialization. This chapter will explore its *personal structures* to provide further context for subsequent chapters to build a more complete picture of the local craft community.

To set the stage for later discussions of *who* local craftsworkers were and how that informed the social relations of their communities, this chapter will consider their origins. We have seen that the demand of employers across industrial sectors for highly trained craftsworkers well practised in the diverse skills of their craft remained continuous, perhaps even intensified. Self-employed craftsworkers also proliferated throughout this period. But from where did this sizable force of craftsworkers come? What attracted them to Hamilton, and what expectations might they have brought with them? Once here, how did their origins mesh, or not, with the men for whom they worked?

This chapter will examine these issues in three sections. The first section will use the Hamilton manuscript schedules of the 1871 Census of Canada to determine the geographic origins of Hamilton craftsworkers. It will show that while some local craftsworkers were born in Ontario and a few were born in the United States, most had immigrated to Hamilton from the British Isles. A second section will assess the literature on international labour migration for some indication of the motivation of these individuals. It will suggest that craftsworkers may have seen in communities such as Hamilton forms of economic opportunity offering a chance to regain control over production processes whose requisite craft skills had been degraded closer to the international economic core, an increased likelihood for social mobility, and a generally more positive experience of the emerging economic system. A third section will show that craftsworkers may have been able to confirm these views once employed in local shops, since almost all the men for whom they worked had themselves risen through the craft ranks to become the proprietors of their own industrial establishments. This section will combine data from the 1871 Industrial Census and various biographical evidence to determine the overwhelmingly artisanal origins of Hamilton industrialists. This survey of the origins of Hamilton craftsworkers will complement the study of the city's economic structures by showing that hard at work within the city's modified but traditional craft enterprise were varieties of craftsworkers, many of them recent immigrants, who sought out more traditional and less degraded work arrangements than they may have experienced closer to the core of the developing capitalist world. Their ambitions for economic betterment may have been bolstered by the fact that almost all their employers were men with the same humble beginnings as themselves – an assertion that later chapters will examine in more detail.

Recruiting Craftsworkers

The labour migration of craftsworkers in nineteenth-century Ontario remains understudied. In a study built largely around the testimony of Ontario workers and employers to the Royal Commission on the Relations between Labour and Capital (Labour Commission), Craig Heron has shown that factory owners in urban Ontario had come to rely on both foreign and domestic supplies of labour by the later 1880s. Each of these labour pools was internally divided. The domestic labour supply included craftsworkers who had trained up through the apprenticeship systems of urban factories and less formally trained workers who had learned their crafts on the farms or in the small village shops of the local countryside. However, domestic supplies could still satisfy only part of their overall demand for skilled labour. In large measure employers continued to rely on two broad sources of skilled male labour from outside the domestic economy: all-round, highly trained craftsworkers from Britain and workers with a narrower, more specialized craft training from the United States.[1]

The evidence here provides some indication of the relative weightings of these pools of labour in Hamilton by the early 1870s.

The manuscript schedules of the 1871 Census of Canada enumeration of 'birthplace' provides some detailed evidence of the geographic origins of Hamilton craftsworkers (see table 2.1). Such evidence provides information about only two fixed points in time (craftsworkers' country of residence at birth and the fact that they resided in Hamilton in 1871) and says nothing of the geographic complexity of their life in between. It does, however, strongly indicate that large groups of craftsworkers born in one geographic location sought their livelihood in another.

As one might expect of a place where high rates of transiency have been identified through this time period, the census evidence suggests that local employers could not rely to any large degree on domestic labour supplies for skilled workers. Ontario was reported as the place of birth of less than 15 per cent of craftsworkers listed on the nominal census. The exact proportions of rural and urban craftsworkers cannot be determined from the evidence, but some comments can be made. For Ontario-born craftsworkers drawn from the countryside, the greater proportion of Ontario-born craftsworkers reported for such occupations as printers (34.7%), carriage and wagon makers (20%) and carpenters (17.3%) appear to support the assertions made by employers and workers before the Royal Commission on the Relations between Capital and Labour over a decade and a half later, about the encroachment of such less-well-trained 'country boys' in these trades in urban areas. The same evidence, however, shows that blacksmiths, another country trade associated with labour migration to Ontario's urban areas, were less likely than average (11%) to have been born and trained in the local countryside and somewhat more likely than average to have come from England or Ireland.[2]

While some craftsworkers born in Ontario may have trained in the local countryside before trying their luck in the city, by 1871 Hamilton's industrial community was sufficiently well established to generate something of an indigenous urban craft workforce. Later chapters will provide a detailed examination of the well-functioning nature of local networks of craft mobility through which apprentices and journeymen passed while rounding out their skills. Local employers, most of whom, as we will see, had received formal craft training, took on apprentices and mentored craftsworkers through the ranks from early in the city's industrialization. The city's early metal shops, for example, began taking on apprentices and recruiting other

Table 2.1 Hamilton craftsworkers by place of birth, 1871

		Canada			British Isles					Other		
	n	Ontario	Other	Total	England	Scotland	Ireland	Wales	Total	U.S.	Germany	Other
1. All craftsworkers (%)	1905	14.0	2.7	16.7	37.5	17.7	17.3	0.7	73.2	5.0	3.3	1.8
2. Selected occ. (a)(%)												
a. Metal												
Blacksmiths	127	11.0	1.6	12.6	41.7	18.1	22.8	0.8	83.4	1.6	1.6	0.8
Boilermakers	28	10.7	0.0	10.7	32.1	39.3	17.9	0.0	89.3	0.0	0.0	0.0
Engineers	45	4.4	0.0	4.4	37.8	42.2	13.3	0.0	93.3	0.0	0.0	2.2
Machinists	256	19.1	2.3	21.4	47.3	16.4	5.9	0.8	70.4	5.1	1.9	1.2
Moulders	121	10.7	5.0	15.7	28.9	14.9	25.6	0.0	69.4	12.4	2.5	0.0
Tinsmiths	53	32.1	5.7	37.8	32.1	9.4	15.1	0.0	56.6	5.7	0.0	0.0
b. Wood/Paper												
Carpenter/joiner	415	17.3	2.9	20.2	35.7	22.2	15.4	0.5	73.8	4.6	2.0	1.2
Carr./wagon makers	40	20.0	2.5	22.5	25.0	12.5	27.5	0.0	65.0	2.5	5.0	5.0
Broom/brush makers	28	17.9	7.1	25.0	50.0	14.3	7.1	0.0	71.4	3.6	0.0	0.0
Cabinetmakers	57	10.5	1.8	12.3	42.1	17.5	5.3	1.8	66.7	0.0	19.3	1.8
c. Clothing												
Hatters	21	23.8	0.0	23.8	38.1	23.8	9.5	0.0	71.4	4.8	0.0	0.0
Shoemakers	194	9.3	2.1	11.3	28.9	11.3	35.1	0.0	75.3	6.7	5.2	1.5
Tailors	114	3.5	0.0	3.5	28.9	21.1	26.3	0.9	77.2	2.6	16.7	0.0

Table 2.1 Hamilton craftsworkers by place of birth, 1871 – (*continued*)

		Canada			British Isles					Other		
	n	Ontario	Other	Total	England	Scotland	Ireland	Wales	Total	U.S.	Germany	Other
d. Building												
Bricklayers	21	14.3	0.0	14.3	57.1	4.8	0.0	0.0	61.9	9.5	9.5	4.8
Masons	67	3.0	0.0	3.0	44.8	23.9	16.4	1.5	86.6	4.5	4.5	1.5
Painters	92	16.3	2.2	18.5	51.1	8.7	14.1	0.0	73.9	7.6	0.0	0.0
Plasterers	30	10.0	0.0	10.0	20.0	26.7	23.3	0.0	70.0	16.7	0.0	3.3
e. Food												
Bakers	51	11.8	0.0	11.8	35.3	23.5	17.6	0.0	76.4	5.9	2.0	3.9
Butchers	51	9.8	3.9	13.7	56.9	7.8	13.7	0.0	78.4	2.0	5.9	0.0
f. Other												
Coopers	45	6.7	8.8	15.5	22.2	26.7	26.7	0.0	75.6	4.4	4.4	0.0
Printers	49	34.7	12.2	46.9	24.5	8.2	10.2	2.0	44.9	2.0	2.0	4.1

Source: ArchiviaNet, 1871 Census of Ontario, Hamilton Manuscripts

craftsworkers through the ranks by the mid-1840s.[3] Similarly, a vibrant community of apprentices had been assembled in the city's printing industry by the 1850s.[4] One limiting factor throughout this time period, however, remained the quite stringent tradition-determined limits on the number of apprentices allowed in local workplaces.[5] Even though local employers trained up what young workers they could in the crafts, this was not yet sufficient to supply an expanding demand for skilled labour.[6]

Overall it appears that most Hamilton craftsworkers were still being drawn through geographically dispersed and highly mobile continental and transatlantic networks of labour migration. Interestingly, the evidence does not show a labour market as yet significantly bifurcated between the United States and the British Isles. Table 2.1 shows that craftsworkers born in the United States represented only 5 per cent of Hamilton's craft workforce. This is hardly a measure of how many craftsworkers had some work experience south of the Canadian border. By this decade North American labour markets had often been integrated into complex craft-based continental networks of labour migration that were commonly interfaced with counterpart networks in Britain and Europe. Craftsworkers crossed freely back and forth across the Canada–United States border in search of work. Some workers, such as iron moulders, arrived in Hamilton after working in a number of other North American cities that were part of an extensive travelling network developed and administered through their unions as part of a fairly effective attempt to coordinate and control continental labour markets in their craft.[7] Other workers kept abreast of continental work opportunities through more informal networks of family and friends that could extend far and wide and on both sides of the border. For example, patternmaker Andrew MacIlwraith used such contacts to find work and even temporary lodging in New York City in 1859 when work opportunities in the Hamilton area dried up.[8] Chapter 3 details a number of local craftsworkers who worked, at least temporarily, in the United States. In all, it is likely that a larger percentage of Hamilton craftsworkers had worked part of their lives in the United States than were born there. It does not appear, however, that large numbers of craftsworkers born and presumably trained in that country had been compelled to settle in Hamilton in the early 1870s.

Rather, it appears that Hamilton employers still had to look overseas, particularly to the British Isles, to attain the skilled workforces they required. About three of every four members of Hamilton's craft workforce in 1871 had been born in the British Isles. Craftsworkers born in Ireland and Scotland each accounted for about a quarter of this total, though in some crafts greater proportions are obvious. Irish craftsworkers were more likely than average to be moulders, shoemakers, coopers, carriage makers, or tailors. Similarly, it is not surprising to find that with an established national reputation in secondary metals, about 40 per cent of all Hamilton's engineers and boilermakers came from Scotland. But the largest component of craftsworkers who shared a national birthplace in Hamilton in 1871 was from England (37.5%). In some cases, such as at the workshops of the Great Western Railway, employers actively recruited these highly skilled British workers.[9] Others came of their own volition, finding a niche for their skills in the city's expanding industrialization. Indeed, the extensive training and more well-rounded skills[10] of the British craftsman would have been a good fit with the diverse product lines still typical of the flexible industrialization outlined in the last chapter.

Why Hamilton?

The remainder of this study will be largely concerned with uncovering the *nature* of the community created by Hamilton's craftsworkers, the core of which came from Britain. As a preliminary step in that direction it is worth considering *why* such workers might have been attracted to Hamilton and what *expectations* they may have brought with them. The literature on the migration of British and European craftsworkers to nineteenth-century North America has begun to uncover more complex reasoning behind craftsworkers' decision to immigrate beyond the mere enhancement of their work opportunities. Threaded throughout much of this work is the suggestion that migrants came to 'escape' the ravaging and immiserating effects of capitalism in their British and European homelands. This was especially pronounced in the realm of agrarian smallholders. Allan Kulikoff has recently shown, for example, that in the colonial period and up through at least the first half of the nineteenth century, primarily British immigrants to the United States came to escape the process of proletarianization so distasteful back home, wishing instead to become contented members of a 'small producer society' mainly as small farmers, a point supported by other studies.[11]

But what of the urban, immigrant artisan or skilled worker of the long mid-nineteenth century? Here, too, it appears that the desire to escape capitalism's alienating tendencies (though not necessarily capitalism itself) was a chief motivational 'pull' towards North

America. A number of British and European craftsmen, seeking to escape progressively degrading conditions in their trades and themselves often only one or two generations removed from the soil, also chose North America for its abundant land. North Staffordshire potters, for example, established an Emigration Society through their union in a twofold attempt to fulfil some members' dreams of small landowning while decongesting the local labour market for others.[12]

Immigrating craftsworkers' aspiration to return to the land was far from universal, however. Workers in crafts decayed by deskilling, increasing divisions of labour, the entry of women, and generally declining wages often found in North America trade conditions that in many respects turned back the clock. As Dirk Hoerder has termed it, 'they "returned" from factory production to craft production.' While a number of their brethren opted for land, for instance, many other Staffordshire potters stayed in their trade and were able to regain control over the work process. Similarly, while emigrating handloom weavers found in places like New England a shift to power looms and the employment of women and children as early as the 1830s, many of them found security in Philadelphia, where handloom weaving was maintained to serve markets for finer handloomed products. There is little surprise that 1851 passenger lists show that half of the emigrating weavers who declared their city of destination were headed to Philadelphia.[13]

A number of these emigrating craftsworkers achieved 'self-made' independence. William Van Vugt's study of wood, food, shoe, and metal trades workers emigrating from Britain to the 'Old Northwest' United States, for example, found that while most of the workers in these crafts emigrated to become farmers, those that stuck with their crafts after they arrived often 'remained at their craft for good and became operators or owners of their own smithy, tailoring shop, butcher shop or whatever.'[14]

Immigrating craftsworkers who remained wage earners, such as those from Sheffield's crucible steel and toolmaking industries,[15] often boasted higher incomes and living standards. Others, such as German artisans immigrating in the 1850s and 1860s, found solace in the numerous positions for foremen and superintendents available in North American factories. Hoerder's conclusion on artisanal migration to mid-nineteenth-century North America is telling: 'For artisans and skilled workers independence meant that craft consciousness and skills could be maintained, that the impact of deskilling could be avoided (at least temporarily), that abusive foremen could be left behind. Emigration has sometimes been interpreted as flight from conflict and class struggle.'[16]

While these immigrants may have been attempting to escape the hard edge of industrial capitalism, this did not mean they were completely without enthusiasm for its prospects. Charlotte Erickson's various studies of emigration from England to North America confirm that while a number of relocated craftsworkers had their eye on the prize of independence, this was not retrogressive step; it often included openness to participation in modern forms of capitalism. Many craftsworkers journeyed overseas not so much as a 'flight of impoverishment' as they did in the 'hope of economic improvement.' In that endeavour there is evidence they were receptive towards such changes as modern technological and 'labour saving' improvements. Craftsworkers such as the carpenter George Martin kept a keen eye peeled for the opportunity to don the mantel of mastership. But, as his case also exemplifies, staying in a relatively high-wage supervisory position could actually provide a preferable position of independence. James Battersby wrote to his brother from the United States in 1853 that 'There is a great pleasure in working in this country inasmuch as you feel as good as your employer and on par with them, saying what you like ... everyone is alike, master and man.'[17] How many emigrants followed a similar path to Scottish ironworker James Sheriffs, who, 'inspired by glowing accounts of the opportunities,' left Banff for America in 1848 to become superintendent of a Minnesota foundry before proceeding into successful self-employment himself with the opening of the Sheriff's Manufacturing Company in Milwaukee?[18]

And improvement – self-improvement – lay at the core of many of these immigrants' activities. In America, commented the handloom weaver Edward Philips, 'the path to science, to wealth and to honour is open to all.' Seen in this light, perhaps craftsworkers decisions to emigrate had less to do with escaping capitalism than with simply going to where they believed their experience of it would be more positive.[19]

These points admittedly run roughshod over a more complex historiographical landscape. But the image of the partially immiserated craftsworker being 'pulled' to centres such as Hamilton for the positive 'image' they offered fits in well with the findings of the chapters that follow. The present study will test this larger hypothesis by showing the great extent to which Hamilton craftsworkers, most of whom were funnelled through these migration networks, found the fulfilment of these expectations in Hamilton. The previous chapter confirms the above view of immigrating craftsworkers in the labour migration literature by showing that, in the context of the industrializing Ontario economy, the types of craft production systems that were being degraded by economies of scale closer to the centre of the expanding capitalist economy, while often adapted and expanded, largely remained intact. Subsequent chapters will show further that craftsworkers saw in communities such as Hamilton a chance to regain control, to benefit from capitalism while at the same time achieving independence.

Who Led Hamilton's Industrialization?

One other way to consider these issues through the lens of the personal structures of industrialization is to examine the social origins of the proprietors of Hamilton's industrial establishments. Did the men for whom these craftsworkers worked, for example, personify any of the possibilities discussed above? Accounts of industrial growth should consider not just *stages* of economic development, but also *paths* to industrialization. A number of historians have noted that early industrialization entailed change for craftsworkers not just in *how* or *where* they worked, but also in *who* they worked for. Studies of industrialization and class formation must take into account the social origins of those men who led the process. Understanding *who* these men (and, in rarer instances, women) were and how they fit in to the social relations of production is crucial to any understanding of continuity or change in the personal structures of industrialization. In many respects, inattention to this has led to a social history of industrialization that is unidimensional. As subsequent chapters will show, the social origins of Hamilton's industrialists had a pronounced effect on the development of class relations in that city. First, however, the origins of this group need to be determined with some accuracy.

Marx pointed towards two roads to industrialization, merchant and commercial redirection of capital into manufacturing or artisan-proprietor's expansion of their small handicraft operations into larger enterprise (what he dubbed the 'really revolutionizing path').[20] However, the divergent social consequences of these two paths have not been adequately problematized, most labour historians being content to treat the 'capitalist class' as a homogeneous category. Many studies of early industrialization in the United States concentrate on industries such as textiles, shoes, and primary iron and steel where merchant and finance capital was the driving force behind their establishment.[21] In Canada, this tendency has been exacerbated by scholarly efforts to show that merchants were not against industry. In their study of the making of Hamilton's 'entrepreneurial class,' for example, Katz et al. described the city's industrialization in the two decades before 1871 as following Marx's first path, being guided by 'a stable group' of merchants and financiers who 'sponsored the industrialization of the city.'[22] Merchant hegemony over industrial enterprise, of course, is presented as one of the big 'changes' brought by industrialization, and for many historians it has provided a suitable backdrop for the consideration of 'conflict' rooted in class differentiation.

However, some scholarship on the social origins of industrialists has placed an emphasis on the artisan-entrepreneur of Marx's second path. Research in the United States has provided some of the deepest and most sustained examination of this phenomenon.[23] Detailed studies of this sort are few and far between in the Canadian literature.[24] Studies of Ontario's early industrialization have only hinted at the artisanal roots of some of the province's manufacturers.[25]

Accounts of Hamilton's industrialists also suggest that the entrepreneurial artisan may have found at least some place in the city's supposed merchant-led industrialization. First, accounts of the city's merchant-sponsored industrialization are themselves not reliable. Katz's view of the industrialization of the city as having been facilitated almost completely through a simple redirection of merchant and commercial capital to industry is based on the misreading of a single project working paper that itself suffers from serious methodological and conceptual flaws.[26] Similarly, T.W. Acheson's study of the social origins of the Hamilton industrial elite between 1880 and 1885 reinforces Katz's findings. He found commercial capital eagerly financing such major Hamilton manufacturing enterprises as Ontario Cotton, Hamilton Cotton, the Ontario Rolling Mills, the Hamilton Bridge Company, and the Canada Screw Company. Based on this evidence he concluded that industrial expansion in Hamilton in the early 1880s 'was simply a continuation of a process which had begun in the preceding generation.' Unfortunately, Acheson's study is based on a survey of only a very select group of Hamilton industrialists, most of whom entered into industry in response to the opportunity opened up by the National Policy. Also, the 'continuation' to which Acheson alludes is not backed up with any evidence, primary or secondary, from the pre-1880 years. In another study, however, Acheson does note the artisanal origins of such Hamilton-area manufacturers as John and Alexander Gartshore, Thomas Wilson, Robert McKechnie and John Bertram.[27]

Other studies also suggest the artisanal roots of at least some city industrialists. Palmer indicates that at least some of Hamilton's industrialists took 'the really revolutionizing path' to success, but does not expand on this theme and goes on to present Hamilton's employers as a static group against which a multidimensional and vibrant group of skilled workers fought for independence and control. John Weaver's excellent study of boosterism, technological diffusion, and regional economic development in the city's early foundry industry provides the most thorough examination of the artisanal origins of some of Hamilton's – and indeed Canada's – industrialists presently available. But while Weaver's study was fairly thorough in its survey of the artisanal roots of the city's founders, there still exists no comprehensive examination of the origins of the city's manufacturing class per se.[28]

How common was it for Hamilton industrialists to have risen from the ranks? Many of the above studies hint that at least some of the manufacturers in a given place could claim artisanal origins. However, none can purport to make this claim based on a thorough and rigorous social scientific survey of that class as a whole.[29] Acheson's study of Saint John shows massive artisanal involvement in the founding of industry in that town, but it offers no statistical proof of the extent of that involvement. David Burley offers copious evidence of the artisanal origins of Brantford's manufacturers, but he too provides no indication of how widespread this phenomenon actually was. Most troubling is Katz's somewhat ambiguous treatment of this subject. In general Katz avoids having to address the potential artisanal origins of this group by suggesting that class leadership remained constant, with commercial men turning their attention towards industry as the city entered the industrial age. In other places, though, Katz and his associates show that movement, both up and down, did take place between the ranks of skilled workers and manufacturers. However, this does not seem to influence their ultimate conclusion about journeyman immobility. They also try to explain away what mobility they do find, arguing that it was 'rare' or that '[most] probably these young people who moved upward were disproportionally sons of men already in the business class.' Evidence for this assertion is not offered. A more serious concern lies with the quality of their data in general. As Katz himself points out, the sources themselves allow for no real distinction between master artisans and those who worked for them except in 1871. After a cost/benefit analysis of righting the sample Katz concludes that, for now at least, artisans-turned-masters will have to be left as 'artifacts of synonymy.'[30]

Table 2.2 Occupational mobility of artisans linked between 1851 and 1871

	Occupational rank in 1871			
	Up (%)	Same (%)	Down (%)	n
Artisans in 1851	16.40	73.00	10.60	256

Source: Katz et al., *Social Organization*, 168. Adapted from table 5.4.

Even though the data of Katz and his associates are admittedly incomplete, a reconsideration of some of their numbers does support the overall thesis that some – and I would argue in this context, probably a significant – portion of the city's manufacturing class rose from the ranks. In their sample of more than 256 artisans for the period 1851 to 1871, in excess of 15 per cent achieved a rise in occupational rank in this period (see table 2.2). This possibility of artisanal mobility is confirmed when reconsidering their findings on the economic ranking of artisans and masters traced from 1861 to 1871. In this case 13 per cent of artisans were able to attain the rank of manufacturer over this decade. Contained within this study group are also those men who started the decade as masters (most likely small) and ended it as artisans – another 12 per cent of the group. The authors are careful to point out that downward occupational mobility (and it is unclear if the move from master to artisan was in all cases downward) was not accompanied by a decline in means. By the end of the decade both groups – 25 per cent of the sample – were significantly better off financially, both individually and collectively, than the skilled worker who worked for wages in both years (see table 2.3). While the data are imprecise, they do suggest that from the bottom up, at least, a number of artisans did make the leap from skilled worker to manufacturer or, at least, to wealthier status.

From the top down the picture becomes clearer. How common was it for Hamilton industrialists to have risen from the ranks? For the time period covered by this study the most comprehensive listing of industrialists available are the Industrial Schedules of the 1871 Census of Canada for Hamilton. This is a particularly rich and rare source since it allows the compilation of a list of all Hamilton industrialists in a given year, from the major employer of hundreds of men and women to the traditional artisan workshop operated by 'self and son.' It also allows a unique glimpse into the state of industrialization in Hamilton close to the terminal date of this study. However, it is also a complex source and should be used with some caution.[31] To con-

Table 2.3 Mobility of masters and artisans traced from 1861 to 1871, Hamilton

Occupational category			
1861	1871	N	%
Artisan	Artisan	190	60.51
Artisan	Master	42	13.38
Master	Artisan	40	12.74
Master	Master	42	13.38
Total		314	100

Source: Katz et al., *Social Organization*, 59. Adapted from table 1.5.

struct a database of the origins of the industrialists listed on the manuscripts I adopted a methodology closely resembling the one used by Gutman in his study of Paterson, New Jersey, and Ross in his Cincinnati study by using a number of local biographical sources to reveal the origins of various manufacturers. The industrial schedules were made machine-readable and then cross-referenced with a number of biographical sources elucidatory of the origins of Hamilton manufacturers.[32]

The database assembled for this study allows the origins of industrialists in all sectors of the city's economy to be traced.[33] In all, this study was able to determine the origins of 233 proprietors of the 328 industrial establishments listed on the 1871 Industrial Census for Hamilton. The results from the Hamilton database are significant. Roughly 95 per cent of Hamilton's industrial proprietors whose origins could be traced could claim artisanal origins in 1871. Only about 6 per cent of the city's industrialists came from the ranks of merchants, bookkeepers, clerks or any other non-artisanal occupation (see table 2.4).

By their nature, the biographical sources listed above tend to leave evidence of only the more successful of the city's artisans and craftsworkers in the historical record. To correct this imbalance, I have included in the sample proprietors of establishments with five or fewer employees who met certain criteria. These individuals were only included if they practised a traditional craft that demanded a degree of skill that was acquired through an established system of apprenticeship.[34]

While the above methodology far exceeds other studies in how extensively it determines the artisanal origins of industrial proprietors

Table 2.4 Origins of Hamilton industrialists, 1871

	All manufacturers		Manufacturers with >5 employees		Manufacturers with >$10,000 prod. val.	
Origins	n	%	n	%	n	%
Artisanal	220	94.42	63	86.30	55	87.30
Merchant/clerk/ bookeeper/ other non-artisanal	13	5.58	10	13.70	8	12.70
Totals	233	100	73	100	63	100

Source: 1871 Industrial Census Database

in one community, it is still unable to account for the origins of a significant section of the sample. More specifically, the origins of those proprietors employing more than five workers but whose 'success' was not sufficient to secure them a place in the privileged historical record of larger concerns cannot be determined. The origins of those largely 'in between' these two poles (roughly one-third of all industrial proprietors[35]) can likely never be concluded from the available evidence.[36] Some members of this unknown group could well have had non-artisanal origins. But the overwhelmingly artisanal origins of those proprietors straddling both ends of this spectrum suggest that the results for this group would not have been out of line with the two-thirds of industrial proprietors that could be identified. Given the evidence presented here, it is much more likely that a number of these proprietors were small shop artisans who had expanded their way out of the criterion for this sample and whose enterprises were located in sectors of Hamilton's industrial economy, such as the metal industry, that generally favoured (required?) artisanal start-ups.

There are important questions to ask of the sample that has been identified. When examining questions of class formation in industrializing society, for instance, should focus be especially centred on those sectors where capital accumulation and the congregation of large numbers of wage earners under one roof was the greatest? As suggested above, it *was* significant that small artisan-proprietors existed – and did so beside larger concerns – to this point in the industrialization process. This persistence must be factored into our understanding of the nineteenth-century industrial city.

However, even if the group of small artisan-proprietors is taken out

Table 2.5 Origins of Hamilton industrialists, by sector, 1871

	Origins				
	Artisanal		Non-artisanal		Total
Sector	n	%	n	%	n
Metal	45	95.74	2	4.26	47
Clothing	50	96.15	2	3.85	52
Wood/paper	42	100.00	0	0.00	42
Agricultural	22	95.65	1	4.35	23
Construction	14	100.00	0	0.00	14
Miscellaneous	14	82.35	3	17.65	17
Chemical	1	20.00	4	80.00	5
Beverage/food	19	95.00	1	5.00	20
Printing	6	100.00	0	0.00	6
Leather	7	100.00	0	0.00	7
Minerals	0	0.00	0	0.00	0
Forest	0	0.00	0	0.00	0
Totals	220		13		233

Note: Sectors are presented in descending order of economic importance. See table 2.1.
Source: 1871 Industrial Census Database

of the sample, the initial results stand. Two criteria were used to separate out from the original sample proprietors of more 'advanced' industry – number of employees and gross product value. Again, the results show a preponderance of proprietors with artisanal origins. For establishments employing more than five people, over 86 per cent of proprietors had started out as artisans. The situation was similar for concerns boasting ten thousand dollars or more worth of annual product. In this case just over 87 per cent of proprietors could claim artisanal roots (see table 2.4). These numbers exceed Ross's survey of the leading 10 per cent of Cincinnati's manufacturers, where he found 74.5 per cent of proprietors to have risen from the ranks.[37] Small or large, the proprietors of Hamilton's industry largely claimed artisanal roots by 1871.

It is also notable that proprietors with artisanal backgrounds were also not heavily concentrated in only a few industrial sectors. In general, the incidence of artisanal origins among industrial proprietors was spaced fairly evenly across the leading sectors of Hamilton's industrial economy. The sectoral origins of Hamilton's industrial proprietors in 1871 are outlined in table 2.5. In the metal, clothing, wood and paper, agricultural products and construction sectors – representing about 85 per cent of the city's value-added industrial production – origins were almost completely artisanal. In these sectors 159 out of 162 proprietors claimed artisanal backgrounds. The predominance of artisanal backgrounds was also heavy in the beverage/food, printing, and leather sectors. Representing about 6 per cent of economic activity in the city, 27 of the 28 industrialists in these sectors started as small masters. The origins of proprietors in sectors representing over 90 per cent of industrial economic activity in the city in 1871 were almost completely artisanal.

Conclusion

In all it appears that the personal structures of Hamilton's craft world by the early 1870s melded well with its economic structures. Labouring away inside the city's numerous small shops and larger manufactories were craftsworkers who applied wide-ranging skills to familiar, though sometimes adapted, work tasks. Most of these men had arrived in the city in search of economic opportunity, the majority from the British Isles. Like their brethren across North America in this time period, their search for a work environment that offered a more positive experience of the emerging economic system than the forms of craft degradation familiar back home could have been satisfied inside the city's numerous craft enterprises. Also echoing more traditional work arrangements was the fact that almost all the men for whom they worked were themselves craft masters. Together, master and man worked in more or less familiar surroundings. Whether or not traditional social relations were preserved in this context will be the subject of subsequent chapters. Chapters 1 and 2 have delineated the economic and personal structures of industrialization in order to *suggest* the potential space for continuity in craftsworker experience. The task of the remaining chapters will be to explore the actual dimensions of craftsworker experience within this broad structure of craft capitalism.

3

Craft Mobility and Artisan-Led Industrialization: Continuity in Symbol and Practice

> Hamilton has quite a bunch of men who began at the bottom of the ladder, but by perseverance, economy, hard work and sticking to the job have moved up to Easy street ... A chapter on these prosperous Hamiltonians would be a suggestive study for boys who are now growing into manhood.[1]

It is easy to dismiss these comments, penned by Richard Butler in 1909, as wishful thinking and construction after the fact. Writing under the nom de plume 'the Old Muser,' Butler repeatedly hammered home this theme in his weekly historical reminiscence column in the *Hamilton Spectator* through much of the first two decades of the twentieth century. But is there fact to be separated from fiction in these accounts? Butler himself rose from lowly printer's apprentice to employer, diplomat, and author. Is there any evidence that his contemporaries – especially those who commenced their work lives as apprentice and journeymen craftsworkers – shared in this experience? If so, perhaps this variety of evidence needs to be reconsidered, read for its 'taint' as a recollection but not simply discounted. When read carefully and measured with other evidence, this chapter will show there was more than a kernel of truth to Butler's musings.

Chapter 2 showed that, contrary to previous accounts of the social dimensions of its initial industrialization, almost all male industrial proprietors in Hamilton rose from the ranks. This finding suggests the necessity of rethinking the basic social arrangements between Hamilton's craftsmen and those for whom they worked by the early 1870s. As such, this chapter will suggest that artisan-sponsored industrialization created a social context in which established patterns of craft mobility appeared to be preserved and even strengthened in an era of new possibilities. It shows that throughout the early industrial period there endured a pre-existing artisanal social structure within which craftsworkers could continue to form identities along the line of an established but revised intra-occupational mobility pattern of apprentice–journeyman–master. It proposes that for craftsworkers the fundamental ingredient of dispossession—the despoliation of their ownership of, or access to, the means of production – was not yet common. It raises the *suggestion* – one examined at length in later chapters – that the social origins of Hamilton's industrial proprietors and the mobility networks maintained in their workplaces had a profound effect on the development of social and class relations in the city. The present chapter documents this continued social arrangement. Later chapters explore its social dimensions.

It would seem evident from the examples of individual men making the leap from craftsworker to manufacturer outlined in chapter 2 that social mobility – or, more specifically, craft mobility – was a fact of life in mid-nineteenth-century Hamilton. As a concept, social mobility has been debated with vigour and many historians remain at odds over its meaning or usefulness as a line of historical enquiry. The major works on Hamilton's initial industrialization have been premised on the idea that rigid and fixed structures of inequality worked to exacerbate class separation in the city.[2] The finding that the city's industrialists predominately 'rose from the ranks,' however, raises questions about this prevailing view of limited social mobility.

Studies of social mobility in other parts of mid-nineteenth-century Ontario and elsewhere have largely supported findings of inequality,[3] though some more recent historiography has challenged it.[4] When considering the more particular case of artisans-turned-manufacturers, the debate becomes somewhat more involved. Michael Katz, Michael Doucet, and Mark Stern argue that in mid-nineteenth-century Hamilton 'journeyman was often a permanent status, not a phase in the life cycle.'[5] This thesis of craftsworker immobility is confirmed in other Ontario studies and generally supported in the international literature.[6]

On the other side of the debate, however, a number of historians, historical economists, and sociologists have noted ample room for artisanal opportunity in nineteenth-century Ontario.[7] But since most of these studies mention the potential of artisanal mobility as something of an aside to their main arguments, it is not surprising that a thorough documentation of its presence is still lacking.[8]

Some of the most fruitful thinking about social mobility in the last twenty-five years has centred not on methodological questions but on the ideological assumptions that lay behind research models in general. James Henretta, for example, suggests that social mobility was likely not a widely held cultural value among large groups of nineteenth-century Americans.[9] However, historians of social mobility also need to come to terms with pre-existing mobility patterns brought forward into the industrial age. For example, mobility had been a deeply entrenched feature of the crafts world since at least the Middle Ages.[10] The progression from apprentice to journeyman to master was based on much older cultural associations and identities than were nineteenth-century notions of the self-made man. Craft mobility, the traditional apprentice–journeyman–master progression, was a reality to Hamilton craftsworkers as late as the early 1870s because their employers were living examples of it. There, the form of traditional craft mobility may have been exaggerated and modified, but it was firmly rooted in craft tradition.

The maintenance of craft mobility also has important implications for reconsidering the fast-growing historiography of masculinity. International studies of nineteenth-century manhood have largely bifurcated into distinct fields of study. While international historical writing on middle-class masculinity has been particularly productive, there are a number of holes yet to fill.[11] Left unproblematized, for example, is the particular masculinity of that section of the parvenu 'middle class' that emerged from the ranks of artisans and craftsworkers, as did so many of Hamilton's industrialists.[12]

Conversely, the literature on craft/skilled-worker masculinity has been conceived almost wholly within the confines of the dispossession model.[13] A central feature of much of this work has been the importance of progress through the craft ranks in the construction of skilled-worker masculinity, presented usually as something that has been disrupted or renegotiated by the jarring impact of industrialization and the hegemony of the wage-earning relationship. While the history of craftsworker masculinity in early industrial Hamilton has not yet been written, implicit in previous studies of the city that posit limited social mobility and the decline of the independent craftsman/artisan is that this traditional avenue of masculine achievement had been closed in large degree.

A central contention of this chapter is that Hamilton craftsworkers not only aspired to mobility but also believed, or at least perceived, it was possible. The life-course work experience of Hamilton's industrial proprietors shows that by the early 1870s craftsmen could still hope to achieve mobility in Hamilton. Their notion of social mobility was not formulated as a new atomistic ideology generated by the modern logic of industrial capitalism. Rather, it was based more on bringing forward traditional conceptions of occupational mobility built into the crafts, albeit in an enhanced form that took account of the new possibilities of the industrial age. Social mobility for Hamilton's craftsworkers by the early 1870s was an outgrowth of craft mobility patterns, but it also surpassed them.

The first section explores the strong cultural symbol of the artisan-turned-industrialist in Hamilton. It argues that the general success of the city's industrial proprietors conveyed a powerful image of opportunity to Hamilton's aspiring apprentices and journeymen. The second section considers how craft mobility served not only as a strong cultural symbol but also as a crucial practised component of Hamilton craftsworkers' work culture. Through at least the early 1870s the perception of opportunity was bolstered by younger craftsworkers' continued, even expanded, ability to climb up to positions of independence through a widening web of craft mobility, a process in which they continued to be mentored by those senior to them in the craft hierarchy. A concluding section offers a reconsideration of class formation in Hamilton based on the findings of the two previous sections.

Symbols of Continuity

Much of the intense debate surrounding social mobility over the past few decades has been reduced to what Henretta has termed 'a quest for technical exactness and statistical finesse,'[14] which has lost sight of other, perhaps less quantifiable, possibilities. Hamilton craftsworkers not only hoped for mobility, they also *perceived* it as a possibility. Charles Stephenson has argued that workers' *desire* to achieve mobility has been bolstered by a real *perception* of opportunity among large segments of the working class. While he asserts that a statistical study would likely show the contrary, 'social mobility occurred often enough for its possibility to be taken seriously by many workers, if they desired it.'[15] As Herbert Gutman found in his study of the social origins of Paterson, New Jersey, manufacturers between 1830 and 1880, 'the rags-to-riches promise was not a mere myth ... So many successful manufacturers who had begun as workers walked the streets of that city then that it is not hard to believe that others less successful or just starting out on the lower rungs of the occupational ladder could be convinced by personal knowledge that

Table 3.1 Large and small artisan-proprietors compared: value added, capital invested and wages paid, Hamilton, 1871

		Small masters (5 or fewer employees)	Large masters (more than 5 employees)	Totals
Value added	$	297,795 10.80%	2,446,888 89.20%	2,744,683 100%
Capital invested	$	460,930 12.30%	3,302,854 87.70%	3,763,784 100%
Wages paid	$	110,503 8.04%	1,264,445 91.96%	1,374,948 100%

Note: Does not include GWR as financial particulars were not reported.
Source: 1871 Census Manuscripts

"hard work" resulted in spectacular material and social improvement.'[16] Likewise, the widespread success of Hamilton's many artisan-industrial proprietors, both large and small, provided a strong cultural symbol of opportunity to local journeymen and apprentices.

Small Masters

Was the 'comfortable competence' of the small master well on its way to becoming to becoming a historical anachronism by the 1870s? The argument that as industrialization proceeded, small masters struggled to keep their dwindling operations afloat before finally being forced into the ranks of the wage-earning proletariat has indeed become the received view in the historiography. Needless to say, the Hamilton example has been a central account of the decline of the small producer.[17]

Was the small master being 'squeezed out' of industrial production in the city, as portrayed in many theses of small producer decline? In terms of share of industrial output and other indicators this would seem to have been the case. As outlined in table 3.1, in terms of value added, capital invested, and wages paid, Hamilton's small masters had lost significant ground to larger-scale enterprise by this point in industrialization. At best, small masters commanded between one-eighth and one-tenth of industrial output in the city in 1871.

However, these numbers leave much unknown about the development and nature of local and regional markets and their impact on the

Table 3.2 Productivity: value added per employee, Hamilton, 1871

	Small masters (5 or fewer employees)	Large masters (more than 5 employees)	Value added production greater than $25,000
Total value added ($)	297,795	2,446,888	1,892,190
No. of employees	460	4299	3003
Value added/employee ($)	647.38	567.17	630.1

Note: Figures do not include Great Western Railway as financial particulars were not reported for this concern.
Source: 1871 Census Manuscripts

viability of varying scales of enterprise across a wide array of industrial sectors. While an examination of these factors demands a study unto itself, there are some important questions that can be asked of the material at hand to help shed light on the lot of the small master by 1871.

First, it needs to be ascertained whether the small master was common in the city in 1871. I have defined small masters as all those industrial proprietors identified on the Industrial Schedules of the 1871 Census of Canada who were in established crafts and employed five or fewer workers. To build a comparison group, a larger subset composed of all industrial proprietors for whom artisanal origins had been determined was isolated from the census data. The comparison of these groups yields strong results. Of the city's 220 manufacturers identified as having artisanal origins on the Industrial Schedules of the 1871 Census of Canada, fully 160 or close to 73 per cent of these men were small masters. In the everyday view of the community, the small master was still, by far, the most common example of industrial proprietorship in Hamilton by 1871. Combined with evidence from chapter 1 that the general opportunity for self-employment was expanding for craftsworkers in the two decades prior to 1871, the suggestion that Hamilton's industrial economy represented to craftsworkers a positive opportunity for self-employment seems likely to have manifested itself in widespread public perception.

It is even more revealing to question how these men were perceived by others. If the small master had become an obvious sign of declining fortune and hand-to-mouth living then indeed the evidence would seem to support the decline of the small producer. However, when Industrial Schedule information is used to compare the businesses of small and large masters in terms of value added per

Table 3.3 Estimated income of proprietors of establishments with five or fewer employees, 1871

Industry	n	Wages ($)	Raw mat. ($)	Prod. val. ($)	Est. income	Est. income per day[a]
1. Primary						
A. Agricultural	19	7,601	80,871	115,678	1,431.89	4.58
B. Forest	0	0	0	0	0	0
C. Minerals	1	0	120	625	505.00	1.62
2. Secondary						
A. Beverages/food	18	11,635	57,713	101,803	1,803.06	5.78
B. Chemical	8	7,200	26,860	68,120	4,257.50	13.65
C. Clothing	40	26,351	41,301	95,905	706.33	2.26
D. Leather	4	1,824	2,506	8,000	917.50	2.94
E. Metal	22	17,649	20,643	55,830	797.18	2.56
F. Printing	3	2,740	2,243	8,000	1,005.67	3.22
H. Wood/paper	29	13,440	20,062	51,145	608.39	1.95
I. Construction	14	16,050	19,710	45,934	726.71	2.33
J. Miscellaneous	13	6,013	11,856	30,640	982.38	3.15
Totals	171	110,503	283,885	581,680		

Note: Est. Income calculated as Prod. Value minus raw Material minus Wages divided by n.
[a] calculated on a 26-day month or 312-day year.
Source: 1871 Census Manuscripts

employee, the operations of small masters appear to have been as productive, or even slightly more so, than those of their large master counterparts (see table 3.2).

More telling are indications of the continued financial viability of small masters' establishments gleaned from the Industrial Schedules. A rough indication of the income of small masters can be calculated by subtracting raw material costs and wages from total product value in a given industrial sector and then dividing the result by the number of establishments in that sector.

The results outlined in table 3.3 indicate the level of yearly income the proprietor of a small industrial establishment in Hamilton may have earned in the early 1870s. Daily income was determined by dividing total yearly income by 312 working days (a working year based on a 26-day month). At the low end, the one producer in the mineral sector earned an average of $1.62 a day. In the wood/paper, clothing, construction, metal, and miscellaneous sectors, artisan-proprietors claimed

Table 3.4 Wage rates per day, selected occupations, Hamilton, 1870s

Occupation	I Summer, 1870[a]	II c. 1873[b]	III 1871 Manuscripts[c] [n]
Blacksmiths	1.75	2.18	1.89 [4]
Bricklayers/masons	2.75		n/a
Carpenters	1.75	1.80	2.32 [2]
Painters	1.63	1.74	3.08 [4]
Plasterers	2.25		n/a
Shoemakers	1.25		2.17 [17]
Wheelwrights		1.91	n/a

[a] Source: 41st Congress, 3rd Session, House Executive Documents, No. 94, 'State of Trade with British North American Provinces,' cited in J.G. Snell, 'The Cost of Living in Canada in 1870,' *Historie sociale/Social History* 12, no. 23 (May 1979): 186-90.
[b] Source: Edward Young, *Labor in Europe and America* (Washington, 1875), cited in Leo Panich, 'Dependency and Class in Canadian Political Economy,' *Studies in Political Economy* 6 (1981): 7-33.
[c] Source: 1871 Census Manucripts, isolated subsectors.

a daily average ranging from $1.95 to $2.56. At the upper end small masters in the leather, printing, agriculture, beverages/food, and chemical sectors show a daily income of $2.94, $3.22, $4.58, $5.78, and $13.65 respectively. These rates should be contrasted with wage rates for the city's skilled workers outlined in table 3.4.

Table 3.4 provides a comparison of small master incomes with (admittedly limited) wage rate information for the city's journeymen craftsworkers.[18] In general it appears that the estimated daily incomes of small artisan-proprietors at least equalled but more often exceeded the wage rates of skilled craftsworkers in the city. Column III of table 3.4 outlines incomes for small owners in categories that best correspond to occupational categories of skilled craftsworkers outlined in columns I and II estimated from the 1871 Industrial Schedules. More telling is the fact that the estimated daily incomes of industrial proprietors presented in table 3.3 fairly uniformly exceed the daily wage rates for skilled workers outlined in table 3.4. More importantly, it should be noted that daily income calculations for small artisan-proprietors are based on full-year employment. If seasonal lay-offs were factored into the above figures,[19] the generally superior earnings (and, therefore, security) of self-employment would emerge even more firmly into evidence. In Hamilton it appears that small masters enjoyed a significantly higher yearly income than their craftsworker counterparts dependent on the irregular wages of seasonal employment.

It is also possible to consider the relative 'success' of Hamilton's small masters through one admittedly less reliable indicator: the comparison of the frequency of employment of their secondary family members with those of skilled workers' families. Did necessity require small masters to send other family members out to waged work at rates similar to families headed by a skilled worker? In making this determination it must be recognized that small masters likely promoted the entry of their sons into the workplace in order to set them on a course to mimic their own success. Nonetheless, problematizing this question does yield some useful results.

To answer this question two data sets were assembled out of census materials to form the basis of a comparison. First, information about labour force participation was compiled from the nominal census manuscripts for all of Hamilton in 1871 for the families of all small masters identified on the census's industrial schedules. A second data set was assembled from the 1871 nominal census for all families headed by a skilled worker in Hamilton's St Mary's Ward, located in the heart of the city's industrial district. Both data sets contain detailed information on the numbers and age of secondary breadwinners in each family.

A comparison of these data clearly suggests that families headed by small masters found it less necessary to send secondary wage-earners out to work than did families headed by skilled workers. Households headed by small masters reported an average of 1.34 workers per family, whereas the average family headed by a skilled worker sent out an average of 1.68 workers.[20] Similarly, while slightly more than 40 per cent of families headed by skilled workers sent out more than one wage-earner, only 25 per cent of families headed by small masters claimed more than one wage-earner.[21] The necessity of requiring additional family members to contribute to family coffers through waged work was evidently less pressing for families headed by small masters than for those headed by skilled workers.

These findings are confirmed when considering the ages of children reported as earning. Between the ages of eleven and fifteen almost 23 per cent of the children of skilled workers had already entered into waged employment, compared with only 8 per cent for children of small masters. By the time they were sixteen or seventeen close to 65 per cent of skilled workers' children had become wage-earners, whereas only about 23 per cent of sons and daughters of small masters had entered the workforce. Over 90 per cent of the chil-

Table 3.5 Children and work: families of small masters and skilled workers compared, Hamilton, 1871

	Age group		
	11–15	16–17	18–21
Small masters			
Total number	50	22	27
Number working	4	5	12
% working	8.00%	22.73%	44.44%
Skilled workers			
Total number	84	33	58
Number working	19	21	53
% working	22.62%	63.64%	91.38%

Source: 1871 Census Manuscripts

dren of skilled workers reported an occupation by the time they were between eighteen and twenty years of age compared with only 44 per cent of the children of small masters (see table 3.5). A closer look at the data reveals the dynamics behind the low employment figures for children of small masters in this age group. In general small master's families preferred to keep their older teenage daughters at home. While all male children in this age group reported an occupation, only one out of the sixteen resident daughters did so.[22] It was likely the flexibility allowed by superior earnings that allowed small masters to make this strategic choice. That small masters would have sent their sons out to work in large numbers likely had more to do with the expectation of independence than economic necessity. Their ability to keep older daughters at home confirms this.

Given the nature of the data it would be unwise to draw too many hard and fast conclusions from the findings presented above. Among other things, one suspects it is hard to tell the true number of sons who worked for their small-master fathers. Some report the same occupation as their father, but no comprehensive record exists confirming their participation in their father's enterprise. One telling source on this subject, however, is the manuscripts to the industrial census. The enumerator for one division of Hamilton's St Lawrence Ward, evidently in an effort to do a more complete job, ignored census convention and actually wrote in to his manuscript entries the employment of sons in smaller enterprises, using phrases such as 'self + son' or 'self + 3 sons' to identify family participation. The nominal census entries for these families sometimes show that father and son had the same occupation, but make no suggestion of the son's employment by his father. More importantly, in other cases the nominal census reports no occupation for the son, suggesting that work within the small family industrial enterprise may have been underreported and that, for some small masters at least, the help of younger family members in a small industrial enterprise would not necessarily be considered an 'occupation' or 'employment' per se.

In a slightly different vein, the fact that over 65 per cent of small master's sons who worked reported the same occupation as, or were listed on the industrial census as having worked for, their father is significant, since the social dynamic of working for one's father, perhaps with a very real expectation of occupational inheritance, would likely be very different from the early work experience of sons of skilled workers. In sum, while the above findings leave open a number of questions, the least that can be deduced from the evidence at hand is that small masters and their families did no worse financially – and in all likelihood, noticeably better – than the families of their skilled-worker counterparts. The evidence is also strong enough to suggest that compared with households headed by skilled workers, the small master's position as the family's primary– and in many cases, sole – breadwinner was more secure. It is likely that from this a greater sense of independence and manly pride would have flowed.

While larger industrial enterprises may have dominated the city in terms of total economic activity, Hamiltonians would have had little reason to consider independent small proprietorship as a relic of the past by 1871. The small industrial concern was still the most common form of industrial enterprise in the city. The standard of living it provided could well have been seen as a step up the ladder for most wage-earning apprentices or journeymen. As Charles Stephenson has suggested, large numbers of nineteenth-century workers 'sought social mobility' in large part as a cure for the 'endemic irregularity of employment.'[23] The relatively high incomes of Hamilton's small-households heading masters also served to hold out the image of the successful male patriarch to those who aspired to their position. Combined with the manly independence of 'being your own boss,' setting up on one's own must have remained a chief aspiration of craftsworkers in the city by the early 1870s.

Large Masters

The city's large industrial proprietors vastly reinforced this image.[24] Their standing in the community and considerable financial power placed them far beyond the 'successful artisan.' Yet, the majority of Hamilton's most successful industrial entrepreneurs had experienced their rise to prosperous independence simply as an exaggerated version of the road to independent artisanal manhood. Most of them had apprenticed to learn a trade and spent a period performing journeywork for someone else before setting up as masters of their own. Once masters, their enterprises were often humble. Few enjoyed initial access to capital. Most grew their enterprise from small beginnings, relying on their own sweat for initial capital accumulation. While virtually none of these men achieved spectacular overnight success, it was common for enterprising artisans to see significant success within their own lifetimes. These men differed from their small master counterparts in how much they accumulated, but they shared common roots. To the aspiring crafts apprentice or journeyman, they must have represented the very real rewards that could accrue from a devotion to craft and hard work.

Apprenticeship was a common feature of the young life of most of Hamilton's large industrial proprietors. Detailed accounts of many of these apprenticeships are lacking. Most common are press reports referring to various manufacturers as 'first-class workmen' or as having attained a 'practical knowledge' of their business. Press descriptions of such sewing and knitting machine manufacturers as Christopher Lockman, R. Peters, C.J. Appleton, and John Nathaniel Tarbox, for example, described these men respectively as a 'practical ... skillful mechanic,' 'a thorough mechanic in every respect,' 'a skillful mechanic in all departments of the work,' and a 'skilled machinist.'[25] Sometimes, apprenticeship can be deduced, such as in the case of F.G. Beckett, proprietor of the large Atlas Engine and Boiler Works, for whom biographical and census information show to have been practically engaged in the business for ten years before arriving in Canada at the age of twenty-five.[26] More direct evidence of apprenticeship is available for many other industrial proprietors. While these accounts show initial training to most often have occurred elsewhere – especially in the northeastern United States, England, or Scotland – a number of manufacturers did apprentice locally. For example, the successful carriagemaker James Miller Williams apprenticed at a carriage works in Camden, New Jersey, while the highly successful tobacco manufacturer George E. Tuckett spent the latter part of his youth learning the cigar-making trade in small Hamilton shops.[27] Such evidence of apprenticeship can be gleaned for proprietors across all sectors of the city's industrial economy. The larger study determines practical origins for over 86 per cent of the city's large employers in 1871.[28] The vast majority of successful industrialists in the city served as living examples of the potentially bountiful rewards an apprenticeship could offer.

The experience of journeywork was also familiar to many of the city's large masters. Evidence of time spent earning wages can be found for a diverse number of men who had become large masters by 1871, including ropemaker Alexander Main, tailor James Foster and boatbuilder Henry Bastien. Such city printers as Tom McIntosh, John Hand, William Nicholson, and Richard Donnelly all worked as journeymen in the city and elsewhere and all served on the executive of the Hamilton Typographic Society before their rise to prominence. Robert Smiley, long-time proprietor of the *Hamilton Spectator*, worked as a journeyman in a government print shop in Montreal before commencing operations in Hamilton in 1846.[29]

Journeywork was also well known to a number of Hamilton iron founders. Edward and Charles Gurney worked at a Utica, New York, foundry immediately before setting up their Hamilton operation. Metal products manufacturer James Turnbull spent a number of years working as a pattern maker at the E. and C. Gurney foundry before opening the Mary Street Foundry with his brother in 1854. The proprietors of the Hamilton Malleable Iron Works also spent a portion of their youths performing journeywork. William Burrow worked briefly at the Gurney foundry in 1859 before going on to employment in a number of towns in the United States. Charles Stewart and John Milne also left Hamilton in the late 1850s to gain experience south of the border. All three partners had returned to work at local foundries by the early 1860s.[30]

The experience of earning wages was also not a short-term affair for a number of future industrialists. Records suggest an experience of wage-earning of a decade or more for such future large masters as carriagemaker Henry C. Cooper, *Spectator* editor-owner David McCulloch, and foundrymen James Stewart and James Jamieson.[31] It took all these men some time to 'work themselves up' to foreman or superintendent within other establishments before becoming masters themselves.

For some, though, the road to mastership was fraught with obstacles, making the straight upward linear progression from apprentice to master harder to achieve. The career of engine and boilermaker Joseph Killey provides one example of this. After completing his Liverpool engineer's apprenticeship Killey worked for a time as a journeyman at the Canning Foundry in that city, eventually becoming foreman. The savings accrued from that situation allowed for the purchase of a partnership in the Windsor Machine Works near Liverpool.

However, this venture failed, leaving a disgruntled forty-year-old Killey out of work and bereft of fortune. Killey immigrated to Hamilton in 1864, where he worked for a number of years in the large engine and boiler works of the F.G. Beckett Company. Some time after this he became foreman at the St Lawrence Foundry in Toronto. By the early 1870s he was back in Hamilton and had commenced manufacturing engines on his own behalf. This time self-employment stuck and Killey's company proved prosperous.[32] Such other successful local manufacturers as foundryman John Milne, printer Richard Donnelly, and planing mill operator William Casey experienced a similarly bumpy ride to self-employment.[33] If fortunes soured, it was not unusual for journeymen-turned-masters to cross the line back to working for someone else. While this period was sometimes brief, it serves to reinforce the idea that the boundary between journeyman and master was still somewhat fluid in this period.

Obstacles to self-employment were sometimes insurmountable. A foray into self-employment might be followed by working for others for the balance of a career. For example, W.H. Finch served as a foreman at the McQuesten foundry in town and had acquired a small interest in that concern by 1854 before applying his capital to the opening of the Copp, Finch, and Copp foundry in Woodstock in 1857. This enterprise failed to prosper and Finch returned to Hamilton 'poorer in purse but richer in experience' by 1864. Here he seems to have served out the remainder of his career as foreman at the Copp's Empire Foundry.[34] While Finch was able to spend the rest of his working life in the relative comfort of a foreman's position, his experience of failure in self-employment was certainly, as Katz and others have suggested, not uncommon. However, it is likely that the example of most large industrial employers in the city having made the successful transition from journeyman-for-someone-else to masters-of-their-own somewhat clouded this reality.

These examples show that the 'tramp' was also an important experience of early work life for many of the men who had become Hamilton's large industrialists by the 1870s. That these men participated in the tramp is not surprising. This practice went hand in hand with journeywork and was well understood as an integral step up the ladder to artisanal independence, to 'competency,' to manhood.[35] Master and man alike would have recognized the strong cultural meaning of the tramp in Hamilton. After satisfying their wanderlust setting up shop for themselves, Hamilton's large masters hired tramping craftsworkers in turn, thereby recognizing and perpetuating the tramp as a culturally significant practice in the life of the craftsman.

The tramping past of Hamilton's large industrialists also suggests that, for North American craftsworkers in general, social mobility was perhaps more likely a function of transiency than of persistence. Instead of fleeing the city due to lack of opportunity, many craftsmen actually were attracted there because of it. For them, Hamilton was either a way station or an end point on the road to upward mobility. Employers like Robert Smiley, the Gurneys, or the Becketts came to Hamilton to set up shop after performing journeywork somewhere else. Others such as Alexander Main, Joseph Killey, James Stewart, and foundryman Matthew Howles continued at journeywork in town before eventually setting up on their own locally. Even to those native to the city, such as James Foster and foundrymen William Burrow, Charles Stewart and John Milne, a lengthy sojourn south of the border could intervene before they returned permanently to pursue self-employment. Harder to determine are the likely considerable number of men who followed the example of printer Richard Donnelly, who apprenticed and performed some journeywork in the city but found success elsewhere. It is not possible to determine exactly how widespread success was or to identify journeymen entering or exiting the city, since information on early work life is missing for so many of Hamilton's successful large masters. However, enough examples can be identified to suggest that many, if not most, of the city's large industrialists spent their wage-earning years on some form of an often wide-ranging journey in search of permanence and success in self-employment. Because of this it is likely that many mobile masters-to-be did not turn up as part of the linked sample in Katz et al's. determination of social mobility among persisters in Hamilton over the two decades he studied. As Peter Bischoff has suggested, the monumental task now facing historians is the reliable quantification of the contours and patterns of geographic mobility, especially among nineteenth-century craftsmen.[36] Even without careful quantification it would be hard to deny that Hamilton's large masters' experience with wage-earning in their younger years provided an important example to successive waves of journeymen in the city. They symbolized the very real rewards that could accrue from years of hard work, skill diversification, and geographic opportunism.

Mastership represented the fulfilment of a dream of masculine independence nurtured through apprenticeship and journeywork. In this, the initial experience of those men who became the city's manufacturing elite seems little different from that of most traditional small masters. Their early years of self-employment demanded a hard-working, parsimonious existence fraught with uncertainty, not too dissimilar from the recent experiences of journey life. Contrary to some accounts of Canada's industrialization, which concentrate on industries requiring substantial capital allotments and employing a large number of workers,[37] much of Hamilton's initial industrial growth took place as skilled proprietors expanded their shops, aided mostly by their own skill and sweat, perhaps with the help of sons or other male family members, and most often without the luxury of copious capital. Much of Hamilton's initial industrial growth was characterized by this 'natural' expansion from the small artisanal workshop to the larger industrial concern. As products of a fairly typical masculine artisanal course of life, most of these men started out in self-employment on their own with little in the way of capital and much in the way of skill. Real growth was often the result of the consistent accrual of sweat equity in the enterprise by the proprietor himself.[38] To the city's aspiring young craftsworkers, these men must have given much cultural currency to the idea that real growth was possible from humble beginnings.

Evidence of this progression is available for manufacturing establishments in most sectors of the city's economy. The large enterprises of printer and *Spectator* owner-editor Robert Smiley, brush maker Charles Meakins, and porkcurer F.W. Fearman all experienced slow growth from small beginnings. Lacking much capital, Alexander Main established a reputation for his ropeworks throughout Ontario and Quebec and as far west as Chicago by the early 1870s, through initial reliance on small amounts of credit granted him by wholesale merchant Colin Ferrie to purchase supplies for spinning. The small tailoring establishment started by Charles Foster with the assistance of his younger brother James in the 1850s had grown by 1871 into the third-largest clothing shop in the city in terms of annual product. The small shops started by shoemakers Robert Nisbet and P.W. Dayfoot around 1850 had become the city's two largest boot and shoe manufactories by 1871, the former employing 175 operatives to produce its $200 000 in product that year.[39]

Such growth was also typical of Hamilton's secondary-metal producers. Benjamin Greening's highly successful Victoria Wire Mills, for example, got its start in the backyard of his Peter Street home, where he and his wife worked straightening wire and making wire cable on a small hand-driven machine imported from England. The large engine and boiler works of Messrs F.G. Beckett and Company had grown from an 'establishment of moderate dimensions' when operations commenced in the mid-1850s to offering employment to 25 men and boys by 1863 and 120 workers by 1871. By this year the $150 000 invested in the operation made it the fourth-largest industrial establishment in the city in terms of total invested capital. As John Weaver has outlined, most, if not all, of the city's substantial foundry operations by the 1870s started as small shops.[40]

Thus far, implicit in this portrait has been the idea that initial capital requirements were small, most growth being realized through reinvestment of profits. More detailed information of the initial capitalization of a few firms supports these findings. When asked by the Labour Commission to explain how he and his partners had financed initial operations, Hamilton Malleable Iron Works partner John Milne explained 'we had no capital only what we worked for,' a sum one city promotional claimed amounted to a meagre $1000.[41] Douglas McCalla has outlined the low fixed capital requirements of the Fisher and McQuesten foundry, which had growth into the immensely successful L.D. Sawyer Agricultural Implement Works by the 1870s.[42] Edward and Charles Gurney's highly successful stove foundry also began life as a small operation. Arriving in town in 1842 with a capital of about $1400 apiece accrued during their journeyman years, the brother's acquired 'a very modest building' on John Street and commenced production early the next year. This humble operation allowed for production of only 'a couple of stoves a day.' In 1847, the Gurney's began the slow expansion of their business by partnering with pattern maker and woodcarver Alexander Carpenter and gradually enlarging the premises as demand increased, turning the foundry into a 'conglomeration of buildings of various sizes and many ages.' When space on the original property ran out the firm expanded into an old church building next door. By 1871 the E. and C. Gurney Company was Hamilton's largest stove foundry, capitalized at $80 000 and offering employment to over a hundred men who produced upwards of $140 000 a year in product.[43]

With capital in short supply, the initial growth of the small enterprises that would one day become the city's major industries was often accrued on the back of the master himself. Sweat equity seems to have been the most common form of initial capital accumulation. Fisher and McQuesten foundry partner John Fisher complained of the time spent trying to find enough skilled labour to allow him to leave the shop floor to attend to office duties.[44] The Gurney brothers commenced foundry operations in town in the early 1840s by performing virtually all the work themselves.[45] The city's early founders were not the only small masters in the city forced to put their back into their work in the early years of their enterprise. The evidence elucidates the practical involvement well into establishment of their concerns of a diverse group of masters, including engine and boilermakers George Northey and Frederick Beckett, boot and shoemaker Robert Nisbet, clothing maker James Foster, and carriage maker Thomas McCabe.[46]

The examples set by large employers growing their businesses from small beginnings usually through practical application of their own muscle and skill must have provided a powerful example to the city's aspiring young journeymen and apprentices that following established craft practice could lead to a level of masculine independence rooted in but well beyond the conventions of craft tradition.

This section does not tout the reality of the 'rags-to-riches' myth, but outlines the continuation of pre-existing forms of craft mobility among Hamilton's craftsworkers. This, in turn, raises important new questions about the realities of early industrialization in Hamilton and in other Canadian and North American cities and towns. By the early 1870s, the continued functioning of craft mobility networks was strongly represented to area craftsworkers through the widespread humble craft origins of their masters, a significant number of whom had recently achieved their measure of success. For the apprentice or journeyman, the idea that it was still possible to start with nothing but a developing set of skills and to transform that into a viable masculine independence still appeared plausible since almost all those who had 'made it' had followed this route. This perception became a strong cultural symbol with a heavy psychological momentum for the practitioners in the craft world, both junior and senior. This weighty symbol was backed up by actual *practice* into the 1870s.

Practices of Continuity

Hamilton's large masters also created workplaces in which important elements of the tradition of craft mobility were nurtured and preserved up through the early 1870s, thereby bolstering the *perception* of opportunity outlined above. Throughout early industrialization it remained common for local craftsworkers to rise and be mentored through the ranks to become their own masters. The opportunities to achieve this masculine independence were significantly opened up in these years with the creation of numerous superintendent and foreman positions that often carried with them some tangible ownership in the means of production, often through part-ownership or anticipated future ownership of the enterprise. These practices were not just typical of the shops of local artisan-industrial proprietors, but were also well-ensconced in the Great Western Railway's car and locomotive shops, where traditional craft production had been significantly revised and lifetime wage-earning had become the standard for the city's largest industrial workforce.

The Road to Self-Employment

Masters, both large and small, served as living reminders of the possibility of craft mobility to the city's aspiring apprentices and journeymen. The use of city shops as launchpads to self-employment showed the craft progression in practice. From early on it was common for masters to graduate from waged work in a city shop to self-employment, becoming visible examples of the smooth functioning of the craft progression to other workers in the craft. Many of the city's most successful industrialists by the 1870s had spent part of their early work lives as apprentices or wage-earning journeymen in city shops at various times over the previous decades.

As John Weaver has shown, after the initiation of the town's first foundries 'former apprentices and journeymen began starting up their own Hamilton furnaces.'[47] The Fisher-McQuesten foundry was particularly prolific in this regard. The proprietors of that establishment found early on that a good way to recruit loyal workers was to train family members. John Fisher's brother Samuel worked at the furnace from at least 1836. Calvin McQuesten's nephews Luther and Stephen trained there as a moulder and machinist respectively from the mid-1840s and had been joined by their brother Payson by the time they assumed control of the firm in 1857. But the McQuesten-Fisher foundry served as a stepping stone to mastership for more than family members. In 1853 moulder and foreman William H. Finch and 'tin man' William Wirt, both long-time employees, were also admitted into the partnership. James Stewart left their employ in 1845 to manage his successful MacNab Street Foundry after ten years working there as a pattern maker and later as foreman of their pattern department.[48]

This pattern was repeated at other city foundries. James Stewart, in turn, employed as a journeyman moulder Charles Stewart (no relation), himself a former McQuesten and Fisher apprentice. Charles Stewart soon traded in earning wages at the MacNab Street Foundry to join with William Burrow to manufacture castings on their own behalf in 1864. Burrow had honed his moulding skills during the

1850s as either an apprentice and/or a journeyman at the city's other early major stove shop, the E. and C. Gurney Company. There, he likely crossed paths with patternmaker James Turnbull, another Gurney employee. In 1854 Turnbull, along with his older brother William (himself a bookkeeper at Gurney's) left to start their successful Mary Street Foundry. Successful foundryman and tin and copperware manufacturer Dennis Moore started his work life as a fourteen-year-old apprentice in Edward Jackson's Hamilton Tin Factory in 1831. A few years later he became a junior partner, eventually gaining control of that firm's operations upon Jackson's death in 1872. Future London, Ontario, founder John McClary also 'became a moulder and learned the art of making stoves from D. Moore Co.'s experience.'[49]

This progression was not confined to the metal industry. *Hamilton Spectator* co-owner and editor-in-chief David McCulloch started his career as an apprentice upholsterer to Hamilton furniture maker James Reid some time around 1850. He used the competency gained there to secure the position of foreman of the upholstery department at the car shops of the Great Western Railway before leaving to become a partner in the *Spectator* in 1870. Soon after his family arrived in town in 1842, seven-year-old George Tuckett was put to work in James Walker's soap and candle factory to learn the trade of tallow chandler. He switched to cigar making soon after, gaining experience in that trade in a number of small city shops during his teenage years. He became a member of Hamilton's cigar makers' union in the last year of his apprenticeship at Hamilton tobacconist Alfred Quimby's manufactory, where he worked as a journeyman for and then partnered with Quimby a short time later. This partnership had been dissolved by the 1870s, when Tuckett had become one of the country's most successful tobacco manufacturers. Henry Cooper apprenticed and worked as a journeyman in carriage maker James Williams's Hamilton Coach Factory from the 1840s, becoming foreman and junior partner of that concern some time in the mid-1850s. By the early 1860s Cooper had become principal proprietor of what was now Hamilton's largest carriage manufactory. Tramping journeyman Alexander Main found employment at a ropewalk near the foot of Mary Street in the early 1850s before deciding to stay and open his own ropeworks a short time later.[50]

This practice was well established by the late 1860s and early 1870s. For example, more than one journeyman had his ticket to mastership stamped while employed at John Gartshore's foundry in nearby Dundas. From the 1860s through the early 1870s such former Gartshore apprentices, journeymen, and foremen as Robert McKechnie, John Bertram, Thomas Wilson, Alexander Barry, Walter Barnstable, David Scott, and Thomas Cowie opened successful metal shops of their own. There is some substance to the assertion that John Gartshore 'succeeded in fathering virtually every major foundry in the south-western Lake Peninsula'[51] Such former moulders in the E. and C. Gurney Foundry as John Milne, Matthew Howles, and Nelson Tallman founded their own successful establishments in these years.[52]

Possibilities of ownership appear to have remained open for men trained in other metal shops. After failing in a related business in Liverpool, Joseph Killey immigrated to Hamilton in 1864 to work as an engine and boilermaker in F.G. Beckett's Atlas Works. He went on to work as foreman in a Toronto foundry in the late 1860s before returning to Hamilton to found his own engine shop under the name J.H. Killey and Company in 1870. Future foundryman James Jamieson worked for a number of years at the R.M. Wanzer Sewing Machine Company after serving a machinist's apprenticeship at that concern. Some time in the late 1870s he pooled his money and skills with Wanzer bookkeeper John G. Bowes to purchase an interest in Adam Laidlaw's Mary Street Foundry. Under this new configuration, Bowes 'had charge of the counting room, while Jamieson, being a practical mechanic, took the shop end.' The two former Wanzer employees withdrew from the Laidlaw firm in 1884 to form their own successful stove concern, styled Bowes, Jamieson, and Company.[53]

There is also substantial evidence that the practice of men graduating from work for others to become independent masters continued in other industries. Before embarking on a successful contracting career by the mid-1870s, Thomas Allen served a carpentry apprenticeship under local builder William Chisholm. Frank Kidner apprenticed at the *Canada Christian Advocate* and worked as the printer at the *Spectator* before opening his own print shop in 1883. Jacob Zingshiem, William Malcolm, and Alexander Souter all found success in self-employment after serving apprenticeships with local furniture maker James Reid. The trend of employees going on to become masters appears to have continued at the Hamilton Coach Works well after Henry Cooper took over control of that enterprise from his former master James Williams. Cooper's two sons took over the business in 1883 after learning carriage making in their father's shop. Two of Cooper's employees, foreman carriage trimmer Richard Morgan and carriage blacksmith John Malloy, went on to found the Dominion Carriage Factory in 1870.[54]

A number of examples suggest that the craft progression had at least some life well after the 1870s. Nathan Glass Boggs served an apprenticeship and worked as a journeyman for tinsmith's tools maker Samuel J. Moore before setting up his own highly successful tinsmith's tools business with fellow Moore journeyman John Mootry Brown in 1890. The Hamilton Industrial Works employed woodworker George Dowswell and his brother Frederick in the manufacture of clothes wringers and washers before the brothers used their savings to buy the company in the mid-1890s, renaming it the Dowswell Manufacturing Company. Before opening their Harper-Presnail Cigar Company in 1913 Thomas and William Presnail had worked at Tuckett's Tobacco as a cigar maker and manager respectively. Their partner, William Harper, had also been 'connected' with Tuckett's 'for many years.'[55]

The men mentioned above entered into small mastership, the continued viability of which we have seen could have been perceived by city journeymen in the generally comfortable living it afforded. But before proceeding further it is also worth noting that the potential still existed even in the late 1860s and early 1870s for some of these concerns to undertake appreciable growth in the following years. While already in business some time by 1871 brewer Leopold Bauer, boat builder Henry Bastien, and coffin manufacturer John Blachford all markedly expanded their operations in the decades to come. Other concerns headed by small masters in 1871 underwent substantial expansion in the 1880s and 1890s, including furniture makers Jacob Zingsheim and J. Pecover, tailor Joseph Woon, wagon maker Edward McGrath, boot and shoemaker George Midgely, bookbinder John Eastwood, and others. Some small masters grew their enterprises into quite large concerns. For example, after 1871, when he gave employment to only two men and a boy, tinsmiths' tools maker S.J. Moore continued to expand his enterprise until 1890, when he retired, selling his concern to former employees J.M. Brown and N.G. Boggs, who soon employed about one hundred workers and sold goods in markets as far away as South Africa and South America.

In the mind of the public, the powerful example of most local masters' achievement of success through craft ranks must have served to strengthen the *impression* that – statistically significant or not – it was still possible in the period up to the early 1870s to expand a small concern into a prosperous enterprise. This powerful social image allowed aspiring young craftsworkers to still perceive various forms of mastership as the natural culmination of apprenticeship and waged journeywork. The fact that a fair number of small masters were still able to push beyond a 'comfortable competence' to achieve greater financial success must surely have strengthened this image and increased its longevity.

These practices likely diminished in decades to follow,[56] a fact that must have become ever more clear to younger craftsworkers. But even then, they likely did not lose their social currency overnight, a fact to which the continued promulgation of the 'rags-to-riches' ideology by Richard Butler and numerous other North American commentators after the turn of the twentieth century attests. The degree to which such an ideology was initially formulated in actual material practice throughout North America is a research agenda first suggested by Herbert Gutman and given further grounding here.[57] The more direct point to make is that by the early 1870s it was still possible for Hamilton craftsworkers to understand that while the context might be new, craft mobility was – and perhaps more than ever before – a well-functioning process.[58]

Master Mentors

Examples of new enterprises developing from the local craft labour force are plentiful, and the examples provided here are by no means exhaustive. It is, of course, simply the fact that the craft progression remained a practice in Hamilton shops by the early 1870s that was the most important marker of this continuity, especially in the minds of aspiring apprentices and journeymen. But the degree to which this practice was still an entrenched feature of the craft world can also be augmented with some evidence that masters still actively facilitated this progression. Evidence of this more in-depth social process is, naturally, more limited. But the weight of the little information that does survive should be balanced with the fact that no evidence could be found in a close reading of the city press of men lamenting the limitation or cessation of either the craft progression or changes in masters' attitudes towards it.

Local press reports by the early 1870s still portrayed the entry into self-employment as the natural culmination of years of apprenticeship and journeywork.[59] More importantly, however, information can be gleaned to show that masters themselves still took a personal interest in helping their charges realize their craft independence. As members of a craft fraternity, nineteenth-century employers felt it a chief part of their duty to mentor members of their own workforce towards self-employment. There is some limited evidence to suggest that masters sometimes provided material aid to former journeymen making their initial forays into mastership. Weaver has suggested, for example, that the Gurney brothers were likely aided at crucial moments in the growth of their fledgling enterprise by supplies of iron from the then more buoyant Fisher and McQuesten foundry.[60] In turn, the Gurneys appear to have played a crucial role in aiding Matthew Howles's initial foray into self-employment in 1867 by providing a large portion of its initial material impulse in the form of credit and supplies.[61] Similarly, Henry Cooper received aid from James Williams when he assumed proprietorial control of his former master's carriageworks in 1859. In this case Williams provided his former apprentice with a mortgage on the factory's buildings, property, and equipment. When Cooper was unable to live up to this obligation some years later, William's briefly reassumed the property before mortgaging it out to Cooper again, this time 'on easier terms.'[62]

More revealing of this material mentoring, though, was the frequency with which masters trained men and then took them into partnership. Masters likely had many and varied reasons to do this. Taking on a partner, especially one you had trained and knew could be trusted, would have provided a skilled anchor in the shop to those masters seeking to expand their operations and/or other aspects of their business. In many cases, it was probably the desire to retire, fully or partially, that provided the impetus. While the elevation of an employee into partnership was a strategy that served the master's interests, it was also intended to bestow a reciprocity of benefits to all involved. It showed the master's continued personal commitment to the craft progression.

Examples of this practice are numerous. Dennis Moore apprenticed and worked in Edward Jackson's tin manufactory and stove shop before partnering in and then assuming principal control of that firm upon Jackson's death in 1872. James Williams took Henry Cooper into partnership in his Hamilton Coach Company around 1856 after the latter had served under him as apprentice, journeyman, and foreman for over decade. Cigar maker George Tuckett joined with his former master Alfred Quimby in a plug tobacco business by 1862. Clothing manufacturer William Sanford brought a Mr Vail, previously his managing cutter, into the firm in 1871. After a number of years in business on his own behalf, Joseph Killey hooked up with F.G. Beckett, his former boss at the Atlas Engine and Boiler Works, to form the Killey-Beckett Engine Company in 1892.[63]

Not surprisingly, in many Hamilton shops the practice of training one's sons with the intention of passing the family business on to them remained a common form of this practice in the city by the 1870s, with such manufacturing families as the Bastiens, Becketts, Caseys, Eassons, Gurneys, Hoodlesses, Meakins, McQuestens, Northeys, Robertsons, Semmen's, J. Stewarts, Tallmans, and many others leading the way.

While intergenerational transference may have intensified in the decades to come, providing one indication of the end of the traditional craft world, by the early 1870s blood ties were not the sole prerequisite for bonds and obligations between masters and men in some Hamilton workplaces. In a work environment where the owner of an enterprise was still often intimately associated with the shop floor and a participant in its culture, features of a paternal labour relationship remained intact. Beyond the facilitation of their apprentices' and journeymen's ascent to masculine independence, it is also important to note that at least some workers, bosses, and community members still took seriously the more broadly paternal aspects of this relationship. Some masters' facilitation of their workers' success spoke of a larger relationship akin to that of father and son. 'Whistler at the Plough' Alexander Somerville, for instance, eagerly attributed Hamilton's industrial success by 1873 to such inspired men as founder John Gartshore, whose dedication to the craft progression had made him 'father, through his apprentices and journeymen, of nearly one-hundred machine factories and foundries in the Dominion of Canada.'[64]

Most telling are the testimonial remarks offered on the occasion of the retirement of partner John Tarbox from the R.M. Wanzer Sewing Machine Company factory in 1872. Tarbox reminded his men: 'It may interest you to know that during the time I have been director of mechanical skill nearly 150 young men passing from under my charge have become heads of departments or manufactories. I have had the pleasure of assisting and promoting many of them, and I hope, Providence permitting, to have the pleasure of assisting and promoting many hundreds more.' In return, employee Mr Greenfield publicly remarked that Tarbox 'had always treated by him more like a father than an employer.'[65]

As Hamilton entered the 1870s, its craft masters' commitment to facilitating their charges' rise in the world remained a key part of their paternal obligations. In a city where almost half the male industrial workforce toiled in enterprises employing fifty or more workers, it is likely that the actual ability of all craftsworkers to make this step was diminishing. However, the continued rhetorical commitment to this paternal interest coupled with its widespread practice was likely still sufficient to outweigh these changes.

New Positions of Craft Leadership

While self-employment remained a very real hope, in the twenty-odd years before the 1870s it was not the only path by which a craftsworker could achieve a manly 'competence.' In the wage-earning context of a larger shop, 'foreman' or 'superintendent'' status brought with it the independence of a relatively high wage and increased proximity to, and often some measurable ownership of, the means of production. These were undeniably new positions, emergent in the industries undergoing the greatest degree of growth and change. But, by this stage of industrialization, it was still possible for craftsworkers to view them as fitting into the cultural attributes of the (admittedly changing) craft world. Their craft legitimacy was rooted largely in a combination of their own skills with the public transference to them by the artisan-owners who employed them of important aspects of craft leadership. In this way, they could be seen as part of the craft tradition even if they were not. Such forms of mobility need to be factored into determinations of social mobility. While David Burley found a constriction in self-employment after 1860 in nearby Brantford, for example, he does not account the addition of new positions of craft leadership.[66]

The need for foremen or superintendents, of course, arose only after various city shops had achieved sufficient size and complexity of production to warrant a new managerial layer. But such a need did not necessarily occur late in Hamilton's industrialization. Men such as James Stewart, Bob Lucas, and Henry Cooper, for example, were respectively employed as foremen in the Fisher-McQuesten foundry, E. and C. Gurney foundry, and Hamilton Coach Works in the 1840s.[67] However, in the decade and a half before the 1870s the city press and other sources began to make increasing reference to the presence of foremen in city shops. The position of foreman brought with it a measure of prestige, especially when considered from the perspective of journeymen and apprentices. Craftsworkers commonly viewed their overseers with at least some sense of veneration. The historiographic view of the foremen as simply the 'hard taskmaster' acting in the interests of capital and bent solely on wresting productive control from his workers or instituting such new managerial regimes as the 'drive system' needs to be reconsidered in this light.[68] Part of this reconsideration needs to be made in recognition of the fact that, in some Hamilton workplaces at least, foremen remained active union members.[69] It makes more sense to understand the foreman's position as developing within the craft progression. Journeymen and apprentices would likely have viewed the foreman's greater job security, higher pay, and closer proximity to the means of production as a relatively new, but definitely real, step on the road to craftsworker independence they themselves hoped one day to follow.

In fact, a foreman's position could well have been understood by Hamilton craftsworkers as a satisfactory end in itself within the craft progression, even within a context of a lifetime of wage-earning. A study of workplace testimonials outlined in chapter 4 shows that foremen were still commonly held in esteem by their charges. While men like Gurney foremen Robert Lucas and James Mason or Gardener Sewing Machine Company foreman William McBeth may have worked for wages all their lives, they likely did so as visible beneficiaries of craft competency.

Their position in the craft hierarchy was also significantly reinforced by the fact that many foremen occupied a crucial and indispensable place in the productive process. In the enterprises of non-artisanal proprietors especially, a foreman's comprehensive practical understanding and de facto control of the productive process might lie almost solely with the craftsman-foreman. Telling is the case of James Brayley, foreman of merchant William McGiverin's hardware manufacturing operations. Not only was this section of McGiverin's business put wholly under the management of a foreman who was 'well known as possessing real mechanical and inventive powers,' but production within McGiverin's well-known saddlery and harness manufactory would not have been possible without the use of 'a peculiar device ... invented by Mr. Brayley.'[70]

Sometimes the crucial productive knowledge possessed by these men earned them the loftier title of 'superintendent' or 'manager.' In 1872 the merchant-directors of the new Hamilton Tool Manufacturing Company boasted their new company's operations would be overseen by Manager John W. Murray, 'who has a large and successful practical experience.' Former forwarder and wharfinger Daniel Charles Gunn, who 'knew nothing about the practical workings of a great machine shop,' placed production at his plant under the full control of Superintendent Kinmond, a 'first class workman.' On a visit to merchant Richard Juson's nail works in 1863, one reporter noted that plant Superintendent D. MacDonald's 'many years experience in the manufacture of cut nails' entitled him to 'hardly less credit than the [firm's] enterprising proprietors ... [in the] successful establishment of this branch of manufacture in Hamilton.' As time went on the usage of various managerial titles would undoubtedly achieve more rigid and hierarchical distinction, with 'foreman' becoming generally subservient to 'manager' or 'superintendent.' It should also be noted that even in artisan-led enterprises, foremen or superintendents were often recognized as occupying elevated and important places in the craft hierarchy of the shop floor. The skilled proprietors of the Atlas Engine and Boiler Works, for instance, took great pride in the fact that '[t]he master workmen in charge of each department are mechanics of the first order.'[71]

Given that these men were so crucial to production, it is not surprising that a number of them either entered into their positions of responsibility as, or were rewarded for a job well done later on with, an interest in the firm which they helped oversee. A number of foremen/superintendents followed the route of Peter Warren, superintendent and partner in the Dennis Moore Foundry and 'a gentleman of long experience as a founder,' by entering a business both as part-owner and overseer. It was, of course, their intimate knowledge of production that made these men uniquely suited to this position. Not only was this type of arrangement functionally expedient for the smooth operation of a concern, but these men's qualifications were also often publicly touted to garner the confidence of a firm's potential customers and creditors in the quality of a company's goods and the general competence of its members. Typical were newspaper reports or credit ledger entries that made special mention of the practical qualifications of a partner/superintendent. On the opening of the Hespeler Sewing Machine Company, for instance, while the *Spectator* named all the partners of the enterprise it paid particular attention to mechanical superintendent and partner R. Peter's qualifications as 'a thorough mechanic in every respect.' Given the crucial position that the foreman/superintendent-owner could play in an enterprise it also appears that it was not uncommon for this individual's skills and abilities to comprise his capital investment in the firm. When J.H. Stone became mechanical superintendent and partner in James Williams's new tinware factory in 1871, for example, the local R.G. Dun credit agent reported that he 'contributed no means, but is the mechanic engaged.' Another common route was to work for a wage when commencing tenure as foremen or superintendent, and then trade up to become part-owner some time later. John N. Tarbox, for example, purportedly began his stay in Hamilton as 'superintendent of the Wanzer factory, and then became a partner in that concern.' It was also not uncommon for a foreman/superintendent to cash in his partial ownership of the firm where he worked and apply the proceeds to the founding of a new concern more completely under his control. For instance, cabinetmaker Joseph Hoodless held a small interest in and served as superintendent of the Edgar and Melville Company, manufacturers of various wood products, before withdrawing to open his own furniture factory in 1872.[72]

Many times, though, foremen/superintendents appear not to have been part-owners of an enterprise they oversaw before making the step to self-employment. Wanzer Sewing Machine Company foremen James Jamieson and Christopher Lockman, for example, had no interest in that concern before partnering respectively in the Mary Street Foundry in the late 1870s and the Wilson, Bowman Sewing Machine Company in 1869. Carriage manufacturer Richard Morgan, foundryman Thomas Cowie, and master printer R.R. Donnelly similarly worked as foremen in city shops before making the foray into self-employment.

However, it must also be stressed that ownership of the means of production was not a prerequisite for craftsworkers' understanding that foremen/superintendents had been fundamentally elevated within the craft hierarchy. Such foremen as James Mason, Robert Lucas, George Sheed, John Taylor, and William McBeth (who will be introduced in more depth in the next chapter) may have remained wage-earners for the balance of their careers, but they did achieve an estimable rise in the craft ranks in the eyes of their contemporaries. The experience of machinist Robert Brick provides another interesting example of this type of rise. Brick experienced his 'first knowledge' of the machinist's trade as an apprentice at Northey's foundry. He then rounded out his skills by working for a number of years as a journeyman at the Wanzer plant. Around 1870 Brick experienced upward movement in the eyes of his peers when he agreed to become superintendent of the new Wilson, Bowman sewing machine factory. According to Joseph Tinsely, an 'old-time' printer active in the International Typographical Union, Brick's rise in the world was plain for all to see. Among other markers of success, Brick was particularly well known for his penchant for 'ultra-fashionable clothes' and such luxurious accessories as diamond shirt studs. Brick's rise in the eyes of his fellow workers, of course, was achieved without obtaining any real ownership of the means of production.[73]

Similar to the foreman or superintendent, the subcontractor may have occupied another such intermediate role in the craft hierarchy in some local workplaces, though evidence of this is sorely lacking. Some historians have viewed employers' use of such individuals as an early form of dispossession, simply 'subcontracting exploitation and management.'[74] It is likely the squeeze of competition may indeed have created such conditions, especially in more developed economies. But in places with different economic conditions, the subcontractor and his employees could well have had a more positive experience. In its first few years of operation the Great Western Railway leased space in its shops to a number of private contractors, though concerns over product quality and financial considerations put an end to this by the later 1850s.[75] The organization of sections of the local carriage industry, outlined in chapter 1, also suggests this possibility. More direct evidence of this practice remains to be uncovered. This finding affirms Craig Heron's wider conclusion that, while some modest examples of this practice could be found in mid-nineteenth-century industrializing Ontario, subcontracting was 'not typical.'[76]

Wage-Earning at the Great Western Railway

The most pervasive example of craftsworker mobility achieved within the context of wage-earning is, of course, found in the elaborate supervisory structures embedded in the shops of the Great Western Railway. The dimensions of paternalism in the GWR shops have been much studied. However, it would be useful to situate the GWR within the larger social context of craftwork in Hamilton.

Lifetime wage employment was a reality for many in the shops of the GWR. Given that the railway shops were, by far, the city's largest employer, this concern would appear to be the major exception to the argument that Hamilton craftsworkers still inhabited a world in which journeymen could expect to achieve more traditional forms of craft 'independence' and where access to the means of production was still often possible or perceived to be so. Yet, while Paul Craven and Tom Traves have argued that the organization of work in GWR shops 'more closely resembled the industrial than the artisanal model,' they also show this to have been a wage-earning context characterized by strong traditions of paternalism that, while 'transitional,' still found much of their rooting in the personal labour relations of the past.[77] Bolstered by relatively high, secure, and year-round wages, this paternalism also stood in stark contrast to other wage-based industrial relations exhibiting forms of conflict often associated with the alienating effects of industrial capitalism. Within this context railway craftsmen climbed through an elaborate set of occupational rungs that represented mobility *within* that enterprise. What this represented to Hamilton craftsworkers – those from within the GWR *and* those from without – was that a variety of mobility within craftwork was possible even inside a large industrial enterprise where wage-earning was the norm.

At the GWR, as in so many other Hamilton workplaces, the craftsworker-foreman -and superintendent became an important symbol of craftsworker success. Craven has pointed out that the company's manufacturing operations were almost wholly overseen by men whose deep practical knowledge established the Great Western 'on the leading edge of mechanical innovation' in Canada.[78]

Both the company and its employees took great pride in the fact that the foremen of the various shops within the mechanical departments represented the crème de la crème of skilled workers. In 1863 the company's fitting shop was headed by a Mr Foster, 'one of the most intelligent and skilled mechanics in the employ of the company.' Overseeing the boilermaker's shops was a Mr McIntyre, 'a very competent workman of long experience.' In the smiths' shop Mr James Stevenson, who enjoyed 'a very high reputation as a mechanic,' was calling the shots. Mr McCulloch, 'one of the most skilled cabinet-makers in Canada,' headed up production in the cabinet workshop, while future *Hamilton Spectator* owner David McCulloch applied his 'artistic skill and good taste' to the supervision of the upholsterer's shop. The carpenter's shop was headed by 'first class mechanic' Henry Childs.

The evidence also shows that the humble origins of a crafts training extended to the company's mechanical superintendents, who themselves commanded much discretion in the daily operation of the shops. Upon his departure from the company in 1856, Henry Yates, the first superintendent of the Great Western's locomotive department, was fondly toasted by the men under his charge as 'one of our own class, having graduated amongst us.' Samuel Sharp, superintendent of the car department from the commencement of operations and after 1862 head of the combined car and locomotive departments, was also a practical man. Sharp started his career as a building trade apprentice at Liverpool, moving on to railway work in his early twenties. Upon his death in 1873 he was remembered as 'essentially a self-made man, and owed his success in life more to the inherent force of his own character than to the advantages of adventitious circumstances.' A 'vigorous' young man who had compensated for his lack of education in childhood through strict attendance at the London Mechanics' Institute, Sharp was proud to exclaim that it was 'the mechanic' in this modern age who 'had set the world thinking.' Sharp's successor W.A. Robinson, the son of a Birmingham hairdresser, was also a 'practical mechanic' whose innovative bent won him several patents.[79] To their journeymen and apprentices, the GWR's foremen and superintendents represented the real rewards that could still accrue from a committed crafts training.

GWR craftsworkers were also not sealed off from the craft mobility networks in other Hamilton workplaces. While perhaps the majority of the GWR skilled workforce were likely recent immigrants, significant numbers were also recruited locally.[80] At least some GWR craftsmen trained at local shops. For example, upholsterer David McCulloch apprenticed for Hamilton furniture maker James Reid, while painter Henry B. Witton worked at J.P. Pronguey's local carriage shop. Some GWR shop employees left the company to pursue other opportunities locally. Upholstery shop foreman David McCulloch, paint shop foreman Henry Witton, and boilermaker Alexander Wingfield went on to successful careers in fields outside their craft. Machinist James Omand, carpenter Henry Bastien, and Mechanical Superintendent William A. Robinson left to pursue self-employment opportunities in manufacturing in fields consistent with their training.[81]

Seen in the above light, the personal management style practised at the GWR should not be understood as an exception to prevailing craft practice, but as a congruent extension of its practice within the specific context of wage-earning. The industrial experience of the GWR, while profoundly new, was still rooted in craft culture and ideology. And while the type of paternalism practised by management in the GWR shops was heading away from the personal labour relations of the past and towards an emerging corporate paternalism, it was still an organic part of the greater culture of craft mobility present in Hamilton.

A central continuity to the Hamilton craft world by the early 1870s was the continued possibility of owning one's own shop or attaining considerable security and economic prestige as a foreman. Self-improving craftsworkers created an expanding cat's cradle of occupational ladders that they built between Hamilton's myriad industrial establishments and climbed within their specific plants. They were often mentored in this endeavour by their own employers, men who had once themselves negotiated this rite of passage. This process showed little sign of slowing down by the early 1870s. As many new plants opened, self-employment was no longer the only road to achieving competence. The numerous foreman and superintendent positions that opened up by the 1860s and 1870s offered new avenues of opportunity and advancement. The inhabitants of this new managerial stratum occupied positions of responsibility understood to be on the upper rungs of the craft hierarchy. Whether these men owned part of the operation that they supervised or simply worked for wages at such places as the GWR shops, they were venerated within their craft. In all, craft capitalism created a social context in which pre-existing practices of craft mobility were preserved and new ones opened up.

Rethinking Craftsworkers and Class Formation in Hamilton

The examination of craft mobility both as symbol and practice suggests a new theory of class formation. What, exactly, was the class status of the Hamilton craftsworker by the early 1870s in light of the above findings? While industrial capitalism was well advanced in the city by this time and the capitalist mode of production had been established in a considerable number of local workplaces, Hamilton craftsworkers were not yet fully situated, materially or ideologically, within that mode. An underexplored current in the historiography in Canada and elsewhere focuses on the role of the Independent Commodity Producer – most often farmers or fishermen – as a particular socio-economic and cultural form.[82] Less attention has been paid to artisans as petty producers.[83] The key question that must be asked of the situation of Hamilton craftsworkers is whether they had been despoiled of their ownership or control of the means of production, or at least their *anticipation* of that ownership. The loss of this ownership is of course the necessary precondition for the fundamental economic relationship of capitalism, a point far too often overlooked when considering the transition to capitalism.[84] In the case of Hamilton, craft mobility – or, perhaps more importantly, the *expectation* or *perception* of craft mobility – still appeared to give craftsworkers access to the means of production. As Marx explained, 'the capitalist epoch is ... characterized by the fact that labour power, *in the eyes of the worker himself*, takes on the form of a commodity.'[85]

Hamilton craftsworkers, however, did not live in a world still wholly pre-capitalist or non-capitalist. They participated in the capitalist economy, but they were also actors who by and large had not yet lost control of the means of production. This point is crucial, because it meant that while capitalist production *was* established and that journeymen might be rewarded by it, they ultimately did not experience its most alienating effects. Many, if not most, wage-earning craftsworkers still maintained the hope, perhaps even the expectation, that they would one day move into mastership or some other craft-based form of independence. Their continuing practice of craft skill in the workplace would have profoundly re-enforced that image. The continuation of a more traditional relationship to the means of production held them back from fully entering the capitalist world and experiencing its attendant social cosmologies. As Allan Kulikoff has said, it is how the non-capitalist and capitalist worlds related to each other that raises 'new questions about both economic behaviour and political and economic ideology.'[86]

A tacit feature of much of the historiography on craftsworkers and industrialization has been that nineteenth-century journeymen understood themselves to be life-long wage-earners, and that it was from this structural position – for better or for worse – that their primary outlook on the world was formulated. But as Gary Kornblith has warned, historians still need to adequately address 'the emergence and contemporary evaluation of wage labor as the predominate form of labor within urban trades. In short, we need to focus our attention more fully on what was for Karl Marx the defining feature of capitalist production and examine what it meant for craftsmen at the time, rather than to some latter-day historian.'[87] For Hamilton craftsworkers, the *hope* of becoming a producer militated against primary wage-earning identifications. Hand in hand with this were the number of opportunities to go up the wage-earning ladder into higher paid and perhaps more secure employment. Either way, Hamilton craftsworkers must surely have perceived a social system in which cultural traditions of mobility might be fulfilled in one way or another. The widespread abuses and immiseration of wage-earning would be experienced by some during this period and on a more meaningful scale later, but the ultimate logic of wage-earning and industrial capitalism was not yet certain. Most Hamilton craftsworkers could still understand their situation within industrial capitalism as one that they could use to achieve their own ends, one they truly believed functioned in their interests and made real their aspirations. This was the defining feature of craft capitalism: unambiguously capitalist enterprise did exist, but the journeymen who participated in these capitalist institutions did so not fully as creatures of capitalism but as social actors who were also situated outside it in pre-capitalist or non-capitalist modes of production.

Hamilton craftsworkers are perhaps best understood as existing on a continuum of mobility with the modest shop of the traditional small producer at one extreme and the work opportunities in such advanced factory-like settings as the Great Western shops, where improvement was possible but wage-earning its context, on the other. Craftwork in Hamilton was transitional. It hung in the balance between two very different worlds. The first was of the modern bourgeois epoch but still decidedly pre-capitalist.[88] It was a world in which craftsworker independence, defined as graduation to master (or quasi-master) status, was still well in evidence. It was the *expectation*, real or not, that one could or would one day control his own means of production that defined this world. The second world was best evidenced by the Great Western shops, where craft mobility survived intact but in the decidedly capitalist context of wage-earning.

It is the fact that the continuum of mobility straddled both these worlds that is most notable. Combined with the ease with which men could move between the two worlds, this fact meant that the capitalist and non-capitalist worlds overlapped. In the mind of the craftsworker, where one world ended and another began was very much obscured by the fact that both worlds offered to craftsworkers elements central to their aspirations, namely, mobility leading to security. It was from this unique position 'in between' that craftsworkers would formulate a particular world view that would inform their role as actors in the unravelling of early industrial capitalism. Exploring the social dimensions of this transmodal position will be the task of the remaining chapters.

4

A Culture in Continuity: Master–Man Mutualism in Hamilton, Ontario, during Early Industrialization

Cultural change is the dynamic resolution of the old and the new. Raymond Williams, of course, best interpreted this dualism in terms of a given culture's 'residual' and 'emergent' elements.[1] What is interesting about the work culture of Hamilton craftsworkers is how the particular transmodal position of its participants allowed it to become emergent in a way as yet unexplored by historians. But before the dimensions of that 'lively and vibrant' aspect of the culture can be examined, it is first necessary to gain a greater understanding of the pre-existing culture from which it emerged.

As the last chapter showed, the linchpin of continuity in the work culture of Hamilton craftsworkers up to the early 1870s remained the uninterrupted, adapted, even expanded practice of craft mobility. But the function of Hamilton masters in the greater work culture did not end there. As scions of a paternalist hierarchy, they also created workplaces that nurtured and preserved other features of the craft tradition of which mobility was a part. This chapter will build on these findings by showing how various other aspects of the pre-existing crafts work culture that fostered a social closeness between master and man were also maintained atop this structural arrangement. It will examine the remarkable degree of craft continuity – of the residual culture – that existed between master and man in Hamilton shops up through the early 1870s.

The first section will assess the sexual demographics of Hamilton industrial workplaces to suggest that a central underpinning of a continuous work culture – the all-male craft workplace – was well intact by the study's terminal date. A second section will show how the unchanged masculine exclusivity of the shop floor enabled important continuities in the communal masculine work experience of masters and men – both on the shop floor and as it was celebrated by them off the job. A third section will examine residential locations to show that masters were still very much part of the organic working communities that took shape around their plants. The central contention of this chapter is that important aspects of pre-existing crafts work culture were brought forward to serve as workable social relations of the early industrial age.

Studies that examine the work culture common to master and man have yet to find a place in the historiography. This situation is likely largely a result of the ambition of much of the 'new' labour history beginning in the 1970s to locate the potential of workers – especially nineteenth-century craftsworkers and skilled workers – to achieve levels of class-consciousness through the matrices of an emerging working-class culture.[2] It is not surprising that aspects of a politically motivated research agenda that threatened to degenerate into a search for the country's first-class conscious worker soon came under criticism, first by practitioners of the so-called old labour history.[3] But soon from the ranks of the new labour history itself a gentler, more trenchant critique arose that questioned the 'class-for-itself' nature of the workplace culture of the nineteenth-century craftsman.[4] These studies suggested that at the very least craftsworkers might not have carried around with them an inherent propensity towards socialist action. This debate has also been played out south of the border, where the distinction of 'consciousness-achieved' or 'consciousness-denied' has dominated much of the debate among historians of nineteenth-century artisanal culture in the early republican United States.[5]

The dispossession model is, of course, the common thread between all these considerations of worker culture. In whatever guise, these accounts generally portrayed craftsworker culture as having undergone a jarring transformation from a golden age of small-scale artisanal production where mutualism and tradition nurtured craft harmony to the capitalist exploitation and industrial degradation of the large modern workplace.[6] The conflict between master and man, rooted in the so-called bastardization of craft,[7] has become the received view of the work culture of the mid- to late-nineteenth-century craftsworker in Canada and elsewhere. The situation is much the same in the literature recently produced by gender historians eager to chart the masculine dimensions of the shop-floor culture of nineteenth-century craftsworkers. In most cases, gender has simply been draped around the conceptual framework assembled by New Left historians a generation before. Most of this writing has focused on the masculine culture of craftsworkers in Britain and the United States, but early Canadian examples appear to follow the same paradigm.[8]

This research agenda has virtually ignored the powerful pre-capitalist cultural ties between master and man (not just those between journeymen) that helped them negotiate their respective entries into the industrial age.[9] While nineteenth-century craftsmen may or may not have shared a culture in common with other wage-earners, attention should also be given to the broader character of the workplace culture that did exist. The focus should be on what shop-floor relations meant to craftsworkers and masters at the time, not to historians a century or so later. It should be similarly recognized that such a research direction should not attempt to compare a craft's deviation over time from some simon-pure 'golden-age' of handicraft production rooted (one assumes) in the Middle Ages. Virtually all crafts changed in innumerable ways at many different points in time. Even from the late eighteenth century crafts in Canada rarely adhered to European guild standards.[10] Some crafts were obliterated by the new technologies of the Industrial Revolution. Others simply absorbed those new technologies by modifying craft routines and weathered the storm intact. In some cases industrial technology called into existence whole new groups of craftsworkers who invented traditions based on the workplace customs of already established crafts.[11]

While work routines may have changed over time, what likely did remain common to masters and men alike at many workplaces was their identification of both themselves and each other as craftsworkers. This mutual recognition flowed out of elements of a personal labour relationship that still fostered a social closeness between masters and men in a variety of workplaces. As the last chapter showed, the key feature necessary for the maintenance of the craft world was the continued ability of craftsworkers with the help of their masters to obtain a form of security and independence through movement upwards within the craft. The continued belief amongst journeymen and masters alike that those who were committed to its ideals could still obtain manly independence within the craft was the key to continuity in the craft world. However, as we shall see below, the continued social closeness between master and man was also expressed in a variety of other situations ranging from a boss's continued participation in the skilled work of the shop floor to his continued residence near his plant and in the community of his workers.

Master and Man: Dimensions of the All-Male Workplace

Historians have often viewed the encroachment of women into the traditional male craft workplace as a key ingredient – perhaps the key ingredient – in male craftsworkers' perceived degradation of their craft and status.[12] Modifications to the sexual demographics of the workplace appear to be intimately and directly linked to changes in work culture. This raises the question of the extent to which women had impacted the masculine exclusivity of the Hamilton craft workplace by the early 1870s.

Michael Katz and his associates have examined this issue in some detail for mid-nineteenth-century Hamilton. Their findings suggest a strong stability in female employment between 1851 and 1871. While the proportion of working women to the general population did not increase in this period, this group did exhibit some occupational redeployment. Rather than moving into traditionally 'male' jobs, this was mostly the result of working women turning their backs on domestic service in favour of industrial jobs that were themselves 'associated with traditional women's work,' such as clothing outworker. Indeed, by 1871, 25 per cent of all employed women worked in dressmaking, tailoring, or related needle trades. This is especially significant given that industrial employment accounted for only 33 per cent of women's employment, leaving just 8 per cent of all wage-earning women working in industrial jobs outside the needle trades.[13] Put another way, women working in the industrial sector but outside the needle trades make up a scant 2 per cent of Hamilton's total industrial workforce by 1871.[14] In most Hamilton shops, the traditional all-male workplace remained well intact by the early 1870s.

To be sure, women workers had entered some industries, especially the ready-made clothing and boot and shoe industries (see table 4.1). In both these cases, though, the creation of new gendered occupational categories such as the male cutter and the female outworker likely helped soften the experience of changing gender demographics by preserving gender hierarchies at least to a degree.[15] In both these industries markets still allowed the small shop run by a male master with a journeyman or two and/or an apprentice to coexist alongside more rationalized enterprise.[16] But beyond this, women's industrial employment was stretched thin across a limited number of workplaces. Bosses in the tobacco industry set the few women they employed to work producing smoking and chewing tobacco, leaving cigar making, with its rich and vibrant masculine work culture, untouched.[17] The nine women and girls employed in Hamilton's very modest bookbinding industry spent their days performing such tedious operations as folding, sewing, and binding.[18] Other modest pockets of female employment were concentrated in such non-traditional or marginal industrial sectors as brush making, photography, paper bag making, or whip making. Except for the clothing industry, women enjoyed only a marginal existence in industrial employment in the city by the early 1870s.

Table 4.1 Profile of female industrial employment, by industry, Hamilton, 1871

				As percentage of industry	
Industry	n (Estab.)	Male (n)	Female (n)	Male (%)	Female (%)
A. Clothing					
Boot/shoe	23	269	60	81.76	18.24
Clothing/tailoring	28	241	473	33.75	66.25
Dresses/millinery	14	1	113	0.09	99.01
Furs/hats	9	64	102	38.55	61.45
Gloves/mitts	1	1	4	20.00	80.00
Shirts/collars/ties	1	2	4	33.34	66.66
Sheets	1	0	3	0.00	100.00
B. Other					
Tobacco	7	133	41	76.44	23.56
Baking	12	43	2	95.56	4.45
Confectionery	10	48	6	88.89	11.11
Harness/saddle	9	78	1	98.73	1.27
Sewing machine	4	477	1	99.80	0.20
Railway car/locomotives	1	983	1	99.89	0.11
Bookbinding	3	12	9	57.14	42.86
Printing/publishing	6	103	4	96.26	3.74
Bags/boxes/paper	2	3	4	42.86	57.14
Brooms/brushes	8	71	22	76.34	23.66
Cabinets/furniture	11	72	1	98.63	1.37
Musical instruments	5	49	1	98.00	2.00
Sashes/doors/blinds	2	24	2	92.31	7.69
Ships	3	14	1	93.33	6.67
Coffins	4	10	1	90.91	9.09
Photographs	5	7	4	63.63	36.36
Mats	1	2	2	50.00	50.00
Whips	1	12	10	54.54	45.45
Meat curing	10	47	2	95.92	4.08

Source: 1871 Census Manuscripts

As firms expanded and rationalized production, did they exhibit a greater tendency to employ women? Table 4.2 compares the female industrial workforce participation rates in small industrial concerns with those of the total workforce. The rate of female participation across all sectors for small establishments closely resembles the levels found in the total industrial workforce. The major exception is the clothing industry, where men became dominant in the case of small

Table 4.2 Male and female employment in establishments with five or fewer employees, Hamilton, 1871

Industry	(Estab.) n	Male (n)	Female (n)	Male (%)	Female (%)	Compared with total workforce	
						Male (%)	Female (%)
1. Primary							
A. Agricultural	19	41	0	100.00	0.00	86.77	13.23
B. Forest	0	0	0	0.00	0.00	100.00	0.00
C. Minerals	1	1	0	100.00	0.00	100.00	0.00
2. Secondary							
A. Beverages/food	19	35	3	92.11	7.89	90.10	9.90
B. Chemical	8	26	0	100.00	0.00	100.00	0.00
C. Clothing	40	70	54	56.45	43.55	43.23	56.77
D. Leather	4	10	0	100.00	0.00	98.73	1.27
E. Metal	22	63	0	100.00	0.00	99.92	0.08
F. Printing	3	8	0	100.00	0.00	90.15	9.85
H. Wood/paper	30	63	11	85.14	14.86	92.81	7.19
I. Construction	14	45	0	100.00	0.00	100.00	0.00
J. Miscellaneous	13	24	6	80.00	20.00	94.10	5.90
Totals	173	386	74	83.91	16.09	84.75	15.25

Source: 1871 Census Manuscripts

Table 4.3 Male and female industrial employment, Hamilton, 1871, 1881, 1891

Year		Male	Female	Total
1871				
	n	4,867	876	5,743
	%	84.75	15.25	[100]
1881				
	n	5,298	1,073	6,371
	%	83.16	16.84	[100]
1891				
	n	6,726	2,883	9,609
	%	70.00	30.00	[100]

Sources: 1871 Industrial Census Manuscripts; 1881 Census of Canada, Volume III, tables XXIX–LIV, 'Details of Industrial Establishments,' 324-497; 1891 Census of Canada, Volume III, Table II, 'Totals of Industrial Establishments, by District,' 383.

enterprise, though still not by much. In aggregate, female industrial workforce participation rates are virtually identical when comparing female workers in small establishments with the female workforce as a whole. This finding suggests that, in the minds of Hamilton working people, the employment of women in larger industrial concerns did not necessarily portend the feminization of the workforce but rather extended more familiar or traditional sexual divisions of labour into new contexts. The use of the sexual division of labour as a tool to rationalize production still lay in the future.[19]

In fact, it was not until well into the 1880s that women's workforce participation rate increased as a proportion of the industrial workforce as a whole (see table 4.3). In both 1871 and 1881 women's work as a proportion of total industrial employment held steady at about 15 per cent of the workforce. By 1891, however, the rate had doubled. One can deduce that the 1880s was the key decade in which family economies and male egos first began to grapple with the noticeable entry of women into traditionally male sectors of industrial employment.[20]

Given that the proportion of women at work actually declined slightly in the twenty years after 1851 and that the jobs women took remained firmly in the sphere of traditional 'female work' even when they were redeployed into industrial work, it appears unlikely that working families in the city were yet facing the assault on family gender dynamics and male breadwinner identities that would likely accompany increased female industrial labour force participation rates in coming years. All this is not surprising, since, as chapter 1 shows, the city's early industrialization had been achieved almost wholly through the expansion of traditionally male crafts. This is in stark contrast to cities such as Cincinnati, where the entry of large numbers of women into industrial employment by 1870 had 'permanently shattered' the exclusive male domain of the craft workplace and 'dramatically altered' traditional forms of family economy by this time.[21] In Hamilton, the traditional male workplace remained a fact in most crafts in 1871.

Cultural Expressions of Master–Man Mutuality

Sharing the Shop Floor

The fact that the complexion of the male workplace had not yet been changed by industrialization meant that many pre-existing craft practices along with their attendant masculine work cultures were similarly preserved. Among the chief participants in craftsworkers' work culture was the craftsman/owner. Contrary to the view that masters had withdrawn themselves from having much in the way of a common identity with their workers by this stage of industrialization, the evidence suggests that masters were still vitally connected to the work cultures at their plants, both on the shop floor and beyond.

The city's masters were not just well versed in the skills demanded by their operations; they often still practised them side by side with their workers. The presence of the master on the shop floor practising the skills he either shared with or was presently imparting to his workers (both directly and through his foremen) would have encouraged the city's younger craftsworkers to reasonably believe that some similar form of independence and security might be realized from their commitment to craft. The masters' intimate connection to the shop floor well into their mature business lives helped perpetuate a work mutualism between master and man that was characterized more by continuity than change.

Examples of successful industrialists having 'made it' from small beginnings through the steady conversion of muscle and skill into masculine independence were outlined in previous chapters. By the early 1870s, the continued presence of masters practising their skills alongside their workers on the shop floor was still most visible in the city's small shops, which represented the majority of industrial establishments in the city. But even in larger establishments, masters remained a common sight on many shop floors throughout the 1860s and 1870s and even beyond. For example, Henry G. Cooper, the proprietor of by far the largest carriage works in the city by the 1870s, had worked as an apprentice, journeyman, and foreman for carriage maker James M. Williams before acquiring control of the operation in the late 1850s. By 1871 Cooper's oldest son William was working in the shop as a carriage maker along with his younger brother Henry, then an apprentice blacksmith. Over the next decade the two sons assumed control over the concern. Following in the footsteps of their father, the firm's new proprietors happily styled themselves as 'energetic, practical and enterprising' young men with a 'thorough knowledge of the details of the business, and fully alive to the most recent improvements in carriagemaking.'[22] Similarly, the McCabe brothers retained a 'personal management and superintendence' of their sizable carriage works through these years.[23]

The assumption of the title of mechanical superintendent by sole owners or partners in a number of Hamilton shops also spoke of their continued application of practical know-how to the day-to-day operations of their plant. The three brother-proprietors of the L.D. Sawyer agricultural implement works each headed up a mechanical department within their works, as did the various junior partners associated with them over the years.[24] Charles Meakins and his sons, 'all practical workmen,' were still a common sight on the shop floor of their brush factory by the early 1870s, with all the work at that plant still 'wholly under the supervision of members of the firm.'[25] John Tarbox's involvement as junior partner and mechanical superintendent of the large R.M. Wanzer Sewing Machine Company also appears to have required the daily application of his machinist training to that concern's productive process.[26]

Reports sometimes allow for a more revealing glimpse of the fact that masters often moved in the same space on the shop floor, practised the mysteries of their craft, and even wore clothes similar to those of the employees they worked beside. Mathew Howles evidently still took a very active hand in the stove, tinware, and refrigerator manufactory he had founded sometime around 1870.[27] Alexander Somerville observed broom factory owner Allan Easson, at his bench, hard at work beside his employees in 1868.[28] The proprietors of F.G. Beckett and Company continued to take a hand in production themselves even after building their engine and boiler works into a successful enterprise. One visitor to the shop floor in 1865 remarked on seeing the proprietors themselves 'mingling in the busy throng with upturned sleeves, and exercising a personal supervision of their business.'[29] Even after foundrymen William Burrow, Charles Stewart, and John Milne accommodated the rapidly increasing demands of the market for the products of their Hamilton Malleable Iron Works by erecting a large new plant in 1871, the partners remained 'personal supervisors of their business.'[30]

The continued presence of masters on the shop floors of many Hamilton workplaces by the early 1870s helped maintain an atmosphere of immediacy sufficient to perpetuate pre-existing forms of craft mutualism between masters and journeymen. This was especially true of the city's many small industrial establishments, but it also appears that even in large workplaces many masters had not yet donned the white collar and attached themselves to the more 'genteel' cultures that shunned the dirt, din, and practice of the shop floor. The masters roaming the floors of the city's larger workplaces had undoubtedly begun to function more as overseers than traditional masters-workmates to their men, but they remained well ensconced in pre-existing networks of shop-floor paternalism rooted in craft practice. Their growing success may have modified their relations with their men, but their continued enlightenment in the mysteries of the craft helped to prevent that relationship from fundamentally transforming.

Celebrating Mutualism: Picnics, Excursions, Testimonials and Parades

The best evidence, however, of how workers and bosses related to each other in this context is provided by accounts of how they reflected on the dimensions of this work culture after the workday was over. The adherence of master and man alike to a common craft world can be gleaned by examining how work mutualism was talked about, understood, and even celebrated off the job. The continued integrity of the craft world was reflected in a myriad of social situations ranging from picnics and excursions to testimonial dinners and parades.

Some historians have viewed craftsworkers' organized leisure activities as forums of a developing working-class consciousness that became increasingly exclusive to journeymen as industrialization proceeded. Other historians have looked more at the mixed nature of these events, often both sponsored and attended by employers, as evidence of a type of paternal labour discipline extended by employers into the realm of leisure. These historians are generally interested in employers' use of leisure activities as efforts to 'restore intimacy to workplace relations' that had been drifting apart on the job.[31] Both these views have been at least partially refracted through the lens of the dispossession model with the a priori assumption of class relations rooted in capitalism. It is important for historians not to lose sight of the fact that these leisure activities were traditional to the crafts. They had long been held with the primary purpose of celebrating the abundance that can accrue from a job well done. To craftsworkers they represented the rewards of mutualism at work and the opportunity to reflect on that mutualism in a more relaxed and jovial atmosphere.

In the summer months, picnics and excursions were the most common examples. For example, Hamilton craftsworkers of all stripes attended the annual events sponsored by the Mechanics' Institute starting in the 1840s.[32] Craftsworkers were also undoubtedly in attendance at the many excursions, picnics, and balls hosted by Hamilton's many fraternal organizations, national societies, temperance clubs, militia units, or fire brigades.

As Hamilton industrial workplaces expanded in the 1850s and 1860s, members of the city press began to marvel at the increasingly frequent spectacle offered in the workplace excursion and picnic. Typical were the city's boot and shoemakers, who held their first annual picnic and excursion as a trade in 1853.[33] By 1860s this event had become an annual affair. But what is notable about an event commonly billed as the 'Annual Festival of the Sons of St Crispin' was its specificity to one workplace, that of Robert Nisbet, proprietor of the city's largest boot and shoe manufactory.

Employer and employee alike attended the event itself. Through at least the early 1870s, Nisbet and his successors in business annually displayed their 'usual liberality' towards the festival by either donating money or chartering a steamer to a choice picnic spot.[34] In return, workers paid eager tribute to their employer, such as in 1864 when after dancing and the 'liberation of a supply of champagne from its confinement' Nisbet was heartily toasted by his employees.[35] This was perhaps the cement of the personal labour relationship, but it was also an opportunity for the community of interests between employer and employed to be touted. In the employer's response at the previous year's festival, for example, high praise was lavished on the superior article turned out by the skilled workforce and the high degree of success that had afforded the establishment.[36]

Workplace mutuality was also a common theme at the various excursions, picnics, and balls held for employees of the city's various sewing machine factories beginning in the early 1860s. As one reporter noted, the 'free, open air gala' on Burlington Beach held for employees of the Wanzer Sewing Machine factory in 1862 was the right atmosphere to contemplate the 'comfortable living' afforded by a successful manufacturing enterprise. Time in these surroundings, he wrote, could best be spent 'relaxing from labor, for the day, and enjoying mutually, employer and employed, the change from labor of the workshop or office.'[37] The Wanzer picnic became an annual fixture, the firm itself picking up much of the expense for the outing. These became occasions when the shop-floor relations of master and men could develop a more social side. At the 1863 company picnic, for example, Wanzer partner John Tarbox's superintendence of the shop floor was eagerly transferred to the organization of and participation in the series of athletic events transpiring throughout the day.[38] These bouts of leisure helped foster a social closeness that built on the craft culture of the shop floor. It is no surprise, then, that at the Annual Wanzer Winter Ball in February 1871 one newspaperman noticed that a jubilant Mr Tarbox 'may well feel proud of the class of men he has gathered around him, and from the way he shared in their festivities last night, we rather think he does.'[39] Similarly, at their second annual Reunion Picnic in 1871, the partners of the Wilson, Bowman Sewing Machine Company 'with their families mingled with the merry-making crowd and participated in their enjoyments.'[40]

Metal workers and their bosses shared this type of mutuality at the annual picnic for the employees of Burrow, Stewart and Milne's Hamilton Malleable Iron Works in the dying days of the nine-hours agitation in 1872. The *Hamilton Spectator*'s man on the ground cheerfully reported how 'pleasant was the presence of the firm and their families, who seemed to vie with their employees in making every one happy.' Annual gatherings such as these, he added, 'must have a most beneficial effect morally and physically, and will do more towards cementing a kindly feeling and introducing a spirit of mutual interest in the business of master and man.'[41] These events allowed workers and owners alike to appreciate the benefits of an industrious mutualism at work, while also allowing them to cultivate its social side in more relaxed surroundings.

Picnics hosted by unions and seemingly exclusive to journeymen and their families were also on the rise at this time. In this it appears that the Iron Moulders' International Union No. 26 took the lead, but only in the late 1860s and early 1870s.[42] Members of the Hamilton tailors' and typographical unions seem also to have followed suit by the early 1870s.[43] But these union-centred social activities did not preclude the continuation of similar employer-sponsored events, such as the excursion to Burlington Beach attended by upwards of 175 workers and their families from James Stewart and Company's MacNab Street Foundry in 1871.[44]

The line between exclusive union events and those involving employers was also fuzzy. In the case of the printers, for instance, it seems more than coincidental that the picnic of '*Spectator* employees' in 1870 took place at the same location (Rock Bay) and on the same weekend as the 'Typographical Union Picnic' the following year.[45] Similarly, the eager endorsement by the city press of the 'Grand Working Men's Picnic' at the Crystal Palace in 1869 happily noted that it was 'the support of several principle employers in the city' that had made the event possible.[46]

In all, there is little evidence to suggest that these early picnics and excursions hosted by journeymen's unions necessarily excluded employers. Among those present at the first picnic of the Cigar Makers' Protective Union in August 1866 were 'a majority of the employers in the tobacco trade.' Indeed, the fact that the cigar bosses attending this event 'participated in the diversions of the day with a relish' shows how fast craftly camaraderie could replace conflict in a trade just a few months before upset by a city-wide strike.[47] Hamilton journeymen would likely have to wait another decade or so until the union excursion and picnic became an event more exclusive to journeymen.[48] Still ascendant by the 1870s, was the trade excursion and picnic in which both employer and employed celebrated the mutual rewards of their labour.

It is from the more intimate situation of the testimonial dinner and presentation that we find more telling evidence of a common appreciation of the continuation and maintenance of craft mutualism on the shop floor articulated by master and man alike. The city press commonly reported these events through at least the early 1870s. The participants in the testimonial dinner and presentation were often drawn together from a specific workplace for the express purpose of honouring someone they considered 'one of their own' at a transitional moment in their lives, such as a retirement or entry into a new job situation or matrimonial life. In these ways the testimonial was often used to recognize an individual's attainment of some important marker of adult craftsworker manhood. Honourees were frequently men who had reached some end point in their struggle up through the craft ranks – craftsworker-industrialists who had reached the end of their work life, craftsworker-foremen who were moving on to 'better' situations, or simply craftsworker-employers in receipt of their workers' high esteem.

The time of day and location at which a testimonial occurred varied. A testimonial might be offered at work either during lunch or at the end of the day. Many were held in the evening, usually in the more comfortable surroundings of a restaurant or bar where a 'sumptuous supper' or liquid refreshment could accompany the proceedings. It was also not unusual for a procession consisting of employers, employees, and invited guests to form at the workplace and march en masse, often accompanied by a marching band, to the home of the guest of honour.

The testimonial presentation itself, though, tended to follow a ritualized format. A congregation would form usually consisting of the honouree's workmates, including their superiors, representatives of the city press, and other invited guests. A chair and a vice-chair directed the ceremony. Especially if dinner and drinks were involved, the monotony of toasts and speeches might be relieved by the inclusion of various entertainments, such as musical performances, the singing of songs, or the recitation of poetry by members of the testimonial party. The celebration itself always culminated in a toast to the guest of honour, usually read by the chair on behalf of the honouree's 'fellow workmates' and the presentation of a handsome gift, often purchased from the receipts of a common collection at the shop. The high esteem of the men was usually reflected in the appreciable value of the gift, be it a meerschaum pipe, a silver tea service, an expensive watch, or a gold chain and locket. Next, the guest of honour would offer a reply that inevitably made known his feelings of mutual good feeling with those present. The event was often concluded with three cheers for the honouree. The proceedings then often gave way to an air of informality, with guests perhaps spending the balance of the evening 'speechifying, singing and drinking toasts.'

It is in the praise offered in the formal toast and its reply that we can view the testimonial as a celebration of a maintained craft mutualism at work. David Burley has identified this exchange as a ritual in which masters and men spoke of their reciprocal obligations as they fit in with the logic of capitalist social relations. While the testimonial may well have been assuming something of that form in Hamilton's larger shops, it was on balance still formulated with the primary purpose of celebrating the continuity of the craft world.[49]

Testimonials were forums for high praise. Toasts would lavish the honouree with high tribute to his conduct, bearing, and comportment at work. Most common were comments on the reason for their success thus far in life, a statement that usually contained reference to the steady application of their superior craft skills and mechanical abilities to a given enterprise. The employees of knitting-machine maker C.J. Appleton proclaimed that their 'sense of confidence' in that enterprise and 'high regard' for its proprietor stemmed from his proficiency as a 'skilled mechanic in all departments of the work.'

Gardner Sewing Machine Company foreman William McBeth was toasted by his men for his 'actions as a man and ... ability as a mechanic.' His men heralded sewing machine manufacturer John Tarbox as a 'liberal master of well tried ability.' One union moulder toasted retiring Gurney foreman James Mason as a 'fellow workman.' On his retirement from the same shop, his journeymen and apprentices lauded foreman Robert Lucas as 'one from whose experience many of us have learned wisdom in our art.'[50]

Those giving testimony also spoke of the atmosphere of shop-floor mutuality that flowed from this shared craft knowledge. Employers and foremen alike were praised for adherence to craftly codes of shop-floor conduct. Gurney moulders expressed appreciation for the always 'kind and honest treatment' bestowed on them by foreman Lucas, 'one of the most indulgent of taskmasters, one who while he expected every man to do his duty, never required anyone to do more.' James Mason was regarded for his 'kindly spirit' and the discharge of his 'duty honorably ... and in the best interest of [his] employers,' which ensured that the 'best of feelings has at all times existed ...amongst ourselves.' Wanzer employees expressed hope that a 'little incident' like the Nine Hours Movement had done nothing to 'mar the good feeling always existing between master and men' under John Tarbox's supervision. C.J. Appleton's men remarked on 'the kindness you have been solicitous to show us and ours upon all occasions ... that excellent feeling which cements man to man in a brotherly regard.'[51]

Indeed, these toasts often revealed something beyond a simple working relationship. Most expressed genuinely warm and friendly feelings towards those being honoured. Upon his 'return to married life,' for example, foundryman John Milne's 'employes and friends' raised their glasses to his 'kind and forbearing spirit' as an employer and his 'social and agreeable' nature 'as a friend.' James Mason's men charged that they were 'losing a friend, who is indeed a friend, and who has by his acts shown himself to be such.'[52]

In his reply, the honouree offered similar acclamations of the skill and craft knowledge of his shopmates, celebrating the mutualism of the workplace. John Tarbox eagerly accepted the testimony of his men 'with the true spirit of a mechanic.' James Mason expressed the 'pleasure of working side by side' with his fellow workmen for many years. Robert Lucas pledged to retain of his workers fond memories of 'the years I worked among you.'[53] Comments such as these offered recognition on behalf of those in charge that production was dependent on a cooperative craftswork atmosphere on the shop floor.

Honourees, too, confirmed their adherence to a shop-floor conduct reflective of their situation as craftsworkers among craftsworkers.

Eloquent on this point was Wilson, Lockman Sewing Machine Company foreman James McInerny: 'I am well aware that a foreman is too often looked upon by the workmen as a person placed over them to play the part of a hard taskmaster, but for my part I shall always endeavor to discharge my duty to my employers in an honest, faithful and efficient manner, and in regard to the workmen I hope I shall never forget that "A man's a man for a' that ..."' Gardner foreman William McBeth also echoed the sentiments of the Scottish poet in stating to his workmates 'I have done my duty towards you. I always endeavor to treat a man as I would like to be treated myself.' The fact that both McInerney and McBeth were founding members of Hamilton's machinists' union gave greater weight to these expressions of craft unity.[54]

Proper shop-floor comportment among masters and men maintained good feeling and reflected their common respect for the craft. While shop-floor conflict sometimes did occur, it was rarely mentioned in these forums. When it was, it was portrayed as rare and fleeting. 'I have had many hundred workmen and mechanics under my supervision,' John Tarbox remarked at his retirement testimonial; 'on but one occasion has their fullest confidence been taken from me.' That 'little incident,' of course, was the Nine Hours agitation occurring just a few months previously. He continued, 'let us hope that circumstances will never again place us in a like position,' reminding his workers that he always endeavoured 'to do justice to all under my charge.' 'If in this I have at any time failed,' he proclaimed, 'my judgment, not my heart, has been at fault.' A high value was placed on maintaining the good feeling between employers and employed. As C.J. Appleton put it to his workers, 'it is my pride, gentlemen, that all is harmony in our works.'[55]

The guest of honour often took harmonious workplace relations beyond its immediate business practicality and personalized his relations with his men, thereby exposing the emotional stock he held in their well-being and friendship. John Doty expressed to his machinists his 'earnest interest in their welfare and happiness.' 'It affords me great pleasure,' announced foundryman John Milne to his moulders, 'to find that I have won the eulogium of those who have had the opportunity of watching my career for a great number of years.' Expressions such as these spoke of a personal relationship with workers that was indeed man to man. Exclamations of feelings could get downright mushy. Gurney foreman Robert Lucas expressed appreciation that he had gained from his moulders their 'esteem and good will' and 'an opportunity to know him thoroughly.' In the darkened din of the moulding shop, a tongue-tied Lucas readily admitted to the assembled throng, 'my feelings are overwhelmed.' William McBeth similarly declared 'my heart swells with emotion,' to the group of assembled mechanics and workmen he preferred to view as 'so large a number of friends.'[56]

The testimonial, then, served as a forum for speaking about and celebrating what remained common between masters and men on the shop floors of Hamilton's industrial workplaces by the early 1870s. That the language of craft mutuality was still commonplace on the shop floors of the city's largest manufactories is especially notable in this regard. Resonating throughout these testimonials was a mutual recognition that it was the skills of those honoured and their commitment to putting those skills to industrious use that had gained them the success in which their fellow workmates hoped one day to share.

Trade processions were another arena in which relations at work were commented on through constructed public statement and display. Bryan Palmer has portrayed these events as decidedly class conscious, terming them the 'most striking assertion of the craft unionists' presence ... in the grand context of class conflict [and the] continuous expansion of the labour movement.'[57] While arguing trade processions were conspicuous for their 'continuous presence' in Hamilton from 1860, he offers the Confederation parade of 1867 as the only real example of this trend before the 1880s. Much is made of this imposing grand procession. Parading butchers, iron moulders, shoemakers, bakers, and other fellow 'unionists' evidently turned this event into 'a proud moment for Hamilton's workingmen.'[58]

A closer look puts this view into question. What is not mentioned is the fact that some trade groups marching in this procession did so as representatives of specific workplaces, such as the Canadian Oil Company, the Hamilton Glove and Mitten Manufacturing Company, the Wanzer Sewing Machine Company, or the Times Printing Company. Neither do these processional groupings appear to have been composed solely of journeymen 'unionists.' This was readily evident, for example, in the elaborate reportage given to the Wanzer display: 'The procession of Messrs. Wanzer's establishment was headed by Mr. J.N. Tarbox, one of the partners, on horseback ... immediately after which marched the four foremen of the different departments ... To them succeeded the mechanics, the labourers, and next the boys, all of them looking very cleanly prosperous and contented.'[59] In some sections of the parade, at least, master and man marched together.

Did those who marched under the banner of their company feel themselves in tense distinction to the parade's trade union element that day? In fact, a strong trade union element appears not to have marched in the parade *at all*. The only evidence that butchers, iron moulders, bakers, and shoemakers were 'unionists,' in fact, is that they were referred to in the city press by the names of their trade rather than with specific workplaces. In no report were these groups referred to as journeymen. The only hard evidence that a trade grouping was not represented by both masters and men was the 'Times newsboys,' who were hardly at the forefront of working-class agitation in the city.

Rather, butchers, iron molders, bakers, and shoemakers were likely trade contingents, composed of all men and boys in the city who shared a common craft, be they journeymen, apprentices, self-employed small masters, or larger manufacturers. The call to organize the 'bakers' contingent, for instance, requested 'a general attendance of city bakers and journeymen.'[60] It is notable that the proprietor of the city's largest bakery, Issac Chilman, took the chair when the meeting commenced.[61] Nothing is known of the composition of the contingents of 'iron moulders' or 'tinsmiths' (whose intention to participate in the parade was not realized). Similarly, no information is given of the 'butchers.' However, one can deduce that participants in that contingent consisted primarily of self-employed masters in what was still a very decentralized trade.[62]

A more detailed understanding is provided by evidence relating to the cordwainers' contingent. Their participation in this event has been offered as strong evidence of a 'solidarity' that was symbolic of a developing consciousness of class among the members of a degraded craft.[63] Closer scrutiny of the backgrounds of those shoemakers that can be identified as having organized and participated in the parade, however, leads to a much different conclusion.

The 'shoemakers of Hamilton' met two weeks before the big day to organize 'a most credible and imposing part of the procession' that would reflect well on their position as 'one of the largest and most influential of the trades' in the city. These 'followers of King Crispin' initially met at the King William Street Engine House, identified as 'a centre of skilled worker's associational life.'[64] However, their second meeting was held at the shop of Robert Hopkins, a master shoemaker and one of Hamilton's largest boot and shoe manufacturers. This suggests that, at the very least, local boot and shoe manufacturers did not view this group as antagonistic.

However, the social composition of the group attending this meeting can be more thoroughly determined. Press reports list the names of the twenty-three members of the committee elected to organize the shoemaker's part in the parade and to hold positions of honour in the contingent. Listed among this number were the names of only six journeymen. The rest of the committee was composed of foremen (3), large boot and shoe manufacturers (3), and self-employed boot and shoemakers (8).[65] Hotheaded journeymen marching in defiance of their employers this group was not.

The mixed nature of the shoemakers' complement is also confirmed when considering those who were elected to lead the procession in the roles of King Crispin and 'sundry other worthys.' Journeyman M. Silver was chosen to don the flowing pink robes and gold crown of the shoemaker's patron saint and M. Dean, another journeyman, was picked to play the part of Aide-de-Camp. But masters, too, found their place among the processional characters. The role of Champion was assigned to small-shop-owner William Ward, while small masters Messrs. Glass and Ryan were to act as Standard-Bearer and Aide-de-Camp respectively. Heading up the procession as Marshall – in much the same style as Tarbox and his sewing machine employees – would be P.W. Dayfoot, the city's second largest boot and shoe manufacturer. Hopkins and Dayfoot formed the committee charged with obtaining the necessary dresses and badges for the occasion. Also present at the second organizational meeting was Robert Nisbet, representing the interests of Hamilton's largest boot and shoe manufactory.[66] The shoemakers' contingent, then, saw large and small masters join with their foremen and journeymen as fellow craftsworkers paying homage to King Crispin. No simple connection can be drawn between this event and the unionization of journeymen shoemakers.[67]

Indeed, craft pride and workplace harmony became the central image of the Confederation Day procession as a whole. At the centre of the butchers' procession was an ox 'profusely ornamented with red and blue rosettes and artificial flowers' proudly displayed atop a wagon. Alongside the ox rode the 'sturdy butchers, all of them well-mounted and exceedingly "old countrified."' The iron moulders' procession was 'not a showy looking; but an exceedingly respectable set of men, and they marched well and preserved good order.' Putting their craft skills to work, the bakers impressed onlookers with an ongoing display of the bread-making process as the centrepiece of their contingent.

The bakers were evidently not the only group exhibiting their craft pride that day. The contingent provided by the Wanzer Sewing Machine Company, one of the city's largest manufacturing establishments, for example, replicated a workplace order centred on craft pride and mutualism. Wanzer machinists could feel proud of their place in the procession. Heading things up was one of their own, company partner and trained machinist John Tarbox, mounted on horseback. Also ahead of them were their foremen, representing an experience and proficiency in the craft to which most of them likely aspired. Their ennobled place in the workplace pecking order was further confirmed by the rows of labourers and boys following up from the rear. This arrangement spoke of a common craft pride embedded in a continued respect for the craft progression.[68]

Hamilton craftsworkers used the Confederation Day parade to make strong statements about their craft pride and the continued shop-floor mutualism upon which it was based. This message was expressed by butchers, iron moulders, bakers, and shoemakers marching in the traditional trade procession but also by Wanzer's machinists and other male employees keeping proud step in the company contingent. In all, the trade procession was another arena in which the continued shop-floor mutualism between master and man was put on display.

The Social Geography of Early Industrialization

Another way of assessing the degree to which masters had extricated themselves from, and thereby disrupted, the craft culture they shared with their men is to consider their residential presence in the craft community outside the walls of their plants. A glimpse of the social geography of the late-nineteenth-century city is easily gleaned in the pages of *Hamilton: The Birmingham of Canada*, an 1892 city promotional. In a lavish photographic collage this publication portrays both Hamilton's multitudinous factories and the opulent, ornate, even ostentatious homes of their owners.[69] Its message was unabashed: Hamilton's manufacturing success was tremendous and ongoing, the 'princely mansions' of its captains of industry a visual testament to the wealth they created. Indeed, by this date, the residential and social segregation of the city had advanced markedly.

In their study of residential patterns in the frontier city just forty years before this, Ian Davey and Michael Doucet found Hamilton's social geography to be 'surprisingly ambiguous,' the city's class differentiation not yet readable in its residential structure. However, even at this early date, shades of things to come could be seen in the lavish stone houses and estates of Hamilton's wealthy merchants nestled in the city's South Central section on the rise close to the mountain.[70] They were the most telling indicator of a residential exclusivity that would come to mark the city in the coming decades. Indeed, many of the featured homes of Hamilton's manufacturers in *Hamilton: The Birmingham of Canada* occupied large lots in an elite district that had developed westward from these arcadian estates of the city's early commercial elite. These behemoths of middle-class domestic tranquillity were located largely in the city's up-and-coming exclusive South West district.

This area was somewhat amorphous, fronted by the homes of such manufacturers as W.E. Sanford and George Tuckett, who resided on the high-and-dry 'hogsback' of land extending south of King Street between Queen and Bay Streets, from there extending south with the greatest development of exclusive homes taking place south of Charlton Avenue between James and Queen Streets.[71] These prosperous manufacturers eagerly bestowed on their homes monikers that bespoke their immensity, permanence, and invented tradition: Alexander Gartshore's 'Rabelston,' George Rutherford's 'Fernhill,' and George Tuckett's 'Myrtle Hall,' to name but a few.

While paragons of Victorian architectural splendour, their style and the modern building technologies that they displayed placed them in contrast to the earlier Georgian and Gothic stone homes built by the city's merchantocracy. In a word, they were new. This observation raises a number of important questions. If manufacturers had only recently moved into these homes and into the elite segregated district in which they were situated, then where did they live before? More particularly, was manufacturers' 'retreat' into exclusivist middle-class suburban domestic bliss a feature of the social geography of the city by the terminal date of this study, the early 1870s? Or, more simply put, in a social context of artisan-led industrialization, when did successful masters separate home from work?

In their study of Hamilton's 'business class' between 1851 and 1871, Michael Katz and his associates did briefly examine the issue of residential separation from work. Their data were assembled, however, to examine the extent to which fathers had actually absented themselves from the home during early industrialization – a test of the validity of the 'haven in a heartless world' paradigm. While some of Katz's numbers are suggestive of the broad residential trends practised by manufacturers, they are, unfortunately, not properly categorized or quantified to help answer the central questions of this chapter.[72] It is necessary to look elsewhere in the historiography to frame this methodological approach.

Social historians and social geographers have paid much attention to, and developed sophisticated methodologies for studying, the generally increasing journey to work of members of the working class as a result of nineteenth- and twentieth-century industrialization.[73] The concomitant social process for industrialists in general, much less master artisans-cum-manufacturers in specific, remains under-explored. The primary intention of those who have studied this phenomenon is to show that part of the process of nineteenth-century class differentiation was spatial, in terms of the withdrawal of the manufacturing class from more modest residences at or adjacent to their work and as part of the same community as their workers to much more affluent, often suburban, surroundings where class convergence was achieved with other elements of the parvenu middle class. Some historians have cited simply the *fact* of manufacturers' residential separation from their workplaces and workers to support arguments for class cleavage.[74] But others have made more of an attempt to elucidate residential withdrawal as part of a larger social *process*.[75]

Where might we locate Hamilton manufacturers on this continuum of residential separation by the early 1870s? Answering this question tells us much about the degree to which, as craftsworkers, Hamilton's employers felt they could disassociate themselves from their workplaces at this stage of industrialization. It speaks directly to Hamilton's artisan-manufacturers' primary identities, whether they are tied to the traditional craft shop and the community surrounding it, or detached from it and seeking some distancing from that community through residential convergence with other sectors of the city's elite. In the eyes of their workers, too, the residential patterns of the employers would have likely spoken volumes about their continued commitment to the craft world.

As chapter 2 demonstrated, Hamilton's artisan-manufacturers did not enter the city in mid-century financially well endowed. Slow growth from small shop to manufactory often took place at work locations at, beside, or near the proprietor's residence. Typical was the case of Benjamin Greening, who by the late 1850s was operating what would one day become a tremendously successful metal wire business from a makeshift shed behind his Peter Street home.[76] By the early 1870s Greening's situation still appears to have been typical for Hamilton's small artisan-proprietors (those employing less than five workers). A perusal of the 1871–2 city directory confirms that Hamilton's small masters did not have to journey far, if at all, to get to work. By this date even Greening had only to walk next door to enter his newly constructed Victoria Wire Mills.

Of course, the initial residential detachment from workplace and workplace community would likely have occurred first among the

Table 4.4 Distance from work to home: Hamilton manufacturers with artisanal origins and five or more employees, 1871

	Number of blocks				
	Same[a]	Within 1[b]	5 or less	10 or less	Over 10
n (64 total)	7	22	16	13	6
Percentage of total	10.9	34.4	26.6	20.3	9.4
Cumulative percentage	10.9	45.3	70.3	90.6	100

[a] Home and work at same location
[b] Home on same, or within one, block of work
Source: 1871 Industrial Census; Hutchison's 1871–2 City Directory for Hamilton

city's more successful master-manufacturers. Again, we are interested to determine how far this process had come by the early 1870s. I therefore cross-referenced manufacturers of artisanal origin who claimed five or more employees on the 1871 Industrial Census with the 1871–2 city directory for Hamilton, which revealed the locations of both home and work. Distance to work was calculated as the number of blocks between home and workplace.[77] While previous historians' attempts to delimit this process with qualitative, often impressionistic, evidence are likely ultimately correct in their conclusions, this study represents the first attempt to systematically examine this process at a given point in industrialization.

Table 4.4 presents strong evidence that Hamilton's large manufacturers had not severed their residential links to their workplaces or the communities that surrounded them by 1871. Residing only ten blocks or less from their places of business were over 90 per cent of Hamilton's large manufacturers. Residential separation between home and work totalled five or fewer blocks for over 70 per cent of the study group. More than 45 per cent of large masters still lived within one block of their shops. Eleven per cent of Hamilton's large manufacturers still resided where they worked.

While most artisan-manufacturers lived closer to their shops, those who resided ten or fewer blocks from their businesses still lived within the bounds of the mixed residential city studied by Davey and Doucet in mid-century. Some of the artisan-manufacturers who did have to walk up to ten blocks to get to work lived in the more socially exclusive South Central portion of the city, but they tended to reside only on its more modest, less affluent streets, closer to the bustle of the city's core. That part of South Central Hamilton in which the city's most successful merchants had chosen to practice the domestic arts (more south than central) generally lay outside the ten-block radius. The baronial mansions of the city's South West district, featured so prominently in *Hamilton: The Birmingham of Canada*, had still to be built by 1871.

Notable in the majority of large Hamilton artisan-manufacturers who had to travel five or fewer blocks to work were the number of proprietors who still lived at their places of business. As might be expected, a number of these were smaller concerns, such as George Copeland's ropewalk employing eight or William Harris's bakery (employing six). What is surprising, though, is that the workforces at most of the establishments in this category were of sizes well beyond that of the small shop. Alfred Greens' brush manufactory gave employment to eighteen men and boys. Nineteen workers were on the payroll at John Semmen's planing mill. James Reid employed twenty-four skilled workmen at his furniture works. Most notable, though, was the sizable brush manufactory of C.W. Meakins and Sons. After throwing aside cabinetmaking for brush manufacture eight years previously, Charles Meakins could boast gross annual sales of $40 000 by 1871, paying his thirty-six employees a total of $12 000 in wages that year. By this time the plant consisted of a number of buildings, which taken together constituted a 'considerable floorage.' Such technical improvements as a steam engine were also in evidence by this time. Meakins and his family resided in the top two floors of the three-storey section that fronted this complex, the first floor and basement of which housed the firm's office, salesroom, and warerooms.[78]

Most numerous, though, were the twenty-two manufacturers who had assembled quite sizable workforces but still lived within a block of their plants. The forty-three employees of Alexander Lawson's *Hamilton Spectator* toiled about a block from the home of that partner in the newspaper. Both T. and F. Northey lived within sight of their Wellington Street machine works, employing thirty-one. Both William Turnbull and Adam Laidlaw lived about a block from their successful Mary Street Foundry. William Burrow lived a block from the original Hamilton Malleable Iron Works at Caroline near York Streets. From his Catherine Street home, it took just a quick shuffle for his partner Charles Stewart to supervise construction of that firm's new Cannon Street foundry, still under construction in 1871. John Stewart, William C. Stewart, and Adam Cook all lived within a block of their McNab Street Foundry, employing sixty-three. James Stewart, the firm's principal proprietor, perhaps as a sign of his inability to shake the journeyman habits of his younger days, lived in a hotel just a few blocks from the plant.[79] The home of agricultural implements manufacturer Samuel Sawyer would have been in common view of that plant's 90 workers as they entered and exited the plant each day.

These manufacturers lived cheek by jowl with their workers in the blocks immediately surrounding their plants. This can be seen in the case of the city's numerous foundries, many of which were located on the outer North Eastern periphery of the central business district. Not surprisingly, the blocks surrounding the homes of such prominent metal manufacturers as Charles Gurney Jr, Nelson Robbins, Charles Stewart, Peter Warren, Adam Laidlaw and William Turnbull were crowded with the homes of moulders, stove mounters, blacksmiths, machinists, and the like.

There were those manufacturers that had, by this time, removed themselves to more affluent surroundings. The sizable homes of iron founders Edward and Charles Gurney, for example, stood above the city on a rise of land nestled against the escarpment on the John Street Road along with the stone houses of well-heeled merchants and professionals. They seem to have followed the example of their former partner, patternmaker Alexander Carpenter, who had built his famed Picturesque Gothic 'Rock Castle' nearby as early as 1848.[80] Similarly, machinist John Nathaniel Tarbox, partner in the wildly successful R.M. Wanzer Sewing Machine Company, resided in a 'magnificent residence' complete with an 'extensive green' on eastern King Street outside the city limits.[81]

But the decision to remove self and family to more well-to-do environs was evidently not made lightly. As Davidoff and Hall found in Birmingham, the initial process of manufacturers' residential separation from their workplaces was achieved only with some degree of unease. Where a manufacturer did move away, they noted, 'often a son, younger partner or manager would move in,' helping to maintain the equilibrium in the factory community.[82] Foundryman and tinsmith Dennis Moore lived on Hannah Street in the south-central section of the city, while his junior partner Peter Warren maintained a residence on Catherine Street across from the plant. Engine and boilermaker F.G. Beckett's absence from his Atlas Works was made up for by the presence of his brother and father within two blocks of the McNab Street plant and a younger brother closer still. What is notable about the greater-than-ten-block removal from his plant was the fact that Beckett chose to live on Catherine Street near Cannon Street in the centre of the city's metal manufacturing district and its surrounding neighbourhoods. Even the Gurneys, perhaps the city's most successful industrialists, were sure to install Charles Gurney Jr in a residence about one block from their John Street Foundry. Boarding with young Charles was his cousin John Tilden, soon to be a partner in the enterprise.

In all, it appears that the choice to separate oneself and family from proximity to the workplace had not been made by Hamilton's artisan-manufacturers by the early 1870s. The domestic society of most of these men was still firmly planted in the mixed residential neighbourhoods surrounding their plants. A few of the most successful industrialists had already withdrawn to more elite districts, but this was far more the exception than the rule at this time. Those that withdrew also made sure that someone representing them still lived close to their plants. The masters that continued to reside near their plants likely lived in grander homes than those of their workers, but not in residences the scale and opulence of those featured in *Hamilton: The Birmingham of Canada* twenty years later. We must also remember that the better homes of masters were themselves a continuity; it was part of the craft progression for a master to live in a finer home than those of his journeymen.

Conclusion

The craft world was still well intact in Hamilton by the early 1870s. The craft workplace remained a domain of male exclusiveness. Even in larger workplaces, journeymen still saw their bosses as fellow practitioners of the craft, both in reputation and practice. Outside the workplace craftsworkers used occasions such as picnics, excursions, testimonials, and parades as forums in which to announce to the general public the continued integrity of the craft world and the maintenance of craft mutualism. The craft community, exhibiting integrated residential patterns of masters and men in proximity to their workplace, was similarly preserved. The evidence simply does not support the increased social differentiation that other historians have suggested characterized relations between masters and journeymen by this time. Rather, craftswork by the early 1870s was still characterized by the common identification by both masters and men of both themselves and each other as craftsworkers. That the work routines and practices of the craft world had undergone a degree of change by this time is not disputed. However, the degree of change had not yet been sufficient to shatter pre-existing identifications between master and men rooted in the craft workshops of previous decades.

5

The 'Self-Made Craftsworker': Transmodalism, Self-Identification, and the Foundations of Emergent Culture

When you speak of the working man in Ontario, you include everybody. We all work. We all began with nothing. We have all got by hard work all we own – and the richest among us still work, and like to do it.[1]

The previous chapter outlined residual aspects of craftsworker culture. The task of the remaining chapters will be to examine the dimensions of this culture's *emergent* aspects. The transmodal nature of craft capitalist development informed Hamilton craftsworkers' understanding of their world. Dispossession and disruption was a marginal social experience at most. Great cultural continuities still thrived, and this was especially true of the functioning of craft mobility, a centrepiece of the craft world. If anything, what had been valued in the past now appeared even more possible. But the key feature of Hamilton craftsworkers' experience – a feature that allowed their culture to expand into the recesses of these new possibilities – was their participation in a type of industrialization where capitalist alienation was itself not yet emergent. The general lack, or at least muting, of this reality allowed craftsworker culture to push forward, preserving yet modifying, their actions guided by capitalism but not yet determined by its ultimate logic.

Previous chapters have shown how craft mobility, a key feature of the material arrangement of craft capitalism in Hamilton, was not fundamentally disrupted during the early industrial period. If anything, its practice expanded. The process of craft capitalist industrialization transformed the collective identity of Hamilton craftsworkers. As historical actors, they responded to this material circumstance – a burgeoning capitalism on the one hand and a preserved system of occupational elevation on the other – by reformulating their sense of themselves within its realities. The identity they developed from the core practice of craft mobility was that of the self-made craftsworker. This chapter will examine how the structural arrangement of craft capitalism in Hamilton provided a base from which craftsworkers derived this collective understanding of themselves. The next chapter will outline how craftsworkers put this identity to active use in the forging of an emergent culture unique to the transmodal material situation of craft capitalism.

This chapter will address the body of research that has taken as its focus nineteenth-century formulations of the self-made man.[2] Chapter 3 suggests that there is good reason to believe that versions of masculinity forged around 'self-made' success were culturally salient to Hamilton craftsworkers. This chapter will examine the dimensions of Hamilton craftsworkers' particular understanding of mobility in the social context of craft capitalism.

The 'self-made man' is itself a slippery concept and needs to be used with some caution. This term is most often associated with the development of strong forms of masculine individualism among male members of the emergent middle class. But how individualist were middle-class versions of self-made success? A number of gender historians have recently shown that at the root of this version of masculinity actually lay forms of class mutualism. Young men's clubs, fraternal associations, and a host of other organizations, as well as the 'feminized' space of home, provided young men with an important collectivist 'solace' to retreat into before and after battling as individuals in the marketplace. Such networks of support could also provide access to credit, partnerships, and business contacts in general, key components in the individual's attempt to 'make it.'[3] At root, middle-class man was 'self-made' only in the sense that he started with relatively little in the way of financial resources and was able over time to achieve a socially recognizable level of financial security through which he could claim an independence, the so-called rags-to-riches story. In actuality, middle-class men appear to have been 'self-made' individuals only through their participation in larger class-based support networks.

Historians often pit versions of middle-class masculinity based on individualism against those of craftsworker/skilled-worker masculinities rooted in the mutualism of craft. The previous chapter argued that transmodal culture found its roots in the mutualism of its residual culture. But again the question arises: craftsworker mutualism was indeed a collective act, but was it wholly *collectivist*? One of the main aims of craftsworker mutualism had long been to secure for the craftsworker *as an individual* a place of competence and independence in the world, at the workplace, in the family, and in the community.[4] Craft mutualism – with the central practice of craft mobility at its core – can be understood as a collective concern to enhance the individual's ability to make himself.

The collectivist/individualist experience of supposedly 'self-made' middle-class males was in some respects similar to the successful craftsworker who participated in the mutualism of craft and travelled its well-worn mobility networks on his way upwards to some form of craftly independence. However, their class experiences were hardly identical. Middle-class men and craftsworkers derived their masculine identities from two very different worlds, each infused with distinct values and cultural practices derived from markedly different material arrangements. While these two groups would have disagreed over what constituted a self-made man, however, they would have at least shared a common understanding of what 'self-made' meant in terms of the collective facilitation of individual success. The 'degraded' craftsworker would not appreciate this convergence of experience, but the transmodal craftsworker likely well could. The point is that the 'self' in self-made had rather more to do with craftsworkers' individual exertions – with them as actors – *within* a culture of mutualism than it did with any truly individualist acts.

In fact, as we shall see, the net result of the recognition of the successful Hamilton craftsworker as 'self-made' formed the base of another type of self-made man not before considered in the historiography. The literature recently produced by gender historians has most often presented the self-made man as a distinctly middle-class formulation.[5] Almost nothing has been said about how craftsworkers or the working class in general related to this middle-class construct.[6] Social historians primarily concerned with issues of class have tended to follow the overall bifurcation of middle-class and working-class histories by viewing burgeoning nineteenth-century images of individualism and self-made success as largely a middle-class phenomenon with which the working class had little affinity.[7] Other historians, sometimes unconsciously, have built some bridges. Some historians have understood sections of the working class as having bought into distinctly bourgeois formulations of self-made success and individualism as part of a larger middle-class project of social control.[8] In these accounts workers may be portrayed as unwitting 'dupes' of the middle class, willingly drinking from a fountain of materiality not particular to their class position.[9] Yet other historians have shown craftsworkers to have resisted middle-class advances, or to have taken from them selectively, creatively adapting aspects of bourgeois ideology to the specific realities of working-class life.[10] In virtually all these cases, though, historians have presented a trickle-down understanding of craftsworkers' full or partial acceptance or outright rejection of ideologies of self-made success whose origins were decidedly middle class (or, at least, reactions well within the confines of the dispossession model).[11] This chapter will offer the contrasting argument that within the specific historical circumstance of craft capitalism, it was craftsworkers themselves who derived their own understanding of successful manhood based on their material experience. This chapter will show that understandings of self-made success developed by Hamilton craftsworkers were distinctive to their particular social experience and not an adaptation of some mythologized typology articulated by another class fraction.

The term 'self-made' presents the historian with a package of problems. We saw above how the general realization that individual success was largely attributable to forms of class mutualism greatly undercuts the term's descriptive usefulness. One of the other chief dangers with employing the term 'self-made' in the present study lies with unwontedly importing a term laden with strong cultural meanings derived from a middle-class context. In one respect, though, it could well have been that convergent understandings of self-made success *between* elements of the emerging middle class and non-immiserated craftsworkers did exist, opening the door to a trans-class usage of the term – a situation in need of enquiry by historians. In the same breath as lofty scion of the Hamilton merchantocracy Allan MacNab could declare, for instance, 'I have made my own fortune, and, thank God, this is a country where every man who has the honesty and (to use the expression) the pluck to live and speak as a man should, can do the same,' he also paid ready recognition to the reality of the 'self-made' craftsworker: 'look at the Bench of the country; there you see the son of a mechanic. Look at the Legislative Council ... there you see the mechanic and sons of mechanics. At the Bar the same is the case.'[12] More importantly for this study, though, one must ask what relevance this term had to craftsworkers. As we shall see, the successful craftsworker self-identified as 'self-made' – the term was in popular use. It is for this reason, coupled with the historiographic qualifications cited above, that the present study will employ the term 'self-made' in its discussion of Hamilton craftsworkers.

This chapter will examine the construction of the concept of the self-made craftsworker in Hamilton. Other social groups, especially the city's middling elements, acknowledged the self-made craftsworker as a distinct social form. Not yet faced with the necessity of justifying their social dominance and the alienation it engendered among the city's workers, this class fraction did not prescribe this masculine typology as much as simply recognize it unfolding before them. The self-made craftsworker was, above all else, a self-identification created by craftsworkers to describe their experience within the emerging craft capitalist order. Not surprisingly, masters articulated this social form, but so too did journeymen poised to partake of its fruits. So normative did this construction become that craftsworkers began to speak of it as an inevitability, even a right. Craftsworkers came to understand, justify, and elevate their new-found place in the world by developing the claim that only with the exercise of certain masculine qualities – independence, perseverance, industry, energy, honesty, hard toil, sobriety, and others – had they achieved their proud new status. These claims further normalized the image of the self-made craftsworker and entrenched it as a social form. They also worked to construct the self-made craftsworker as the preferred masculine form to which all craftsworkers should aspire. In this endeavour, this image was given added potency through its repeated presentation as the more manly alternative to other masculine models, particularly that of the loosely defined 'aristocrat.' Craftsworkers argued that what made a man was not simply wealth, but how that wealth was attained. They elevated their particular version of manhood through repeated presentation of the less manly, even feminized 'aristocrat' in contradistinction to the more manly craftsworker, who had laboured to achieve his station. Through all this, Hamilton craftsworkers came to understand their self-made selves as a discrete masculine social form.

Recognizing the Self-Made Craftsworker

As previous chapters have suggested, substantial wealth was not a necessary precondition to definitions of craft success. The achievement of any social position from millionaire industrialist on down through buoyant small master, superintendent, foreman, or even well-paid, respectable journeyman could symbolize the successful craftsman. One could fall at any point along this continuum of success to understand oneself and be understood by others as self-made. Practices of craft mobility and self-identifications built around understandings of self-made success became easily conflated in a trans-modal social environment where the possibility of success appeared available to all those who worked for it.

The image of the self-made man enjoyed great cultural currency among Hamilton craftsworkers and others. Hamiltonians, craftsworkers and non-craftsworkers alike all came to recognize the self-made craftsworker as a distinct masculine social form. This is not to say that the self-made craftsworker represented the only version of self-made masculine success in the city through the middle decades of the nineteenth century. Like so many other North American cities of this time period, an ideology of self-made masculine success reflective of middling class experience was also well in evidence, particularly among members of Hamilton's mercantile elite, of which Allan MacNab's celebration of his own 'pluck' is but one example.

But while the origins of the concept of the self-made man among the city's commercial classes and other middling groups demands a study in its own right, what is most relevant to the present discussion is the fact that these groups and the broader non-craftsworker community recognized and commented on the self-made craftsworker as a distinct social form. MacNab was one of many from outside the craft world to comment on the self-made craftsworker. The number of craftsworkers-cum-industrialists attending the annual dinner of the St George's Society of Hamilton in April 1857 likely also keenly appreciated one 'gentleman's' reference to the 'fact that individuals who now occupied prominent positions, who kept their carriage and spent large amounts for luxuries sake, had come to Hamilton penniless and in the greatest want.'[13] Similarly, 'Occulus,' self-styled as 'neither an employer or an employee,' added his perspective to the Nine Hours agitation of 1872 by pointing out to protesting journeymen that their employers were 'almost, to a man, from the same ranks as those of yourselves.'[14] He was backed in this sentiment a few days later by 'Old Settler,' who asked Hamiltonians to recall 'how many of our most respectable citizens of this present day are the men who did the work on these small means, who built the city ... men who were mechanics in every sense of the word.'[15]

City newspapers published a number of accounts of those who rose from the ranks. This often took the form of long lists of men – craftsworkers and not – who had become 'Self-Made Men' or 'Great Men Who Rose from the Ranks.' In an effort to provide 'A Stimulus for the Young and the Industrious,' these accounts could cover the better part of a page. 'TRY, and you will do wonders,' declared one newspaper before its listing of a hundred-odd representative 'Self-Made Men.'[16]

Also interesting was the repeated comment paid to self-made craftsworkers in the pages of the short-lived *City Enterprise*, a publication heavily oriented to a commercial readership. This newspaper featured a number of morality tales of industrious, hard-working mechanics made good. Typical was the story of Washington Wilberforce who, while still a carpenter's apprentice, used his self-taught draughting skills to draw up a submission for a contest to design a new State House. When a gentleman from the prize committee appeared at the shop the next week to confer upon the 'architect' a prize of two thousand dollars, he was astonished to be presented with a boy still half-trained in his trade.[17] Another fictional account told of two Russian diplomats who were so impressed with the small factory operations of a mechanic who was already modestly self-made that they lavished upon him huge contracts promising handsome profits.[18] The *City Enterprise* cheerfully summarized its view of the general prospects of the modern mechanic in another article: 'by the power of his good right arm, the poor boy of yesterday ... has become the talented young man today.'[19]

The above comments reflect in part a developing middling class conception of the self-made man as measured by the accomplishment of wealth. As will be shown below, while craftsworkers could surely appreciate such a marker, their conception of the self-made man placed much greater emphasis on quality of character. Stripped of their prescriptive definitions, the above comments reveal that Hamilton's commercial elite and other non-craftsworkers well understood the very visible social process through which they saw so many craftsworkers passing.

The reality of the self-made craftsworker was much more than simply a middle or middling class prescription. The reality of this social form was centrally voiced by craftsworkers themselves.

It is no surprise that those who had benefited from it most, namely, masters, amply articulated this social fact. The craftsworker-supervisors of the Great Western Railway, for example, offered their employees constant reminders that the social elevation of the craftsworker was fact in Canada. Speaking at the GWR Mechanics' Annual Festival in 1855, Locomotive Superintendent Henry Yates held up for his men the examples for such self-made craftsworkers as Watt, Arkwright, Fairbairn, and Stephenson as demonstration that 'all great improvements of our time have proceeded from the working classes.' It was with the 'inventive genius' of men who had 'sprung from the working classes,' he explained, that the 'great cities of the West' were built and 'innumerable benefits and blessings' bestowed on mankind.[20]

Yates's enthusiasm for the self-made ideal was self-fulfilling. When he left the GWR to pursue his own private business interests in 1856, he was fondly toasted by the men under his charge as 'one of our own class, having graduated amongst us.'[21] Samuel Sharp, mechanical superintendent of the GWR and himself a former mechanic, was proud to declare, as chair of Yates's 1872 retirement testimonial, that his good friend 'came to the country 15 years ago, then a comparatively poor man; but, as you are aware, by honesty and integrity he has amassed for himself a considerable fortune.' Yates's return to England in retirement, Sharp commented, would show that country 'what this Canada of ours can do for deserving men.' He proudly concluded, 'my friend is entirely a self-made man.'[22]

Sharp himself offered periodic public pronouncements on the ever-rising social fortunes of the mechanic in Canada. He proclaimed to the assembled mechanics at the 1857 Annual GWR Festival, for example, that 'were one of the grisly mechanics of old, whose creed was – "There's nothing like whisky," to come into that hall, and asked if he took the company to consist of mechanics, he would answer, "No, no," with an incredulous smile.'[23] The social elevation of the mechanic in Hamilton, it appears, was plain for all to see.

The proprietor-editors of some city newspapers offered similar comment. As owner-editor of the *Gazette*, former printer Richard Bull railed against his 'Yankee neighbours' who suggested upward opportunity for Canadian craftsworkers was limited. 'In Canada,' he asserted, 'the road to promotion is equally open to every virtuous subject of Queen Victoria.' He pointed gleefully to the decision of 'the Governor General to appoint a SHOEMAKER to be Registrar of the County of Waterloo' to illustrate his point.[24]

The most persistent trumpeter of the self-made craftsworker was undoubtedly *Spectator* owner-editor David McCulloch, himself a former upholsterer. As we shall see below, McCulloch became one of the central propagators of the image of the self-made man and self-improving craftsworker. 'Self-Made Men,' an article published under his editorship (and, one suspects, likely authored by him), was typical of the position of the *Spectator* on this issue. This article recounts the steady movement upwards in the world of a John Smith from the 'rude hamlet' of Ancaster who started his ascent to success by processing and selling catnip before parlaying his modest accrued capital to book publishing, 'by which he cleared many thousands of dollars a season.' The *Spectator* asked its readers rhetorically, 'in a country offering the advantages of Canada, what earthly excuse can be offered for the toil and poverty which offends the spirit of independence?'[25] Beyond this, one has simply to consider the body of newspaper articles related to the concept of self-made success cited in this chapter to get some idea of how pervasively city newspapers touted this as social reality.

Other craftsworker-employers also presented a normalized view of the self-made craftsworker. In his testimony before the Labour Commission in 1887, iron founder John Milne was asked to recount the opportunities open to craftsworkers in the previous few decades of the city's industrialization. He replied that the general 'demand for new industries' fifteen or twenty years ago afforded plenty of 'opportunity [for the craftsworker] to make a successful start.'[26] Particularly eloquent on this subject was machinist-manufacturer John Tarbox, a mechanical superintendent and partner in the R.M. Wanzer Sewing Machine Manufacturing Company. 'Nothing could please me more,' he explained to his machinists on the occasion of his retirement, 'than to see you all succeed and have sunshine with you always.' Success was self-made, he reminded them, the product of the proper application of self to enterprise: 'With energy and determination, success is before you.' More interestingly, Tarbox pushed beyond this, publicly articulating the fact that individual, self-made success was rooted in broader networks. He took great pleasure in reminding the assembled throng, for instance, that during his tenure 'nearly 150 men passing from under my charge have become heads of departments or manufactories ... and I hope, Providence permitting, to have the pleasure of assisting and promoting many hundreds more.' In Tarbox's formulation self-made success was real enough, but at its base lay forms of mutualism.[27] It was hardly a stretch for craftsworkers who had already tasted the fruit of self-made success to speak of it as the prevailing social condition.

The embeddedness of the concept of the self-made man in the psyche of Hamilton craftsworkers was also evident in the public voice of still-aspiring craftsworkers, especially journeymen. 'Look down the broad roll of fame,' wrote one mechanic in the *Ontario Workman* in 1872, 'and you will find that the majority whose names are inscribed on it, worked their way up from the ranks.'[28] One *Ontario Workman* poem offered as its central message that 'Honest industry will prosper' and allow craftsworkers to 'attain a station.'[29] The *Spectator*'s reprint of 'Workman's View of Canada,' offering the observations of an Ottawa stonemason on Canadian social realities, further reinforced this theme. 'There is plenty of room for all,' declared the optimistic mason, especially to those 'energetic and industrious men who are now hopelessly toiling and living from hand to mouth in the old country.' Canada offered them an ample opportunity to 'better their condition' and a 'progress [that was] sure and certain.'[30]

Journeymen also reflected on their expected rise both as individuals and as part of a collectivity of craftsworkers at various public events. Their public pronouncements often expressed a general understanding that this process had become so normative that it now contained an element of inevitability. Journeyman metalworker Matthew Howles received a warm reception when he told fellow craftsworkers attending the annual festival of the Hamilton Co-Operative Society in 1866 that cooperation would help facilitate the 'progress and advancement of the working classes to that position which everyone felt they were one day destined to occupy.'[31] Boilermaker Alexander Wingfield, whose celebrated verse was commonly delivered at craftsworkers' dinners, festivals, and celebrations, triumphantly declared that in Hamilton,

> The busy hum of industry upon her streets is heard,
> And Science vies with Art, and Toil brings home a fair reward;
> Her artizans have earned a place upon the scroll of fame,
> And Europe's sons have learned to pay respect unto her name.[32]

But the degree to which success had come to be conceived as the entitlement of the hard-working mechanic was perhaps most forcefully expressed by William Mitchell, secretary of the Amalgamated Society of Engineers (ASE). Mitchell struck a chord with the large number of mechanics in attendance at the ASE's annual dinner in 1871 with his declaration that 'in a world whose wealth is being produced by mechanical excellence and engineering skill,' the 'raising' of craftsworkers to 'that local position' was now a 'right.'[33]

Perhaps most telling of how widespread was the belief among craftsworkers of their continued ability to rise in the world are accounts left by former journeymen that reflect back on this era after the fact. Nowhere is this evidence more copious than in the voluminous reflections offered in weekly columns by two 'old-time printers' in city newspapers after the turn of the twentieth century. Their recollections were no doubt tainted by reading back in time their experiences of how the concept of the self-made man had developed by the early twentieth century. Coupled with the other evidence presented here, however, their accounts can be taken as further validation of the widespread social phenomenon of the self-made craftsworker in the mid-nineteenth century.

The first of these men was Joseph Tinsely, who, writing under the pseudonym 'Jaques,' offered glimpses into the city's past in his weekly column for the Hamilton *Herald* between 1902 and 1914. Tinsely started his tenure in the local newspaper industry working as a printer for the *Times* likely sometime in the early 1860s. He served a number of terms as president of the Hamilton local of the International Typographical Union. Tinsely's historical reflections often took the form of short biographies of well-known Hamiltonians. Many of these stories shared the rags-to-riches theme. They most often told tales of young men short on capital but long on skill, determination, and innumerable other qualities. Their hard work was always shown to have paid off in financial security in their now old age and an assured position of respect within the community.[34]

The second and more prolific author in this regard was Richard Butler. Self-styled as the 'Old Muser,' Butler's historical reminiscences appeared in the Saturday edition of the *Spectator* for much of the first two decades of the twentieth century. Butler started his work life in Hamilton as an apprentice printer in the *Journal & Express* office as early as 1849. He worked as a journeyman at the *Canadian Christian Advocate* by the early 1850s, during which time he played a considerable part in re-forming the Hamilton Typographical Society and serving on that union's executive in various capacities for a number of years thereafter.[35] Like Tinsely, Butler devoted much space in his lengthy Saturday columns to profiling men who had risen from modest circumstances, many of whom had started their working lives as craftsworkers. The presentist taint of the early twentieth century was often well in evidence in these recollections. The attainment of great wealth, for instance, was often a central point to his writings and strongly reflected in his frequent stories of the spectacular success of such self-made men as Andrew Carnegie or F.W. Woolworth, whose road to riches would have lain well outside the experience of the mid-nineteenth-century craftsworker.[36] This taint likely reflected the new use to which the concept of the self-made man was being put at a time when such elite elements as artisan-industrialists had found it increasingly necessary to de-emphasize the communal aspects of their roots and play up the more mythologized aspects of their success to justify their positions of dominance in a much more decidedly alienated capitalist social order.

Interspersed with these more spectacular examples, however, were accounts that more accurately reflected the values of realities of the crafts world of Butler's youth. He frequently cited the ascent to success from small beginnings of native Hamiltonians, in a number of cases providing industry-by-industry glimpses of the humble origins of the city's early industrial pioneers. One article, for example, took an in-depth look at the craftsworker-manufacturers who founded Hamilton's nineteenth-century metal industry. Butler charted the rise of such prominent metal manufacturers as John Fisher and the Sawyer brothers, the Copp brothers, Burrow, Stewart & Milne, William and James Turnbull, the Gurney brothers and Alexander Carpenter, Edward Jackson and Dennis Moore and others, to show in grand detail that 'with but one exception the shops have all been started by men of limited capital.'[37] Similar treatments were provided for nineteenth-century artisan-proprietors of Hamilton's sewing machine, shoemaking, printing, boat building, and other industries. As a collective portrait of Hamilton's nineteenth-century industrial growth, Butler offered his readers the repeated and amply documented message that, at that time at least, the rise of the mechanic was the norm.[38] 'Hamilton has quite a bunch of men who began at the bottom of the ladder,' Butler constantly reminded his readers, 'but by perseverance, economy, hard work and sticking to the job have moved up to Easy Street.'[39]

The Character of the Self-Made Craftsworker

Butler's assertion in the above passage that self-made success was made possible through the exercise of certain masculine qualities speaks to another important feature of the self-made craftsworker in the Hamilton of his youth. The material experience of Hamilton craftsworkers had taught them that individual success – self-made success – was not only possible or probable, but perhaps even inevitable (according to some even a right) to the individual craftsworker who aspired to achieve such a position. The question then became, simply, what were the actions necessary to individual achievement.

Rather than concentrating on detailed business advice, much of the discussion related to this question centred on the proper exercise of an amalgam of masculine qualities that defined the self-made craftsworker's essential 'character.' The road to self-made status, it came to be understood, was open to the aspiring craftsworker able to exert healthy doses of such personal qualities as independence, perseverance, industry, energy, honesty, and sobriety in his craft development. Beyond simply recognizing the self-made man as one of their own, Hamilton craftsworkers and others also assigned meaning to that fact. In doing so they constructed an image of the self-made craftsworker that both rationalized his ascent and gave justification to his newfound place in the world. In ideological terms they began to understand the self-made craftsworker as possessing an elevated and noble type of masculinity. To meet with success the craftsworker had to possess not only superior craft skills but also the highly masculine qualities demanded by the modern industrial world.

Explanations for the self-made success of craftsworkers were often presented as a function of their adherence to an amalgam of values through which masculine independence was best facilitated. Independence as a quality in its own right, of course, was a strong component in this mixture. One *Ontario Workman* correspondent advised that the surest way for the craftsman to achieve success was to 'Fight your own battles. Hoe your own row. Ask no favors of anyone.'[40] A full-page morality tale in the short-lived *Workingman's Journal* recounted the fictional making of industrialist Haydn Brown, whose success was only achieved once a healthy independence was established from the orbit of his father and the dependence and frivolity that entailed.[41] Another city periodical declared emphatically 'Let every man fight his own battles, with his own good lance.' To attain material success, it added, one most first be rich in 'self-resources.'[42]

Other qualities were of course necessary to complement the craftsworkers' fierce sense of independence. McCulloch's *Spectator* offered that self-made success was only possible when independence was coupled with a determination to 'face the world boldly like a Durham bull going for a bran mash.'[43] Perseverance, industry, energy, and general hard toil were also key ingredients to success. 'It is folly to suppose a man who is born poor must need be so always,' declared one early city newspaper, 'Nothing is impossible to perseverance and industry; mountains sink before them.'[44] In a public lecture titled 'Success and its Conditions'and delivered in 1869, the Reverend A.B. Simpson outlined to the audience many men who had 'achieved their own distinction.' 'These men all rose from the ranks,' he explained; 'by perseverance alone can the mountaintops of achievement and success be attained.'[45]

That Hamilton manufacturers had achieved this topographic feat was easily discerned in numerous accounts in which newspaper reporters and promotional writers reflected on the success of the city's thriving manufacturing plants. A long series of articles, 'Hamilton Manufactories,' published by the *Times* in the early 1860s connected the success of their artisan proprietors with the qualities of perseverance, energy, hard work, and determination with mantra-like regularity. The success of the Hamilton Coach Factory, for example, was 'in no small degree ascribed to [the] energy, perseverance and skill' of its proprietor Henry Cooper.[46] In another report, the 'active' and 'enterprising' qualities exhibited by the proprietors of the Atlas Engine and Boiler Works were said to account for that firm's prosperous condition.[47] Industrial promotionals offered similar accounts of success. John Gorvin, for instance, had secured himself 'among those prominently engaged' in the manufacture of boots and shoes through eighteen years of 'steady perseverance and good workmanship.' Similarly, the harness manufactory of Jas. Philip and Son had become 'widely known' as a result of its partner's 'excellence in workmanship, and ... straightforward and upright dealing.' The recent transference of the above business to one of the partner's sons, the promotional warned, should be no cause for alarm since 'Mr. Philip (Jr.) is a young man of much energy and "go"'[48] Another promotional attributed stove manufacturer Matthew Howles's 'many ... prosperous and pleasant years' in business to his possession of 'native enterprise' and the 'right go.'[49]

An unflagging allegiance to skill and hard toil became part of this equation for success. 'You must not be afraid to work if you want health and wealth,' counselled the *Ontario Workman*.[50] The same journal declared that 'in America, labor is the key which unlocks wealth's great storehouse, and opens the road to honor.'[51] Indeed, discussions of the sturdy mechanic frequently cited his almost mythical capacity for toil as a key feature of his masculinity. Mary A. Denison, for example, paid tribute to the evidently attractive physicality of 'The True Mechanic':

Yonder he goes, with steady tread,
Toiling for his daily bread,
While the city is hushed,
Sleeves unrolled and cheeks health-flushed;
O! the strong mechanic!
The sinewy-armed mechanic![52]

Such stories forged a discourse profiling the masculine qualities that were widely believed to help engender success.

But success was not attained through brute force alone. Rather, it was strongly understood that prosperity would result only when the mechanic's brawn was intelligently applied to his craft knowledge. The effect of this potent combination was vividly illustrated in the

Spectator's story of the rise to riches of David Maydole. This 'roadside blacksmith' from Norwich, New York, achieved his greatness through his simple craftly ambition to produce 'A Good Hammer.' Maydole sold his first hammer to a visiting carpenter. The next day he received orders from the carpenter's five companions, who had been amply impressed with his superior product. After that, word spread quickly until a New York City tool merchant 'left an order for as many such hammers as David Maydole could make.' Before he knew it the modest blacksmith had 115 men on his payroll. Throughout all this Maydole kept his nose to the grindstone and his character intact: 'His only care ha[d] been to make a perfect hammer.'[53]

Men such as David McCulloch were evidently so convinced of the social possibilities of these qualities that they would stand behind such statements of unbounded optimism as 'with the proper energy and perseverance every young man would become a millionaire and a member of Parliament.'[54] But the lofty place to which these values could elevate craftsmen was perhaps most eloquently expressed in the *Ontario Workman's* poem entitled 'Persevere':

Young man, toiling on obscurity,
Struggling 'gainst an adverse tide.
With a high and honest purpose
Which the mocking world deride ...
... Persevere! Gain a station
With the gifted and the great;
Those who now scorn thy vocation,
Then will gladly kiss thy feet.

Persevere! Unceasing effort,
Humble though, and weak it be,
May o'ercome whate'er opposes,
And work miracles for thee;
Be assured reward will follow,
Good will come to him who delves,
Honesty industry will prosper.
Heaven helps those who help themselves.[55]

The idea that only 'honest industry' would prosper was also central to craftsworkers' understanding of the key values that would enable their success. The qualities of honesty and integrity were often pivotal to explanations of the rise to independence of local masters. It was John Semmen's 'strict honesty of dealing,' for example, that accounted for his rise to one of the Dominion's foremost manufacturers of baby carriages.[56] The decision of the two Russian diplomats to bestow large contracts on a modest locomotive works, as outlined in the *City Enterprise* morality tale earlier, was made as a result of the 'frank, attentive and unsuspicious manners' displayed by the humble craftsman-owner towards them upon their unannounced and incognito visit to the plant.[57] Similarly, it was journeyman carpenter-turned-lumber merchant William Chisholm's 'steady industry and sterling integrity of character [which] commanded in due time, the success these qualities deserve.'[58]

Sobriety, too, was touted as a necessary precondition to success. GWR mechanical superintendent Samuel Sharp's comment to his men that the creed of the mechanic of old was 'There's Nothing Like Whisky!' was offered in an effort to equate the more temperate attitude of the modern mechanic with his success.[59] Hamilton temperance advocates and clergymen frequently made the general connection between temperate habits and success. 'The seeds of death, ruin and debauchery were sown' by drink, the Reverend David Inglis declared to a meeting of the 'friends of temperance' at the Mechanics' Hall in 1859, and would prevent 'a young and growing country ... to be behind in social advancement and progress'[60]

But more direct connections were made for Hamilton craftsworkers between temperance and success. The public declaration of printer James Davidson outlining the evils of his past intemperance made a particular impact in this regard. Once editor and proprietor of the *Niagara Mail*, Davidson soon found himself beggared by the 'extravagance and evil crosses' of drink. His route downward was slowed briefly by his short tenure as editor of the *St Catharines Post*, 'a paper published by men who had formerly been my apprentices.' As the excess of drink continued, Davidson soon found himself unemployed, without fortune, and living above a Hamilton saloon. His father's own death from the effects of intemperance finally pushed Davidson to take the pledge. Part of his personal penitence for his years of inebriated existence was to publish a long letter outlining the life of a now reformed 'Infidel, Drunkard and Gambler' in the pages of the *Spectator*. Central to Davidson's reflections on his pitiful past acts was a deep concern with the poor example he had provided his past apprentices and journeymen: they had 'by steadiness worked themselves up to station and respectability while I was going downward and devil-ward like a shooting star!' Distraught and ashamed, Davidson explained further 'I was editor for my former workmen[!] ... and I say that one of my worst sins against God was the evil example I set in the community.'[61] In this case, sobriety was not simply a precondition to personal success; it was part of a larger responsibility of masters towards the future prosperity of their charges.

The exercise of these masculine qualities – independence, perseverance, industry, energy, hard toil, honesty, fair-dealing, sobriety, and others – allegedly accounted for the success of so many Hamilton craftsworkers. But once self-identifications were built along these lines, the reverse also came to be true: success presupposed these masculine qualities. The larger point here is that craftsworkers in Hamilton explained their own success – the achievement of 'improvement' by their own definition – in their own terms. The self-made craftsworker became, in this formulation, its own distinct social form.

Michael Kimmel has presented the rise of the self-made man in nineteenth-century America as a process that pushed to the margins such pre-existing masculine forms such as the independent artisan. In his version, the 'restless, insecure, striving, competitive and extraordinarily prosperous' self-made man supplanted the tradition-bound 'Heroic Artisan,' who had based his masculine identity on such outdated character trademarks as hard work, honesty, industry, fierce independence, and others. The example of Hamilton crasftworkers suggests that the story of the self-made man in nineteenth-century America was likely not as simple as the replacement of one version of manhood with another. It was, rather, a complex process that involved the gradual convergence of differing concepts of the self-made man as the middle class was itself made. In mid-nineteenth-century Hamilton, however, this middle class – and a working class – had yet to be made. The self-made craftsworker was a fresh construction built out of material experience and as yet undiluted by competing versions of self-made success held out by other middling class fractions.[62]

Differentiation and Definition: Craftsworkers and 'Aristocrats'

To construct a distinctive image of their self-made selves, Hamilton craftsworkers frequently differentiated themselves from other pre-established masculine models. Through this exercise craftsworkers elevated their particular vision of ideal manhood above all others. Self-made success was presented as the distinguished road to be taken. On his ascent, the self-made craftsworker demonstrated qualities that marked his type of success as loftier and nobler than versions of success achieved by different means. In this respect the ideology of the self-made craftsworker was most often presented in contradistinction to inherited, non-productive wealth. In particular, craftsworkers pitted (and constructed) their image of success against versions of the loosely conceived aristocratic man.

This discussion sometimes took the form of craftsworkers talking of supplanting an old aristocracy by a new. 'The New Aristocracy,' a poem published in the *Weekly Times* in 1870, laid out this fact plainly to its readers:

A title once could only show
The signs of noble birth,
And men of rank were years ago
The great ones of the earth ...
Now look abroad! The light of truth
Is spreading far and wide,
And that which fills our English youth,
Must shame our ancient pride.
'Tis mind alone can wield the sword,
In spite and wealth and rank:
The artisan may face a lord,
With thousands in the bank.[63]

H.F. Gardner similarly remembered his friend H.B. Witton in 1922 by situating the former GWR shop worker as a member of the broad 'aristocracy of labour' that existed in the city during the 1860s and 1870s.[64]

Much more common, however, were discussions of the 'aristocracy' that presented it as an obsolete social form which craftsworkers should be loath to either recreate or emulate. The creation of this oppositional dynamic can be partly attributed to a developing understanding rooted in the realities of transmodalism that in the modern political economy it was no longer necessary for wealth to beget wealth. 'Help Yourself,' explained one *Ontario Workman* correspondent, 'men who have made fortunes are not those who had five thousands dollars given them to start with, but boys who have started with a well-earned dollar or two.'[65] The *City Enterprise* chimed, 'to sigh or repine over lack of inheritance is unmanly, [e]very man should strive to be a creator instead of an inheritor.'[66] Again, it was David McCulloch's *Spectator* that laid out to craftsworkers most forcefully the possibilities of the modern age: 'There are many young men who are in the habit of excusing their idleness and inefficiency with the plea that they can do nothing without capital ... These persons forget one important fact ... That nearly all rich men in the country were once poor. That nearly every personal fortune they can enumerate is the product of its owner's toil and skill ... There are other forms of capital besides accumulated money; brains, muscle, industry.[67]

It was upon this framework that craftsworkers developed a concept of masculine success built in part by the contrast of their own self-made experiences with those of the inherited wealth of the loosely conceptualized aristocracy. A large part of this process entailed denouncing wealth as a simple indicator of manhood. What became more important in constructing 'true manhood' was *how* wealth was achieved, not simply its *fact*. The *Canadian Illustrated News*, a journal edited and written in large part by Great Western shop workers, complained in 1863 that '[t]here seems to be an idea pretty prevalent that money makes the gentleman.' It continued, 'yet still there remains a class whose only ideas of gentility are connected with wealth and station, and who cannot think of virtue, honor, and education as proper attributes of a gentleman, without being accompanied by birth and wealth ... we would sooner seize the rough, unwashed hand of an honest mechanic than take the tip of the white-kidded fingers of a fop: the former we respect, but the latter we despise.'[68] Men were made from the virtues attained and the values practised on the ascent from rags to riches. The author of Samuel Sharp's obituary remembered the 'essentially self-made' mechanic's rise to the position of superintendent of the Great Western Railway's Car and Locomotive shops from a Liverpool building trades apprenticeship as a product of an 'inherent force ... of character' that, among other things, 'abhorred pretentiousness.'[69] One poem published in the *Ontario Workman* declared that what made 'The True Mechanic' an exemplar of manhood to his sons was his

Giving his babes what God gave him,
Force of muscle and vigor of limb,
Scorning the fear that his boys shall be
The pampered weaklings of luxury ...[70]

In another article, this journal implored the young mechanic to eschew the 'fine clothes and better fare' of those who 'slept in mansions and palaces,' and opt instead for a 'stern manliness' with the declaration 'I have come here to make my own way' as its central tenant. The young man who vowed to be 'no man's pauper,' to 'exercise self-denial,' to 'dress plainly,' and to practise 'honesty and simplicity' would receive 'a discipline worth a university education [and be] educating himself in the very elements of manhood.'[71] Yet another article presented the 'castle-builder,' the man whose fortune relies on the assistance of others and his own belief that 'the world owes [him] a living,' as the practitioner of a shallow manhood who 'forgets that to attain wealth and respectability he must be honest, energetic and persevering ... forgets that every man should get an honest living from industry.'[72] The reward of wealth in these instances was presented as somewhat ancillary to the achievement of manhood.

The condition of self-made craftsworker came to be understood as an elevated type of manhood through its repeated presentation as the preferred masculine alternative to the decidedly less manly aristocrat. The *Ontario Workman*'s reference to the 'pampered weaklings of luxury' speaks to the heart of this construction. So too does imagery provided in the 1866 *Spectator* poem 'Honor to Our Workmen,' which presents the 'hardy sons of toil – The heroes of the workshop, And Monarchs of the soil' in sharp distinction to the 'pampered child of fortune.'[73] Another contribution to the *Ontario Workman* vented against those who expressed pity for or thought of themselves as 'somewhat of a superior being when compared with the "poor tradesmen."' Such individuals, the article's author added, were 'generally to be found in the class known as "counter-hoppers," "quill-drivers," & c.' whose ornamental manhood quickly evaporated in the presence of the more masculine mechanic: 'Mark the swagger of that dry goods clerk as, arrayed in his best suit, for which he has not yet paid the tailor, he sallies forth in the evening to take a stroll in the "pawk" or sponge on his more affluent acquaintance. Do you not mark his lordly mien, how like a true noble he daintily steps aside to let past the sturdy blacksmith whom he encounters on his way.' The station claimed by such pretenders, the writer continued, was wholly artificial. 'Is not the money made at blacksmithing as good as the money made by your two-penny clerk,' he queried, 'and does not the blacksmith always get more pay?' He concluded by pointing out that most of the real inhabitors of Canada's 'roll of fame' were in fact those who had 'worked their way up from the ranks, and obtained their first lessons from the book purchased by the money earned by the sweat of their brow.'[74] Printer and columnist Richard Butler carried his variation of this attitude into the twentieth century: 'the man born to inherit wealth grows up to be one of the world's idlers, and prefers to sweat at golf or as a ball tosser in a baseball club rather than in the workshop.'[75]

The portrayal of the loosely defined aristocratic man – the fop, the idler, the pampered weakling – as *less* masculine than the self-made craftsworker speaks of different forms of abstracted manhood, of multiple masculinities. Craftsworkers' presentation of their masculinity in this dynamic was part of a hegemony project that sought to push aristocratic forms of manhood into recession, to convert them to marginal masculinities. Kimmel has noted the marginalization of the aristocratic 'fop' by the self-made man in nineteenth-century America. In his story, however, it was most often members of the parvenu commercial and financial middle classes that were doing the maginalizing. In Hamilton, the tables were turned: craftsworkers asserted this version of manhood against these same middling elements, especially clerks. While Allan MacNab and other commercial men had begun to articulate some notion of the self-made man, as evidenced earlier, it is interesting to note that Hamilton craftsworkers still observed the pretensions of this bourgeois group to this older aristocratic form of manhood. This likely related to a different and somewhat slower process of middle-class development in that city than in the urban centres of the northeastern United States.[76]

It was also the case that by defining their version of manhood as the most masculine, craftsworkers marginalized competing versions of masculinity to the realm of the non-masculine. In subjective terms, they defined their masculinity as non-femininity. Part of the hegemonic project of their emergent masculinity, then, became 'feminizing' those masculine forms they sought to displace. As R.W. Connell phrases it, 'the terms "masculine" and "feminine" point beyond categorical sex difference to the ways men differ among themselves ... in matters of gender.'[77]

Craftsworkers, then, did not simply construct aristocratic versions of manhood as 'less masculine' than their own, but as distinctly feminine. This project became a central component in craftsworkers' efforts to elevate their own self-made versions of masculinity. The contrast of the 'pampered weaklings of luxury' with the 'hardy sons of toil' feminized one version of masculinity while masculinizing another. This oppositional dynamic was also robustly displayed in the poem 'The Labourer':

Ah! Let the silken dandies scorn
The toilers of the land;
But let me feel the worker's heart,
His hard and wrinkled hand:
And let me labour for his class,

And win his honest thanks;
And I will own a joy unfelt
In fashion's pampered ranks.[78]

In another article, the *City Enterprise* lauded the man who made his own way by the 'power of his good right arm.' Such men, it continued, 'made the country ... bring it whatever iron sinew and unfailing spirit is possesses.' How did the 'stuff' of such men compare with that of others? The answer was clear: 'the little finger of an upright young man is worth more than the whole body of an effeminate and dishonest rich man.'[79]

The difference between the feminized 'aristocrat' and the masculine craftsworker was brought into particularly bold relief in the fictional story of pampered-child-piano-virtuoso-turned-independent-successful-craftsworker Haydn Brown, covering the whole front page of the 18 June 1864 edition of Hamilton's *Workingmen's Journal.* This morality tale outlined the process by which young Haydn Brown emancipated himself from the pampered home life provided by his rich and foppish father by deciding to go it alone and make his own way in the world by learning a craft and ascending the ladder of wealth and independence by his own devices. The thick description of the home life of Haydn's young adulthood builds the sense that he was headed on an unmanly, feminine course. His proper physical development had been stunted in an atmosphere of too many piano exercises. He walked with 'a listless air – a vacant, purposeless carriage.' His budding manhood was further insulted by his sweetheart's rejoinder – 'I don't like to see a man at the piano.' Exasperated, he declared to her, 'Celia, I am nothing but a boy ... and whatever manliness belongs to me has been stunted by compression. I'm sick, disgusted and desperate.' To resuscitate his journey towards proper manhood, Haydn defied his father and turned his back on all the accoutrements of inherited wealth, travelling to the 'city' with no resources at his disposal except his own willingness to work hard and learn a trade. It was not long before his immersion in that 'Titanic stir' awoke a 'new vitality' in the young man. The rest of the story is a tale of masculine advancement. Commencing at 'the bottom round,' Haydn uses his developing craft skills and newfound self-reliance to push himself ever upward to become his own man with his own factory and fortune. Once set firmly on this course he 'felt something commence to expand in him.' The central elements of 'true manhood' soon began to accrue – 'sharp' eyes, 'quick and invigorated' brain, 'strong ... contact with obedient matter,' the 'key of intelligence.' At their next meeting, Celia viewed a man transformed: 'He was taller and broader and heavier. He stood erect and self-reliant; there was, too, the master's expression in his eye; the speaking consciousness of purpose that is strength, and the pride of intellect self-exhumed.'[80] Haydn Brown had achieved emancipation from feminized aristocrat to manly craftsworker-industrialist.

Conclusion

By viewing themselves and being viewed by others as self-made, Hamilton craftsworkers assigned meaning to their material experience of craft mobility. The image of the self-made craftsworker was further normalized through its repeated presentation as an inevitability or right. By explaining its achievement as the result of the exercise of a variety of supportive qualities and values, craftsworkers justified and rationalized its practice and ensconced it further as a social form. This image also gained strength and refinement through its repeated presentation in contrast with completing masculine forms, such as the loosely defined 'aristocrat.'

By the early 1870s the self-made man in Hamilton was no 'myth.' Rather, it was a viable identification built on the base of an expanding social practice and material situation. As such, craftsworkers constructed this image to make sense of their social experience. But, as we shall see, they also used the self-made craftsworker as the primary identity upon which to construct emergent cultural forms. As the next chapters will show, the self-made identity derived from the experience of craft mobility provided the base from which the equally pervasive image of the self-improving craftsworker was elaborated.

6

The 'Self-Improving Craftsworker': Dimensions of Transmodal Culture in Ideology and Practice

Outlined in the previous chapter were the qualities to which the Hamilton craftsworker aspired to secure a position of 'self-made' masculine respectability in the modern industrial world – independence, perseverance, industry, energy, honesty, hard toil, sobriety, and others. This chapter will show that the orbit within which these qualities – as well as other key ingredients of the masculine craftsworker – could be practised, was expanded considerably in this period. Central to craftsworkers' ideological development during early industrialization was the growing belief that, in this modern age, manual skills and physical capacity needed augmentation with the power of knowledge in order to reach their full and proper potential. No longer was the simple acquisition of a craft's age-old 'mysteries' during an apprenticeship considered sufficient to provide the individual craftsworker with the requisite 'skills' to successfully practise his craft for the entirety of his work life. Rather, as participants in the rapidly advancing mechanical age, craftsworkers embraced the need for continuous updating of skill sets and craft knowledge.

Self-improvement was increasingly portrayed as a key ingredient in the facilitation of self-made success. The self-improving craftsworker expressed himself in both thought and practice. His penchant for self-improvement was declared most forcibly in an unbending optimism and enthusiasm for self-education, the unravelling of the 'mysteries' of the modern age through enlightened enquiry. Conversely, while it was the individual who undertook self-improving activity, the culture within which he gained inspiration to do this was collectivist, rooted in local craftsworkers' residual culture of mutuality. The collective concern to 'improve' fundamentally differentiated this culture from more strictly individualist bourgeois cultural forms.

This chapter will focus on how self-improvement was manifested in craftsworkers' self-educational activities in mid-nineteenth-century Hamilton. The first section will consider the development of the self-improving craftsworker at the level of ideology. It will show that in mid-nineteenth-century Hamilton growing numbers of craftsworkers sought a wide-ranging education as the key to cultivating mental as well as manual skills. This educational process was believed to be most beneficial when initiated concurrently with apprenticeship, thereby establishing a practice that would best extend throughout one's work life. Its active pursuit was recommended as a chief leisure activity for craftsworkers. While these understandings were developed as part of a larger transatlantic ideology of craftsworker self-improvement, they achieved special resonance in Hamilton's transmodal social environment. Craftsworkers imagined Hamilton as a place where self-improvement had a special link to craft advancement. To become 'self-made,' it was argued, the craftsworker must first become 'self-improving.' As part of their age-old concern to point their younger members in the proper direction, area craftsworkers issued grave warnings of failure or worse to those who neglected to follow this preferred road to improvement.

The self-improving craftsworker did not simply exist within the realm of ideas; he was also a practised construction. A second section will assess the extent to which local craftsworkers put their ideas of self-improvement into practice at the institutional and community level through involvement in the city's wide array of educational organizations. The Hamilton & Gore Mechanics' Institute (HGMI) will receive particular scrutiny. The HGMI will be reconsidered as a community organization with the mission from its founding to serve a broad constituency – one that included mechanics but also all other classes of the community. Chronic debt perpetually limited its ability to act in the interests of mechanics and all its members. In spite of this, it will be shown that local craftsworkers did use the institute as a venue of self-improvement and took an appreciable hand in its direction. The Mechanics' Institute was, however, only one – albeit the largest – of a host of educational organizations in the city through which local craftsworkers put their penchant for self-improvement into practice. This section will also outline the patronage by local craftsworkers of the city's wide variety of reading rooms, literary, mutual improvement, and scientific associations, and debating clubs. The fact that there was undoubtedly some degree of negotiation between craftsworkers and other social groups in the shaping of these organizations is not disputed here and, in light of the findings of this study, warrants further investigation elsewhere. This chapter will show that, while craftsworkers were participating in a culture and cultural institutions made in part by others both locally and internationally, they were in large degree able to use and shape it for their own purposes commensurate with their own particular material experience.

Self-improvement was mediated and made possible through the hybrid class position of transmodalism, but its experience was often manifested to craftsworkers in gendered terms, as the core component of their masculinity. Historians have recently taken increasing note of those aspects of craftsworker culture that were distinctly masculine. However, they have generally taken as their focus either demasculinization as a corollary of craft degradation under industrial capitalism or forms of remasculinization stemming from the re-articulation of pre-existing masculine craft practices into a decidedly capitalist context. In the latter case they have shown that it was often the existence of strong unions, favourable labour market conditions, the articulation of a family wage ideology, or continued control over crucial points of the productive process that were portrayed as the strengths that allowed craftsworkers and skilled workers to confront class realities head-on and carve out new positions of respect within evolving capitalist structures.[1] Needless to say, both these processes are based on the dispossession model, a concept this study seeks to look beyond. In a related vein, it should also be noted that many of these same historians have understood craftsworker masculinity as something principally derived from the acquisition and practice of manual skills. This study will suggest that during 'the mechanical age' the mind, too, became a primary locus of craftsworker masculinity. In general terms, it will show that Hamilton craftsworkers understood and acted upon their material experience in gendered terms, through the construction of their own masculine model, the self-improving craftsworker.

Craftsworker self-improvement has most generally been considered in the historiography as a key element in the construction of the 'respectable' craftsworker. Much of this discussion was germinated in the extended debates over the nature and existence (or not) of a labour aristocracy in nineteenth-century Britain. Aspects of craftsworker self-improvement have been paid particular attention in the work of Geoffrey Crossick and R.Q. Gray. In his study of mid-nineteenth-century Kentish London, Crossick examined how a 'status-conscious elite stable of skilled workers, with its own life style and aspirations [and] activities and ideology,' asserted strong values of self-respect, particularly notions of independence, through such institutions of working-class respectability as mechanics' institutes, mutual improvement societies, and other self-education institutions, political groups, friendly societies, cooperative and building societies, and trade unions.[2] Similarly, Gray has outlined how a 'syndrome of attitudes and behaviour patterns, linked to the values of "respectability," contributed to the cultural formation of an upper-artisan stratum' in Victorian Edinburgh by scrutinizing the popular recreations (such as soirées and various sporting pastimes) and participation in various voluntary associations (such as the Mechanics' Library, Workingmen's Clubs, or the Volunteer Movement) of that city's craftsworker elite.[3] Through their respective examinations of craftsworker respectability, Crossick and Gray added 'ideology and values' to a debate previously concentrated on such structural issues as high and stable wages and/or authority in the workplace as determinants of the labour aristocracy.[4]

It is also important to note that much of the debate over the labour aristocracy has centred on the degree to which, and the process by which, this mid-nineteenth-century stratum of 'elite' workers accommodated to capitalism. The theory of the labour aristocracy was initially developed, according to Alastair Reid, 'in an attempt to give the process of social control some kind of material basis.'[5] This Leninist project, undertaken most elaborately in the work of E.J. Hobsbawm and John Foster, sought to explain, among other things, how the labour aristocracy became 'the Victorian bourgeoisie's instrument within the working class.'[6] Gray and Crossick have also provided the first important correctives to this one-sided understanding of social control. In their reconstruction of the practices of self-improvement and respectability they proposed that labour aristocrats were not just passive receivers of elite values, but in fact actively shaped these concepts to their own world view within the limits of the dominant culture. These studies supplanted simple social control views with a more complex theory of 'bourgeois hegemony.' Nonetheless, as Gregor McLellan puts it, 'the "ideas" involved remained those that accommodated the class to capitalism.'[7]

Alongside this line of the debate, a number of studies also began to question the very notion of a labour aristocracy. Some scholars questioned the culturally absolute notions of respectability supposedly held by these workers.[8] Others questioned whether such an elite stratum could be identified within the working class at all.[9] More interesting for the present purposes, however, is the suggestion that an identifiable stratum at the upper level of the working class might have actually acted in the interests of their class and rejected elite attempts at social control, bourgeois hegemony, or embourgeoisement. This view is clearly articulated in Bryan Palmer's study of skilled workers in Hamilton. Instead of accommodating to the emerging bourgeois order and imbibing its notions of self-improvement, he argues, Hamilton's skilled workers directed their 'persistent involvement ... in the class struggle' to construct a conscious class culture all their own.[10]

A related issue dividing historians in their consideration of the labour aristocracy has been the social mobility of craftsworkers. Gray's study of Edinburgh, for instance, suggests that limited practices of craftsworker mobility worked as a partial tool of class quiescence. There, he argues, skilled workers' subscription to 'the whole cluster of "respectable" behaviour patterns' was made in the hope of upward mobility, though to positions still within the 'artisan social world.' Edinburgh craftsworkers understood that their adherence to certain bourgeois values and practices could win them greater security in occupation and level and regularity of earnings.[11] Palmer questions this social process in his study of Hamilton, pointing out that while some leaders of the labour movement did settle into elevated positions, they provided only a marginal 'stumbling block' of conscious class activity, which therefore 'hardly demonstrates the existence of a section of the working class actively functioning in the interests of capital.[12]

While historians considering the labour aristocracy have been embroiled in various arguments over its size, shape, function, and existence, they do share a unanimity of opinion on one point: this stratum of craftsworkers was acting and being acted upon within a decidedly capitalist context. Whether they were victims of social control, subject to some form of negotiated bourgeois hegemony, practitioners of outright class defiance, or accommodated (or not) under the rubric of mobility, these craftsworkers are universally portrayed as functioning within a social structure with well-developed capitalist class relations. All the above theorizing about the labour aristocracy has little purchase, then, in the class environment of transmodalism outlined thus far in this study. The 'self-improving' or 'respectable' craftsworker was not, of course, a social form particular to the material situation of mid-nineteenth-century Hamilton. Unlike the experience of the British craftsworkers cited above, however, ideas and practices of 'self-improvement' and 'respectability' took on a special meaning for Hamilton craftsworkers because they were commensurate with the class realities of the city's hybrid class situation. Hamilton's transmodal social environment provided particularly fertile ground in which emerging liberal conceptions of respectability and self-improvement – put forth as part of a general 'age of improvement' in the United Kingdom and North America – could grow and flourish as both an idea and a cultural practice.[13] Perhaps the attraction of so many craftsworkers from the British Isles to Hamilton, outlined in chapter 2, partially fulfilled the aspirations for mobility and self-improvement of the British 'labour aristocrat'. This chapter will outline the dimensions of this culture. The following chapter will determine that this culture was the dominant culture of Hamilton craftsworkers by the early 1870s.

The Ideology of Self-Improvement

Historians have paid close attention to craftsworkers' identification with their manual skills as a core component of their masculine self-image. Less well studied has been the mid-nineteenth-century movement on behalf of a large number of craftsworkers towards a growing emphasis on the intellect and the brain as a key component in masculine self-actualization. Self-improvement came to be elevated to a position of social consideration as part of a developing understanding that the well-rounded craftsworker – the well-rounded man – exercised the proper balance of 'hand and brain' in the execution of craft. The *Iron Molders' International Journal* explained in 1866, for instance, that in the modern world it was necessary for the mechanic to 'devote "head-work" as well as body-work to the business.'[14] 'The man who polishes heart and mind / While he frames the window and shapes the blind,' offered the *Ontario Workman,* 'Is a nobleman among / The noble band of mechanics.'[15] The *Journal of the Board of Arts and Manufacturers* (*JBAM*), the government-sponsored voice of mechanics' institutes in Canada West/ Ontario, explained in 1865 that it was now imperative that 'Working and Thinking' be integrated: 'we want one man to be always thinking, and another to be always working, and we call one a gentleman and the other an operative; whereas *the workman ought often to be thinking, and the thinker often to be working; and both should be gentlemen* in the best sense' (emphasis in original).[16] This dual cultivation of manual and mental skills had obvious benefits. 'Men who labour with their hands all the time,' explained the *JBAM*, 'used to be ... disinclined to employ their minds.' However, those who did submit to 'engage their minds ... find that they are able to do their work with more pleasure, with less labour, and at an increased pecuniary value.'[17]

Self-Education

Self-education or, to use the contemporary term popularized by Samuel Smiles, 'self-culture' became widely understood as the proper avenue through which the brain could achieve this expansion. By the middle years of the nineteenth century, Hamilton craftsworkers were exhorted to expand beyond the simply physical in their quest to make themselves more complete. 'Manual labour is a great good,' conceded the *Ontario Workman*, but only in 'its just proportions ... It must be joined with higher means of improvement, or it degrades instead of exalting.'[18] That 'higher means,' of course, was the active improvement of the mind through continued education. 'The men of the next generation,' declared the secretary of the Toronto Mechanics' Institute, '*must* devote their time, their energies, and their means to the acquisition of knowledge now.'[19] To attain this craftsworkers were urged to buy books or borrow them from their local mechanics' institute, read them voraciously, attend the local reading room, listen to lectures, enrol in classes; in short, undertake any opportunity to foster learning. Self-improvement, then, was best facilitated through self-education.

These forms of 'mental training' were best begun, it was believed, during an apprenticeship, as a natural extension of any previous schooling. The potentially dangerous interruption of schooling by the necessity of work was widely recognized by commentators. 'Large numbers of our youth who have received a fair amount of rudimentary training, but who left school at an early age to engage in the more active duties of life,' complained the *JBAM* in 1864, 'are thus apt to forget in those engagements what they have previously learned.'[20] This sentiment was shared by one member of a local young men's mutual improvement club, who expressed his concern in a letter to the *Times* that 'many of the young in cities are obliged to leave school to engage in some active employment, before they are half through with their education.'[21] This is not to suggest, however, that work was viewed as an impediment to educational attainment. In some cases masters were exhorted to encourage their young charges to further education outside work hours with such inducements as tickets to lectures, employer-sponsored evening classes, and the like. But more common was the sentiment that this was the time in a young man's life when responsibility for further education was turned over to the individual. In a public lecture entitled 'Self-Education,' for instance, a Mr Freeland of Toronto put forth that 'when a man was not in a position to embrace the advantages held out by schools, colleges and Universities, he ought not despair of obtaining a high degree of education by his own individual exertions.'[22] The *Canadian Illustrated News,* owned by printer and former Hamilton Typographic Society officer R.R. Donnelly and Alexander Lawson and purportedly utilizing the writing services of 'a number of young men, many of whom were connected with the Great Western Railway, officers and heads of mechanical departments,' agreed that the best way for the 'human intellect' to grow was through 'its own action ... Every man must therefore, in an important sense, educate himself.'[23] G.S. Tiffany expressed this sentiment forcibly in his lecture 'On Mechanics' Institutes' delivered in 1848. 'No man can have or ever can become great or renowned in any department of human knowledge or usefulness, solely by means of what is taught in classes,' he declared, 'this is merely an assistance to him in his own solitary studies.'[24]

Youth was touted as the most appropriate time for craftsworkers to inculcate self-improvement as a habit for later life. 'Youth is the season to begin the great work of self-culture,' the Reverend John Potts explained in a lecture 'Our Young Men,' delivered under the auspices of the Hamilton YMCA. If this duty was neglected, he added, 'the penalty will be endured all through life.'[25] In a similar vein, the *JBAM* reminded its readers that 'The apprenticeship is the foundation of the great mechanical edifice; and surely, if the foundation of a structure be not firm, the structure itself crumbles and falls to earth. Then, young friends, persevere; be studious and attentive; study well at the branches of your business, both practical and theoretical.'[26] But self-improvement was not simply a vocation of youth; its practice was urged continuously throughout one's work life. The nature of the modern, 'civilized' world, urged the *Ontario Workman,* required constantly that 'study, meditation, society and relaxation should be mixed up with physical toils.'[27] As an 1871 editorial in David McCulloch's *Spectator* remarked, the need for this was obvious; the 'mechanic or engineer must keep posted on the latest improvements of the day.'[28]

This last sentiment exerted particular strength in the Hamilton craftsworker community. While all branches of knowledge were fair game, most commentators conceded that craftsworker self-education should be a directed activity. 'I fear that not a few who might excel are doing serious damage to themselves by reading too much on too many subjects,' the Reverend John Jennings warned those attending his lecture on reading and literature at the Mechanics' Hall. 'A jack of all trades is seldom master of any,' he added.[29] To become well rounded, it was argued, the young craftsworker should first educate himself in all matters relating to his trade. 'Young men to excel in any business must read works particular to their calling,' offered McCulloch's *Spectator*.[30] The *JBAM* concurred that upon the 'ordinary rudiments of a common education' young men should next add 'more intricate studies that would be found useful to them in their several occupations.'[31] Samuel Sharp urged the 'present mothers' and 'future mothers' in attendance at the 1855 GWR Mechanics' Festival to provide their children with an education 'not only in reading, writing and arithmetic' but also in certain 'higher branches of education, in something that will be highly useful to them' in their future work lives.[32]

The attainment of occupational enlightenment did not preclude acquisition of a broader knowledge. Once secure in his occupational knowledge, the intelligent young craftsworker was urged to pursue what Samuel Sharp's eulogizer termed 'a many-sided culture.'[33] The Reverend Simpson expressed this sentiment most succinctly in his lecture 'Mental Culture': 'make yourself master first of what concerns your business and then of all available and useful knowledge; make yourself familiar with the facts of history, science, literature, philosophy and religion; train your mind to think, reason and judge and men will respect you.'[34] Another lecturer also conceded the place for a broader knowledge: 'it is the general effort of the respectable youth of the age to be "well-informed"; to know something about every country, to have a general idea about the leading facts in history and science, and to be acquainted with a kind of light literature.'[35]

Given the long hours of work, of course, self-education was a practice to be pursued during the few scant hours of leisure available in the day. While it was generally conceded that leisure should also include sufficient time for 'meditation, society and relaxation' in just measures,[36] self-education leading towards self-improvement was widely promoted as the best use of that time. 'After the business of the day is over,' urged one member of the Hamilton Young Franklins Institute, craftsworkers and other young men should 'spend their evenings in improving study.'[37] Rev. Simpson counselled his listeners to 'spend those hours of leisure, which so many waste in folly, and hundreds prostitute to sin, in cultivating that field of your own intellect.'[38] Age and marital status had a major determining effect on craftsworkers' ability to do this. Few married craftsworkers with families would have found much reality, for example, in Mr Freeland's exhortation to devote 'all spare time, every unoccupied half-hour' to educational endeavours.[39] By the same token, however, spending time with one's family could be put to productive advantage. A fair share of the 'time for relaxation which [the workingman] finds in the bosom of his family,' the Reverend David Inglis commented in his lecture 'Labour, Its Blessing, Its Curse,' delivered at the Mechanics' Hall in 1856, should be spent 'in the instruction of his children,' in the reproduction of the self-improving craftsworker.[40]

The Particularity of Place

Hamilton craftsworkers' burgeoning enthusiasm for such forms of self-improvement as self-education did not erupt spontaneously. The craftsworkers believed that self-improvement was the hallmark of the modern age and would lead to social advancement of themselves as individuals and as a class. The social advancement of the modern craftsworker was broadly defined and intimately associated with emerging liberal conceptions of respectability and self-improvement elaborated from the idea popular in Britain, Canada, and the United States that this was the 'age of improvement.'[41] GWR car department superintendent Samuel Sharp, like many of his contemporaries, considered the nineteenth century 'the mechanical age,' an epoch of invention and social improvement fuelled and directed chiefly by the intelligent craftsworker. 'It was to the mechanic,' he explained to his men, that society 'owed most of its comforts.' This was the era, he declared triumphally, when 'the mechanic had set the world thinking!'[42]

This new age had been largely facilitated through the general enhancement of educational opportunity. G.S. Tiffany claimed that it was 'the general diffusion of useful knowledge amongst a people' in the present day that had 'improve[d] their moral and intellectual condition.'[43] Samuel Sharp's eulogizer remembered his friend as an enlightened man of the age who 'took a deep interest in the diffusion of knowledge, and social improvement of the working classes' from which he himself had sprung.[44] This was an age like no other, declared Rev. Simpson: 'Education is fast becoming the birthright of every man. Higher culture, which a century ago was the privilege of the few, is now within reach of millions. Let us then urge you my young friends, as the men of the age, to cultivate your minds to embrace these rare facilities for improvement your fathers could not enjoy, and prepare to take your place abreast of your time in the great onward march of this intelligent and progressive age.'[45]

This new reality was especially beneficial to the mechanic. Standing under the ornamented names of Gray, Huskisson, Watt, Awkwright, and Fulton at the 1857 GWR Mechanics' Festival, shop worker Mr Hargreaves proposed to his assembled brethren a toast to 'The progress of intelligence among working men,' commenting that 'a wonderful improvement had been made of later years to this particular.'[46] For the 'respectable youth of the age,' exhorted Rev. Jennings, 'penury is not the insurmountable obstacle that it is often thought to be, for by stern purpose, mind can escape the barriers that would cage it in ignorance, and beneath the humble cottage roof, where it must gather its own means of success, men have lived and studied.'[47] Education was even touted as the great class-leveller. The *JBAM* confidently declared, 'education and manner alone constitute the difference – in our day – between the classes.' The journal proposed that availing oneself of the opportunities of self-education afforded the modern craftsworker a new masculine imperative: 'Young men! Assert your manhood! ... by improving your mental and educational acquirements.'[48]

Hamilton craftsworkers' enthusiasm for the place of self-improvement in the modern age was indeed part of a larger transatlantic ideological development surrounding the 'age of improvement.' The wide dispersal of this idea among craftsworkers was likely a function of the fact that, in this period of high craftsworker geographic mobility, the craftsworker took his ideas with him. GWR painter Henry Witton, one of the leading advocates of craftsworker self-improvement in Hamilton, for example, looked back fondly on the opportunities for improvement of which he had availed himself during his early work life in England: 'At that time in Manchester, special care was taken to supply opportunity for obtaining intellectual culture by the mass of the people. An excellent free public library was established ... Extra provision was made for Art education, and at evening schools, able teachers, for a nominal fee, directed through extended courses of study in chemistry, and many branches of applied science. Moreover, the Athenaeum and other organized societies provided courses of lectures in various branches of Literature.'[49] GWR locomotive superintendent Richard Eaton joined his workmate in this sentiment, recounting to those assembled to celebrate the completion of the first locomotive at the GWR shops 'his early life' in England, remarking that 'for his success he was indebted under Providence to the instructions received through the instrumentality of a Mechanics' Institute.'[50]

However, the self-improving craftsworker was not simply a diffused ideology that carried the same meanings in Manchester, Boston, London, or New York as it did in Hamilton. This emergent ideology took root locally in the fertile ground of Hamilton's transmodal social environment, where it gained a discernible specificity. Local craftsworkers came to realize that, while craftsworkers everywhere should seek self-improvement, its practice in Hamilton would yield particularly ripe and tender fruit. They came to 'imagine' their community – to borrow Benedict Anderson's terminology – as a special place where self-improvement led to social advancement for craftsworkers.[51] Hamilton craftsworkers believed that the failure to achieve the markers of manhood, even with a strict devotion to self-education, was the lot of those from when they were geographically distinct. In Hamilton, the circumstances for success were intact.

Indeed, a strong sense of place pervaded Hamilton craftsworkers' understandings of self-improvement. Commentators frequently expressed the view that workingmen's prospects in Canada were greater than those available to them in the old country. 'Anglo-Canadian,' for instance, cheerfully declared in a letter to the *Spectator* that 'in a country like Canada ... there is a wider scope and easier chances for the attainment of social and honorable positions.' Not only were 'wages ... actually higher in Canada than at home,' he continued, but 'hard working and ambitious men ... have in very many cases risen to a high social position.'[52] Another article in the short-lived *People's Journal* also trumpeted the superior wages North American working men obtained over their British and European counterparts.[53] David McCulloch initiated a hearty vote of thanks to Dr Lille after a lecture he delivered at Hamilton's Mechanics' Hall in which he argued that, like the United States and unlike Britain and Europe, the 'position we occupy is particularly favorable.' It was the 'power of self-reliance' that had kept Canada 'growing steadily,' he declared.[54] The rewards of self-reliance also informed stonemason Thomas Connolly's glowing report on artisans' prospects in Canada to the British reading public. The Ottawa mason declared with lively and manifest delight that, not only were workingmen's wages higher and their cost of living lower in Canada than Britain, but 'the artizan here has less competition in the labour market ... and has a better chance to become an employer himself, or to acquire a little property, because much capital is not so much needed here.'[55]

More interesting was the link that many commentators made between the Canadian (and specifically Hamilton) craftsworkers' predisposition for prosperity and his active pursuit of self-improvement. GWR locomotive superintendent Richard Eaton urged 'all young men of Hamilton to avail themselves of the advantages' of such organizations as the local Mechanics' Institute since 'he considered Canada the first field in the world for mechanical enterprise.'[56] In a lecture entitled 'Labour' delivered at the Mechanics' Hall, the Reverend David Inglis held that in Canada there existed for the workingman the potential to escape the 'curse' of labour, 'its grinding down man's body with toil and thus humiliating his mind.' 'Few countries occupy in this respect a more advantageous position than Canada,' he explained, 'fields of labour are open on every side to the industrious.' It was in the uniquely 'fertile' ground of this country, he exclaimed, that 'man should be raised above ... degradation ... by bringing into exercise his inventive powers.' Giving every man the 'time for that intercourse with the wise and good of all ages, which he finds in books,' he concluded, would allow 'the evils of labour to be remedied.' These 'evils,' it was made clear, were what plagued workingmen in the old country.[57] The *Times* editorialized that in Canada 'where we generally consider ourselves in advance of the old country,' the normative 'proper, orderly, and salutary arrangement' was one in which 'the operative, when his detailed duties of labour are done, can perform his ablutions, and in decent and respectable garb appear in the lecture-room, the library, or the reading room.'[58] Prof. Wilson spoke to those assembled at his local Mechanics' Hall lecture entitled 'In Education Lies the Hope for the Future of Canada' of the creation of a 'young and mighty Canadian Empire.' Canada's rightful road to prosperity and its 'real hope for the future' would be obtained, he lectured, not through the simple 'accumulation of wealth for physical enjoyment' but in the development of 'the means for intellectual culture,' of which Hamilton's local Mechanics' Institute was but one shining example.[59]

More than all others, however, it was GWR upholsterer David McCulloch who most clearly articulated an imagined sense of both Hamilton and the Canadas as the place from which the self-improving craftsworker could best realize his full potential. At a mass meeting of Great Western mechanics to consider their involvement in the Hamilton Mechanics' Institute, he declared: 'There are many circumstances by which we are surrounded, conducive to the carrying out of such mental improvement, for we are not here as in the mother country, disturbed by the strife of contending parties, nor of war's alarms, such being our fortunate position, we should avail ourselves of it, and at once take a step for our general advantage and advancement. The age we live in, too, is one of progress, and our motto should be "Onward."'[60] McCulloch again, and in ample measure, expressed his enthusiasm for the potential of the enlightened mechanic in Canada to his fellow workmen at the third annual GWR Mechanics' Festival in 1857:

> Canada, aided by the skill of her mechanics, was peacefully pursuing a course which would eventually render her one of the foremost nations of the world. A commerce worth millions was now carried on between the

> cities on the lakes formerly fringed by impenetrable forests, the undisputed possession of the wolf and the bear. Where formerly the slow stage coach jolted over mud roads and corduroy bridges, now the luxurious railway car rushed along the iron track with the speed of the wind. And in producing these astonishing results, no class of men had been more instrumental than the mechanics, who, it was hoped, would push on the course of improvement.[61]

McCulloch's ongoing and growing commitment to this ideology up through his years as reporter, editor, and part-owner of the *Hamilton Spectator* is well represented throughout this chapter. In Hamilton, craftsworkers' application of self-improvement to mechanical enterprise was represented as an amalgam with the particular potency of place.

Self-Education and Craft Mobility

As these imaginings suggest, the emergence of the self-improving craftsworker as an ideological form in the city was centrally connected to a developing conviction that educational attainment was a crucial component in craftsworkers' social elevation. The passages above suggest that self-education was widely promoted to enhance one's career prospects. Self-improvement was grafted onto craftsworkers' self-made identifications discussed in the previous chapter. 'Knowledge elevates man in the social scale,' decreed one GWR mechanic.[62] The *Canadian Illustrated News* offered that the 'maker of his own mind [was] the master of his own fortune.'[63] According to the *JBAM*, it was the young man's willingness to avail himself of such educational opportunities as mechanics' institutes that would 'enable him to rise to the top of his profession.'[64] Toronto Mechanics' Institute secretary George Longman explained that 'If the men of the next generation are to fill their respective positions better than their fathers did before them, they *must* devote their time, their energies, and their means to the acquisition of knowledge now.'[65] Rev. Simpson argued that young men of the age had within themselves resources for advancement that could only be accessed 'if rightly improved' by education: 'Young men, your best start in life is education – the best element of your success in life, a cultivated mind – your best capital, not your money, or your friends, but your head ... The true capital is brains.'[66] A 'Young Franklin' explained to the *Times* that young men understood this social reality: 'On looking around they see self-made men ... to follow these examples they feel a little more learning is necessary.[67] G.S. Tiffany argued in his speech on mechanics' institutes that 'those who became distinguished chiefly through their own industry and perseverance, and raise[d] themselves from obscurity by the force of their genius, [and] are commonly called self-made men' were proof-positive of 'the importance which self-culture is to all men.'[68]

Commentators also commonly held up for their readers and listeners real-life examples of self-taught, self-made men, providing copious illustration of their conviction that self-improvement would afford a version self-made success. 'Look down the broad scroll of fame,' urged the *Ontario Workman*, 'and you will find that the majority of the men whose names are inscribed upon it, worked their way up from the ranks, and obtained their first lessons from the book purchased by the money earned by the sweat of their brow.'[69] In its review of the lecture 'Privileges and Duties of Young Men' delivered at the Mechanics' Hall, the *Spectator* noted that the Reverend Dr Murray had 'adduced a number of noble instances of the careers of young men who had risen from obscurity to true greatness by their own assiduity and perseverance.'[70] The same newspaper reported that such illustrative examples also abounded in Mr Freeland's lecture 'Self-Education,' delivered at the Mechanics' Hall: 'Herschal and Faraday, who had risen, the one from the position of a poor drummer, the other from a bookbinder's apprentice, were ... held up as examples of what perseverance could effect, as were also Hugh Miller, the stonemason of Cromarty, and Elihu Burritt, the learned blacksmith.'[71] If such successful men as Hugh Miller had not pursued a well-directed self-education, declared Rev. Jennings in the same hall three months earlier, then he 'would have remained a mason still.'[72] In an article that proclaimed 'Shoemakers, Straighten Yourselves!' the *JBAM* outlined the advance to prominence from a humble shoemaker's apprenticeship of such men as Linnaeus the botanist, the theologian David Pareus, the scientific scholar Joseph Pendril, Gifford, the founder and editor of the *London Review*, and many others.[73] Flanked on either side by names of those who 'in their day and generation had been preeminent in mechanical science,' a self-satisfied locomotive superintendent Henry Yates prompted those assembled at the annual GWR Mechanics' Festival to 'look at your Watts, Awkwrights, Fairbairns, and Stephensons, men who sprung from the working classes.' Speaking after Yates was his close friend Samuel Sharp, who added that this situation could be attributed to the remarkable change that had taken place 'in the habits of workmen since his recollection ... the time was when he paid more attention to his pipe and pot, than to the study of

Arts and Science, which would have elevated him to his proper sphere.'[74] G.S. Tiffany punctuated his own assertion that self-culture fostered success by listing the names of fifty-odd self-educated and self-made men in his lecture on mechanics' institutes. 'I could fill pages by citing the names of self-taught and self-made men,' he concluded. 'It is enough to say, without fear of contradiction, that, without an exception, all who have become eminent in any branch of science, literature or art, owe it in a chief degree to their own patient, thoughtful persevering study and industry.'[75]

General discussions of craftsworker self-improvement often contained grave warnings of the dire consequences awaiting those craftsworkers who chose not to follow the path of modern self-improvement. Rev. David Inglis, for example, urged young men to eschew 'the quick excitement of Bachanalian joy' and opt instead for 'mental culture and moral improvement.'[76] The apprentice who failed to follow the path of learning, warned the *JBAM*, will 'grow up in ignorance, and very often into vice and all kinds of immorality.'[77] Young craftsworkers were constantly cautioned to avoid those leisure activities bound to lead to dissipation and vice. The *Gazette's* exhortation for young men to avoid 'the saloon or gaming table,' for instance, was repeated with mantra-like regularity by many contemporary commentators.[78]

It would, however, be a mistake to view this caution only as an attempt on behalf of middling elements to maintain discipline over an emerging working class. It was common for these warnings to originate from voices within the craftsworker community. The *JBAM* commented, for example, that it was through active self-improvement that 'many young men are saved from the drinking and gambling saloons, from loitering at street corners, or spending their time in idleness, during the most dangerous period of life.'[79] This advice was most often meted out in an attempt to satisfy craftsworkers age-old concern to guide their younger members on a course of their own improvement within craft ranks. As GWR mechanic Mr Turner ex-plained during a meeting to consider his fellow workers' association with the local mechanics' institute, 'as knowledge elevates man on the social scale, so ignorance depresses and degrades him, and even has a downward tendency. Impressed with such a conviction, it is our duty to reclaim man from such downward tendency, and to point him to those noble aspirations and attainments for which he was created ... it is by the advantages of education that we desire to improve ourselves and our children.'[80] David McCulloch's *Spectator* was even more to the point on this issue in its proclamation that 'young men who wish to make their mark in this world must eschew the billiard room and the saloon, it is not from such a school that we may expect to get a future Newton, a Brewster, a Stephenson, a Darwin, a Huxley, or a Tyndall.'[81] Young craftsworkers' rejection of the pool room and saloon was urged by their contemporaries not in an attempt to discipline them as a future workforce but out of craftsworkers' ongoing sense of responsibility to direct their younger members on the correct road to craft mobility.

The Practice of Self-Improvement

The Hamilton and Gore Mechanics' Institute

The exhortations of lecturers and other commentators to craftsworkers on how they should act (and whether craftsworkers actually listened to this advice) can only be determined by looking at the degree to which craftsworkers actually practised such advice. If the world of the self-improving Hamilton craftsworker can be said to have had a primary focus, it was the local mechanics' institute. The Hamilton & Gore Mechanics' Institute (HGMI) was founded at a public meeting at John Bradley's on Court House Square on the evening of 27 February 1839. It came to occupy a place of central importance in the Hamilton community for over forty years until, beset by financial problems, it was forced to close in 1882.[82]

A number of historians have considered the place of mechanics' institutes – including the HGMI – in the nineteenth-century world. A number of these studies have concentrated on the role of mechanics' institutes in early adult education.[83] However, a debate has emerged more recently that considers the functioning of these institutes in terms of class. Along this line of enquiry, historians have generally occupied themselves with considering the extent to which mechanics' institutes functioned on a nascent working class as a tool of class quiescence. In a number of ways this line of enquiry has built on related studies of the expansion of state-run education systems in this time period.[84] A number of historians have followed the lead of Engels by viewing mechanics' institutes as a more or less segmenting influence on the development of a working-class consciousness among their constituents.[85] An opposing school of thought holds that, while mechanics' institutes may have by and large been controlled by 'middle class' elements, they still functioned as sites through which worker-participants could and did express distinctly class-conscious views. In his examination of the

HGMI, for instance, Bryan Palmer has proposed that while 'merchants, manufacturers and clerks could often control local institutes ... workingmen utilized the services and facilities for their own purposes.'[86] Other historians have considered self-improvement institutions of this sort for their role in the process of middle-class formation.[87] The present work, however, suggests that it would be a mistake to consider the HGMI (and likely many other mechanics' institutes) as organizations embedded in specifically capitalist social relations. As we shall see, Hamilton craftsworkers' enthusiasm for and use of their local mechanics' institute was a function of the particularity of their transmodal class experience.

To properly understand craftsworker involvement in the HGMI it is first necessary to consider the extent to which this organization was actually intended for craftsworkers' exclusive use. Indeed, from the institute's inception, members of the city's commercial and professional classes played a considerable role in both the management and patronage of the HGMI.[88] But it would be a mistake to simply view the involvement of commercial or professional men in a 'mechanics' institute' as primary evidence of some degree of social control. One major reason these men were involved in the institute was because they and members of their communities were among its constituents. It was with great pleasure, for example, that S.B. Freeman initiated the warmly received motion at the opening celebration of the Mechanics' Hall: 'That this Institution is recognized as for the benefit of all; its constitution providing that, for a small annual subscription, all classes – the *Mechanic* or the *Professional Man*, the *Merchant*, the *Tradesman* or the daily *Laborer* shall enjoy the privileges afforded by the *Library*, the *Lectures*, or the several *Classes*.'[89] As the discussion of membership detailed below will demonstrate, commercial and professional men and clerks were also no strangers to membership in the HGMI. Indeed, from early on the HGMI board also kept itself open to association with organizations of a decidedly commercial character.[90]

It is perhaps most useful to understand the HGMI as an institution in the service of a broader community that included mechanics. The institute named in their honour was formed during the mid-nineteenth-century period of enthusiasm for the organization of mechanics' institutes across Britain and North America. In a community the size of Hamilton, where it was only feasible from an economic and patronage standpoint for one large self-improvement association to gain the support necessary for a physical presence, the HGMI became the enduring institution.[91]

If the HGMI existed as an institution of the community broadly conceived, it is no wonder that it failed to function at all times in the specific interest of mechanics. Throughout much of its existence, in fact, the institute was hamstrung in its ability to act boldly in any group's interest. The illusions of grandeur held by a number of its directors set the institute from the late 1840s on a course of financial turbulence that plagued it through the remainder of its existence. Underlying these troubles were financial obligations generated by an overambitious building and general improvement program, extending out of the directors' resolute civic boosterism.[92]

The directors' efforts at parsimony occasioned comment from the community as to the HGMI's real usefulness. 'An Old Friend of the Institute' chiding against the directors' repeated decisions to upgrade the hall's facilities in order to maximize rental income. He complained in 1866 that the true self-improvement interests of the institute had long been lost sight of in the directors' perpetual effort to 'hire out a spacious hall for the use of Christy's minstrels and travelling showmen'[93] This course of action also inflamed the passions of its mechanic constituency on occasion. Nowhere was this situation more vividly illustrated than with the HGMI's sometimes tense relationship with the mechanics in the employ of the Great Western Railway. The arrival in town of a sizable workforce to man the newly erected GWR shops coincided with the immediate aftermath of the building of the Mechanics' Hall and the institute's encumbrance by debt. As committed enthusiasts of mechanics' institutes while in Britain, the GWR management moved in 1854 to commit funds for support of the HGMI. This support was thrown into question, however, when less than a year later GWR mechanics held a meeting to express their dissatisfaction with the institute. Chief among their complaints was the institute's exclusionary membership fee and policy. At issue was the hefty £5 fee to become an incorporated member of the institute, the effect of which, upholsterer David McCulloch explained to his assembled co-workers, 'was to exclude Tom, Dick and Harry ... the Directors in passing such a Rule did virtually declare that they did not wish to have Mechanics within that Hall.' The raising of the fee to this exclusionary level, however, appears to have had more to do with the institute's efforts to service its debt and be equitable to those who had subscribed to the building fund than with any conscious efforts at exclusion. As painter and HGMI president Neh. Ford explained to the meeting of GWR mechanics: 'Again, as to the Rules, and the entrance fee of £5, some explanation is due. When the building was completed the Committee were Thousands of pounds in debt. A few gentlemen came forward and passed their notes of the amount, and it was considered that those coming in at a later period and receiving the full benefit of all the advantages should contribute towards these general advantages, and not receive the benefits on the same terms as those who had assumed the responsibility, and that the sum of £5 should be paid before becoming an incorporated member.'[94]

When, towards the end of the meeting, GWR managing director C.J. Brydges proclaimed to the cheers of his men that there was substance to their grievance, the very real threat of the loss of the ongoing support of the railway significantly bolstered the workers' position and seems to have spurred the institute's directors to action. Sometime during the next few weeks the fee was lowered to the still appreciable £2 10s. At a special meeting in February 1856 institute members considered a proposal to do away completely with both the entrance fee and a three-year probationary period for new members and institute a modest annual fee instead. Given that the amendment was voted on by a membership who had contributed handsomely to the new building, it lost. This appears to have been a temporary setback, though, for at the annual meeting held the following month it was reported that the £5 fee had been rescinded and replaced with a $3 fee. The directors, it appears, had moved to appease the disgruntled GWR mechanics.[95]

High membership fees were not the only complaint of the GWR men. They also bemoaned the institute's lack of proper services for the benefit of the modern mechanic, such as a proper scientific and mechanical library and classes providing mechanics with 'various means of improvement.' To facilitate the latter, it appears that the directors were again willing to act. Three months later the directors announced that classes had been organized and subscribed and now simply required suitable rooms where they could be held. Over the course of that year the directors committed £240 to the renovation of the institute's basement for that purpose. At the 1857 annual meeting it was reported that classes, which were all taught by GWR employees, were now under way in a variety of subjects, including mechanical and architectural drawing taught by GWR employee Arthur Ayres. How long these classes lasted is unclear. One later institute president remembered their disintegration due to lack of interest. But their fate also appears to have been bound up with the space requirements of the institute. The institute's perpetual attempts to beef up revenues through rental appears to have pre-empted use of the basement for classes by the early 1860s. A Mr Macallum suggested to the

1863 annual meeting that the institute approach municipal authorities for space to hold a revitalized course of classes. However, the institute's increasing financial pressures by the mid-1860s seems to have prevented this action. While the directors were lobbied to restart classes all through this period, it was not until 1868 that financial troubles were temporarily allayed and the Provincial Legislature had passed an act matching funds put towards such a venture that they again considered their feasibility. At no point in the HGMI's existence, however, do evening classes appear to have thrived.[96]

The relationship of the GWR and its workers to the Institute was always a complicated one. The directors do appear to have acted on the shop workers' complaints. But the extent to which they did this out of a genuine sense of duty to mechanics or simply to maintain the GWR's substantial annual grant the sources do not tell. The GWR management came to the aid of their men by allowing the withholding of this grant as a bargaining chip in the 1855 dispute with the institute, making it clear that if the conflict could not be resolved the men would be enabled to open their own reading room associated with the road.[97] In the end the GWR men found it expedient to set up their own reading room, but it is not at all clear if this was undertaken as an 'act of protest,' as Bryan Palmer has suggested. It appears more likely that this step was taken as part of a greater effort to increase access to the means for improvement to all employees of the GWR.

The library originated from a donation provided by the Prince of Wales to the employees of the GWR upon his visit to Canada in 1860. David McCulloch and Henry Witton were elected from their ranks to 'dispose of the donation' for the purposes of assembling a 'scientific library.' The location of this new library and reading room in the GWR's Hamilton store's department allowed GWR employees from up and down the line borrowing privileges. The establishment of such a travelling borrowing system was understood by both GWR management and workers as more beneficial to all the company's employees and would have been an impracticable service for the HGMI to provide.[98] The GWR's Hamilton Library and Reading Room also appears to have been the first step in a broader initiative to provide these services to the company's dispersed workforce.[99] The redirection of the GWR's annual $400 grant from the HGMI to their own library did throw the institute into a major financial panic. However, nowhere was this talked of as a move made to 'punish' the institute. Indeed, McCulloch, the driving force behind the creation of the GWR library, remained supportive of the local mechanics' institute throughout his tenure as editor of the *Spectator*.

In all, it is important to recognize that in communities such as Hamilton it is unlikely many mechanics' institutes did – or even could – thrive for the exclusive benefit of mechanics, or that they were even intended to serve such a specific constituency. The HGMI was a community institution from its inception and throughout its four decades of existence. The overambitious civic boosterism of its directors saddled it from early on with a debt that perpetually limited its ability to enact bold programs for any groups seeking to participate. These points provide context for the institute and outline its limitations.

It is equally important to understand that while the institute was never constituted exclusively for or by 'mechanics' and operated under appreciable fiscal constraints, craftsworkers could find value and place within it and exerted some control over it. The willingness of the institute's directors to accede to the GWR shop workers' demands is but one example. Palmer has suggested that even though its leadership was decidedly 'middle class,' the HGMI did still function as a central institution for Hamilton craftsworkers. That craftsworkers did indeed use the Institute will be outlined below. But the evidence does not support his view that its affairs were 'directed by men far removed from working-class life.' Palmer presents a list of four middle-class 'local businessmen and promoters' to support this assertion. In fact, two of these men, Thomas McIlwraith and C.W. Meakins, were former craftsworkers, both having apprenticed as cabinetmakers before respectively becoming manager of the Hamilton Gas Works and proprietor of a large brush manufactory. As this study has suggested, it is premature in this era to separate master craftsmen from their men, as their culture of mutuality was still firmly intact.

'Mechanics' were represented on the institute's executive throughout its history. On the original executive sat painter Neh. Ford, chandler James Walkers, and a cabinetmaker, Mr Wright. After this, craftsworker-employers continued as part of the institute's leadership. Participation in the direction of such an association was part of the paternal obligation of masters and one that they were likely honoured to perform. Such a position worked to reaffirm their success and standing in the community and to symbolize to their own charges a position to which they themselves might one day aspire. The real financial responsibilities and organizational demands taken on by the directors would have been understood to be taken on by men with demonstrated experience in aspects of business.

While the occupations of all directors cannot be determined, especially in the institute's early years, a number do stand out. From the late 1840s through the 1870s, the institute's board of directors contained a virtual 'Who's Who' of craftsworker-industrialists. Many of them served multiple-year terms, including: James Stewart, P.T. Ware, James Reid, James Miller Williams, Alexander Carpenter, Edward Gurney, J.B. Dayfoot, Robert R. Smiley, Neh. Ford, Edward Jackson, Hugh Melville, Anthony Copp, George Murison, William Farmer, Thomas White, C.W. Meakins, Thomas McIlwraith, William Turnbull, Richard White, William Young, David Edgar, John N. Tarbox, Alexander Gartshore, George Sharp, and William Leitch.

These men often held the institute's two executive positions. Carriage maker J.M. Williams served as vice-president of the institute through much of the early 1850s, until being replaced by iron founder John Fisher in 1855. Fisher maintained that position through 1856 with master painter Neh. Ford serving as president. That same year, likely as part of the effort to appease the railway mechanics, GWR general manager C.J. Brydges and car department superintendent Samuel Sharp were elected to the board. This move was augmented in 1859 by the appointment of GWR upholsterer David McCulloch to a three-year term as director. In 1857 Sharp moved to the vice-president's chair. The following year the vice-presidency was assumed by brush manufacturer C.W. Meakins. In the wake of the merger with the Hamilton Mercantile Library Association (HMLA) and amid rumours that craftsworker directors had unfairly benefited from contracts let by the institute, it appears no craftsworker-employers held executive positions (though a number remained directors) until 1865, when Thomas McIlwraith took over the president's chair for what turned into a five-year term. In 1874 former machinist and Wanzer mechanical superintendent J.N. Tarbox capped off a three-year tenure on the institute board with a term as vice-president.

When craftsworker-employers were not serving as directors, they were certainly still active in the institute's affairs. In 1849 W.H. Finch, McQuesten Foundry foreman and partner-to-be in the ill-fated Copp brothers foundry in Woodstock, passed a motion at the annual meeting to thank that year's lecturers. At the 1858 annual meeting brushmaker Alexander Easson moved for the adoption of the directors' report. Printer Tom McIntosh served as scrutineer in the board election of 1862, a position held by David McCulloch the following year. The delegation elected to represent the HGMI at the Board of Arts and Manufactures Meeting in Toronto in 1858 included such master craftsmen as Anthony Copp, Charles Meakins, William Farmer, James Reid, and J.M. Williams. Most telling is the participation of a number of manufacturers and master craftsmen in the building subscription campaign in 1853. Topping this list was the Fisher McQuesten foundry, which pledged £100 to the building fund, by far the largest amount pledged by anyone. James Williams, J.B. Dayfoot, Dennis Moore, James Stewart, Robert Smiley, and the Gurneys also contributed substantial amounts ranging from £20 to £50 each. Smaller sums were committed by brewer Peter Grant, soap manufacturers James Walker and John Judd, carriagemakers H.C. Cooper and J.P. Pronguey, furniture manufacturer James Reid, baker and confectioner W.T. Ecclestone, and metal manufacturers Alexander Carpenter and E. Moore.[100] Hamilton's craftsworker-employers took an active interest and played an appreciable part in the direction of their local mechanics' institute.

Craftsworker-employers contributed to the institute financially and played a prominent part in directing its affairs as part of a greater paternal obligation they felt to their journeymen and apprentices to show them the way to craft improvement. If it could be shown that these masters led but their men failed to follow by becoming members or availing themselves of at least some of the institute's services, then the argument that there existed a culture of mutualism with a modern propensity towards self-improvement would be undercut. Throughout the mid-nineteenth century, however, the heavy use of the HGMI by men as well as masters can be determined.

Contrary to those who have argued that we must speculate as to the degree of craftsworker involvement in the HGMI, the existence of membership listings for the years 1862–4 does allow this point to be determined with some accuracy.[101] A cross-referencing of this list with the corresponding city directories for these years yielded a list of 395 HGMI members for whom occupations could be determined. Out of this subset two subgroups were isolated. One included those members broadly defined as 'craftsworkers.' This group included both craftsworker-employers and those who worked for them. Considering these members as a distinct group allows consideration of the relative proportion of 'craftsworkers' (as it has been defined throughout this study) to members of other social groups who were members of the institute. However, to generate some idea of craftsworker-employer membership in relation to those who worked for them, a second subgroup was assembled that included only those members who could be identified as masters.

The findings are significant. Fully 170 members could be identified as craftsworkers, representing 43 per cent of the total identified membership. Of the craftsworker group only forty-eight members could be further isolated as craftsworker-employers, representing only 28 per cent of the total craftsworker membership and only 12 per cent of the total identified membership of the Institute.[102] That the craftsworker community represented over 40 per cent of the total membership of the HGMI – especially in the years immediately following its amalgamation with the HMLA – and that of this group the vast majority were not craftsworker-employers demonstrates the appreciable attraction of area craftsworkers to their local mechanics' institute. Their high degree of involvement in membership of this community institution is highly demonstrative of their active commitment to self-improvement.

Membership figures also do not show the true extent to which craftsworkers involved themselves in their local mechanics' institute. They do not reflect, for instance, the likely considerable number of craftsworkers whose high geographic mobility allowed them to have only a passing association with the HGMI. It is likely that a fair portion of the 273 men whose names appeared on the institute's 1862–4 membership list but for whom neither residence nor occupation could be determined were craftsworkers who may not have remained in town long enough to have their particulars registered in the annual city directory.[103] Nor do these listings account for the number of craftsworkers who were paid-up members of other institutes but availed themselves of the services of the Hamilton institute while passing through town on a work sojourn. Mechanics' institutes appear to have followed the same policy as many nineteenth-century craft unions in recognizing the frequent geographic movement of their constituents through the implementation of a portable membership policy. Article 11 of the HGMI's 1849 Articles of Incorporation, reaffirmed in 1867, codified the provision that 'members of other Mechanics' Institutes in Canada ... upon production of their ticket of membership, be entitled to all the privileges of the Institute, except that of a vote in its management.'[104] Being admitted 'by card' to the services of a local union or mechanics' institute was a commonplace among many nineteenth-century travelling craftsworkers.

This practice is difficult to discern from the available records. However, one qualitative example is elucidatory. Pattern maker Andrew McIlwraith availed himself of the services of mechanics' institutes in Sarnia, Hamilton, Dundas, Galt, and New York City in a period of just over three years. He notes purchasing a membership in the Dundas Mechanics' Institute while employed at the Gartshore Foundry in that town, but appears to have patronized the HGMI interchangeably, likely as a travelling member, during frequent visits to his brother in Hamilton during this period.[105]

The directors also appear to have made concerted efforts to increase craftsworker usage of the institute. These initiatives were often undertaken with an eye towards increasing and maintaining craftsworker membership. The reduction of the membership fee from five pounds to three dollars annually in 1856, outlined above, was one such effort to render the institute more accessible to craftsworkers. For the craftsworker who could not afford even that more modest lump-sum payment, a quarterly payment of seventy-five cents would gain immediate use of the reading room and, after a period of one year, allow an individual's admittance to full membership.[106] This rule would have in particular provided the craftsworker just passing through with an inexpensive, short-term, and non-committed access to the privileges of membership. It was also a form of formal affiliation with the institute, which would not record his name in the official membership list unless he remained in town as a paid-up user for a full year. The directors also enacted a further reduction in the 'mechanics' yearly subscription' to $2.50 in 1866 with the hope that 'this reduction ... will have the effect of very largely increasing that class of members.'[107] To entice a more youthful patronage, the directors created a special 'Junior' membership category which allowed 'apprentices and persons under eighteen years of age ... all the privileges of the Institute, except a vote in its management' for a sum that stood at $1.50 annually by 1867.[108]

The directors also displayed some eagerness within the mandate of their wide constituency to tailor the institute's various services to the special interests of mechanics. There is some evidence to suggest that the board took special care to acquire works for the institute's library that were of a character suitable for craftsworker self-improvement. Indignant GWR mechanics had complained in 1855 that while the library and reading room of the institute were 'well-stocked with newspapers and with the most distinguished periodicals of the day' they did not contain works that were on the whole 'suitable to the requirements of the mechanic.'[109] Compounding this problem was the institutes' continual financial problems, which always severely hampered the acquisition of books and was sometimes cause for the cancellation of periodicals.

Within the limitations of a modest budget, however, some progress was made. The institute was able to add 120 volumes to its library in 1856, many of which, reported the president, were 'reference works of great value, and necessary to the elucidation of the subjects taught in the [mechanics'] classes.'[110] 'In consequence of the depressed state of the funds,' however, no new works were added for the next two years.[111] The merger with the HMLA in 1859 netted the institute 1270 volumes, almost doubling its collection. In the mechanic's interest, it was reported that thirty-five volumes had been acquired that year through the Board of Arts and Manufactures' subscription to the institute.[112] When funds again permitted no new works to be added the following year, the board 'commended this important subject ... to the earnest attention of our successors.'[113] Upon presentation of the GWR's annual grant to the institute in 1862, and in an apparent effort to remedy this situation, GWR general manager C.J. Brydges specified that $100 be committed exclusively to the acquisition of books, of which a fair portion were to be 'thoroughly practical works which, though of little interest to the literary reader, are of great importance to the mechanic and manufacturer.' Through the middle of that decade the institute added between 36 and 180 books to its collections annually, some purchased, some donated. But by 1867 the total collection still only marginally exceeded its size after the HMLA donation of 1859. After a somewhat successful debt-relief campaign that year, however, the directors were finally able to turn their 'earnest attentions' to the state of the library, by selling a number of less-used works and apportioning funds for the purchase of a number of 'new popular and standard works.'[114] The complete reorganization of the library and its cataloguing system was one result of this.

In 1868 the directors proudly published in the *Spectator* the names of the fifty-nine new works purchased that year. Over 80 per cent of these works were of a soundly mechanical or scientific nature, including such titles as *Manufacture of Paper and Boards, Brass and Iron Founder, Tin, Sheet Iron and Coppersmith Worker, Hand-Turning Wood, Guide for Puddling Iron and Steel, Guilder and Varnisher's Companion, On Heat and Steam*, and many more.[115] By the time of the 1869 annual report, works of a strictly 'scientific or mechanical' nature reportedly made up close to 20 per cent of the institute's library.[116]

A major book acquisition program was initiated in 1870 when the more buoyant financial condition of the institute coupled with a government grant facilitated the purchase of 547 new volumes. In reporting the addition of 561 volumes the following year, the directors noted with pleasure that these recent additions had been accompanied by an increase in demand among borrowers for 'a higher class of works,' including those on 'Mechanics.'[117] Listings of books acquired over the following two years published in the *Spectator* also attest to the continuing commitment to collecting works of a scientific and mechanical nature.[118]

A similar effort appears to have been kept up through these years in the institute's news room to stock periodicals relevant to mechanical pursuits. The news room was not spared from the institute's perpetually tight financial situation. The institute's 1859 annual report notes, for instance, that 'several newspapers and Periodicals have been discontinued ... with a view to reduce the expense of the room.' Though downsized, it reassured that 'members can always find on its tables the latest news from all parts of the world, as well as the latest magazines and scientific works.'[119] A brief and incomplete glimpse at the News Room's holdings provided through annual reports through the 1860s and early 1870s details the availability of such journals of interest to craftsworkers as *Practical Mechanics' Magazine*, *Engineer, Journal of the Board of Arts and Manufactures, Scientific Magazine, American Builder*, and *Scientific American*.[120] As the most frequented service by members of the institute, the news room's hours of opening – from 7 pm until 10 pm – were conveniently timed to provide craftsworkers a venue for self-improvement.[121]

Craftsworkers did not attend the local mechanics' institute, of course, strictly for indulgence in the study of mechanical or general science. As suggested above, their prescription for self-improvement encompassed a much wider area of study of which these subjects were the core. The fact that the news room offered 'the principal English newspapers and periodicals [containing] news from all parts of the world' and that the library's 'higher class' holdings included works of biography, history, poetry, drama, reference, voyages and travels, religion, and fiction[122] would have meshed well with the educational aspirations of the self-improving craftsworker. Similar in this regard were the institute's many and varied lectures, covering such diverse but widely appealing subjects as 'The Study in the Life of Shakespeare,' 'On Mary, Queen of Scots,' and 'Astral Wonders,' to name but a few.[123] These topics were chosen partly in an effort to appeal to the institute's wide cross-class constituency. But they were also chosen for their ability to attract enough paying attendees to keep solvent the institute's lecture series, which more than once had to be cancelled due to its 'high cost.'[124] These factors did not, however, preclude lectures on topics of more specific interest to the scientific and mechanical-minded craftsworker, such as 'On Mechanics' Institutes,' 'On Mines and Mining,' 'On the Best Way of Supplying Towns with Water,' among others. Eliuh Burritt, 'The Learned Blacksmith,' attracted a large crowd, many likely craftsworkers, when he lectured at the Mechanics' Hall in 1857 on United States politics. It is likely that the number of lectures focusing on subjects to do more directly with self-improvement and mobility, such as Dr Lille's 'Self-Reliance' or Henry Giles's 'The Necessity of Great Men to an Age,' also attracted a number of craftsworkers.[125] The other feature attracting craftsworkers to lectures was their relatively low cost, which provided a more affordable opportunity to patronize the institute.

There are numerous other examples of craftsworker use of the institute outside of the bounds of membership. In addition to lectures, many craftsworkers likely passed through the institute to attend the many concerts, performances, curiosity shows, and other entertainments offered in its spacious hall.[126] The rental of the hall to house large social functions, however, seems to have been the most direct external use of the institute's services by craftsworkers who may not have been members. The hall was certainly an attractive venue for this type of function. The renovation and frescoing of the hall undertaken in 1858–9 to increase its rental potential transformed it into an even more appealing meeting place for mechanics: 'The Hall is the largest in the city, and by far the most suitable for public occasions ... The walls are painted to represent panels, in some of which full length portraits of a few of the great mechanical and scientific celebrities have been introduced. The faces of these are excellent. Among them we have Stephenson, Watt, Newton and Franklin. Above the cornice there are several heads, such as Shakespeare, Byron, Burns, Scott, Moore and Goldsmith ... on each side of the windows are emblems of the Arts and Sciences.'[127]

Craftsworkers made frequent use of the hall for their annual festivals and celebrations. Beginning in 1854 the annual GWR Mechanics' Ball was held there for many years. The Brotherhood of Locomotive Engineers No. 133 held their annual festival in the hall for a number of years after their formation in the early 1870s. The city's masons held their annual festival at the newly constructed hall in 1853. The annual ball of the employees of the Wanzer sewing machine factory had also reached a size that warranted the rental of the Mechanics' Hall by the early 1870s. Local 26 of the Iron Molders' International Union held their first annual ball in the hall in 1863 and continued using it for that purpose in the early 1870s. The craftsworker-run Hamilton Co-operative Society held their first annual celebration at the hall in 1866.

Given that there were other halls available in the city by the 1860s, the fact that craftsworkers so willingly made use of the Mechanics' Hall – especially under the auspices of their unions – provides implicit evidence of some basic identification with it as an organization that reflected their interests. Indeed, craftsworkers' understanding that the Institute provided an arena in which they could express their particular interests – or was, at least, not antagonistic to them – continued up through 1872 with the use of the hall by the Nine Hour League for its two 'mass meetings' and by the moulders' union for its annual ball.[128] In all, craftsworkers found in the local mechanics' institute a responsive and accommodating space and atmosphere in which their burgeoning commitment to self-improvement could be actively pursued or reflected upon in a more relaxed environment of social intercourse.

Other Self-Improvement Venues

It would be short-sighted to stop with the HGMI when considering the practice of self-improvement by Hamilton craftsworkers. It is also necessary to look beyond this institution to appreciate the true scope of craftsworkers' pursuit of these ends. While the HGMI was the primary locus for Hamilton craftsworkers' activities of self-improvement, these practices were also carried out in a variety of other locations and forms. The local craftsworker could also pursue these activities within the city's various other reading rooms, in literary, mutual improvement, and scientific associations, and debating clubs.

In the era before the first public library, the mechanics' institute provided craftsworkers with the city's largest and most visible – but not its only – library and reading room. As was common in other cities, local newspaper offices likely often provided space for a reading room that, for a modest fee, provided access to a wide array of newspapers and periodicals. This made good business sense, recouping some or all of the appreciable expense printer-publishers already committed to these subscriptions each year in an effort to furnish various current 'foreign news' and other non-local items for their local newspapers. Hamilton's first newspaper reading room was likely opened by A. Crossman, editor of the *Canadian Casket*, in 1832, which reportedly offered the public 'fifty different newspapers from Upper Canada and the United States, and political and literary publications.'[129] Booksellers, too, found they could achieve some liquidity in a business otherwise beset by the slow turnover of their relatively expensive stock by enacting similar measures. Messrs. J. Ruthven & Company, Booksellers, for example, opened the city's first recorded circulating library, offering 'the best assortment of scarce books,' in 1833. An annual membership fee of $5 would gain an individual access to this collection.[130]

A number of other libraries and reading rooms were established in mid-nineteenth-century Hamilton. The Calliopean Library Association was one such early organization. No information exists on this organization except the donation of its library in equal shares to the HGMI and HMLA upon its closing in 1851.[131] The HMLA also accrued an impressive library and opened a reading room shortly after its founding in the mid-1840s.[132] Whether any craftsworkers made use of the facilities of this organization founded in the specific interest of clerks cannot be determined from the evidence. The fact that clerks and merchants saw little social stigma to attending the local mechanics' institute around this same time suggests that there may have been little rigidity in the patronage of either organization by fixed occupational groups. One modest piece of evidence further suggests this fluidity. Hamilton pattern maker Andrew McIlwraith became a member of both the local mechanics' institute and the Mercantile Reading Room while on a New York City sojourn in 1859–60.[133] Indeed, it is of note that the books of the HMLA news room for 1849 showed that it had been 'appreciated' by upwards of 350 'strangers' to the city over the course of that year, an impressive figure considering the association boasted a total membership of only 210 for 1850.[134] GWR mechanics, of course, enjoyed the patronage of their own reading room and library after 1865, where for a 'nominal sum' they had access to close to two thousand books and a wide selection of newspapers and periodicals hand-picked by their representatives.[135]

The other self-improvement facility that served to attract young local craftsworkers was the reading room and library of the local Young Men's Christian Association (YMCA). The first attempt to found a local YMCA appears to have been made sometime in 1856, five years after the founding of North America's first YMCA in Boston. While this organization was initially quite active, offering prayer meetings, evening sermons, and public lectures, it had faded away by about 1860. The local branch was re-formed in 1867 and endures to this day.[136]

The YMCA first advertised its intention to open a library and reading room as early as 1856, but nothing seems to have come of this. Immediately upon its reorganization in 1867, however, the YMCA's officers announced plans to secure rooms for a meeting hall and the 'opening and furnishing of a reading room.'[137] Within a few months rooms were secured and donations of books, periodicals, and the city's daily newspapers enabled the opening of a small library and reading room. Young men seem to have been drawn immediately to this new facility. Especially attractive to young craftsworkers would have been the YMCA's commitment to make this service 'open and free to all young men.' Its hours of opening – typically nine o'clock in the morning to ten o'clock at night – also provided craftsworkers with ample opportunity to patronize this establishment during their leisure hours. Within three months of its opening YMCA officers found it necessary to articulate the need for more commodious rooms since 'the Free Reading Room was being more and more frequented by the young men of the city.' A month later it was reported that the YMCA had successfully obtained a new larger free reading room that was 'attractively adorned with pictures, texts, maps & c ... and well furnished with the leading secular and religious newspapers, periodicals and illustrated newspapers ... A large number of books has also been contributed.' These new rooms also soon proved insufficient to demand and had to be 'greatly enlarged and improved' within the year. A.B. Forbes, chairman of the room and membership committee, reflected on the success of the reading room, remarking with pride 'it is computed that about a hundred and fifty, daily resort to them.' The YMCA officers reported again in 1872 that this level of demand had rendered the rooms 'entirely inadequate to our requirements.' To facilitate the construction of 'a larger, better ventilated, better furnished Reading Room,' they initiated a building fund. Funds for a new building were still being solicited the following year when it was reported that 'in the Reading Room on many evenings there has not been a vacant chair nor an unoccupied space around the newspaper stands.' With a library that now boasted over 700 volumes, the YMCA's free library and reading room provided a well-attended resource to Hamilton craftsworkers and others.[138]

The argument that Hamilton craftsworkers likely appreciated the services of the YMCA's free reading room and library is strengthened when the involvement of various craftsworkers in the direction of the organization and the part they played in its other self-improvement activities is considered. There exist very few references to those men who were involved in the direction and support of the YMCA. The one available listing of association officers for 1867, however, shows tinsmith and founder Edward Jackson elected to vice-president and master shoemaker P.W. Dayfoot as a member of the management committee. A short list of contributors to the new library and reading room published the following year contains the names of such local craftsworker-employers as Thomas McIlwraith, bookbinder John Eastwood, furniture manufacturer James Reid, and master plumber William Farmer. Iron founders and tinsmiths Dennis Moore and

Edward Jackson were listed as part of the small contingent of 'influential men' enlisted by the association in 1868 to advise them on the feasibility of purchasing their own building.[139]

Craftsworker involvement in the YMCA can also be gleaned by considering the other self-improvement activities offered through the association. A number of craftsworkers were likely attracted to attend one or more of the regular series of lectures offered by the YMCA. A number of these lectures – often delivered by religious men – concentrated on topics of interest to the self-improving craftsworker, with titles such as 'Genius and Toil,' 'Success and its Conditions,' and 'The Perils of Young Men in City Life.' The lecture by 'The Learned Blacksmith' Eliuh Burritt, considered by many of his contemporaries as the quintessence of craftsworker self-improvement, entitled 'The Social Age: Its Tendencies and Fallacies' in 1872 was likely especially well attended by area craftsworkers.[140]

The evidence also suggests that area craftsworkers were attracted to the YMCA's weekly 'mutual improvement meetings,' where attendees took turns presenting essays on various subjects in a moderated and strictly non-confrontational environment of debate and discussion. Craftsworker involvement in this aspect of the YMCA is confirmed by the one surviving list of the association's course of essays for 1858–9. The essay presentations included 'Old Testament Biography' and 'Who Is the Ruler of the Universe?' by machinist Robert Parker, 'Popular Amusements' and 'Canadian Patriotism' by GWR upholsterer David McCulloch, the painter D.D. Robertson's 'The Inspiration of Scripture,' stonemason Angus Sutherland's 'Joseph, An Example to Young Men,' and 'Life' by printer and founding member of the local typographical union R.R. Donnelly.[141] In attendance at least two of the 1859 essay discussions was pattern maker Andrew McIlwraith. Accompanying him to Mr Allan's essay 'The Morality of Burns' was Jack Stewart, likely the son of foundryman James Stewart and himself an iron moulder. McIlwraith also attended the Dundas YMCA in company of such men as Robert McKechnie, a benchmate from the Gartshore Foundry, and Alexander Somerville, printer and editor of the *Dundas True Banner*.[142]

The YMCA's employment service also attracted young craftsworkers to its rooms throughout the day and evening. Some time around 1870 the YMCA's 'Employment Committee' set to work matching up young men in need of work with the list of vacancies they compiled with the aid of local employers. In the early 1870s the committee pridefully reported an average annual procurement of between 250 and 300 jobs for its applications. Craftsworkers appear to have been particularly well served in this, one report declaring the committee 'found no difficulty in procuring work for mechanics and labourers. The only class of people they failed to find work for are those who know no trade, such as salesmen, bookkeepers and clerks.'[143] The free library and reading room with its generous opening hours would have also provided the out-of-work craftsworker with what would have been considered a constructive use of time idle from work.

Self-improvement was also practised by craftsworkers through a variety of literary, scientific, mutual improvement, and debating societies. In contrast to the HGMI or the YMCA, these organizations generally did not aspire to a highly visible institutional presence in the community, the erection of substantial buildings or amassing of impressive libraries. Though their meetings were structured, they were often held in more informal space, often rented or loaned. They appear to have achieved public face infrequently, through the sporadic sponsorship of public lectures or an occasional newspaper item. Rather, they tended to concentrate their efforts on inward self-improvement, through the encouragement of their own members' participation in such activities as the presentation of readings, the recitation and criticism of essays of their own composition, or debate. These organizations were also often, but not exclusively, composed of young, unmarried men. As Charles Tyner, chairman of the 1866 anniversary dinner of the Burlington Literary Association, remarked to his associates, 'we had lost but one member by death, but unfortunately they had lost many by marriage.'[144]

Evidence of these organizations is limited usually to newspaper accounts that simply confirm their existence but provide little additional information, especially pertaining to membership. Anna Brownell Jameson noted in her travels through Upper Canada in 1836 that, in addition to a reading room, Hamilton was also home to a literary society. It is possible that she referred to the Young Men's Association (YMA), which in 1840 had lobbied the HGMI for use of its facilities. Whether or not the YMA formed the nucleus of the HMLA is also unclear. By 1848, however, both the HMLA and a Young Mens' Mutual Improvement Association (primarily a debating society) were operating in the city. Just five years later, though, one city editor bemoaned the city's general lack of a mutual improvement association for young men.[145]

The most enduring of these organizations was undoubtedly the Hamilton Association for the Advancement of Literature, Science, and Art (Hamilton Association), formed in 1857 and still in existence at the turn of the twenty-first century. Those considering themselves the leading scientific and literary men of the community patronized the most 'serious' of all these organizations, the Hamilton Association. Members were frequently solicited to give serious papers on various aspects of natural history, science, literature and the arts. Many were original works intended for publication. Indeed, as the nineteenth century progressed, the Hamilton Association published its own journal. Unlike similar societies, it also appears to have attracted a more adult male patronage.[146]

The ambitious program of the Hamilton Mutual Improvement Society (HMIS), formed in late 1862, quickly brought it to the attention of the press. In short order, the HMIS initiated a variety of undertakings, including a series of readings, essays, and debates presented by its members, a series of public lectures and night classes in such subjects as mathematics, English grammar and elocution, German, vocal music and bookkeeping.[147] These efforts were likely overly ambitious and the HMIS's activities appear to have been scaled back to the more realistic and sustainable level of semi-private essay readings and debates by the end of 1863, rendering its further activities and longevity obscure to the historical record. Also functioning in the city by the early 1860s was the St Andrew's Literary and Debating Society, about which little is known.[148]

The Hamilton Literary Association (HLA) functioned out of rented rooms in the city's Good Templars' Hall by the spring of 1864, with its primary activities apparently focused on recitations and debate. Identified only by one short article and two letters to the editor from one of its members, the ultimate fate of this organization also remains unclear.[149] The press account of the Burlington Literary Association's anniversary dinner in 1866 failed to specify how many years its members were celebrating, but its president did characterize it as a 'society not started with very ambitious designs. The members thought that if they met week after week and discussed the prominent questions of the day, that they would be benefited.'[150] A few press reports in the early 1870s suggest the affiliation of a number of literary societies with local churches, including the Literary Association of the John Street Wesleyan Methodist Church, the Young Men's Mutual Improvement Association of Knox's Church, as well as similar societies within the Centenary and St Thomas Churches.[151] The little information that can be culled about the above societies generally appears in the form of newspaper articles announcing or recounted their newsworthy and public functions. Given that the primary focus of this type of popular organization was recitation or debate amongst its members, it is likely that a number of other similar small organizations existed through the mid-nineteenth century but failed to elicit the attention of the local news media.

The limited evidence also sheds very little light on the individuals who participated in these organizations. The few brief references that can be uncovered of those individuals who served as officers or participated in the meetings of these various organizations, however, do suggest their use by some area craftsworkers as venues for self-improvement. Information on the Hamilton Association, for whom the most extensive documentation is available, contains no record of membership. A detailed recording of its officers for the late 1850s and early 1870s does confirm at least some craftsworker involvement. GWR locomotive department superintendent Alexander Braid served as a member of council in 1857. Thomas McIlwraith was installed as first vice-president in 1860. An attempt to solicit donations of articles to stock a museum in 1859 found few takers but did include C.J. Brydges and Samuel Sharpe of the GWR. McIlwraith assumed the duties of librarian and curator and took a seat on the council in 1873. The printer A.T. Freed joined the council in 1872 and became second vice president the following year. GWR painter and Dominion M.P. Henry Witton took a turn as first vice-president in 1872 before assuming the duties of president the following year. Citing the original registers of the Hamilton Association, the printer Joseph Tinsely recounted in the early twentieth century that Witton, McIlwraith, and foundryman Calvin McQuesten had all been founding members of the organization. He also recalled participation in the association at various times between 1857 and 1881 of such men as David McCulloch, furniture manufacturer Joseph Hoodless, cigar manufacturer George Tuckett, carriage maker and oilman J.M. Williams and foundryman A. Leitch. It is also of note that, while out of work as a pattern maker, Thomas McIlwraith's younger brother Andrew spent much of his free time aiding City of Hamilton engineer Charles Robb in the drawing of maps and illustrations for his upcoming lecture to the association, entitled 'On the Geology of the Region 'round the Head of Lake Ontario.' The younger McIlwraith also set his drawing skills to work in the design of a seal for the fledgling association.[152]

Particularly attractive to craftsworkers from early on was the general emphasis of the Hamilton Association on scientific and mechanical subjects to the neglect of the literary and arts portions of its mandate. Natural history and physical geography made up a fair share of the society's early papers, but members also listened to such treatises as Mr Charnock's 'On Breakages of Parts of Locomotives During Extreme Cold.' In his inaugural address as president of the Hamilton

Association in 1871, William Proudfoot reminded the membership of the 'many branches of industry springing from inventions and discoveries of new and useful arts, machines and manufactures, deriving all their value from the skillful application of mechanical or scientific principles which afford a wide field for inquiry and investigation.' It appears that the Hamilton Association could indeed satisfy the quest for self-improvement of at least some mid-nineteenth-century craftsworkers. The printer A.T. Freed, for instance, reflected upon the meaning of his long and active membership in the organization by recounting to those attending the Hamilton Association's fiftieth anniversary dinner in 1907 the great scientific and technical advances of the nineteenth century and crediting such men as 'humble colliery operative' George Stephenson for their facilitation. Freed's own paper 'On Iron and Steel' in the association's 1882 proceedings exemplified his modest contribution to this social process. Indeed, it appears that the early meetings of the association provided craftsworkers with a level of comfort, even alongside members of more 'lofty' background. Henry Witton recalled, for instance, 'fifty years ago a dozen citizens, deeming the time was opportune for concerted action, met together and organized the Hamilton Association. The meetings of the foundation-men were informal, and their doings were devoid of ostentation.'[153] It is significant that craftsworkers found a place in what was likely nineteenth-century Hamilton's most learned society.

A number of craftsworkers also appear to have been involved in various associations formed in the 1860s and early 1870s. The Hamilton Mutual Improvement Association (HMIA) appears to have been a more informal organization than the Hamilton Association and one that catered to a younger membership. It is of note that through the first few months of its existence this organization dubbed itself the Hamilton Institute for Young Franklins. Noted in the press for its 'American origin and connections,' this organization was more than likely inspired by or affiliated with one or another of the various Franklin Institutes functioning in the United States by that time. It is likely that those seeking to found an organization characterized by heavy mechanic and manufacturer involvement south of the border were themselves craftsworkers.[154] No reason is given for the change in name to the HMIA in February 1863. The list of officers published two months later, however, does show the painter T.H. Bartindale and carpenter Addison Pratt elected recording secretary and corresponding secretary and treasurer, respectively. A meeting of the HMIA held the next month was conducted by T.L. McIntosh, printer, publisher of the *Times*, and founding member of the Hamilton Typographical Society. At the opening of the HMIA's fall season in September 1863 a 'respectable number of ladies and gentlemen' were treated to an essay prepared and read by printer Charles Tyner, a reading by tailor Charles Foster, and other similar entertainments. A number of local clerks also appear to have involved themselves in this organization, but the scant evidence does show that craftsworkers found a place here, too.[155]

Evidence relating to the Hamilton Literary Association, formed the following year, is even more limited. However, one brief account of a debate held by the HLA does detail the involvement of marble cutter John Egan, 'a young man, I should say of strong practical sense.' Boot and shoe manufacturer P.W. Dayfoot chaired this same event in which his son H.W. Dayfoot delivered a recitation 'in his usual pleasing style' entitled 'The Shores of Tennessee.'[156] Similarly, the one account of the 1866 anniversary of the Burlington Literary Association shows printer, and by then also *Times* editor, Charles Tyner conducting the proceedings from the president's chair.[157] John Hoodless, the son of cabinetmaker Joseph Hoodless and himself a furniture manufacturer, is revealed as founder and outgoing president of the Young Men's Mutual Improvement Association of the John Street Wesleyan Methodist Church in 1873. Brass founder Hugh Young was among the members of this organization saluting him upon his departure from office.[158]

One would be hard-pressed to find a literary, scientific, mutual improvement, and other self-improvement association in mid-nineteenth-century Hamilton in which craftsworkers did not play a part. Indeed, their frequent assumption of leadership positions suggests their deep involvement in these various societies. Craftsworkers' wide integration into these organizations is testimony to their burgeoning commitment to the practice of self-improvement. It is also likely that the evidence fails to provide a true portrait of just how widespread the institutional practice of self-improvement by craftsworkers really was. Smaller organizations of a more informal character whose modest meetings and events were not sufficient to garner public attention are likely lost forever to the historical record.

A rare insight into one such smaller organization in nearby Dundas is, however, provided through the diaries of pattern maker Andrew McIlwraith. The entries relating to his involvement in the Dundas Mechanics' Debating Club (DMDC) speaks volumes about craftsworkers' commitment to self-improvement in nineteenth century Canada. The twenty-seven-year-old McIlwraith started work as a pattern maker at the Gartshore Foundry in Dundas on 3 March 1858 after searching in vain for work in his trade in Hamilton. Apparently well received by his co-workers, he was pleased to exercise their invitation to attend the evening meeting of 'a Debating Club composed of Foundry workmen' only two weeks into his stint at Gartshore's. At the next meeting on 1 April he was pleased to note making his 'maiden speech' on the question 'Whether had War or Intemperance caused the greatest misery to the human race.'

The DMDC appears to have been a very active organization, holding its well-attended weekly meetings at that town's old engine house. Like similar associations in Hamilton, its activities were generally split equally between the debate of important contemporary questions and the presentation of essays by club members on a wide range of subjects. Indeed, the diverse array of topics considered by the DMDC speaks directly to the self-improving craftsworkers' ambition to complement their trade skills and technical knowledge with a wide range of enquiry. Debate covered such diverse subjects as 'Should Military Spirit Be Encouraged among Young Canadian Men?,' 'Whether Geology or Astronomy Furnished the Best Evidence of Supreme Being,' 'Whether Is Physiognomy or Phrenology the Surest Means of Testing Character,' and 'The Character of James the First.' Essays prepared and presented by club members focused on a similarly wide range of subjects and included such titles as 'Daniel Webster,' 'Commerce,' 'Imagination' and 'On Goldsmith.' Club-goers also considered aspects of political economy. Occupying much club time during McIlwraith's first four-month sojourn in Dundas were two long-running debates on the question 'Would Federal Union Be Advantageous to the British Provinces in America' and 'Whether an Increase of Duties in Imported Manufactures Would Benefit Canada.' It is interesting to note that in the debate on the tariff question club members voted that 'the present protection is sufficient for manufactures for home consumption and that it is too expensive for Canada to turn exporter.' Interestingly, this debate and another on 'Whether Scotland or America Introduced the Steamboat' was as close as the DMDC got to consider questions more directly related to mechanics.

The diaries also document the involvement in the DMDC of a number of Gartshore employees for whom practices of self-improvement evidently became connected to their future successes as self-made craftsworkers in their own right. After marrying the daughter of its proprietor, McIlwraith himself moved on to help run the Goldie Foundry in nearby Galt. Long-time Gartshore employee John Bertram, who left to form the very successful Canada Tool Works in partnership with fellow Gartshore employee Robert McKechnie Jr by the mid-1860s, was also active in the DMDC, attending the recitations and debates and even contributing his own essay, 'Astronomy,' for the consideration of the membership in January 1859. McKechnie's father, Robert Sr, also a long-time Gartshore employee, took an even more active hand in the club, making notable contributions to debates, serving as club vice-president, and presenting his own essay, 'Goldsmith,' to the membership in June 1858.[159] Future foundryman John Inglis also served as DMDC vice-president for a term in 1858. Given the upward direction in which so many club members were evidently heading, it is interesting to note that McIlwraith chose as the topic for his essay presentation to club members 'Wilson, the Ornithologist,' a former weaver whose rise to the status of 'self-made man' was triumphed by Samuel Smiles and others.[160]

An organization of this character, confined, as it seems to have been, to the employees of one workplace, would likely have received little or no coverage in the local press. Indeed, McIlwraith's entries about the DMDC provide a rare glimpse into the associational world of self-improvement of the nineteenth-century craftsworker that would otherwise have remained obscure to the historian.[161] It is also unlikely that this particular organization was an anomaly in the mid-nineteenth-century craft world. McIlwraith himself makes no mention that the existence of such a club was in any way unusual and, when he leaves Dundas, simply picks up his interest in these affairs by attending the debating club of the mechanics' institute in his new home of New York City. Evidence of a similar mechanics' debating society in nearby Galt has also been uncovered.[162] It would be surprising, then, if a city the size of Hamilton did not play host to a number of similar organizations that received even less public attention than the city's larger but still quite obscure community-wide self-improvement associations.

Conclusion

The culture of self-improvement was expressed by Hamilton craftsworkers in both ideology and practice. It was, in certain respects, a culture rooted in the craft mutualism of the past, part of an age-old concern to facilitate the ascent of younger craftsworkers up the ladder of craft mobility. But to do this it necessarily looked forward, embracing liberal conceptions of self-improvement associated with the modern capitalist world. As such, this was an emergent culture, proactively adapting to modern socio-economic exigencies. It was not an isolated culture; currents of self-improvement flourished throughout the Western capitalist world in this period. However, it was a culture shaped and strengthened in the specificity of its local environment. Hamilton craftsworkers developed a particular enthusiasm for self-improvement out of their transmodal social experience, one in which capitalist and non-capitalist worlds overlapped, where the continued functioning of familiar occupational elevation networks enabled many journeymen to understand that, while wage-earning had become a widespread practice, it was not necessarily permanent. In short, this material arrangement did not *yet* provide sufficient grounds upon which ideologies of dispossession had become dominant. The long hours, occupational diseases and accidents, cyclical unemployment, and other contradictions of capitalism would not have been unknown to these craftsworkers, but the apparent opportunities that early industrialization in Hamilton offered these men were still attractive enough to outweigh these drawbacks. Their particular experience was also coincident with their understanding of capitalism's more advanced and socially degraded stages elsewhere. This provided local craftsworkers – many of whom had likely recently come to Hamilton to 'escape' capitalism – with a powerful point of contrast in which their imagined community came out best. Here, craftsworkers viewed the unfolding of modern capitalism with hope, with optimism about the relative number of opportunities it offered them to achieve security as craftsworkers and as men. They understood this age to have been brought about through the aggregation of individual devotion to self-improvement, to the studious expansion of the mechanical arts, to applied science, to invention. The real genius of the age, however, lay in craftsworkers' subscription to the broader ideas of the enlightened individual. Self-improvement provided not just the road to social elevation along the lines of a modernized craft progression, but also the potential for the craftsworker to make himself a more complete, informed, and well-rounded individual along the way. Craftsworkers developed a dual understanding of their social elevation. On the one hand, they viewed their advancement up through the craft ranks to a position of security and respect with great hope. But they were optimistic, too, that they were in the process of elevation as a class. Their devotion to a far-ranging program of self-improvement was undertaken both for their personal elevation and to provide them with the resources to properly function as informed, newly elevated citizens alongside the other respectable classes of the community.

7

Transmodal Culture in Apogee: 1872 Revisited

The development of industrial capitalism in mid-nineteenth-century Hamilton did not result in an entirely Pollyannaish social experience for craftsworkers. Conflict born from the contradictions of this economic system must have been familiar to many craftsworkers. Some had undoubtedly fled the hard edge of capitalism in places where it was more advanced – such as the large industrial centres of Britain and the northeastern United States – and brought that experience with them. Some craftsworkers must also have experienced failure in self-employment, prolonged wage-earning, and other such frustrations of capitalism. Perhaps symptomatic of all this was the fact that unions and strikes were an increasing feature of Hamilton industry through this period. But just how common were they?

Workers in some crafts had formed unions before the flurry of organization connected to the Nine Hours Movement of 1872. Local stonecutters founded a benevolent society as early as 1845. The Hamilton Typographic Society was formed by journeymen printers in July 1846 but lasted only a few months. It was re-formed in 1852 and again (this time permanently) in 1854. The Journeymen House Carpenters & Joiners and the Journeymen Tailors' Protective Society were both active in the early 1850s. A local cigar makers' union may have been functioning, according to one twentieth-century reminiscence, as early as 1854, though contemporary press reports do not reveal its activities until the mid-1860s. Some shop craft workers at the Great Western Railway (GWR) affiliated with the British-based Amalgamated Society of Engineers (ASE) in 1857. The organization of moulders, machinists, and bakers occurred sometime around the early 1860s. A number of these societies had centralized some of their efforts in a local trades assembly by 1864. Local shoemakers appear to have formed a union by 1867. At the GWR, puddlers and locomotive engineers organized associations in 1870 and 1871. During the 1860s and early 1870s a number of local unions also established (or brought with them) membership in such international unions as the Iron Molders' International Union, the Machinists and Blacksmiths International Union, the Brotherhood of Locomotive Engineers, and the Knights of Saint Crispin. The early days of the Nine Hours agitation in 1872 saw the re-formation of local carpenters and joiners into a local of the Amalgamated Society of Carpenters and Joiners, the creation of a Friendly Society of Boilermakers, a tinners' union, and a society of saddle, harness, trunk, and collar makers.[1]

While unions had been established in some crafts, strikes involving local craftsworkers, while not absent from the historical record, hardly had come to occupy a central place within it. More to the point, on only nine occasions had area craftsworkers collectively withdrawn their labour in protest against their employers in the whole quarter century before 1872. Aside from one notable exception, these strikes appear to have lasted only a matter of hours or days.[2]

These few strikes were hardly explosive affairs with employer and employee arrayed against each other in determined conflict. Rather, they tended to unfold well within the bounds of traditional craft mutuality. Journeymen house carpenters and joiners striking for higher wages in 1953 took great pains to inform the public through the local press that their demands were 'honorable and our actions just' and made only 'in consideration of the advanced prices of provisions.' They backed up a resolution that 'the actions of Employers and Journeymen should be for mutual benefit' by respectfully presenting their employers with a memorial appealing to their 'sense of justice' and requesting a meeting where both sides could resolve this issue peaceably.[3] Paul Craven and Tom Traves have shown how GWR Managing director C.J. Brydges was able to rely on the strong bonds of paternalism and mutuality among his shop workers to resolve a strike precipitated by the dismissal of a popular shop foreman by the new superintendent of the locomotive shops in November 1856.[4] Similar to their house-building brethren, factory carpenters complained to their employers in May 1864 of their inability to sustain themselves or their families on wages of $1.25 a day. A deputation of journeymen visited the city's principal employers to make the case for a raise of twenty-five cents a day. They made careful gestures towards the prevailing mutualism of the craft in their memorial to their employers: 'We come not before you with insolent demands; we come to you for relief ... We do not wish to injure you, knowing that your interest is our interest, and when you suffer we suffer also.' Journeymen were encouraged when, in response to the memorial, 'not a single one of the employers objected to its terms.' However, over the course of a week or so journeymen became disgruntled as 'things remained exactly as they were – one employer waiting for some other to take the initiative.' Journeymen carpenters decided that the only way to break this deadlock was to withhold their labour from any employer who would not pay the new rate. This strategy was generally successful: a number of employers acceded before the deadline and others within hours or one or two days of the commencement of the strike. Outlining their position in the local press, the journeymen adopted a tone of regret at having to institute the strike, one of them explaining that 'I do not see that any other position was open ... If the employers had resisted the demand for increased wages as unjust, and had positively refused to grant such an increase, it might be said we were endeavouring to force them into doing that which they considered wrong and unfair. Such, however, was not the case. They agreed as one man that what we asked was fair, but kept hesitating and procrastinating.'[5]

The schisms that resulted from these strikes were also quickly and amicably patched up. Just a few months after the 1856 GWR shopworkers' strike, company officials, department superintendents, foremen, and shop workers celebrated together under a banner declaring 'Success to Mechanical Enterprise' at the annual festival of the GWR railway mechanics. A 'majority of employers in the tobacco trade' participated 'with a relish' in the Cigar Makers' Protective Union picnic at Oakland's Park only a few months after a strike over wages had disrupted that trade. Even as tensions over the issue of the nine-hour day heated up in the spring of 1872, rolling-mill hands still saw fit to present their retiring superintendent – with whom they were embroiled in a strike about a year earlier – with a silver tea service and many thanks for his 'kind and courteous dealings' with them throughout the years.[6]

These conflicts offered little in the way of a developed vocabulary of class-consciousness. A campaign against excessive night work among bakers resulted in the formation of the Journeymen Baker's Association in July 1862 and perhaps occasioned the extensive comment in the local press of any issue dividing master and journeyman before the Nine Hours Movement of 1872. The vocabulary of struggle in this instance charged 'barbarous and cruel' employers adhering to the night system with a 'high, unbending attitude of imperious mastership' set on 'gratifying of a morbid and contemptible taste for exercising the power of oppression over their fellow man.' Isaac Chilman, proprietor of one of the city's largest bakeries (though not a baker himself), who reportedly referred to own protesting journeymen 'white slaves,' was told that, in the end, it was he who would have to 'bow and submit.' Importantly, it was the *Hamilton Times*, a publication controlled by a number of local Reform merchants, who offered these comments. It may have been this newspaper's general support for the early-closing movement among city clerks through these years that informed its position in this instance. The journeymen bakers' role appears to have been much less confrontational, beginning with their presentation of a circular to their employers on 1 July which, adhering to traditions of mutualism, carefully stated 'that their was no disposition whatever on the part of anyone present to infringe upon the interests of the Master Bakers.' A number of local employers granted the day system immediately, and the Journeymen Bakers' Association does not appear to have withheld their labour from employers convinced of the necessity of night work. The *Times* continued the battle in print for a couple of months. In their defence, the offending masters declared that, while they indeed supported the principle of day work, it was the public's demand for fresh bread that necessitated the continuation of work at night.[7]

In general, it is necessary to rethink how direct the link was between the creation of unions and developing class awareness among journeymen. Historians need to explore in much more depth the multiple functions that unions served in the context of early industrialization to broaden their understanding of such organizational forms. To what extent, for example, did unions take shape or function as protest organs, and to what extent as benevolent societies or vehicles for mutual assistance? To what extent was their initial function that of a travelling society, as an organized network facilitating geographic mobility? The 'tramp,' for example, certainly predated industrial capitalism.

As the preceding suggests, unions were organizations with a history and not simply products of industrial capitalism. Rather, their roots lay in such traditional craft forms as the guilds. As organizational forms they did, at some point, adapt to industrial capitalism by transforming to act against it. But does this not also presuppose that other adaptations were possible to other material situations, to different stages of development?

It is also not unreasonable to ask, in light of the hope with which some journeymen came to view the early industrialization outlined herein, to what extent journeymen came to view unions as vehicles through which they could gain more lucrative positions in a modern political economy. A system, it might be added, that many of them may have supported. 'We were all in the same boat, master and man,' reflected Richard Butler on his journeyman days as a Hamilton printer in the 1850s. Given what this study has thus far shown, it is likely significant that the only remaining union membership list from this period, that of the Hamilton Typographic Society, shows that a number of early members went on to become employers or prominent men in the community in their own right in the years that followed, including John Hand, William Nicholson, Richard Butler, A.A. Sheppard, Charles Kidner, Richard Donnelly, and A.T. Freed.[8] Gary Kornblith has suggested researchers need to take pay attention to 'those aspects of capitalist social relations that originally appeared liberating' by, among other things, taking seriously the ways in which early journeymen's organizations sought to turn the new rules of the game 'to their own advantage.'[9]

Perhaps the haste to find the seeds of what came after has largely obscured these possibilities from historians' view. The truer explanation of what followed – its nuance, its complexity – is more likely to be found in the more inclusive research agenda. All this is an admittedly wide row to hoe. As one modest contribution to that effort, this chapter will examine the character of by far the largest of the 'conflicts' to take place in Hamilton's craftsworker community in the period under study – the Nine Hours Movement of 1872 – and to do so with the type of open mind suggested by the questions above. It is not denied that some craftsworkers brought to that struggle – and into the few strikes and unions that preceded this – a developing sense of alienation rooted in the decidedly capitalist aspects of the system under which they laboured. But it is arguable that this was still a marginal social experience. This chapter will make the point that, by this study's terminal date, the character of such conflict was predominately rooted in craftsworkers' transmodal experience of developing craft capitalism.

Craft capitalism opened up a wealth of possibilities to Hamilton craftsworkers. As a material arrangement, it allowed fundamental continuity in mutualistic aspects of craftsworker culture. But it also encouraged the formulation of emergent ideologies and modes of action. These emergent aspects were themselves flavoured by the peculiar material situation in which Hamilton craftsworkers found themselves – one which muted that economic system's alienating tendencies while appearing to offer a measure of security through the apparent preservation, perhaps expansion, of traditional avenues of craft mobility. They manifested themselves in such particular formulations as the 'self-made craftsworker' and its complement, the 'self-improving craftsworker.' But craft capitalism was also a larger and more powerful force.

Thus far I have delineated the broad outlines of the transmodal culture particular to craft capitalism. The present chapter will show how this culture manifested itself and exerted its power in a particular historical situation. Hamilton craftsworkers' experience of transmodalism was born in industrial expansion and increasing economies of scale occasioned by the opening of the Great Western Railway (and its workshops) in the mid-1850s, and its development proceeded apace through the 1860s. Its singularity as a culture by the early 1870s, however, had reached a coherence that represented this culture's fullest expression and, likely, its apogee. It is with the events of 1872, in particular, that one can appreciate most fully the extent to which as historical actors Hamilton craftsworkers had embedded themselves in this social context. The events of that year represent transmodal culture's fullest elaboration and display its depth of character as an emergent cultural form. As a culture in apogee, however, it did display pits and fissures that, while still easily patched up, were likely to become widening cracks in the years to come.

This was also not a static culture. Its emergence was ongoing, expanding with craftsworkers' optimism that their elevation within their craft was an enduring component of a healthy liberal political economy. It was a culture with momentum, with a built-in anticipation of linear improvement, an understanding that things had already improved considerably and should rightfully improve more. It was a culture of expectation.

As the profiles of the 'self-made' and 'self-improving' craftsworker suggest, it was a culture that also engendered in craftsworkers an emergent sense of their rights as free actors in its unfolding, rights perhaps best understood under the broad rubric of 'industrial citizenship.' This was a developing form of organic citizenship constructed from craftsworkers' growing understanding of themselves as chief contributors to the building of modern industry, the economy and society. The fulfilment of this responsibility was only possible if craftsworkers could maintain rights dictated by the emergent culture of craft. The events of 1872 illustrate just how far craftsworkers had developed this budding sense of rights and the extent to which they had committed to defend, preserve and enhance them. The Nine Hours Movement is best understood as a contest over these rights – a contest over how to best maintain the transmodal world. It was in large part a battle against what craftsworkers perceived to be obnoxious obstructions to the right and proper functioning of the modern liberal economy and society and to their right to operate as free actors within it. They chafed not against capitalism's contradictions and alienating features, but against those impediments they believed inhibited its smooth functioning. The events of 1872 were more an expression of emergent notions of rights and citizenship nurtured in transmodal class experience than they were the expressions of capitalist class conflict other writers have perceived them to be.

At the same time the issue of the nine-hour day was rooted in the aspirations of the individual craftsworker, it also found footing in the pre-existing collectivism of the craft world. It was a contest that exposed the differing opinions between some masters and men over just how the collective playing field should be levelled in order to maximize the potential for individual achievement. Harmony was maintained at most Hamilton workplaces, but the debates that developed between some masters and journeymen exposed somewhat different ideas about how the bonds of mutuality and expectations of obligation should be best shaped to facilitate this. What the debate between select numbers of masters and journeymen broke down into were differing (though not fundamentally different) conceptions of how this collective playing field should be shaped. Each side appropriated differing visions of craft identity to press their points. But what this boiled down to was the fact that each side had a vision, commonly rooted in the mutualism of their pre-existing culture, of how best to achieve what they *all* still universally valued – the ability to gain their independence in the overall context of an improving crafts world. For the Hamilton craftsworker, improving one's self was intimately connected to the obligation to improve the craft as a whole.

'... the great lever of our prosperity'

Many of the debates of 1872 were framed in terms of craftsworkers' perceived place in the modern political economy. Indeed, as the burgeoning commitment to self-improvement outlined in the previous chapter suggests, the self-improving craftsworker had become centrally preoccupied with the study of political economy and he and his companions' place within it. It became an integral part of the 'broader knowledge' contemporaries argued constituted the self-improving craftsworker. Hamilton mechanics could and did, through their patronage of the city's many self-improvement societies, indulge their interest in this subject through everything from current periodicals to full-length treatises to lectures and debates.

Pattern maker Andrew McIlwraith provides but one example of how a craftsworker could, through varied activity, satisfy his aspirations to practise this aspect of his 'many-sided culture.' McIlwraith remained constantly informed on the events of the day through the reading of newspapers and current periodicals. At home after work or while work itself was scarce, he spent hours, often full days, feet on the fender, reading local and foreign newspapers, or such longer treatises as 'How to Do Business.' This activity was complemented by frequent visits to the local library newsroom, where he perused current newspapers and periodicals, often in the company of his co-workers. The spirited discussions that followed these sessions can only be imagined, but they likely touched on many of the same points discussed 'upon the Tariff question,' or North American commercial union, in the hall of his debating society. He also attended lectures on topics ranging from 'upon the capabilities and productions' of Kansas to 'the English Merchant,' to simple 'manufacture.'

McIlwraith was not alone in his engagement with these questions; his diaries hint that many of his fellow mechanics actively engaged in similar pursuits.[10] In the second decade of the twentieth century printer and journalist H.F. Gardiner similarly looked back fondly upon one group of workers who were especially notable for their diligent interest in questions of political economy. He recalled in 1922 how

> in the Great Western Railway shops, fifty years ago, there was what might be described as an aristocracy of labor, largely composed of Englishmen who, before coming to Canada, were familiar with the speeches of Cobden, Bright, Bentinick, Earl Derby and Benjamin Disrali; with the writings of Smith and Malthus, of Ricardo and of Mill. Mr. Witton found congenial companions in this group, including Messrs. Charlton, Simons, Hannon, Pinch, Archibald, McCulloch and Hall. They had a well-stocked library for their reference, and in their conversations and debates much useful information was acquired and disseminated.[11]

Interest in such questions came naturally to a group who understood themselves as the prime movers – indeed, as the chief architects – of the modern political economy. As the previous two chapters have shown, self-improved, self-made craftsworkers took great pride in their contributions to the modern world. They consistently spoke about, and festooned their meeting halls with, images of the great 'mechanical geniuses' – men of their own class – who had ushered in 'the mechanical age' through invention. Common were refrains, such as that made by GWR locomotive superintendent Henry Yates to his men, that 'all the great improvements of our time have proceeded from the working classes.' It was with the 'inventive genius' of craftsworkers, he explained, 'that the great cities of the West' were built and 'innumerable benefits and blessings' bestowed on mankind.[12] 'It was to the mechanic' concurred his friend Samuel Sharp, 'that society owed most of its comforts.'[13]

Craftsworkers logically developed an understanding that this collective contribution entitled them to certain new-found rights in the functioning of the modern polity. As equal participants in the modern age, argued the *Journal of the Board of Arts and Manufactures*, the mechanic or artisan could no longer be 'considered by the commercial and professional classes as belonging to a lower caste of society' but should now rightfully 'take his place amongst them without any feelings of inferiority.'[14] Hamilton's mayor proclaimed to the craftsworkers assembled to celebrate the first anniversary of the Hamilton Co-Operative Society, that 'the mechanics are the great lever of our prosperity, and they have a right to the opportunities of raising themselves to a position in which their voice can be felt in the management of state affairs.'[15] William Mitchell, secretary of the local chapter of the Amalgamated Society of Engineers, declared to his co-workers his support for 'raising the skilled machinist to that local position he has a right to claim in every nation of the world whose wealth is being produced by mechanical excellence and engineering skill.'[16] A number of years earlier his workmate Mr Turner argued that the modern mechanic 'had a perfect right to take their share in the political movements of the day.' In these statements we view aspects of a developing labour theory of value that other commentators have interpreted as presaging working-class consciousness.[17] As we shall see, however, they actually portended a much different understanding of class.

While craftsworkers' emergent sense of rights and of citizenship was in many respects a mid-nineteenth-century transatlantic phenomenon, it was also a formulation with a local specificity. This was especially evident in the enthusiasm with which craftsworkers viewed the sale of their labour as a commodity. Labour historians usually take a much different attitude towards this realization, often viewing it as an integral early step in the building of working-class identities out of an experience of being subordinate actors within capitalist social relations. As explained in chapter 2, however, craftsworkers' location within capitalism in Hamilton was by no means straightforward. Their situation in the social relations of production, in fact, militated against emergent identifications built simply out of a dispossessing capitalism.

Through the lens of their transmodal position, Hamilton craftsworkers actually celebrated the commodification of their labour as a key and necessary ingredient to their proper functioning as diligent individuals in the modern polity. The flourishing state of their networks of occupational elevation prevented the realization of their commodified labour as being anything more than a temporary condition. These smoothly functioning networks, in fact, helped craftsworkers put a positive spin on selling their own labour power. In the liberal polity they viewed their paid labour as their own capital, to be accumulated and used to secure for themselves positions of security. In a lecture entitled 'Crispinism' in 1870, Mr Daniel rhetorically asked his Toronto audience, 'now what is the workman's capital but his labor?'

Two distinct possibilities are offered by this observation. The first, following the logic of the labour theory of value, is that the workingman's withholding of this commodity is his best weapon with which to negotiate the conditions of his employment with the employer of his labour (i.e., capital). Capitalist social relations are the most likely arrangement to breed this sentiment. The second possibility is that, in the right social environment, the idea that wages represent accumulating capital represents potential. Given that Hamilton was stocked (and being constantly restocked) with masses of workers with different and varying experiences of capitalism – some with experience of its alienation elsewhere and resigned to its inevitability, some fleeing these tendencies with the hope of escaping them, some whose experience of its alienation had not yet been formed and who were steeped in the ethos of independent commodity production, or eager for a non-alienating capitalism, or somewhere in between – it is likely that both these understandings of labour commodification were held in varying measures by different groups of workers in this period. However, as this chapter will show, it was the cultural force of the latter – the optimistic view of wages as accumulating capital – that still held sway in Hamilton by 1872.

Unravelling the meaning craftsworkers assigned to their particular conception of their labour power as a commodity better delineates this situation. In a social environment where the ability of the craftsworker to start with nothing and achieve success was accepted as fact and endlessly expounded upon, where enterprise was commonly founded upon 'journeyman's wages,' it was perhaps inevitable that young craftsworkers would view the sale of their labour power with optimism. 'Men who have made fortunes,' declared the *Ontario Workman*, 'are not those who had five thousand dollars given them to start with, but boys who have started with a well-earned dollar or two.'[18] Not only was it no longer necessary in the modern world for wealth to beget wealth, as chapter 4 has outlined, but this arrangement was in fact preferable, more virtuous. The connection between journeymen's use of this commodity to secure future success was made repeatedly. David McCulloch's *Spectator* offered, for instance, that 'nearly all rich men in the country were once poor ... nearly every personal fortune they can enumerate is the product of its owner's toil and skill ... There are other forms of capital besides accumulated money; brains, skill, muscle, industry.'[19] The *City Enterprise* concurred that it was 'the power of his good right arm' that had transformed the 'poor boy of yesterday into the 'talented young man today.'[20] Instead of alienation, craftsworkers understood the application of their skills to paid labour in their journeyman years as capital, as simply the natural starting point for their own capital accumulation through which they would gain independence.

The great complement to the young craftsworker's conversion of muscle into capital, of course, was his active pursuit of self-improvement. His overall chance at achieving success and independence, it was understood, was greatly augmented when the reinvestment of the proceeds of his labour was properly combined with 'improving' activity. Chapter 7 outlined the strong connections Hamilton craftsworkers made between the pursuit of self-improvement and their own social elevation. The self-made, self-improving craftsworker, then, became a potent amalgam.

Craftsworkers' emergent sense of rights was fuelled by this powerful combination. As outlined above, it formed the nucleus of their growing sense of citizenship rights – the right to be equal actors in the modern polity. However, this broad set of rights was derived from a more immediate sense of rights formed in their individual efforts to achieve independence. Craftsworkers came to understand that it was right and just that the modern polity be governed in such a way as to protect, perhaps even enhance, their own 'elevation rights.' A common understanding emerged that presented craftsworkers' ability to elevate themselves as an inalienable right of the modern age. Hamilton's mayor, for instance, expressed to those assembled to celebrate the first anniversary of the Hamilton Co-operative Society that 'the surest way of making the mass of people happy and contented was to give them those privileges to which they were justly entitled, and to surround them with the means for developing their intellects and elevating their position in society.'[21] The smooth functioning of elevation networks was presented as normative time and time again. David McCulloch, for instance, moved a lusty vote of thanks from the audience at the local Mechanics' Hall for Dr Lille, whose lecture 'Self-Reliance' posited that 'Everything around us has been growing steadily ... throw to the winds the idea that you are tied down by fate to this or to that. You are fated to nothing except to reap as you sow. Exert the powers that have been bestowed on you; make a wise, generous use of the faculties bestowed on you.'[22] Toronto Mechanics' Institute secretary George Longmann similarly prompted young mechanics to 'devote their time, their energies, and their means to the acquisition of knowledge now' if they wished to fulfil the dream of the modern age whereby 'men of the next generation are to fill their respective positions better than their fathers did before them.'[23] The Reverend A.B. Simpson reminded the number of young craftsworkers attending his lecture at the local YMCA 'to embrace the facilities for improvement your fathers could not enjoy, and prepare to take your place abreast of your time in the great onward march of this intelligent and progressive age.'[24]

As the body of this text has shown, Hamilton craftsworkers lived in an optimistic social milieu in which the traditional craft progression from apprentice to journeyman to master had not yet been eliminated. It also inculcated them with a developing belief that this was an experience, as long as they worked both hand and brain, to which they were entitled. Conflict, however, arose when the smooth operation of this system was disrupted. Craftsworkers chafed not against the inherent conflicts of the capitalist wage relationship, but against perceived obstacles to their elevation within the craft community. This sentiment was expressed perhaps most succinctly by metalworker Matthew Howles in his capacity as president of the Hamilton Co-operative Society. Speaking to his fellow craftsworkers on the occasion of the society's first anniversary, Howles assured his brethren that 'the cooperation of the working classes did not arise from any morbid feeling of jealousy towards those whom fortune had favoured with wealth and high positions in society.' Its ambition was rather more subtle and noble; it 'warred against the elements which obstructed the progress and advancement of the working classes to that position which everyone felt one day they were destined to occupy.' Reminding his fellow mechanics of the mutuality of interests between capital and labour, he added, in a slightly different vein, that the purpose of their activities was to war 'with the monopolies that obstruct the physical, moral, intellectual growth of man, because that obstruction is destructive of independence and competence.' Reinforcing Howles's sentiment was GWR worker James Charlton, who added that in this new country one must 'try all promising experiments and give the laborer every fair chance to elevate himself.'[25] It is worth noting that, only two years later, Howles opened what became one of Hamilton's most substantial stove and tinware manufacturing business. It is within this frame of reference that the events of 1872 unfolded.

The Nine Hours Movement in Hamilton: Scale and Scope

The Nine Hours Movement has received much historiographical attention, rendering a complete narrative of these events unnecessary here.[26] The remainder of this chapter will offer an interpretation that emphasizes the character of this event within the social context of transmodalism over the prevailing understanding of it as a 'benchmark ... in the evolution of Canadian working-class consciousness.'[27] Instead of celebrating the episodic aspects of this event, this chapter will take a longer, more inclusive view, situating it in the broader development of transmodal culture.

Hamilton craftsworkers' involvement in the Nine Hours Movement has been viewed as 'a central component of the matrix of control mechanisms' expressed as part of the 'initial stirrings of Canadian working-class consciousness.'[28] A cursory examination of the evidence easily provides a sense of widespread craftsworker involvement in the movement: union locals were founded in many trades; the 'labour question' received frequent attention in the press; strikes and lockouts were staged; a massive parade of craftsworkers held on 15 May 1872 virtually shut down industrial production in the city. Indeed, accounts of the movement have generally emphasized its episodic aspects – strikes, lockouts, parades. The natural starting point for this examination, then, is to gain perspective on the movement by re-examining the depth and character of the schisms it engendered in the city.

The actual disruption wrought by the Nine Hours Movement was most evident in the wave of strikes and lockouts that occurred in various city shops between February and May 1872. A close scrutiny of their frequency and duration, the number of workers involved, and the circumstances of certain specific occurrences prompts a reconsideration of the depth and character of these disruptions. The few strikes that did result from the demand for shorter hours were generally short in duration and involved a very small percentage of the city's total industrial workforce.

The first and largest of these resulted from the firing of a Mr Bland by the owners of the Wilson, Bowman sewing machine manufactory when he attempted to petition them as a representative of his fellow employees on the nine-hours issue on the morning of 20 February. Bland's dismissal immediately precipitated a strike by the firm's 130 male employees in a show of support. What followed was a relatively brief event, lasting about a week. This was not a strike over the nine-hour workday, however. It was, rather, a job action fought out in terms of employees' right to memorialize their employers. Even when a 'mass meeting' of the Nine Hours League voted to 'contribute to the support of the workingmen of Messrs. Wilson, Bowman & Co.' a few days after the strike began, they did so expressly to support these workers' 'right to petition' their employers. The strike itself reached a speedy resolution when the firm agreed to rehire Mr Bland. Soon after the men returned to work, the firm decided to grant their men's request for nine hours.[29] While this event did expose a difference of opinion between masters and men regarding proper adherence to craft norms, it did not unfold laced with the rhetoric of capitalist class relations, and mutuality was quickly restored. This situation bore some similarity to that at the GWR shops. As Paul Craven has shown, the granting of nine hours by GWR management was not a simple matter of acceding to a reasonable request but the result of a (likely financially) calculated response to considerable 'agitation' on behalf of the men. The railway escaped a possible strike and mutuality was again maintained.[30] The only other strike connected with the movement commenced on 13 May 1872 when marble cutters in the employ of Hurd & Roberts and a Mr Rice walked off the job in protest against their employers' refusal to concede nine hours. Again, this strike appears to have lasted about a week and involved only fifty hands.[31]

Much more disruptive of industrial activity were a number of lockouts instituted by employers shortly before the Nine Hours League's 15 May deadline for shorter hours. Indeed, from quite early on in the struggle it appears that employers, too, had banded together to reinforce their opposition to the movement. A list of 145 employers in favour of the ten-hour system published in the *Spectator* in mid-February provided the first sign of employer cooperation against the Nine Hours Movement. These lists, published a number of times throughout the struggle, reflected employers' combined resolve to resist the movement. And indeed, much mention was made of employers banding together for the purpose of fighting one combination with another.[32] It was only a small fraction of this group, however, that felt any necessity for action extending beyond simple debate with their employees. Perhaps most conspicuous in their opposition to the Nine Hours Movement were the proprietors of the R.M. Wanzer sewing machine factory, who locked out their approximately four hundred employees on 10 May in an effort to provide their employees pause for reflection upon their intended unilateral implementation of the nine-hour day a few days later. It was for this same purpose that the city's foundry operators banded together to lock out their men the next day. Most of the city's foundries were closed, including Gurney, Moore, Stewart, Copps', Gurney and Ware, Turnbull, Sawyer and Northey. This lockout alone cast about 450 men out of work.[33] Thomas McCoombs, proprietor of a small marble works, jumped on the bandwagon that same day by locking out his ten employees.[34] Altogether, then, about 860 men and boys, or less than 18 per cent of the city's male industrial workforce, were on the streets by the time of the workingmen's demonstration on 15 May.

While employers loyal to the ten-hour system, particularly iron founders, exhibited a fair degree of uniformity in their opposition to the nine-hours agitators, some notable successes were made in breaking these ranks. The Great Western Railway shops, employing about 20 per cent of all male industrial workers in the city,[35] conceded nine hours to its men in mid-April. Also acceding to the demand for nine-hour work days were most of the city's sewing machine shops, including Wilson, Lockman, Gardner, Appleton, and Hespeler, whose combined workforces represented a further 8 per cent of the city's' male industrial workforce.[36] Also notable for their granting of nine hours was the machine works of F.G. Beckett and Matthew Howles's stove and tin works, employing 129 men and boys between them.

In all, then, the days leading up to the 'mass demonstration' on 15 May are somewhat ambiguous. On the one hand, about 18 per cent of the city's workers had been locked out to reflect on their demands. On the other hand, nine hours of labour had become an established fact for just over 30 per cent of Hamilton's male industrial workforce. In other city shops – representing approximately 50 per cent of the city's male workers – the nine-hours issue, if it was an issue at all, had not reached a level of seriousness for either side to feel the necessity for such drastic action as strikes, lockouts, or even threats. While the nine-hours issue created ripples in the mutuality between masters and men at select local workplaces, at most shops masters, too, either subscribed to the vision of shorter hours or were able to settle their differences with their workers over it amicably.

The movement itself culminated in a 'grand workingmen's procession' on Wednesday, the 15th of May, the day after which, it was declared, 'nine hours shall constitute a day's work.' This parade has often been viewed as the Nine Hour Movement's culminating act of defiance against recalcitrant employers. Indeed, the men locked out of the city's foundries, Wanzer's sewing machine factory, and the various marble works did comprise a marked element in the procession. The members of Iron Molders International Union No. 26 particularly were 'a body of men who mustered strongly.' Taken together, however, a generous estimate of this contingent places it as no more than 700 or 800 men and boys, or roughly a quarter of the estimated 3000 parade participants.[37] Almost twice as numerous among paradegoers that day were men and boys from shops having already acceded the nine-hour request. The men of the GWR shops, the Beckett Foundry, and various sewing machine shops, if indeed they did march 'en masse' as reported, might have accounted for as many as 1500 of the marchers.[38] The remainder of the contingent, which included goodly numbers of boot and shoe makers, brush makers, and other trades, was composed of men and boys who, while marching in support of the nine-hours issue, seem to have done so without much formal opposition from their employers.

Indeed, especially notable was the rapidity with which industrial relations returned to normal in the city in the wake of this disruption. Only one day after these same workmen trudged four abreast along the five-mile parade route, the *Mail* confidently reported 'the excitement over the nine-hour demonstration yesterday has entirely subsided, and everything in this city has donned its wonted appearance, with the exception of a certain number of workshops where the men were on strike [or] locked out' a few days before.[39] By the following Monday – only three workdays after the 15th – the *Spectator*'s listing of all shops in the city that were open for business included all the foundries and marble works affected by strikes and/or lockouts the previous week. Even the L.D. Sawyer Foundry, identified as one of the nine hours men's most bitter opponents, reported that 'most of their old employees had returned their allegiance' and were running the plant at full capacity within two weeks of the strike.[40]

The movement's main detractor, the Wanzer Sewing Machine Company – having ostensibly taken advantage of this idle time to make 'extensive repairs' to its building and machinery – lagged slightly behind the general back-to-work movement in the city. It, too, however, had opened its doors to employees by Thursday. It also appears that this was the only establishment in which the men held out for their demands. By 29 May, only 95 of the reported 400 workers subject to lockout had returned. The determination of the Wanzer men is likely explained by the fact that this was the only sewing machine shop in the city not to grant nine hours to its employees. Striking workers did stage two or three 'rowdy' protests outside the plant over the next two or three weeks, but the press reported that even some of those 'having been strong advocates of the shorter hours movement' had returned to work by early June.[41] As evidence of this plant's return to normalcy, historians often point to the retirement testimonial given to Wanzer partner and mechanical superintendent John Nathaniel Tarbox just two months later, when his men offered their 'regret' that 'this little incident' might 'mar the good feeling ... kindness and gentlemanly manner in which you have invariably treated your men.[42] The rapidity with which normalcy was restored at the Wanzer plant – by all accounts the very centre of conflict over the nine-hours issue – reveals the general lack of depth and inertia that differences between masters and men had in the overarching context of craft mutuality.

The quick death of the nine-hours fervour is further revealed in the report that scarcely a month after it had unfurled its flag in mass procession on Hamilton's city streets, the Nine Hours League could muster only 300 men for a 'mass meeting' in Market Square, 'one half of whom,' hopefully noted the *Spectator*, 'have no sympathy with the movement.' The purpose of outlining the limits of the Nine Hour Movement's actual disruption is not to belittle it or to question the sincerity of its adherents, but to provide a starting point to question further the nature of the disruption it caused.

The Nature of the Nine Hours Movement

What emerges from this portrait of craftsworker activity in Hamilton in the spring and early summer of 1872 is an image of craft mutuality maintained. This is not to argue that some journeymen did not realize their idea of craft practice had diverged, at least on this issue, from that their masters. This view is further strengthened when one considers the language craftsworkers used to express themselves in this situation. Some bold assertions pertaining to the inevitable conflict between capital and labour can be identified. Not surprisingly, select commentators in the *Ontario Workman* most forcefully expressed working-class understandings of the Nine Hours Movement. 'Slowly and gradually, but earnestly and successfully,' held one contributor, 'labor is freeing itself from the thralldom of capital.'[43] Another commentator declared that 'employers seldom if ever look at trade questions from their workingmen's standpoint, consequently their view of trades questions are generally inimical to the true interests of the men.'[44] The same issue occasioned the insights of another observer on the growing divergence of fortune between masters and men: 'the rapid increase in wealth through the introduction and improvement of machinery, capitalists becoming millionaires in a few years, building themselves palaces, living in luxury, while the workingmen who make the wealth cannot raise themselves homes of their own, prove there is "something rotten in the state."'[45] The leadership of the Nine Hours Movement aired similar pronouncements. Toronto nine-hours activist John Hewitt declared to the assembled delegates of the newly formed Canadian Labor Protection and Mutual Improvement Association in Hamilton's Temperance Hall in early May, for example, that 'too long had the workingmen been the tools of capital.'[46]

Hewitt was well known for strong statements in recognition of class conflict. However, as John Battye has noted of Hewitt in particular and the rhetoric of the Nine Hours Movement in general, strong statements of class conflict were far more the exception than the rule.[47] The fact was that assertions reflective of working-class experience, while not absent, were by no means dominant in this struggle. Far more common were exclamations that stressed the mutuality of interests between employers and employed.

Statements of mutuality often originated with capitalists themselves. Prominent merchant, railway promoter, and hardware manufacturer Colonel William McGiverin, for instance, declared that, while he could not support a cause that involved 'secret organizations and combinations,' he did support the nine-hours idea in principle as long as its implementation was congruous with 'that perfect harmony and those cordial relations which should always exist between employers and employed.'[48] David McCulloch, himself having recently made the transition from wage-earning craftsman to craftsman-employer, pressed this point repeatedly on the editorial page of the *Spectator*. Anticipating the negative impact of the idea on social relations in Canada during the early days of the movement, McCulloch warned local craftsworkers against recreating 'the unfortunate collisions between capital and labour which have taken place in other countries' over this issue. Masters and men in Canada, he added, 'have been hitherto free' of such fractious social relations.[49] McCulloch echoed these sentiments repeatedly through the rise and decline of the movement. As tensions grew in the few days before 15 May, he editorialized, 'we regret deeply the rupture of the friendly relations which have hitherto existed between employers and their men. In no country of the world have these been more satisfactory than in Canada.' If this divisive course continued, he added, the damage to workplace relations would be considerable 'and in all probability it would take years to restore them.' It is worth noting the great relief expressed by McCulloch over this issue only a week after the mass procession: 'We are glad to see this has been a good-humoured fight, and that neither party have lost their tempers over it. In a short time we hope to see the old cordial relationships re-established and the work of the season proceeding as usual.'[50]

Such detached observers of the Nine Hours Movement as 'Occulus,' self-styled 'neither an *employer* nor *employee*,' also worked to reinforce craftsworkers' culture of mutualism. Evidently responding to an attack on Hamilton employers levied by one workingman likely in the rival *Hamilton Standard*, Occulus issued a sharp rebuke to any divisive class-bound view of the city's industrial social relations: 'I have yet to know which of the employers of Hamilton are "tyrants" and treat their employees as "serfs"; which of them live in luxury, on "boned turkey, rich wine, etc."' Rather, he exclaimed, 'Everyone knows that they [employers] are almost to a man from the same ranks as yourselves, and have risen to their present position by their own achievements in industry, and not by stinting their labor to nine hours a day.' Denying the true nature of Canada's industrial relations and adopting such a short-sighted course as that seen in the 'continually recurring *strikes* in England,' he added, would have the effect of simply driving work out of the country.[51] It is no surprise that exclamations of craft mutualism were such a common feature in the debate over the nine-hours idea, since, as chapter 3 has shown, this culture was still firmly in place in Hamilton by 1872.

Many craftsworkers involved in the movement – including most of its leaders – still framed their world view in these terms. GWR shop worker Robert Parker, a prominent player in the Hamilton Nine Hours League, reassured his mass brethren assembled to consider the nine-hours issue that 'this was not a revolt against properly constituted authority.' More directly articulate on the issue was Nine Hours League secretary James Ryan, the prime mover of many of the events of 1872. Ryan could not have been clearer: 'There is no real antagonism between capital and labour, but mutual dependence.'[52] This is not to suggest that one or another of these views became exclusive to Hamilton craftsworkers that year, but that the culture of mutualism was still hegemonic. The faint cracks that were discernible between masters and men were understood by most craftsworkers as atypical of Hamilton or Canada (or as more typical of other parts of the more mature industrial world, such as the old country) and generally glossed over with the brush of the dominant culture. The remainder of this examination of the Nine Hours Movement will consider the dimensions of this hegemonic culture in more depth.

From its beginning – and contrary to the notion that 'the movement came under immediate attack'[53] – the nine-hours idea was generally accepted as a principle on virtually all fronts. A number of members of the city's elite, for instance, publicly declared their support for the cause at the movement's founding meeting in late January. The merchant T.C. Watkins's unflagging support for the movement has been amply documented. Such notable members of the local elite as Colonel William McGiverin, A.T. Wood, and John Winer also pledged support that day. McGiverin, a hardware merchant, politician, railway promoter, and local saddlery hardware manufacturer, declared to the workingmen and others assembled at the Mechanics' Hall that 'his heart was in the movement,' and urged organizers to make their local push for nine hours a national movement. Proclaiming that it 'was in the interest of employers not to work their men to death,' he declared his steadfast belief that employers across Canada would 'cheerfully comply' with the men's request. Following McGiverin on the platform was merchant, politician, and railway promoter Andrew Trew Wood, who proclaimed that 'the matter at stake was an important one' and readily added his endorsement to the movement. Local druggist and glass and patent medicine manufacturer John Winer also 'heartily indorsed [*sic*] the nine-hours movement' that day.[54] McGiverin and Wood's reasons for jumping on the nine-hours bandwagon likely had at least something to do with political expediency. However, their support must also be considered as but one small representative element of the appreciable number of employers in Hamilton who expressed at least some degree of endorsement of this idea by the more direct method of granting nine hours to their men (begrudgingly or not), thereby reinforcing in the minds of most masters and men that their respective notions of craft had not diverged.

David McCulloch's *Spectator* also supported the nine-hours idea. This may seem surprising, given that this publication became the source of some of the most scathing attacks on the Nine Hours

League as winter turned to spring that year. As we shall see in more depth below, however, while the *Spectator* came to disapprove of the movement's methods it did support its principles. In alerting its readers to the initial meeting of the movement, McCulloch conceded that nine hours was an 'important question,' but cautioned the movement's leaders that its implementation should be 'handled with ... wisdom.'[55] Another staunch supporter of the nine hours idea was A.T. Freed, the newspaper's assistant editor. While he supported the cause, however, he could not endorse the methods of its leaders. He had particular differences with James Ryan, whose publicly grandiose tactics he deplored.[56]

The reasons why the Nine Hours League lost the endorsement of the above supporters will be addressed in detail later on. This broad support, however, first compels a more in-depth look at the character of this struggle. The nine-hours struggle was, by and large, a debate over the defence, maintenance, even expansion of craftsworkers' place in the modern polity. Champions of the cause envisioned widespread social advances if they prevailed. While glimpses at their vision are provided in other studies, it is important to reiterate them here.

Many supporters argued there was a direct connection between the implementation of nine hours and the enrichment of family life.[57] This sentiment had been a feature of the Hamilton shorter-time movement since at least the mid-1850s. The Reverend David Inglis received rave reviews for his lecture 'Labour, Its Blessing and Its Curse' at the Mechanics' Hall in 1856. Speaking to local 'masters,' he urged that they 'give the workingman time for relaxation which he finds in the bosom of his family, in the instruction of his children.'[58] Sentiments of this sort were often front and centre in speeches from those extolling the nine-hours cause a decade and a half later. Prominent nine-hours delegate and GWR boilermaker Robert Parker moved a resolution at the 29 January mass meeting that read in part that 'the time thus gained' from the shorter working day would allow workingmen to better carry out 'the various duties and responsibilities of fathers and Citizens.' Nine hours was a social necessity, proclaimed Dr Hall to the workingmen assembled an important league demonstration at Queen's Park in early April. The working class, he argued, must enjoy the requisite time for them to 'instruct their families in the general ways of sobriety and good order.' A burdensome work schedule unjustly prevented a working man from 'putting on his best clothes and going out with his family' except on Sundays, when doing so meant not attending church.[59] League secretary James

Ryan's declaration that 'we also wish time to cultivate social and domestic virtues' was equally forceful on the issue.[60]

The issue of how the nine-hour day related to family life received perhaps its most eloquent and detailed expression in a letter to the *Ontario Workman* from a 'printer's wife' in early May. Railing against *Globe* editorials suggesting men's presence at home an hour earlier each day would be ill-received by women for its infringement upon their 'alone' and 'gossiping' time, this commentator held that more time at home would increase a family's overall level of enjoyment. She explained that her own 'worse half' had recently been granted an extra hour of leisure each day. The result: 'an extra hour in mutual improvement ... The extra hour is spent at home ... in the shape of gardening, fixing up things generally, or reading and writing, and – miserable fellow – playing with the children.' As a parting jab, this feisty woman suggested that while this arrangement had an almost universally positive application, it might not suit a select few. She could well understand, for instance, why George Brown's wife might not wish an extra hour a day in the company of her 'arbitrary and overbearing' life mate.[61]

Mentioned even more than extra time in mutual improvement with one's family, however, the nine-hour day could be fruitfully applied to other kinds of 'improving activity.' An hour less labour each day would have an additionally positive bodily effect on the craftsworker. It was partly in an effort to 'better our physical constitutions,' explained league secretary James Ryan, that area craftsworkers lobbied for shorter hours.[62] Calling overwork 'Labour's Curse,' Rev Inglis had laid this sentiment down to Hamilton craftsworkers a decade and a half earlier: 'Let there be no overworking. Let the master forbear from forcing such physical toil upon his men as will drag them down in utter weariness of body.'[63] The *Times* similarly added its support to local journeymen bakers in their struggle for shorter hours in 1862, explaining that 'spare time ... is indispensable to health and the sustaining of physical energy.'[64] In the context of the nine-hours' struggle the merchant Thomas Watkins defended Hamilton craftsworkers' need to 'spend their time so as to improve bodily health.'[65] In the dying days of the movement, a dejected Ryan complained that 'we are degenerating and sometimes spoiling our health by overwork at the anvil or vice.'[66]

This argument was usually packaged with warnings of another, perhaps more catastrophic, effect of longer hours of labour. The mind, too, was a victim. Rev Inglis made this connection directly: 'Labour's curse is its grinding down man's body and thus humiliating his mind.'[67] To Ryan's urging of bettering 'our physical constitutions' was attached the exhortation to 'increase our mental power.' 'We want not more money,' he added, 'but more *brains*.'[68] 'With more leisure,' he explained in an address to the Dundas Nine Hours League, 'would come more mental power.'[69] In the parlance of the day, it was in the cultivation of 'mental culture' to which an extra hour of leisure would be best applied.

Some form of structured educational activity was necessary to facilitate this goal. Boilermaker Robert Parker held that too many hours of labour left the workingman in gross 'want of instruction.' He moved the unanimously accepted resolution at the league's foundation meeting 'that the time thus gained [from shorter hours] is necessary to enable us to improve our education.'[70] Indeed, the application of wanted leisure time to various forms of study became a common feature of virtually all declarations of support for the movement. A variant of Ryan's oft-cited cry 'We want more time to study and learn' was repeated in myriad forms by the league secretary throughout the struggle. The pro-nine hours Hamilton *Standard,* too, lobbied for 'time for recreation and study.'[71]

The previous chapter outlined Hamilton craftsworkers' strong penchant for self-improvement through self-education. Nine-hours advocates consistently echoed this fundamental association between mental improvement and craftsworkers' increased abilities to contribute to general social and material improvement. Central features of the arguments for nine hours of labour included consistent reference to such positive benefits of augmented mental activity as increased 'productive power' or 'inventive genius.'

Providing craftsworkers with adequate study time, it was proposed, would add directly to their own and the country's productive potential. 'Our country, though young, is destined to be great and glorious,' proclaimed league secretary James Ryan. To keep the momentum going in this direction, he added, craftsworkers must have extra time to 'study and learn' to become 'more skilled in the use of ... machinery.' National competitive advantage would thus be aided by the increased 'mental power' of Canadian mechanics: 'so if we cannot equal our Yankee neighbours in the variety of our undertaking, we can at least compete with them in the artistic finish of our productions.'[72] Sustaining this 'fast-rising and very enterprising country' would be impossible, argued the carpenter C.F. Cole, without the further cultivation and 'cooperation of the skilled hand and intellectual mind of the artisan.'[73] The *Standard* made the connection direct: 'time for recreation and study would enable [workingmen] to increase their productive power.'[74] Nine-hours advocates, moreover, offered a liberating vision of more production with less labour. 'If [craftsworkers] had an extra hour a day,' exclaimed C.F. Cole, 'they would be able to introduce mechanical improvements which would much reduce the demand for manual labour.'[75] By spending leisure hours devising mechanical improvements, the *Standard* argued, 'the deficiency in production would not be proportionate to the shortening hours of labour' for craftsworkers.[76]

It is interesting to note that this identified need for mental improvement in the name of increased competitiveness was often promoted as part of a general enthusiasm for the introduction of modern machinery into the craft workplace. Allowing more time each day for workers to cultivate their 'inventive genius' by applying their mental power became a key component of the shorter-hours argument. The craftsworker who improved his 'mental culture,' declared T.C. Watkins, would inevitably 'add largely to the cultivation of the arts and sciences by improving the present and inventing new machinery.'[77] C.F. Cole bemoaned the fact that men 'who had ideas for new inventions or improvements in machinery, were now so exhausted by their day's labor, and had so little time, that the ideas were often lost.' According to Watkins, fostering inventive capacity was the only true road to competitive advantage. At the founding meeting of the movement he argued that workingmen's 'interchange of ideas with others of their draft' led directly to improvement: 'Thus workingmen rise to the highest positions, new inventions are found out and the world is enriched by the products of genius thus developed.'[78] Watkins stuck to his guns in the movement's Indian summer, arguing that workingmen must be provided sufficient time to 'improve their inventive faculty; without which they cannot advance and make that progress which the present period demands.'[79] More time for cultivation of the mind would do away with labour's drudgery while heightening its competitive value in the economy by allowing craftsworkers to apply their own smarts to improvement of the production process.

Time for the mental improvement of the young craftsworker would help effect his social elevation. The craftsworker's ability to 'rise to the highest positions' was a key concern of nine-hours advocates seeking the smooth functioning of the modern polity, and who were themselves steeped in the culture of the local transmodal social environment. It is worth noting, for instance, that a number of leaders of the movement, men such as league president and shoemaker John Pryke, the president of the newly formed tinners' union W.R. Spencer, and the printer A.T. Freed were men who achieved varying degrees of success either in self-employment or within larger organizations in the period surrounding 1872.

The granting of the nine-hour day as it related to craftsworkers' general social elevation received frequent comment. E.K. Dodds exclaimed to an excited crowd of nine-hours supporters gathered at Queen's Park in April that in Canada 'they had no aristocracy, but the aristocracy of labour, and the man who by the sweat of his brow made himself a position, stood equal to any man in the country.' Sometimes this elevation was presented in general terms, as an uplifting and multifaceted 'good time to come.' James Ryan, for example, chimed to a Dundas audience that with shorter hours would come 'more mental power, more moral strength,' which would in turn 'accelerate the speed of the good time coming and confer upon themselves, their children and their country, a permanent and invaluable blessing, that physically, intellectually and socially would repay them a thousandfold.'[80] But more often the connection to personal mobility through the craft ranks was made explicit. Commenting on a local co-operative stove and general castings foundry scheme, the *Hamilton Standard* opined that these men 'whose skill, ingenuity and labor have made their employers rich ... if properly directed the same time and talents can enrich themselves.'[81] Whether productive power, inventive capacity, the metering of bodily strength, attention to family, or the cultivation of the craftsworkers' mental aspects of skill through study, shorter hours was consistently touted as necessary to social elevation.

As an earlier section of this chapter demonstrated, commentators often spoke of craftsworkers' elevated place in the modern world, a position to which the properly motivated craftsworker was well within his rights to expect. These sentiments fit firmly into the orbit of the self-made and the self-improved craftsworker that Chapters 5 and 6 showed were still firmly embedded in the Hamilton crafts landscape by 1872. Indeed, as both those chapters amply document, much of the most penetrating discussions of craftsworkers' social elevation – and their right to it – occurred during the months of that year when the nine-hours question was in full consideration and often appeared in organs born out of the movement such as the *Ontario Workman*.

That craftsworkers had a right to pursue these lofty goals that nine hours of labour would bring was explained repeatedly. According to James Ryan the position of Canadian workingmen in this struggle was a matter of them 'simply arousing themselves to their position in unison with their power.' Echoing many of his contemporaries, he argued that such antiquated forms of control as aristocratic power had no place in Canada: 'labour was at one time the slave of aristocracy, but now it is fast becoming the patent of nobility.'[82] The time and social environment was now ripe, argued his compatriot Robert Parker, for workingmen to 'fulfill with credit to ourselves and advantage to the State, the various duties and responsibilities of Fathers and citizens.'[83] What workingmen wanted from decreased hours of labour was the perpetuation – indeed, the expansion – of a social environment they had sampled and wished to cultivate further. In the era of self-improvement, time to 'study and learn' would allow the diligent craftsworker to assume his rightfully earned place of respect in the modern social structure. Consistent improvements to technology brought about by the constant exercise of inventive powers uninhibited by unceasing toil would create an upward spiral in which all craftsworkers could partake of the fruits not just of social elevation in the realm of work, but also in family life and citizenship. Removing the barriers that obstructed the smooth operation of this system was a central aspiration of the 'nine-hour pioneers.'

The above were precepts, as previously noted, that were generally accepted within the craftsworker community. To argue that, in this light, the nine-hours agitation was not characterized by a fair degree of conflict, however, would be to deny the historicity of these events. Schisms *did* occur. Their nature, however, needs delineation.

Much of the conflict that did occur was itself confined within the broad culture of self-improvement. To begin with, it is important to recognize that the very question of nine hours itself was set up and considered by various members of the craft community – as were other questions within the broad culture of self-improvement – in the classic style of the debate. As chapter 6 demonstrated this was a convention with which a good number of local craftsworkers were quite familiar. In the case of the nine-hours question it was a form of exchange of ideas that was transported out of the somewhat abstracted and private forum of the debating or literary society onto the public stage, where opposing sides made claims and rebutted counter-claims in open forum under the ever-watchful eye of the media and also exercised their emergent notions of the proper masculine practice of public citizenship.

As was customary in the semi-private functioning of the debating society, the public stage for consideration of the nine-hours issue was expected to be one in which the dialectical presentation of well-considered opinion untainted by emotion would allow Hamilton's great mass of self-improving, level-headed men to arrive at some unanimity of opinion as to which line of reasoning should rightly prevail. Upon hearing of the first mass meeting to consider the nine-hour's question, for instance, David McCulloch, Hamilton's leading arbiter of self-improvement, warned this meeting's participants that 'this, it will be admitted, is a very important question, and its consideration ought to be approached in a spirit of dispassionate inquiry.'[84] McCulloch was backed up in this sentiment on the podium at the meeting by hardware merchant Andrew Wood, who, in expressing his support for the nine-hours principle, warned the assembled workingmen to 'ask it on just and reasonable grounds. It must be a matter of reciprocity between the employers and employees which they should discuss among themselves calmly and dispassionately.'[85] When the nine-hours issue ignited its first workplace confrontation at the Wilson, Bowman shop in February, McCulloch's *Spectator* repeated its warning: 'We earnestly entreat the thoughtful among the workingmen to look this question calmly in the face and study all its bearings.'[86]

It was within this framework that the greater debate about the nine-hours issue transpired among thoughtful members of Hamilton's craft community. As stated before, virtually all commentators on this question agreed in principle that nine hours was a desirable object that, if instituted thoughtfully, would lead directly to craftsworkers' personal and social betterment. This speaks volumes about the general and continued unanimity in craft values between masters and men. Opinions differed, however, over the practicalities of its implementation.

Much of the debate over the practical implementation of the nine-hours system revolved around issues of political economy. Here, members of the craft community brought the full force of their knowledge honed through self-improved study and private debate into public scrutiny. Time and again those railing against the Nine Hours League and their allies for their attempts to force local and, at best, regional employers to grant their request raised the bogey of damaged competitive ability to bolster their argument against what they saw as a limited, narrow, and short-sighted implementation of an otherwise laudable idea.

Some months before the movement began to congeal, the *Times* declared the issue of shorter hours to be a topic of 'world-wide interest ... and probably the most important social problem which lies in the pathway of the future.'[87] Offering editorial counsel to local workingmen on the eve of the foundational meeting of the league some months later, David McCulloch too conceded this to be 'a very important question.' But to this he added a stern warning to meeting participants regarding the folly of any rash and narrow action: 'We presume there is no intention to make it merely a local movement. It will be obvious to all that the adoption of the system in any one locality without its being adopted generally would be ruinous to the manufacturing industry of that locality by placing its manufacturers at a disadvantage in competing with their rivals in other localities.'[88] Andrew Wood, who lent his support to the cause and also exclaimed 'the matter at stake was an important one,' gave the assembled workingmen a similar caution and echoed this sentiment on the meeting dais. The movement for shorter hours, he urged, 'should not be confined to Hamilton, for if other places such as Montreal, Kingston or any manufacturing place kept up the old ten-hour system, Hamilton would not be able to compete with them, and they would then have to leave Hamilton.' Urging nine-hours organizers to broaden the scope of their thinking, he cheerfully added that he had 'no hesitation in saying that if the movement was made universal the employers would cheerfully accede to the request.'[89]

Indeed, it appears the leaders of the movement did take these concerns to heart, at least to a degree. They assembled a regional coalition in support of the nine-hours cause that was unprecedented among Canadian workingmen to this date. They also offered the fairly consistent rebuttal argument that Canada was lagging behind international trends in regards to hours of labour. If Canada's two main competitors – Great Britain and the United States – could find the wherewithal to put shorter hours into practice, then why not Canada? 'England has conceded the principle of our claim,' noted James Ryan at the same meeting where Wood aired his sentiments, 'What is right *there* cannot be wrong *here*.'[90] John Drysdale, in his capacity as chair of the grand nine-hours celebration at the Crystal Palace on 15 May, noted 'the movement ... had spread throughout Great Britain and the United States and was now spreading here.'[91] The *Ontario Workman* also noted this: 'The competitors of Canadian manufacturers in foreign markets have consented to a reduction of the hours of labor among their men, so that the reduction here entails no extra hardship, for it simply places the manufacturers of both places upon the same footing as they were before the agitation commenced in either country.'[92]

Those sceptical of the league, however, remained unconvinced. While movement organizers had made impressive inroads in towns and cities throughout central Canada (mostly southern Ontario), these roots did not run deep. Nor did they involve much more than a declaration of intention by one party (workingmen) to implement a system the problems of which their employers had not been given sufficient time to consider on their merits. As 'Occulus' explained, 'the question involved is not the ability of the workingman to exercise absolute *right* as to his working or not working under the only conditions he chooses to prescribe, but it is one of *expediency* and *safe experiment*, concurrent with the acquiescence of those whose enterprise and capital give him the source of employment.' Taking a jab at the argument of league allies that the implementation of this system in other countries justified its introduction in Canada, he added, 'the curtailment of ten hours work a day to nine hours is a problem yet to be solved. It is now upon trial in the Mother-Country; but whether it will eventuate beneficially to the workingman or the community generally, or operate disastrously, by alienating from home that enterprise and capital to cheaper markets of labor abroad, remains to be seen.'[93]

Indeed, when league officials issued their unilateral intention to implement nine hours as a set days work in Hamilton on and after 15 May, league critics were quick to offer a sharp rebuke to what was to them an obviously retrograde step. McCulloch's *Spectator*, as usual, led the charge. Desperately urging that the issue be returned to the bounds of respectful and balanced debate, this journal cautioned: 'We earnestly entreat the thoughtful among the workingmen to look at this question calmly in the face and study all its bearings; the attempt to introduce the system in Hamilton on a day which can now be named we cannot think but is ill-advised.'[94] McCulloch was joined in his sentiments shortly thereafter by Colonel McGiverin, who similarly withdrew his hearty support for movement with the declaration 'I cannot give further countenance or support to a movement which I am now convinced ... must prove disastrous to the prosperity and best interests of the city, as well as a dire calamity to the workingmen and their families.'[95]

The unanimity of opinion against the tactics of the league and its allies – as well as the general acceptance of the competitive-damage argument – was perhaps best represented in the preamble to the resolution preceding the first long published list of Hamilton manufacturers vowing their opposition to the Nine Hours Movement and avowal to stick to the ten-hours system:

> Whereas, Certain of the Mechanics and Workingmen of Hamilton propose to initiate the Nine Hour system in this city, and as the introduction of such a system would be most disastrous alike to Employers and Employees by retarding our Manufacturing and Commercial advancement, giving Competitors throughout the Dominion an advantage over us, so that Hamilton

> would now lose her proud position as the First manufacturing City in Ontario, thereby inevitably crippling our industries. Therefore, be it resolved That we, the Manufacturers, Builders, and other Tradesmen of the City of Hamilton feel it our duty to oppose this movement.[96]

It was upon this issue that the lines of battle over the nine hours of labour were solidly drawn.

Wider support in principle for the nine-hours idea diminished as the actions and proclamations of the league and its close allies unfolded in the early months of 1872. Critics of this group offered increasingly low opinions of the rash action of the league and its supporters, critiquing the absence of cool, rational debate and arguing that its leaders were increasingly influenced by destructive and ill-considered emotions. When 'Occulus' pleaded with league members to back off and allow 'safe experiment,' he was urging the nine-hours men to return to the realm of reasoned debate. His call to consider the cause's 'expediency' was a plea for a return to detachment. A similar light was cast upon this schism when printer and *Spectator* assistant editor A.T. Freed explained his waning support for the movement to his readers in late February. 'Personally I am in favour of the Nine Hour Movement, and I expect to remain so,' he explained. His problem, however, lay with the style and tactics adopted by those heading up the league: 'The difference between Mr. Ryan and myself is that while I prefer to seek the attainment of the object in view by quiet organization ... he has a great predilection for speech making at public meetings which certainly can do no great good, and appears to have done some harm.'[97] While remaining a supporter of the nine-hour day, Freed distanced himself from what he considered to be the short-sighted and hasty decisions of the league leadership.

Straying outside the accepted conventions of the culture of self-improvement, however, was not the only front upon which the league and its allies received the disapproval of members of the local craft community. The nature of the sources themselves favours the voice of masters in this dissent. But this should not be mistaken for evidence of class conflict. While less evident in the literary record, it must also be remembered – as evidenced earlier in this chapter – that the league did not receive the overwhelming support of the city's journeymen. Resistance to the nine-hours idea also arose from men who, while recognizing social elevation aspirations and rights, did not subscribe as heavily to the general culture of self-improvement. This group appears to have been constituted of men more steeped in the side of transmodal culture that emphasized the 'self-made craftsworker,' men who subscribed to the perhaps older notion that craft success in work and life was a product of good old-fashioned hard work as opposed to more modern notions of theoretical education and its ingenious application to productive enterprise.

This group is more rightly considerd to embody a variation on craftsworker thought, rather than be as a coherent group of individuals committed to one vision of craft community as opposed to another. In general, this group appears to have argued that the successful craftsworker must exercise a balance between indulgence in modern self-improvement and old-fashioned toil, industry, and prudence. As an ideological position, this was a critique that could be made both by wholehearted advocates of self-improvement or more traditional masters who had worked their way to the top through time-honoured methods. David McCulloch, for instance, was one of the city's pre-eminent advocates of self-improvement. But he, too, counselled shorter-hour advocates who clamoured for the elevation they expected to get from more time in the reading room not to lose sight of where success was ultimately made. Asking the nine-hours advocates to reflect more deeply on their grandiose visions of more time to study and learn, for example, he exhorted: 'Let the workingmen become their own employers, and they can work just such hours a day as their inclinations and the industrial conditions which surround them may determine.'[98] Put in the position to which they evidently aspired, argued McCulloch, workingmen would soon realize their claims for more study time, though laudable, were exaggerated and impractical. After all, McCulloch himself – and a number of other local self-made craftsworkers – had found adequate time for self-improvement within their busy traditional work schedules to facilitate their own personal enlightenment and rise through the ranks.

There was, nonetheless, a more traditional strain to this line of thought that appeared with some consistency throughout the struggle. Furniture manufacturer James Reid – a skilled craftsworker in his own right and former master to a number of self-made craftsworkers in the city – took issue with an article that appeared in the *Standard* in late January which offered the logic that if shorter hours were granted the net result would be that workingmen would get more done in nine hours than they had in ten. He commented that the only workingmen capable of such a feat were 'dishonest scoundrels who can put ten hours' work into nine.' Declaring the statement a 'gross libel upon workingmen,' he explained such a pace would be unnatural to production; 'no honest man can do it except for a day or two at a push; but it could not be kept up.' According to Reid, ten hours was the system tried and tested to best accommodate the proper work rhythms of the 'honest man.'[99]

The point of view was given its best definition by 'Occulus,' who opined shortly thereafter on the reasons for Hamilton's success thus far as a manufacturing centre. Rebutting the inflated rhetoric of an unidentified nine-hours supporter, he thundered that almost all local masters had 'risen to their present position by their own achievements in industry, and not by stinting their labour to nine hours a day. Go ye and do likewise, but in order to do so you must abandon this nine-hours idea.'[100] 'Occulus' did not decry self-improvement activities, but without hard work and commitment manifested in long hours of labour, the young craftsworker could not expect the elevation that he so sought. A letter from 'Old Settler' ('who works from sun-rise to sun-set, and feels all the better for it') printed in the *Spectator* a few days later was even more forceful on the issue:

> Workmen of Hamilton of the *present day* beware what you are about. When under the providence of God I came to this town, expecting, at least hoping, to better my condition in life, I found that the best mechanics were working for seventy-five cents a day, and were contented and happy; and as the town expanded, and genuine labour became more in request, wages rose to a dollar a day, all was peace and contentment, and reviewing that time and recalling to my mind how many of our most respectable citizens of the present day are the men who did the work on these small means, who built the city, and actually the cause of its existence by their industry; men who were mechanics in every sense of the word, men who could do an honest day's *labor* for an honest day's pay ... These are the men who by perseverance made Hamilton, and who are now called by pretenders, upstarts and warts on the face of society.
>
> Now, if these pretenders to being laboring men would follow the example of these upstarts and warts, it would be much better for themselves and the public.[101]

The picture that emerges from all this is that of a generation of craftsworkers who attributed their success to hard work and were put out with a younger generation's seeming unwillingness to do the same. In a dynamic that has been often repeated throughout history, this older group expressed a deep-seated concern that their younger counterparts risked succumbing to one of the traits of character inimical to the self-made craftsworker – laziness. One *Spectator* article, for example, offered its opinion on one of the potentially harmful effects of trade unions. 'Why will honest and industrious workingmen,' it asked, 'continue to tax themselves for the support of the idle and incapable members of the order? And why should employers be forced by trade unions to give place and pay lazy fellows who do not earn their salt?'[102] The proprietors of the Wilson, Bowman Sewing Machine Company used similar reasoning in defending their decision to stand fast against the strikers at their plant in February. 'We regret exceedingly that things should have come to pass, but the blame rests not on our shoulders,' but rather, they explained in a public letter, 'on the shoulders of the lazy and unprincipled agitators, who never performed one honest day's labour.'[103] That this group viewed the goals of the nine-hours advocates as existing outside the bounds of the accepted conventions of self-made craftsworker manhood is revealed somewhat obliquely in one humorous aside published in McCulloch's' *Spectator* in late February: 'A stylish young man riding on a splendid grey horse with all the harness rolled in a conglomerated mass about the horse's shoulders, created quite a sensation among the farmers on the Wellington Square Road last Friday. Some of the ignorant yeomen thought him the advanced guard of the nine-hour delegates from Toronto, but we have since learned he was a commercial traveler whose buggy broke down.[104] Indeed, the use of the nine-hours delegate as young fop is significant as it served as a universally identifiable signifier of youthful laziness and waste. It was with similar glee that McCulloch inserted a poetic postmortem for the Nine Hours Movement (the '*h*infant') into his newspaper that again touched on this theme:

Had our *h*infant but lived, we ne'er might
Have worked,
But sponged on its earnings, and labor have
shirked;[105]

The Nine Hours League and its defenders attempted to weather this storm by standing firm against its critics. In this endeavor the league was particularly eager to (re-)establish its vision of the self-made, self-improving transmodal craftsworker as being a concept with a place within the recognized conventions of level-headed and dispassionate debate. To facilitate this, the league turned the tables on its transgressors and accused them of straying outside established convention. Nowhere was this more in evidence than at the grand workingmen's celebration on 15 May. There, speaker after speaker held up for public view the balanced, well-considered, and socially positive image of the league. John Drysdale, chair of the celebration, explained to the crowd that it was the 'bosses' who had failed to see reason:

> We have proposed to our bosses to meet us on a platform and discuss this question with us but they have refused to do so. We have seen that the Movement came from the East, from which direction all great and moral movements come, and is now spreading over the west ... Without assuming any higher position than our station affords we asked the bosses to meet us and discuss the question and they refused. Consequently we had to form a platform of our own and we have done so ... We said that the 15th of May should be the day on which we should expect an answer from them, and from which time nine hours should constitute a day's work. The people of Hamilton have shown that that day has come.[106]

John Hewitt, visiting from Toronto, picked up on this theme, pointing out that when this great social question was initially taken up by local workingmen, 'would the employers come forward and discuss the subject with them? No. They had been asked to do so but refused.' It was the ill-considered action of employers, argued Hewitt, that forced workingmen to turn to the respectability of unionism to boldly state their considered position.' Offering particularly penetrating insight on this issue that day, as usual, was James Ryan, who declared to the workingmen thus assembled 'praise is due to you for the manner in which you have conducted yourselves in regard to this movement.' In contrast to their employers, he continued, 'you have shown today how you can treat meetings of the capitalists, held in garrets and taverns, by your open conduct.' It was workingmen, claimed Ryan, who were the ones to state boldly their convictions and stand by them in public 'like men.'[107]

Conclusion: If Not Now, When?

Read one way it is tempting to see debate over this issue – with master and men, arrayed as they were, in opposition to each other – as signifying a growing oppositional climate between them. It is likely that in the experience and minds of some craftsworkers a more class-conscious variant of craft culture was taking shape. But while such understandings could compete with older, more hegemonic craft ideologies, they could also co-exist with them. To conclude that the Nine Hours Movement signified or presaged some sort of opposition rooted in the class relations of capitalism would be premature – but not by much, as will be suggested below. What emerged from this debate was the sense that what some masters and men considered the norms of their mutualistic culture were diverging, though this divergence hardly represented an essential rupture. The contrast here of some master's vision of self-improvement being combined with continued hard work and some journeymen's vision of self-improvement involving less time for work does not signify any fundamental break (or even much in the way of the constituent elements of a future break). Rather, what it points to is a continued variety of paternalism exercised by some masters in the interest of their charges, to whom they still felt a responsibility to nudge off any misguided track. To this point must be added the fact that, at its deepest, this debate did not represent a division between most masters and men in Hamilton, but only a select few. In most Hamilton workplaces, as earlier sections of this chapter have demonstrated, debate over the nine-hours issue, if it was a debate at all, took place well within the shared values and norms, the mutualism, of the craft workplace.

In the end, the panacea offered by the more militant members of the Nine Hours League – whose articulation of and proposed solution to the problem was a partly British and partly American import – did not make sense to most Hamilton craftsworkers, steeped as they were in the local transmodal environment. The promises it did offer – time for improvement, both domestic, physical, and mental – did have the broad approval of the local craftsworker population, but as a total package the drastic actions towards its implementation proposed by the league was understood by large numbers of craftsworkers as impractical and, on the whole, failed to illicit their active support. The players in this production – masters and men – all liked the tune but some of them disagreed on the arrangement. And, as this movement reached its crescendo, little did they know this was their swansong.

The contours of what unfolded after the early 1870s is not within the purview of this study. In conclusion, however, something in the order of an informed suggestion as to the likely 'fate' of the transmodal world of craft capitalism is in order. Capital concentration, market integration, mercantile participation, increasing economies of scale, and other features of mass production *would* come to typify industrial development in Hamilton sometime after the early 1870s. But when was this transition made and what were its contours? It seems most likely that these changes occurred as a prolonged process with roots in the economic depression of the mid-1870s but not fully dominant in the city until the 1890s or, perhaps, the turn of the twentieth century.

The lean years immediately following the terminal date of this study brought the harsh reality of capitalist contraction into sharp focus for craftsworkers of all stripes both in Hamilton and throughout Ontario. Unemployment became an immediate problem for large numbers of craftsworkers, but the depression appears to have also brought with it some important forces of structural economic change that knocked much industrial enterprise out of comfortable markets and more craftsworker-friendly modes of production. Some employers dealt with the downturn defensively, laying off workers, downsizing, or shutting down parts of their operations. Others faced the economic calamity with offensive manoeuvres, by seizing larger markets, introducing 'improved machinery,' or attacking labour costs. Needless to say, the intensified competition and move to concentration buried in these measures did much to erode the structural situation of craft-based enterprise.[108]

However, more significant concentration within Canada was impeded by a factor much more alarming to craftsworkers and industrialists alike – vastly increased competition from firms based in the United States. The cutting off of southern markets to Canadian goods through the reimposition of American import tariffs in 1866 compounded the ill fortunes of Canadian producers once the boom of the early 1870s wore off, and cheap American goods began to 'slaughter' the Canadian market.[109]

The answer to this problem for many Canadian producers, of course, was protection. As Craig Heron has suggested, however, in the minds of many manufacturers the promise of protection was limited and the realization that streamlining productive systems was a long-term necessity was pronounced.[110] A parliamentary committee investigating the condition of manufacturing in Canada in 1874, for example, reported that a protective tariff would allow smaller Canadian concerns to grow to the size of their 'unnatural' American competitors and, by adopting their modern productive efficiencies 'naturally,' build up large operations capable of producing cheaply for the consumer market.[111]

Hamilton craftsworkers experienced at first hand many features of the economic downturn. Wage reductions were commonplace. Unemployment was chronic. In an effort to alleviate this situation the *Spectator* began publishing the names of those seeking work.[112] The situation was further compounded by instability of employment at the Great Western Railway shops, heretofore the city's most secure workplace. The relocation of the GWR car shops to London in 1874 – an event unrelated to the depression – had a profound effect on the upward of 500 employees and their families affected by that move. Four years later, the GWR's remaining shop workers were given the choice of a four-day week or a one-third reduction in pay.[113] That animosity could result from this bleak economic situation was best evidenced in a strike/lockout between the Iron Molders' International Union and most of the city's founders that lasted from the late summer of 1874 through to the early spring of the next year.[114]

While a number of local firms succumbed, some did prosper. The local sewing machine industry provides one example. The Hespeler Sewing Machine Company, reportedly running at full steam and set for expansion in 1872, was idle and boarded up less than two years later. On the flip side was the Wanzer Company, which took the downturn as an opportunity to expand into the Maritimes, set up an American plant to bypass the U.S. tariff wall, and introduce a number of 'labour-saving' mechanical innovations to its local plant.[115] Already jangled by unemployment, then, there was also good evidence to local craftsworkers that their employers might be heading down a path that was hardly lined with their best interests. But it is likely this was simply the start of the process. As Ben Forster has concluded, there were still plenty of small producers around to benefit positively from the protective tariff when it was introduced after the economic recovery became apparent.[116]

However, this was likely the start of something, and it was accompanied by a number of other subtle but accelerating changes, many of which became increasingly evident by the 1880s. In this decade local competition intensified, especially after numerous local producers began to battle to open up Western markets.[117] Established industrial enterprise continued to grow. In the decade before 1881 capital invested in local enterprise increased a staggering 214 per cent, most of this likely occurring in the buoyant years at either end of the depression.[118]

This trend was intensified by the inducements held out by the National Policy. This happened in traditional sectors. American interests, for example, bought and invested heavily in the dormant GWR rolling mills in 1879. But the tariffs also brought new sectors into existence. The city's industrial complexion was most fundamentally altered with the addition of an appreciably sized cotton textile industry in the form of the Hamilton Cotton Company (1880) and the Ontario Cotton Company (1881).[119] These operations were capital-intensive, a slap in the face to the trend of slow growth from small beginnings.

Indeed, to area craftsworkers all this growth, concentration, and move to large-capital enterprise by the 1880s was likely rightly perceived as a significant heightening of barriers to entry. Telling are John Milne's comments to the Labour Commission later in that decade:

> Q. – Can you tell us how many of the foundries in Hamilton were started by men who had been mechanics or workingmen? A. – I think nearly all of them were.
>
> Q. – Do you think that a mechanic in your line of business today has the same opportunities, or that a number of them joined together have the same opportunities for establishing a business as existed when you established yours? A. – I think there is hardly the same chance today.[120]

Coming from a man who had himself risen through the local ranks, these comments likely reflected a growing and widespread sentiment in the craft community that the keystone of the transmodal world – opportunity for advancement – was fast becoming dislodged.

A number of other factors also worked to increase the separation of the city's manufacturers from its craftsworkers during this decade. The sheer size and capital requirements of industry began to require a new and more impersonal style of ownership. The joint-stock company fast became the preferred vehicle through which this was achieved. The Hamilton Tool Company had adopted this style of ownership as early as 1873.[121] But as the 1880s unfolded the list grew long to include such local industrial fixtures as the Hamilton Bridge Company, Ontario Cotton Company, Hamilton Cotton Company, Canada Screw Company, Hamilton Forge Company, Ontario Tack Company, and many more.[122] Needless to say, in these concerns the immediacy of the artisan-headed concern was compromised.

Among already-established family-owned companies it is also likely that this was the decade in which first-generation craftsworker-proprietors began turning the reigns of ownership over to younger family members in significant numbers. The Gurney Brothers, among the city's earliest industrial proprietors, had begun to transfer responsibility to younger family members such as Edward Gurney Jr and John Tilden beginning in the mid-1870s. It is likely the Gurneys' slightly younger counterparts followed suit shortly thereafter. Joy Parr has outlined how this generational transfer could effectively disrupt the organic culture of the craft workplace in her study of the Knetchel Furniture Company in Hanover, Ontario.[123] Testimony given to the Labour Commission by Edward Gurney Jr gives some idea of how this change may have been experienced in local workplaces: 'When I built the present foundry I built a room (against the opinion of my father, who had more knowledge of such things than I), so that the men might have a place to wash in. I fitted it up with warm and cold water and everything of that kind. The men would not go there; they washed in the pots in the foundry, as they always had done, and as their fathers did before them. I got well laughed at, and by none moreso than the men.'[124]

The other important change easily discernible after the implementation of the National Policy tariffs was in the type of individual attracted to invest in industry. During the 1880s commercial and financial money was finally induced to flood into local industrial enterprise in a substantial way. Such men as hardware merchant Andrew Trew Wood, his partner Matthew Legatt, wholesale merchants James Young and Donald McInnes, the merchant-politician Adam Brown, contractor and railway promoter William Hendrie, and others acquired interests, assumed directorships in, and tirelessly promoted many of these new larger industrial concerns. In turn, a number of established industrial proprietors with artisanal origins became increasingly involved in the world of the merchant and financier. In league with local mercantile and financial interests, the Gurneys were the motive force behind the establishment of the Bank of Hamilton in 1872. Edward Gurney Sr served as a director of the bank from 1872 until 1884 and also sat on the first board of directors of the Hamilton Provident and Loan Society. Fellow foundryman Dennis Moore held directorships at various times in the Bank of Hamilton, the Canada Life Assurance Company, the Hamilton Cotton Company, the Traders' Bank, the Land Banking and Loan Company, and the Hamilton Provident and Loan Society. Clothing manufacturer William Sanford served as vice-president of the Hamilton Provident and Loan Society and as a director of the Exchange Bank.[125] The integration of business interests of men of artisanal, commercial, and financial backgrounds, as we know from chapter 3, was also reflected in patterns of residential convergence that took place sometime after 1871 and before the early 1890s. (The degree of intermarriage between the sons and daughters of these elite elements would also be an interesting research avenue.)

As these elite factions came together, as they agglomerated their capital, and as barriers to entry for small producers became increasingly insurmountable, a capitalist class was made. The making of a working class from journeymen craftsworkers, the other side of this equation, was likely expedited by the progressive choking off of networks of craft mobility – the discontinuation of access to the means of production – as part of this same process. It is no coincidence that it was during the 1880s – both in Hamilton and elsewhere – that labour conflict became at all common within and across industrial sectors.

Had all these factors combined to sweep away the transmodal world of craft capitalism by the early 1890s? Again, the answer is likely mixed. Craftsworkers did work under substantively different circumstances in many city shops. But journeymen's protest, expressed through their craft union and in the trade assemblies of the Knights of Labor, was still heavily steeped in producer ideology, the contours of which might be reassessed in light of this study.[126] In relative terms, the changes of the 1880s were also still new. Many of the old faces – craftsworkers who had started their own concerns in the 1860s or early 1870s – remained firmly entrenched in the industrial landscape. The momentum of the past would have still weighed heavily on the minds of local craftsworkers. As chapter 3 explained, there were still examples of local craftsworkers founding their own concerns (though likely in much smaller numbers) up through this decade. Small producers were admittedly on the decline by the 1890s, but as a number of studies have shown their persistence should not be underestimated. Market integration was still a going concern.[127]

Craftsworkers' circumstances may have been altered by this time but even more decisive change lay not far ahead. The turn of the twentieth century brought with it a number of factors that would have driven to dust the remnants of the transmodal world – a vast acceleration in corporate concentration, new elaborate and impersonal managerial systems, the recruitment of large, ethnically diverse new pools of labour, the importation of American-style production systems in the form of branch plants, a firm commitment to introduce mechanization and assault the skills of the craftsman wherever possible. This 'second industrial revolution' fundamentally involved the systematic and widespread introduction of the elements of mass production to the newly consolidated Canadian market.[128] The seeds for this change were sewn as early as the economic depression of the mid-1870s, but the marginalization of flexible specialized enterprise and the social world it spawned were the consequences of a process that likely took several decades.

Conclusion

Craft capitalism best describes the variant of industrialization and the social relations it engendered between and among artisans and craftsworkers in Hamilton up through the early 1870s. The city's impressive industrial base had largely been built by this time from craft-based enterprise following a flexible specialized path of growth within a climate of limited regional markets and variable demand. More than this, however, the term most fittingly describes craftsworkers' social experience of this situation. This structural arrangement opened up to them a more or less hopeful experience of industrial capitalism.

This optimism was rooted in the fundamental preservation of traditional patterns of craft mobility. As former craftsworkers themselves, the city's industrial proprietors symbolized to their aspiring charges the fruits of craft training, the maintenance of the apprentice-journeyman-master progression. However, the overall context of a vastly expanding industrialism and its consequent aggregation of opportunity also allowed city masters to inject this symbol with substance. Up through the early 1870s the perception of opportunity was put into practice in Hamilton workplaces. Perhaps more than ever, craftsworkers were able to climb up to positions of independence through an expanding web of craft improvement. Mastership small and large remained a desired end-point to craft improvement, but new positions signifying elevation within a craft such as foreman or superintendent were also available in ever-increasing numbers. Younger craftsworkers continued to be mentored throughout this whole process by those senior to them in the craft hierarchy. These practices were also replicated in such places as the shops of the Great Western Railway, by far the city's largest industrial establishment and a place where one could experience this mobility but in the decided context of lifetime wage-earning.

All this was bolstered through the continued vitality of the mutualistic culture of the craft workplace. The shop floor remained an exclusive male preserve, a place where employers were still regarded by their men as master practitioners of the craft. The vibrancy of this culture was celebrated repeatedly by master craftsworkers in a wide array of work-based picnics, excursions, testimonials and parades. The residential world of masters also remained tightly focused on the working communities surrounding their shops.

These cultural continuities, combined with the perception that wage-earning was still just a stage of the craft life cycle, situated many local craftsworkers within capitalism without subjecting them to its ultimate alienation. As such, their class position straddled the capitalist and non-capitalist worlds. This transmodal position had a profound effect on their social experience, creating modes of understanding and experience influenced by capitalism but not fully of it or completely determined by its logic.

It was from this transmodal class position that local craftsworkers constructed identities and modes of behaviour. The smooth functioning of craft mobility networks easily lent credence to the construction of a specific masculine typology, the self-made craftsworker. That formulation, rooted as it was in a positive experience of capitalism and combined with a burgeoning enthusiasm for the elevating effects of science, technology, and other modern forms of mental education, provided the basis, in turn, for another typology, the self-improving craftsworker. These constructions were discernible in their own right but could and often did overlap each other in varying measure. They also extended beyond mere ideological constructions to become practised components of craftsworker culture.

Conflict rooted in capitalist class experience, while present, was not yet dominant. The Nine Hours Movement, as it manifested itself in Hamilton's craft community, was not a struggle against alienation at the point of production, but was a function of craftsworkers' attempts to push the frontiers of the transmodal world. Whether to gain time to spend in family-based leisure or self-improving study, the Nine Hours Movement demonstrated craftsworkers' willingness to act as equal participants in the modern polity and to push it further in an already pleasing direction. Dispossession was not the lot of most Hamilton craftsworkers by the early 1870s.

This study has challenged the dispossession model, but it does not seek to cast it aside. It proposes that in Hamilton the alienation of craftsworkers was pre-dated by a period offering a more positive experience of the emerging economic system. This is not simply an argument about timing. Rather, its contributes greater complexity and nuance to our to our understanding of craftsworkers' experience of, and role in, the rise of industrial capitalism. It suggests that while dispossession may have been a feature of the early industrial period in some economies, other experiences may have characterized the unfolding of early industrialization elsewhere. Hamilton craftsworkers were eager participants in the unfolding of industrialization because their situation within it allowed them to understand themselves and to act as its beneficiaries.

Dispossession did become a common experience to them in time, but how that came to be needs to be reconsidered in light of the evidence presented here. In the mind of the craftsworker, the line between the transmodal world and one offering alienation at the point of production would have been neither neat nor complete. Chapter 7 suggests the material structures of the transmodal world also endured, in slowly decreasing proportion, into this new age, further complicating experience and action. Rather than being swept into oblivion, craftsworkers' transmodal experience would have profoundly informed their assessments of and reactions to more modern developments. It is hoped that further explorations of the possibilities examined herein will help bring greater understanding and foster new approaches to examining the behaviour of the actors who shaped nineteenth-century industrialization.

The nature of the first Industrial Revolution in Canada, especially as conceived by labour historians over the past few decades, could be reconsidered in this light. Again, this would be partly a reconsideration of timing, but also of complexity, of the nature of contests of 'control,' managerial innovation, early workers' organizations and activities, paternalism, the masculine experience of craftsworkers, the functioning of social control mechanisms, and much more. The last section of chapter 7 suggests that the transmodal world could well have remained influential long enough for historians to reconsider the contours by which Canada's first Industrial Revolution interfaced with its second.

In these ways the evidence should urge us to think about the effects of the transmodal world on what came after. The possibilities for such reconsideration are many, but two will be mentioned here. As chapter 7 has suggested, the nature of such a labour organizations as the Noble and Holy Order of the Knights of Labor, especially as its adherents used their material experience to devise dreams of what might be in Hamilton and similar communities, could be reconsidered. Also, the findings on craft mobility and the artisanal nature of industrial proprietorship suggest it is important to rethink the 'rags-to-riches myth.' In the thirty-odd years since Herbert Gutman urged historians to more widely test this popular ideology, only scattered studies have attempted to uncover the extent to which industrialists worked their way up through the ranks.[1] The myth gains at least some substance from this study. These findings suggest that its explanatory power deep into the decidedly capitalist worlds of the twentieth, or even twenty-first, centuries was based on something beyond simply a controlling construct of the elite, but had some material basis.

This was a local study. Hamilton experienced a particular kind of industrialization, one characterized by limited markets and variable demand, the preservation and expansion of the craft workplace and its attendant mobility networks, and the creation of a craft community that built its identity on such a material experience. But it is unlikely that this experience was unique. In fact, as the historical alternatives and related literature suggests, communities whose industrialization was similar to Hamilton were likely common throughout North America and other parts of the Western capitalist world. The nature of the industrialization of these communities and the social relations that took shape within them needs to be explored and compared to the example provided here. This line of enquiry could be usefully extended forward to consider the social consequences resulting from the endurance of flexible enterprise into a second Industrial Revolution more typically considered for its mass-production industries.

In the same vein, these findings should also urge us to look more broadly at the international dynamics of capitalist expansion. As sections of chapters 2 and 6 suggest, there was a geographic dimension to craftsworkers' experience of industrialization. Harold Innis urged us long ago to consider 'the discrepancy between the centre and margin of western civilization.'[2] The hypothesis that craftsworkers were attracted by pre-capitalist social and economic forms on the periphery of an expanding industrial capitalism – forms that were themselves dynamic creative components of that economic system – is supported by the evidence presented here and deserves further testing by historians of labour migration and labour and business historians studying communities on the periphery of Western capitalism.

The fact that craftsworkers may have been coming to North American communities such as Hamilton, as chapter 2 suggests, to escape capitalism – or, more specifically, its alienating features – offers a framework (one that I will only very briefly elaborate here) for understanding the broadest contours of the expansion of industrial capitalism in the Western world, the patterns of migration it engendered, the nature of societies that grew on its ever-expanding periphery, and much more.

The macro-process this suggests is also outlined on a theoretical level by Karl Marx. Either completely ignored or highly under-explored have been aspects of his writing relating to the place of independent commodity producers in the unfolding of historical modes of production and their place in the process of nineteenth-century colonization. This study has shown that Hamilton craftsworkers, while no strangers to capitalism, were by no means fully of it. They retained many of the essential pre-conditions of independent commodity producers. As Marx argued, this was a pre-capitalist social and economic form, one that would be eventually 'dissolved' by capitalism proper, through the expropriation of the means of production by capitalists from workers without equivocation. He recognized that small producers – mainly farmers, but also artisans – colonized places such as North America to find economic and social conditions enabling the continuation of pre-capitalist social and economic forms such as independent commodity production – forms that had already been largely subsumed in their British or European homelands. He explained:

> In western Europe, the homeland of political economy, the process of primitive accumulation has more or less been accomplished. Here the capitalist regime has either directly subordinated to itself the whole of the nation's production, or ... has at least indirect control of those social layers ...
>
> It is otherwise in the colonies. There the capitalist regime constantly comes up against the obstacle presented by the producer, who, as owner of his own conditions of labour, employs that labour to enrich himself instead of the capitalist.
>
> ... So long, therefore, as the worker can accumulate for himself – and he can do this so long as he remains in possession of the means of production – capitalist accumulation and the capitalist mode of production are impossible. The class of wage-earners essential to these is lacking.

Emigration to 'the colonies,' he continues, functions as a process where from core to periphery 'today's wage-earner [becomes] tomorrow's independent peasant or artisan, working for himself.'[3]

What emerges both from the literature on labour migration surveyed in chapter 2 and in Marx's writings on independent commodity producers and the colonies is an interesting theory of capitalist expansion. The negative experience of immiseration at the core of advancing capitalism in such places as Britain had the effect of propelling outwards varieties of emigrants who re-established on the periphery social and economic forms now unviable in the core. While Marx and most other writers have considered this process mostly for its application to peasants and farmers, this study has considered it among artisan-craftsworkers. And, for such emigrants, the *periphery* to which they 'escaped' is probably best thought of as an *industrial periphery* where craft-based enterprise had (for a limited time at least) the ability to grow from small to large in a way that *did* offer reasonable amounts of opportunity and optimism. This was, of course, a transitory process – capitalist exploitation would come, but escaping to the margins forestalled this. As we have seen, while they existed, modes of production on the periphery that were not fully capitalist served as centres of social creation. When the margin was finally subsumed, it is also not hard to imagine that new peripheries with their own specialized social relations were created in turn. Capitalism's life force – its endless expansion – was likely historically highly dependent upon the repeated creation of non- or pre-capitalist modes of production on its periphery that were repeatedly subsumed and re-created farther on. This is a key process to factor into any theory of the international dynamics of capitalist growth. In this could well lie a good part of the explanation for the general stability of an expanding industrial capitalism as well as a better understanding of how the groups of workers that made this possible transnationally developed different modes of behaviour, different organizations, and so on. At the feet of this process likely lies much of the explanation of the differing paths and timings of the economic and social development of nations and regions touched by Western industrialization. When considering artisans and craftsworkers, close attention to the development and movement of the industrial periphery in Canada, the United States, or wherever will better reveal industrialism's true textures. The forward logic of capitalism, in this light, can be partly understood as the perpetual creation, destruction, and re-creation of economic and social forms not of itself but intrinsic to its existence.

Notes

Introduction: Artisans, Craftsworkers, and Social Relations of Craft-Based Industrialization

1 A partial list of these works includes Michael Hanagan, *The Logic of Solidarity: Artisans and Industrial Workers in Three French Towns, 1871–1914* (Urbana: University of Illinois Press, 1980); Joan Wallach Scott, *The Glassworkers of Carmaux: French Craftsmen and Political Action in a Nineteenth Century City* (Cambridge, MA: Harvard University Press, 1974); E.P. Thompson, *The Making of the English Working Class* (London: Penguin, 1964, 1984); E.J. Hobsbawm, *Labouring Men* (New York: Basic Books, 1964); Herbert Gutman, 'Work, Culture and Society in Industrializing America, 1815–1914,' *American Historical Review* 78, no. 3 (June 1973): 531–88; David Montgomery, 'Workers' Control of Machine Production in the Nineteenth Century,' *Labor History* 17 (1976): 486–509; Alan Dawley, *Class and Community: The Industrial Revolution in Lynn* (Cambridge, MA: Harvard University Press, 1976); Sean Wilenz, *Chants Democratic: New York City and the Rise of the American Working Class, 1788–1850* (New York: Oxford University Press, 1984); Bruce Laurie, *Working People of Philadelphia, 1800–1850* (Philadelphia: Temple University Press, 1980) and *Artisans into Workers: Labor in Nineteenth Century America* (New York: Hill and Wang, 1989); Stephen J. Ross, *Workers on the Edge: Work, Leisure, and Politics in Industrializing Cincinnati, 1788–1890* (New York: Columbia University Press, 1985); Susan E. Hirsch, *Roots of the American Working Class: The Industrialization of Crafts in Newark, 1800–1860* (Philadelphia: University of Pennsylvania Press, 1978); Howard B. Rock, *Artisans of the New Republic: The Tradesmen of New York City in the Age of Jefferson* (New York: New York University

Press, 1979); Paul G. Faler, *Mechanics and Manufacturers in the Early Industrial Revolution: Lynn, Massachusetts, 1780–1860* (Albany: SUNY Press, 1982). See also Sean Wilenz, 'Artisan Origins of the American Working Class,' *International Labor and Working-Class History* 19 (Spring 1981): 1–22.

2 The earliest example is British. See Cynthia Cockburn, *Brothers: Male Dominance and Technical Change* (London: Pluto Press, 1983). Another good British example is Keith McClelland, 'Masculinity and the "Representative Artisan" in Britain, 1850–1880,' in *Manful Assertions*, ed. Michael Roper and John Tosh (London: Routledge, 1991). American examples include Ava Baron, 'Acquiring Manly Competence: The Demise of Apprenticeship and the Remasculinization of Printers' Work,' in *Meanings for Manhood*, ed. Mark C. Carnes and Clyde Griffen, (Chicago: University of Chicago Press, 1990); Ava Baron, 'An "Other" Side to Gender Antagonism At Work: Men, Boys, and the Remasculinization of Printers' Work,' in *Work Engendered: Towards a New History of American Labour*, ed. Baron (Ithaca, NY: Cornell University Press, 1991); Baron, 'Questions of Gender: Deskilling and Demasculinization in the U.S. Printing Industry, 1830–1915,' *Gender and History* 1, no. 2 (Spring 1989): 178–99; Mary H. Blewett, 'Manhood and the Market: The Politics of Gender and Class among the Textile Workers of Fall River, Massachusetts, 1780–1880,' in *Work Engendered*, ed. Baron; and Patricia Cooper, *Once a Cigar Maker* (Urbana: University of Illinois Press, 1987). For a Canadian example that follows the dominate paradigm – especially that established by Baron in the United States – see Christina Burr, *Spreading the Light: Work and Labour Reform in Late-Nineteenth-Century Toronto* (Toronto: University of Toronto Press, 1999) and 'Defending "The Art Preservative": Class and Gender Relations in the Printing Trades Unions, 1850–1914,' *Labour/Le Travail* 31 (Spring 1993): 47–74. For a Swedish example see Ella Johansson, 'Beautiful Men, Fine Women and Good Work People: Gender and Skill in Northern Sweden, 1850–1950,' *Gender and History* 1, no. 2 (Summer 1989): 200–12.

3 This account was presented most forcefully in studies of craftsworkers and class formation in Toronto and Hamilton released in the late 1970s and early 1980s as part of the first wave of Canada's 'new' labour and working-class history. Synthetic accounts have since, by and large, adopted this model. See Gregory S. Kealey, *Toronto Workers Respond to Industrial Capitalism, 1867–1892* (Toronto: University of Toronto Press, 1980); Bryan D. Palmer, *A Culture in Conflict: Skilled Workers and Industrial Capitalism in Hamilton, Ontario, 1860–1914* (Montreal

and Kingston: McGill-Queen's University Press, 1979) and *Working-Class Experience: Rethinking the History of Canadian Labour, 1800–1991* (Toronto: McClelland & Stewart, 1992). See Burr, *Spreading the Light*, for a recent account built upon this view.

4 The classic European account is David Landes, *The Unbound Prometheus: Technological Change and Industrial Development in Western Europe from 1750 to the Present* (Cambridge: Cambridge University Press, 1972). In the United States this is best represented in the organizational synthesis that has taken shape around the work of Alfred Chandler Jr. See Chandler, *The Visible Hand: The Managerial Revolution in American Business* (Cambridge, MA: Belknap Press, 1977). For the dominant theoretical account of the deskilling of craftsworkers by modern industry – in many ways a virtual companion volume to Chandler – see Harry Braverman, *Labor and Monopoly Capitalism* (New York: Monthly Review Press, 1974). For influential sectoral accounts, see David Brody, *Steelworkers in America* (New York: Harper & Row, 1960); and Dawley, *Class and Community*. For similar interpretations of American economic development, see Naomi Lamoreaux, *The Great Merger Movement in American Business, 1895–1904* (Cambridge: Cambridge University Press, 1985); David Houshaell, *From the American System to Mass Production* (Baltimore: Johns Hopkins University Press, 1984); Susan Strasser, *Satisfaction Guaranteed: The Making of the American Mass Market* (New York: Pantheon, 1989); Nathan Rosenberg, *Technology and American Economic Growth* (New York: Harper & Row, 1973); O. Mayr and R.C. Post, eds., *Yankee Enterprise: The Rise of the American System of Manufactures* (Washington, DC: Smithsonian Institution Press, 1981); H.J. Habakkuk, *American and British Technology in the Nineteenth Century: The Search for Labour-Saving Inventions* (Cambridge: Cambridge University Press, 1962); and Nathan Rosenberg, *Perspectives on Technology* (Cambridge: Cambridge University Press, 1976).

5 Charles G. Sellers, *The Market Revolution: Jacksonian America, 1815–1846* (New York: Oxford University Press, 1991), 25.

6 Raphael Samuel, 'Workshop of the World: Steam Power and Hand Technology in Mid-Victorian Britain,' *History Workshop Journal* 3 (Spring 1977): 6–72. For a related comparative account of industrialization in Britain and France see Patrick O'Brien and Caglar Keydar, *Economic Growth in Britain and France, 1780–1914: Two Paths to the Twentieth Century* (London: Allen & Unwin, 1978). See also Ronald Aminzade, 'Reinterpreting Capitalist Industrialization: A Study of Nineteenth-Century France,' *Social History* 9, no. 3 (October 1984): 329–50; and Maxine Berg, *The Age of Manufacture, 1700–1820:*

*Industry, Innovation and Work in Britain (*London: Routledge, 1994). For a summary discussion of combined and uneven development in the United States, see Walter Licht, *Industrializing America: The Nineteenth Century* (Baltimore: Johns Hopkins University Press, 1995), esp. chap. 2. In Canada, Craig Heron, in particular, has suggested a new periodization of capitalist industrialization that demarcated distinct phases, rather than a single path of proletarianization. In this view the 'first' industrial revolution (roughly 1840–90) is characterized for its particularly limited changes. See Craig Heron and Robert Storey, 'On The Job in Canada,' in *On The Job: Confronting the Labour Process in Canada*, ed. Heron and Storey (Kingston and Montreal: McGill-Queen's University Press, 1986), pp. 3–46. For a more recent treatment, see Craig Heron, 'Factory Workers,' in *Labouring Lives: Work and Workers in Nineteenth-Century Ontario*, ed. Paul Craven (Toronto: University of Toronto Press, 1995), 479–594.

7 James R. Farr, *Artisans in Europe, 1300–1914* (Cambridge: Cambridge University Press, 2000), 291; O'Brien and Keydar, *Economic Growth in France and Britain*; Samuel, 'Workshop of the World,' 10. A similar point to the above is made in Charles Sabel and Jonathan Zeitlin, 'Historical Alternatives to Mass Production: Politics, Markets and Technology in Nineteenth-Century Industrialization,' *Past and Present* 108 (August 1985), esp. 133–42.

8 For the influence of combined and uneven development on the Canadian literature, see Kealey, *Toronto Workers Respond to Industrial Capitalism*; Palmer, *Culture in Conflict;* Ian McKay, 'Capital and Labour in the Halifax Baking and Confectionery Industry During the Last Half of the Nineteenth Century,' *Labour/Le Travailleur* 3 (1978): 63–108; and Craig Heron, 'Factory Workers,' 479–594.

9 The seminal article in this field is Sabel and Zeitlin, 'Historical Alternatives to Mass Production.' The viability of craft production was also examined in Michael J. Piore and Charles F. Sabel, *The Second Industrial Divide: Possibilities for Prosperity* (New York: Basic Books, 1984). For more up-to-date reflections on this research direction, see Sabel and Zeitlin, 'Stories, Strategies, Structures: Rethinking Historical Alternatives to Mass Production,' in *World of Possibilities: Flexibility and Mass Production in Western Industrialization*, ed. Sabel and Zeitlin (Cambridge: Cambridge University Press, 1997), 1–36, and Zeitlin, 'Productive Alternatives: Flexibility, Governance, and Strategic Choice in Industrial History,' in *Business History around the World,* ed. Franco Amatori and Geoffrey Jones (Cambridge: Cambridge University Press, 2003). A large body of international research has since been spawned by the historical alternatives approach, including Jonathan Zeitlin and

Gary Herrigel, eds., *Americanization and Its Limits: Reworking US Technology and Management in Post-War Europe and Japan* (Oxford: Oxford University Press, 2000); and Jonathan Zeitlin, ed., 'Flexibility in the "Age of Fordism": Technology and Production in the International Automobile Industry,' *Enterprise and Society: The International Journal of Business History* 1, no. 1 (March 2000): 4–8; Gary Herrigel, *Industrial Constructions: The Sources of German Industrial Power* (Cambridge: Cambridge University Press, 1996); Jonathan Zeitlin, 'Why Are There No Industrial Districts in the United Kingdom?,' in *Small and Medium-Size Enterprises*, ed. Arnaldo Bagnasco and Charles F. Sabel (London: Pinter, 1995), 98–114; ibid., 'Flexibility and Mass Production at War: Aircraft Manufacture in Britain, the United States, and Germany, 1939–1945,' *Technology and Culture* 36, no. 1 (1995): 46–79; Whitney Walton, *France at the Crystal Palace: Bourgeois Taste and Artisan Manufacture in the Nineteenth Century* (Ithaca, NY: Cornell University Press, 1992); Andrew Popp, *Business Structure, Business Culture and the Industrial District: The Potteries, c. 1850–1914* (London: Ashgate, 2001); and Steven Cobrin, 'Two Paths of Industrial Adjustment to Shifting Patterns of International Competition: The Political Economy of Flexible Specialization and Mass Production in British Textiles,' (PhD thesis, Harvard University, 1990).

10 Sabel and Zeitlin, *World of Possibilities*, 5.

11 Sabel and Zeitlin, 'Historical Alternatives to Mass Production,' 164–71.

12 See, for example, Gerald Berk, *Alternative Tracks: The Constitution of Industrial Order in America, 1865–1917* (Baltimore: Johns Hopkins University Press, 1994); Marc Jeffrey Stern, *The Pottery Industry of Trenton: A Skilled Trade in Transition, 1850–1929* (New Brunswick, NJ: Rutgers University Press, 1994); and Philip Scranton, 'Diversity in Diversity: Flexible Production and American Industrialization, 1880–1930,' *Business History Review* 65, no. 1 (Spring 1991): 27–90.

13 Philip Scranton, *Endless Novelty: Specialty Production and American Industrialization, 1865–1925* (Princeton, NJ: Princeton University Press, 1997).

14 The incorporation of flexible specialization in the United States into their theory, for example, is amply evident in Sabel and Zeitlin, 'Stories, Strategies, Structures,' and Zeitlin, 'Productive Alternatives.'

15 See Aminzade, 'Reinterpreting Capitalist Industrialization'; Alan White, '"We never knew what price we were going to have till we got to the warehouse": Nineteenth-Century Sheffield and the Industrial District Debate,' *Social History* 22, no. 3 (October 1997): 307–17; Clive Behagg, 'Masters and Manufacturers: Social Values and the Smaller Unit of Production in Birmingham, 1800–1850,' in *Shop-*

keepers and Master Artisans in Nineteenth-Century Europe, ed. Geoffrey Crossick and Heinz-Gerhard Haupt (London: Methuen, 1984); Behagg, 'Myths of Cohesion: Capital and Compromise in the Historiography of Nineteenth-Century Birmingham,' *Social History* 11, no. 3 (1986): 375–84; Maxine Berg, 'Small Producer Capitalism in Eighteenth-Century England,' *Business History* 35 no. 1 (1993): 17–39; Lars Magnusson, *The Contest for Control: Metal Industries in Sheffield, Solingen, Remscheid and Eskilstuna During Industrialization* (Oxford: Berg, 1994); Tessie P. Liu, *The Weavers' Knot: The Contradictions of Class Struggle and Family Solidarity in Western France, 1750–1914* (Ithaca, NY: Cornell University Press, 1994). For a related point, see Zeitlin, 'Productive Alternatives,' 14.

16 See, for example, Daniel Samson, ed., *Contested Countryside: Rural Workers and Modern Society in Atlantic Canada, 1800–1950* (Fredericton, NB: Acadiensis Press, 1994); Rusty Bittermann, 'Farm Households and Wage Labour in the Northeastern Maritimes in the Early 19th Century,' *Labour/Le Travail* 31 (Spring 1993): 13–46; Sean T. Cadigan, *Hope and Deception in Conception Bay: Merchant–Settler Relations in Newfoundland, 1785–1855* (Toronto: University of Toronto Press, 1995); Allan Greer, 'Fur-Trade Labour and Lower Canadian Agrarian Structures,' Canadian Historical Association *Historical Papers* (1981); Marjorie Griffin Cohen, *Women's Work, Markets and Economic Development in Nineteenth-Century Ontario* (Toronto: University of Toronto Press, 1988); Bittermann, 'The Hierarchy of the Soil: Land and Labour in a 19th Century Cape Breton Community,' *Acadiensis* 18, no. 1 (Autumn 1988): 33–55; Rosemary Ommer, *Merchant Credit and Labour Strategies in Historical Perspective* (Fredericton, NB: Acadiensis Press, 1990); Linda Little, 'Collective Action in Outport Newfoundland: A Case Study from the 1830s,' *Labour/Le Travail* 26 (Fall 1990): 7–36; and some essays in R.J. Brym and R.J. Sacouman, eds., *Underdevelopment and Social Movements in Atlantic Canada* (Toronto: New Hogtown Press, 1979).

17 Patrick J. Joyce, *Work, Politics and Society: The Culture of the Factory in Later Victorian England* (Sussex: Harvester Press, 1980); D. Roberts, *Paternalism in Early Victorian England* (London: Croom Helm, 1979); Paul Craven and Tom Traves, 'Dimensions of Paternalism: Discipline and Culture in Canadian Railway Operations in the 1850s,' in *On The Job*, ed. Heron and Storey, 47–74. See also H.I. Dutton and J.E. King, 'The Limits of Paternalism: The Cotton Tyrants of North Lancashire, 1836–1854,' *Social History* 7 (January 1982): 59–74.

18 Raymond Williams, 'Base and Superstructure in Marxist Cultural Theory,' *New Left Review* 82 (November–December 1973), reprinted in

his *Problems in Materialism and Culture: Selected Essays* (London: New Left Books, 1980). Kealey and Palmer employ this concept in large degree in their study of the Knights of Labor. See Kealey and Palmer, *Dreaming of What Might Be: The Knights of Labor in Ontario, 1880–1900* (Toronto: New Hogtown Press, 1984). I also believe this sort of thinking informs Palmer's discussion of reform thought and producer ideology in chapter 4 of his *Culture in Conflict.*

19 Sabel and Zeitlin, *World of Possibilities* brings together a large number of papers by international scholars building on the historical-alternatives approach. These participants workshopped papers in two meetings at Lyon's Maison Rhone-Alpes des Sciences del l'Homme, one presumes in the late 1980s (but is never told) in an effort to set the historical alternatives approach in firmer ground. Sabel and Zeitlin's introduction provides the most recent and penetrating survey of their approach.

20 For a useful summary of this debate, see Allan Kulikoff, 'The Transition to Capitalism in Rural America,' *William and Mary Quarterly*, 3rd series, 61 (1989): 120–44.

21 Michael Merrill, 'Putting "Capitalism" in Its Place: A Review of Recent Literature,' *William and Mary Quarterly*, 3rd series, 52, no. 2 (April 1995): 315–26. In contrast to Henretta and Kulikoff's work, Merrill holds up Christopher Clark's work on families in the Connecticut River valley as a singular example of the fruits this 'alternate approach' can bear. See James Henretta, *The Origins of American Capitalism: Selected Essays* (Boston: Northeastern University Press, 1992); Allan Kulikoff, *The Agrarian Origins of American Capitalism* (Charlottesville: University of Virginia Press, 1992); and Christopher Clark, *The Roots of Rural Capitalism: Western Massachusetts, 1780–1860* (Ithaca, NY: Cornell University Press, 1990).

22 See especially Eugene Genovese, *The Political Economy of Slavery: Studies in the Economy and Society of the Old South* (New York: Vintage, 1965), *The World the Slaveholders Made* (New York: Pantheon, 1971), and *Roll Jordan Roll: The World the Slaves Made* (New York: Pantheon, 1974); and Elizabeth Fox-Genovese and Eugene Genovese, *Fruits of Merchant Capital: Slavery and Bourgeois Property in the Rise and Expansion of Capitalism* (New York: Oxford University Press, 1983).

23 Marx wrote: 'The transition from the feudal mode of production is twofold. The producer becomes merchant and capitalist … This is the really revolutionizing path. Or else, the merchant establishes direct sway over production.' See Karl Marx, *Capital,* vol. 3 (New York: International, 1967), 334. For a later attempt to gives Marx's observation some empirical legs, see Maurice Dobb, *Studies in the Development of Capitalism* (London: Routledge, 1946, rev. 1963), esp. chapter 4.

24 Herbert Gutman, 'The Reality of the Rags-To-Riches "Myth": The Case of the Paterson, New Jersey, Locomotive, Iron, and Machinery Manufacturers, 1830–1880,' in *Work, Culture and Society in Industrializing America*, ed. Gutman (New York: Vintage, 1977), 211–33; Susan E. Hirsch, 'From Artisan to Manufacturer: Industrialization and the Small Producer in Newark, 1830–60,' in *Small Business in American Life*, ed. Stuart W. Bruchey (New York: Columbia University Press, 1980), 80–99; and Stephen J. Ross, *Workers on the Edge: Work, Leisure, and Politics in Industrializing Cincinnati, 1788–1890* (New York: Columbia University Press, 1985). For other considerations of artisanal industrialization in the United States, see Thomas C. Cochran, *Frontiers of Change: Early Industrialism in America* (New York: Oxford University Press, 1981), esp. chap. 4; Philip Scranton, *Proprietary Capitalism: The Textile Manufacture at Philadelphia, 1800–1885* (Cambridge: Cambridge University Press, 1985); and Gary J. Kornblith, 'The Craftsman as Industrialist: Jonas Chickering and the Transformation of American Piano Making,' *Business History Review* 59 (Autumn 1985): 349–68.

25 See Ross, *Workers on the Edge* for one such interpretation.

26 See Clive Behagg's work on Birmingham for this interpretation. See Behagg, 'Masters and Manufacturers' and 'Myths of Cohesion.'

27 In Marx's words, 'the skill of the craftsman thus continues to be the foundation of the production process.' See Marx, *Capital*, vol. 1, 458. For the identification and limited application of the stage of manufacture in the Canadian context, see Palmer, *Culture in Conflict*, chapter 1, and McKay, 'Capital and Labour in the Halifax Baking and Confectionery Industry,' esp. 76–80.

28 The emphasis by practitioners of the 'staples approach,' notably Harold Innis, on primary resource export as the main engine of national economic growth left little or no room for consideration of domestic industrial development. Mel Watkins's staple theory of economic growth is still among the most satisfying frameworks to conceptualize the growth of industry in the linkages of Canada's staple economy. See M.H. Watkins, 'A Staple Theory of Economic Growth,' *Canadian Journal of Economics and Political Science* 29, no. 2 (May 1963): 141–58. One of the first applications of the staple economy's 'multiplier-accelerator' affect on domestic industrial development was provided in Gordon W. Bertram, 'Economic Growth in Canadian Industry, 1870–1915,' in *Approaches to Canadian Economic History*, ed. W.T. Easterbrook and M.H. Watkins (Ottawa: Carleton University Press, 1997 [1967]), 74–98.

29 R.T. Naylor's thesis was first outlined in his essay 'The Third Commercial Empire of the St. Lawrence,' in *Capitalism and the National Ques-*

tion, ed. Gary Teeple (Toronto: University of Toronto Press, 1971), 1–42 and further elaborated in his two-volume *The History of Canadian Business* (Toronto: Lorimer, 1975). For an insightful critique of Naylor's argument, see Douglas McCalla, 'Tom Naylor's *A History of Canadian Business, 1867–1914:* A Comment,' Canadian Historical Association, *Historical Papers* (1976): 249–54. For a related explanation of the stifling of industry by merchants and bankers, also from within the 'new political economy' school, see Wallace Clement, *Continental Corporate Power* (Toronto: McClelland and Stewart, 1977).

30 The seminal studies are Kealey, *Toronto Workers Respond to Industrial Capitalism*; Palmer, *Culture in Conflict*; and Kealey and Palmer, *Dreaming of What Might Be*. For early Marxist treatments that recognize nineteenth-century Canadian industry, see Stanley B. Ryerson, *Unequal Union: Confederation and the Roots of Conflict in the Canadas, 1815–1873* (Toronto: Progress Books, 1968) and H. Clare Pentland, 'Labour and the Development of Industrial Capitalism in Canada,' (PhD thesis, University of Toronto, 1961). For an early non-Marxist study of nineteenth-century industrialization, see also Gordon W. Bertram, 'Historical Statistics on Growth and Structure of manufacturing in Canada, 1870–1957,' in *Canadian Political Science Association Conference on Statistics, 1962 and 1963*, ed. J. Henripin and A. Asimakopolas (Toronto, 1964) and Edward J. Chambers and Gordon W. Bertram, 'Urbanization and Manufacturing in Canada, 1870–1957,' in *Canadian Political Science Association, Conference on Statistics, 1964*, ed. Sylvia Ostry and T.K. Rhymes (Toronto, 1966).

31 Craig Heron, 'Factory Workers.'

32 Neoclassical discussions of Ontario's economic growth and market limitations include Douglas McCalla, *Planting the Province: The Economic History of Upper Canada, 1784–1870* (Toronto: University of Toronto Press, 1993); McCalla and Peter George, 'Measurement, Myth and Reality: Reflections in the Economic History of Nineteenth-Century Ontario,' *Journal of Canadian Studies* 21 (Fall 1986): 71–86; and Ben Forster, 'Finding the Right Size: Markets and Competition in Mid- and Late Nineteenth-Century Ontario,' in *Patterns of the Past: Interpreting Ontario's History*, ed. Roger Hall, William Westfall and Laurel Sefton MacDowell (Toronto and Oxford: Dundurn Press, 1988), pp. 150–73. For Elizabeth and Gerald Bloomfield's findings based on the quantification of the industrial schedules of the 1871 census, see *Industrial Leaders: The Largest Manufacturing Firms of Ontario in 1871* (Guelph: University of Guelph, Department of Geography, Canadian Industry in 1871 Project, 1989) and their numerous other papers in this series. For an introduction to the Canadian Industry in 1871 Project,

see Bloomfield and Bloomfield, 'Mills, Factories and Craftshops of Ontario, 1870: A Machine-Readable Source for Material Historians,' *Material History Bulletin* 25 (1987): 120–32. For the few studies that speculate on artisan-led industrial growth, see Jacob Spelt, *Urban Development in South-Central Ontario* (Ottawa: Carleton Library No. 57, 1972), 127–8; John McCallum, *Unequal Beginnings: Agriculture and Economic Development in Quebec and Ontario until 1870* (Toronto: University of Toronto Press, 1980), 91, 101; McCalla, *Planting the Province*, 115; McCalla, 'Tom Naylor's *A History of Canadian Business: 1867–1914.* A Comment,' Canadian Historical Association *Historical Papers* (1976) 249–54; and David Burley, *A Particular Condition in Life: Self-Employment and Social Mobility in Mid-Victorian Brantford, Ontario* (Montreal and Kingston: McGill-Queen's University Press, 1994).

33 Farr, *Artisans in Europe*, 283.

34 Marx, *Capital,* vol. 3, 334.

Chapter 1. The Structure of Hamilton's Early Industrialization: Continuity and Change

1 John Weaver, *Hamilton: An Illustrated History* (Toronto: Lorimer, 1982), 16–23; Douglas McCalla, *The Upper Canada Trade, 1834–1872: A Study of the Buchanans' Business* (Toronto: University of Toronto Press, 1979); Michael Doucet and John Weaver, 'Town Fathers and Urban Continuity: The Roots of Community Power and Physical Form in Hamilton, Upper Canada, in the 1830s,' *Urban History Review* 8, no. 2 (October 1984): 75–90.

2 Doucet and Weaver, 'Town Fathers'; McCalla, *Upper Canada Trade.*

3 John C. Weaver, 'The Location of Manufacturing Enterprises: The Case of Hamilton's Attraction of Foundries, 1830–1890,' in *Critical Issues in the History of Canadian Science, Technology and Medicine*, ed. Richard A. Jarrell and Arnold E. Roos (Thornhill: HSTC, 1983); 197–217.

4 Weaver, 'Location of Manufacturing Enterprises.'

5 Upon enquiry into both the 1851 and 1861 Return of Mills and Manufactories it was determined that this source needs to be used with extreme caution. In many categories it was apparent that the census significantly underenumerated the number of establishments operating in the city at this time. It also failed to list whole industrial subsectors. These omissions negate the usefulness of the census to determine the true patterns of industrial diversification between decennial periods. Rather, as I have done above, its usefulness as a source lies primarily

with providing limited and somewhat subjective evidence regarding industrial diversification at one given point. For a penetrating discussion of the Canadian census during this time period, see Bruce Curtis, *The Politics of Population: State Formation, Statistics, and the Census of Canada, 1840–1875* (Toronto: University of Toronto Press, 2001).

6 Katz, *People of Hamilton*, 23. Katz does not separate artisanal or manufacturing establishments from other business types in this calculation. He finds that out of the 282 'artisan shops, stores, offices, and manufactories' listed on the 1851 census 52% reported no employees, 8.9% reported listed only one, and 21.8% listed between two and five employees. Only thirty establishments reported between six and ten employees and 'but a handful' reported more than ten. Given the reported size and complexity of the city's commercial enterprises by this time, it is likely they account for most of those establishments reporting more than ten employees.

7 Paul Craven, 'Labour and Management on the Great Western Railway,' in *Labouring Lives: Work and Workers in Nineteenth Century Ontario*, ed. Craven (Toronto: University of Toronto Press, 1995).

8 HPL, Joseph Tinsely (pseudonym: 'Jaques') 'Old Hamiltonians Scrapbook,' 103–8; Weaver, *Hamilton*, 49–50.

9 *Spectator*, 6 August 1853; *Gazette*, 5 September 1853.

10 HPL, Clipping file, H.F. Gardiner, 'The Beginning of Hamilton Industry,' n.d.

11 *Spectator*, 4 January 1858; *Times*, 7 March 1859; Palmer, *Culture in Conflict*, 14; HPL, Typescript, Robert R. Brown, 'Canadian Locomotive Builders: Part II – Dan. C. Gunn, Hamilton, 1857–60.'

12 The major exception to this trend was, of course, the GWR shops whose developing paternalism including holding onto skilled labour by providing work through economic downturns. See Paul Craven and Tom Traves, 'Dimensions of Paternalism: Discipline and Culture in Canadian Railway Operations in the 1850s,' in *On The Job: Confronting Labour Process in Canada*, ed. Craig Heron and Robert Storey (Kingston and Montreal: McGill-Queen's University Press, 1986), 47–74; and Craven, 'Labour and Management on the Great Western Railway.'

13 Weaver, *Hamilton*, 54.

14 The terminal date of this study – so close to the decline of the Nine Hours Movement of 1872 and the slip into the deep economic depression starting the next year – is neatly coincident with the taking of the Dominion's first formal census of industrial establishments in 1871. The manuscripts to this census survive and have proved an invaluable source for historians since their release in the early 1970s. See Eliza-

beth Bloomfield, 'Using the 1871 Census Manuscript Industrial Schedules: A Machine-Readable Source for Social Historians,' *Histoire sociale/Social History* 19, no. 38 (November 1986): 427–41. A number of historians have relied on these schedules for painting their own portraits of industrial activity in mid-nineteenth-century Canada. A partial list includes Gregory S. Kealey, *Toronto Workers Respond to Industrial Capitalism* (Toronto: University of Toronto Press, 1980); Michael Katz et al., *The Social Organization of Early Industrial Capitalism* (Cambridge, MA: Harvard University Press, 1982); and L.D. McCann, 'The Mercantile-Industrial Transition in the Metals Towns of Pictou County, 1857–1931,' *Acadiensis* 10, no. 2 (1981): 29–64.

15 Please note for figures throughout that a careful quantification of the industrial manuscripts yields somewhat different totals in various categories than the published aggregate census. Most glaring is the discrepancy in number of hands employed, with the manuscripts clearly listing 5743, whereas the published aggregation lists only 4456. It should also be noted that it is extremely difficult to obtain any really accurate sense of change over time in terms of number of industrial establishments in the city. The aggregate 1861 census, for example, reports only fifty-six industrial establishments. Even a hasty examination of the sectors in which these few enterprises were located, however, leads one to realize that many establishments were not enumerated.

16 Paul Craven and Tom Traves, 'Canadian Railways as Manufacturers, 1850–1880,' Canadian Historical Association *Historical Papers* (1983): 254–81.

17 *Times*, 26 January, 8 June, 19 November 1864; *Spectator*, 30 March, 24 November 1864; 1871 Industrial Census. See also Paul Craven, personal communication to author, 17 March 2003, and Craven, 'Maintaining the Way: Iron, Rolling Mills, and the Transition to Steel Rails in Canadian Railway Operations, 1850–1880,' presented to the New History Society, Toronto, October 1986, and to the Symposium in Canadian Economic History, Toronto, University of Ottawa, November 1986.

18 *Spectator*, 14 September 1857, 15 September 1865; *Times*, 5 October 1863, 27 June 1865, 12 October 1866.

19 Hamilton City Directory, 1853/4, 1870/1; *Times*, 24 February 1862, 9 October 1863.

20 *Spectator*, 21 October 1857, 6 December 1872, 29 December 1923; HPL, F.H. Armstrong, 'Edward Gurney,' *Dictionary of Canadian Biography* typescript entry.

21 *Times*, 2 August 1861, 22 July 1863, 16, 17 October 1871; *Spectator*, 8 April, 31 July 1869, 30 August 1870, 3 September 1870, 6 July, 11

October 1871, 19 February, 22 October 1872; *Hamilton Weekly Times,* 1, 8 September 1870. See also Martha Beckmann Brent, 'A Stitch in Time: Sewing Machine Industry of Ontario, 1860–1897,' *Material History Bulletin* 10:1–30.

22 *Times,* 24 February 1862, 20 July 1863, 7 August 1865; *Spectator,* Carnival Edition (1886).

23 *Times,* 4, 9, 14 September 1863.

24 *Spectator,* Carnival Edition. (1886); HPL, Joseph Tinsely, 'Old Hamiltonians Scrapbooks,' n.d.; *Industries of Canada, Historical and Commercial Sketches, Hamilton and Environs* (Toronto: M.G. Bixby and Company, 1886), 76.

25 *Spectator,* 13 September 1871.

26 This figure is based on a survey of Ontario urban centres with at least one hundred industrial workers and above-average industrial significance compiled in Elizabeth Bloomfield, 'Using the 1871 Census Manuscript Industrial Schedules,' 432.

27 Elizabeth Bloomfield and G.T. Bloomfield, *Industrial Leaders: The Largest Manufacturing Firms of Ontario in 1871*, Research Report No. 8 (Department of Geography, University of Guelph, 1989). I have added James Williams' Canadian Oil Company located next to Hamilton in Barton Township and commonly touted as a Hamilton enterprise in the Broomfield and Bloomfield list of eight Hamilton manufacturers.

28 Bloomfield and Bloomfield, *Industrial Leaders*.

29 See, for example, Gregory S. Kealey, *Toronto Workers Respond to Industrial Capitalism, 1867–1892* (Toronto: University of Toronto Press, 1980); Bryan D. Palmer, *A Culture in Conflict A Culture in Conflict: Skilled Workers and Industrial Capitalism in Hamilton, Ontario, 1860–1914* (Montreal and Kingston: McGill-Queen's University Press, 1979); and Kealey and Palmer, *Dreaming of What Might Be: The Knights of Labor in Ontario, 1880–1900* (Toronto: New Hogtown Press, 1984).

30 Craig Heron, 'Factory Workers,' in *Labouring Lives: Work and Workers in Nineteenth-Century Ontario*, ed. Paul Craven (Toronto: University of Toronto Press, 1995), 484.

31 In Ontario, industrialists' ability to expand and specialize their production facilities remained constrained by limited domestic markets up through the latter decades of the nineteenth century. Elizabeth Bloomfield and Gerald Bloomfield, for example, have shown that in 1871 the aggregation of these small producers accounted for the lion's share of industrial output in the province. The mean size of industrial establishments that year was still less than five workers. Other important discussions of Ontario's economic growth and market limitations include

Douglas McCalla, *Planting the Province: The Economic History of Upper Canada, 1784–1870* (Toronto: University of Toronto Press, 1993); McCalla and Peter George, 'Measurement, Myth and Reality: Reflections in the Economic History of Nineteenth-Century Ontario,' *Journal of Canadian Studies* 21 (Fall 1986): 71–86; and Ben Forster, 'Finding the Right Size: Markets and Competition in Mid- and Late Nineteenth-Century Ontario,' in *Patterns of the Past: Interpreting Ontario's History*, ed. Roger Hall, William Westfall, and Laurel Sefton MacDowell (Toronto and Oxford: Dundurn Press, 1988), 150–73. For Elizabeth Bloomfield and Gerald Bloomfield's findings based on the quantification of the industrial schedules of the 1871 census, see their *Industrial Leaders,* and their numerous other papers in the series Canadian Industry in 1871 Project.

32 Pointing to such industrial concerns as Wanzer's, Wilson, Bowman and Company, Gardner & Company, the Copp Brothers Foundry, and McPherson's Boot and Shoe Manufactory, among others, Palmer does concede that these establishments were 'interspersed with innumerable smaller concerns' but fails to integrate this observation into his overall analysis of the social relations of production. See Palmer, *Culture in Conflict*, esp. 12–17. This is also evident in Kealey's study. For example, after providing probably the most detailed portraits of uneven industrial growth yet produced in the historiography, Kealey proposes that 'by the 1870s modern industry had come to Toronto.' While he does go on to declare that 'the unevenness of industrial development had major repercussions for the emerging working-class movement,' this insight does not fundamentally influence his subsequent discussion. See Kealey, *Toronto Workers Respond to Industrial Capitalism,* 24, 30.

33 Ian McKay, 'Capital and Labour in the Halifax Baking and Confectionery Industry during the Last Half of the Nineteenth Century,' *Labour/Le Travailleur* 3 (1978): 63–107. A major exception to this is Craig Heron, 'Factory Workers.'

34 The format of the 1851 and 1861 census does not allow quantification of this.

35 See, for example, Samuel, 'Workshop of the World,' and Richard Stott, 'Artisans and Capitalist Development,' 105.

36 See Palmer, *Culture in Conflict*, 15, and Craven and Traves, 'Dimensions of Paternalism: Discipline and Culture in Canadian Railway Operations in the 1850s,' *On The Job*, ed. Heron and Storey, 53, 69.

37 *Times* 19 November 1864. See also Craig Heron, *Working in Steel: The Early Years in Canada, 1883–1935* (Toronto: McClelland & Stewart, 1988), 34–40; Heron, 'Factory Workers,' 501, 507–8; and Samuel, 'Workshop of the World,' 43–4.

38 *Spectator,* 9 June 1869.
39 For the persistence of the work routines of moulders and an explanation of the mechanization of this craft in the early twentieth century, see Kealey, *Toronto Workers*, 28–9 and 64–82; W. Craig Heron, 'Working-Class Hamilton, 1895–1930' (PhD diss., Dalhousie University, 1981), 127. The Archivanet on-line 1871 census lists only two stovemounters and no coremakers in Hamilton in 1871. The 28 fitters listed in the city were likely dispersed widely across a number of shops and, while no yet a common feature, portended things to come. See also Heron, 'Factory Workers,' 502–3.
40 *Spectator,* Carnival Edition (1886); *Times,* 30 September 1863; *Hutchison's Hamilton City Directory,* 1871–72.
41 *Spectator,* 9 June 1869.
42 Kristofferson, 'Craft Capitalism,' chap. 5.
43 See *Spectator,* 1 May 1871, for a description of the Wanzer plant. For the maintenance of machinists' skills and customary work habits in Toronto, see Kealey, *Toronto Workers*, 28–9, 77–9.
44 Sabel and Zeitlin, 'Historical Alternatives to Mass Production,' 138.
45 *Times,* 5 October 1863, 27 June 1865; *Spectator,* 15 September 1865; *City Directory* (1871–72); Samuel, 'Workshop of the World,' 42.
46 The city's five blacksmithing establishments reported on the 1871 Industrial Census were uniformly small, employing between one and six hands each. Notably, 120 blacksmiths are listed on the Archivanet 1871 census database for the city.
47 Hamilton's tin and sheet iron products and tinsmithing subsectors in 1871 employed 1–5 hands, except D. Moore, who employed 30 hands in his tin, japan, pressed-ware, and copper operations.
48 This information was culled from product descriptions provided on the 1871 Industrial Schedules.
49 *Times,* 20 July 1863, 7 August 1865, 17 October 1867; *Spectator,* 19 December 1864. See also Kealey, *Toronto Workers*, 28, 37–52; Heron, 'Factory Workers,' 504; Mary H. Blewett, *Men, Women and Work: Class, Gender and Protest in the New England Show Industry, 1780–1910* (Urbana: University of Illinois Press, 1990).
50 Kealey, *Toronto Workers,* 28, app. I, table 1.3.
51 Two hundred and eighty-nine tailors are listed on the 1871 census, as opposed to 103 in 1861.
52 *Times,* 21 July 1863, 23 June 1871. The combined and uneven development of Canada's larger clothing industry is further outlined in Mercedes Steedman, 'Skill and Gender in the Canadian Clothing Industry, 1890–1940,' in *On The* Job, ed. Heron and Storey, 162–76; Steedman, *Angels of the Workplace: Women and Gender Relations in the Cana-*

dian Clothing Industry, 1890–1940 (Toronto: Oxford University Press, 1997); and Ruth A. Frager, *Sweatshop Strife: Class, Ethnicity, and Gender in the Jewish Labour Movement of Toronto, 1900–1939* (Toronto: University of Toronto Press, 1992).

53 *Times*, 1, 2, 3, 4 September 1963; *Canadian Illustrated News*, 14 February 1863; Craven, 'Labour and Management on the Great Western Railway,' 347–55; and Craven and Traves, 'Dimensions of Paternalism,' 52–60.

54 *Times,* 11 July 1871; *Spectator,* 2 January 1868.

55 This should especially be contrasted with the Jacques and Hay facility in Toronto. See Kealey, *Toronto Workers*, 19–20.

56 *Spectator*, 17 May 1861, 25 February 1868.

57 The self-description of the Hamilton Coach Factory in the 1871–2 city directory presents the Grayson and Aitcheson concerns as part of the firm's operations. Neither Grayson nor the Aitchesons were listed on the industrial census schedules that year. However, both these concerns advertised and appeared to accept orders in their own right. The Aitcheson concern emerged as its own sizable operation some years later. For a description of the artisanal pooling of skills before the advent of the modern integrated industrial operation in the nineteenth-century Ontario carriage industry, see David Burley, *A Particular Condition in Life: Self-Employment and Social Mobility in Mid-Victorian Brantford, Ontario* (Montreal and Kingston: McGill-Queen's University Press, 1994), 31–3.

58 *Times,* 8 September 1863, 17 July 1867; *Spectator,* 30 December 1863, 11 July 1871; Kealey, *Toronto Workers*, 29.

59 *Times,* 13 September 1864; *Spectator,* 15 April, 29 August 1871, 8 December 1924; Miss Lottie M. Jones, 'Early American and Canadian Glass,' *Wentworth Bygones* (Hamilton: Head-of-the-Lake Historical Society, 1975), 57; Samuel, 'Workshop of the World,' 32–4.

60 Forster, 'Finding the Right Size,' 150–73; Heron, 'Factory Workers,' 495.

Chapter 2. Personal Structures: Craftsworkers and Industrial Proprietors by 1871

1 Craig Heron, 'Factory Workers,' in *Labouring Lives: Work and Workers in Nineteenth-Century Ontario*, ed. Paul Craven (Toronto: University of Toronto Press, 1995), 511–16.

2 For information of the development of the domestic sources of skilled labour, especially by the later 1880s, see Heron, 'Factory Workers,' 512–16. Not all skilled workers recruited from the countryside were

poorly trained. For a study of the continuation of formal apprenticeship among countryside blacksmiths in mid-nineteenth-century Ontario, see William N.T. Wylie, 'The Blacksmith in Upper Canada, 1784–1850: A Study of Technology, Culture and Power,' in *Canadian Papers in Rural History*, vol. 7, ed. Donald H. Akenson (Gananoque, ON: Langdale Press), 50–3.

3 John Burt to Unknown, 16 September 1874, Hamilton Public Library; *Spectator,* 5 September 1870, Carnival Edition (1886); John Weaver, 'The Location of Manufacturing Enterprises: The Case of Hamilton's Attraction of Foundries, 1830–1890,' in *Critical Issues in the History of Canadian Science, Technology and Medicine*, ed. Richard A. Jarrell and Arnold E. Roos (Thornhill, ON: HSTC, 1983), 208–11; in *The Dictionary of Hamilton Biography* (hereafter *DHB*) vol. 1, 'Stewart, Charles' ed. Thomas Melville Bailey (Hamilton, ON: Dictionary of Hamilton Biography, 1981), 187 See chapter 3 for more extensive documentation of systems of apprenticeship and other forms of craft mobility in Hamilton workplaces.

4 *Spectator,* 13 April 1913, 16 July 1921; Richard Butler, *Saturday Musings,* Hamilton Public Library, micro #121, vol. 3: 94, 188, 201–2.

5 The continued strength of apprenticeship systems in Hamilton workplaces through the early 1870s is outlined in Bryan D. Palmer, *A Culture in Conflict* (Montreal and Kingston: McGill-Queen's University Press, 1979), 74–9.

6 Heron, 'Factory Workers,' 515.

7 Peter Bischoff, 'Another Perspective on Labour Migrations: The International Iron Molder's Union' s Influence on Mobility as Seen through Their Journals, 1860s to 1930s' (unpublished paper); Bischoff, 'D'un atelier de moulage à un autre: les migrations des mouldeurs originaires des Forges du Saint-Maurice et segmentation du marché du travail nord-américain, 1851–1884,' *Labour/Le Travail* 40 (Fall 1997): 21–4; Bischoff, '"Traveling the country 'round": migrations et syndicalisme chez les mouldeurs de l'Ontario et du Québec membres de l'*Iron Molders Union of North America*, 1860 à 1892,' *Journal of the Canadian Historical Association* 1, no. 1. (1990): 37–71; Patricia Cooper, *Once a Cigar Maker* (Urbana: University of Illinois Press, 1987); David Bensman, *The Practice of Solidarity: American Hat Finishers* (Urbana: University of Illinois Press, 1985); Heron, 'Factory Workers,' 511.

8 Diaries of Andrew McIlwraith, 1857–1862, typescript, Kitchener Public Library, 179–266.

9 Paul Craven, 'Labour and Management on the Great Western Railway,' in *Labouring Lives*, ed. Craven (Toronto: University of Toronto Press, 1995), 334.

10 Heron, 'Factory Workers,' 512.

11 Allan Kulikoff, *The Agrarian Origins of American Capitalism* (Charlottesville: University Press of Virginia, 1992). See also Kulikoff, *From British Peasants to Colonial American Farmers* (Chapel Hill: University of North Carolina Press, 2000).

12 Horst Rossler, 'The Dream of Independence: The "America" of England's North Staffordshire Potters,' in *Distant Magnets: Expectations and Realities in the Immigrant Experience, 1840–1930,* ed. Dirk Hoerder and Horst Rossler (New York: Holmes and Meier, 1993). For the similar aspirations of Scottish miners, see John Laslett, *Nature's Noblemen: The Fortunes of The Independent Collier in Scotland and the American Midwest, 1885–1889* (Los Angeles: Institute of Industrial Relations, University of California, 1983).

13 William E. Van Vugt, *Britain to American: Mid-Nineteenth-Century Immigrants to the United States* (Urbana: University of Illinois Press, 1999), 63.

14 Ibid., 70.

15 Geoffrey Tweedale, *Sheffield Steel and America: A Century of Commercial and Technological Interdependence, 1830–1930* (New York: Cambridge University Press, 1987).

16 Dirk Hoerder, 'Labour Migrants' Views of "America",' *Renaissance and Modern Studies* 35 (1992): 5–6, 16: Rossler, 'Dream of Independence'; Hoerder, 'German Immigrant Workers' View of "America" in the 1880s,' in *The Shadow of the Statue of Liberty: Immigrants, Workers and Citizens in the American Republic, 1880–1920*, ed. Marianne Debouzy (Urbana: University of Illinois Press, 1992), 17–33.

17 Van Vugt, *Britain to America*, 12.

18 Ibid., 67.

19 Charlotte Erickson, *Invisible Immigrants: The Adaptation of English and Scottish Immigrants in Nineteenth-Century America* (London: Weidenfeld & Nicholson, 1972), 233, 237, 256, 271, 296–9, 320; Erickson, *Leaving England: Essays on British Emigration in the Nineteenth Century* (Ithaca, NY: Cornell University Press, 1994), esp. introduction, chaps. 3 and 6; and Erickson, ed., *Emigration from Europe, 1815–1914: Selected Documents* (London: Adam & Charles Black, 1976), 52–6, 148–51.

20 By the first road, merchants redirected capital from commerce into manufacturing, establishing 'direct sway' over production by subordinating master artisans and other producers to their centralized control. By the second road, master artisans took the 'really revolutionizing path' by using accumulated capital to expand their enterprises and take to trade themselves. See Karl Marx, *Capital: A Critique of Political*

Economy, vol. 3 (New York: International, 1967), 334. See also Maurice Dobb, *Studies in the Development of Capitalism* (London: Routledge and Kegan Paul, 1946; repr. New York: International Publishers, 1963), chap. 4.

21 Alan Dawley, for example, has outlined the process by which the small master shoemaker in Lynn, Massachusetts, was 'done in' by increasingly aggressive local shopkeepers after the turn of the nineteenth century, allowing industrialization of that industry to take place 'under the auspices of merchant capitalism.' Alan Dawley, *Class and Community: The Industrial Revolution in Lynn* (Cambridge, MA: Harvard University Press, 1976). For other discussions of merchant involvement in the industrial development in the American Northeast, see George Rogers Taylor, *The Transportation Revolution, 1815–1860* (New York: Rinehart, 1962); Glenn Porter and Harold Livesay, *Merchants and Manufacturers: Studies in the Changing Structure of Nineteenth-Century Marketing* (Baltimore: Johns Hopkins University Press, 1971); David Brody, *Steelworkers in America* (New York: Harper and Row, 1960); Robert F. Dalzell Jr, 'The Rise of the Waltham-Lowell System and Some Thoughts on the Political Economy of Modernization in Ante-Bellum Massachusetts,' *Perspectives in American History* 9 (1975): 229–68; Peter J. Coleman, 'The Entrepreneurial Spirit in Rhode Island History,' *Business History Review* 37 (Winter 1963): 319–44; Caroline F. Ware, *The Early New England Cotton Manufacture: A Study in Industrial Beginnings* (Boston: Houghton Mifflin, 1931); and Frances W. Gregory and Irene D. Neu, 'The American Industrial Elite in the 1870s: Their Social Origins,' in *Men in Business: Essays on the Historical Role of the Entrepreneur*, ed. William Miller (New York, 1962). For an interesting interpretation of the development of the 'other' New England textile industry, see Jonathan Prude, *The Coming of Industrial Order: Town and Factory Life in Rural Massachusetts* (New York: Cambridge University Press, 1983).

22 Michael B. Katz, Michael J. Doucet and Mark J. Stern, *The Social Organization of Early Industrial Capitalism* (Cambridge, MA: Harvard University Press, 1982), 12, 18, 30–5, 51, 58–61, 161; Michael J. Katz, *The People of Hamilton, Canada West* (Cambridge, MA: Harvard University Press, 1975), 143, 196.

23 See, for example, Herbert Gutman, 'The Reality of the Rags-to-Riches "Myth": The Case of the Paterson, New Jersey, Locomotive, Iron, and Machinery Manufacturers, 1830–1880,' in his *Work, Culture and Society in Industrializing America* (New York: Vintage, 1977), 211–33; Susan E. Hirsch, 'From Artisan to Manufacturer: Industrialization and the Small Producer in Newark, 1830–60,' in *Small Business in Ameri-*

can Life, ed. Stuart W. Bruchey (New York: Columbia University Press, 1980), 80–99; and Stephen J. Ross, *Workers on the Edge: Work, Leisure, and Politics in Industrializing Cincinnati, 1788–1890* (New York: Columbia University Press, 1985). See also Gary J. Kornblith, 'The Craftsman as Industrialist: Jonas Chickering and the Transformation of American Piano Making,' *Business History Review* 59 (Autumn 1985): 349–68; Kornblith, 'From Artisans to Businessmen: Master Mechanics in New England, 1789–1850,' (PhD diss., Princeton University, 1983); and Thomas Cochran, *Frontiers of Change: Early Industrialism in America* (New York: Oxford University Press, 1981).

24 In his study of Montreal entrepreneurship between 1837 and 1853, Gerald Tulchinsky has shown that merchants put off by a long-term tie-up of capital left much of that city's early industrialization open to artisans, many of whom profited handsomely in their efforts to expand their operations. See Tulchinsky, *The River Barons* (Toronto: University of Toronto Press, 1977), esp. chap. 12. It should be noted that Tulchinsky does not argue for a pervasive artisan-based industrialization, finding that merchants did invest in such sectors as transportation, shipbuilding, and marine engine industries. T.W. Acheson has found that much early industrial growth in Saint John, New Brunswick, can be attributed to artisanal expansion. See: Acheson, *Saint John: The Making of a Colonial Urban Community* (Toronto: University of Toronto Press, 1985).

25 Graham Taylor and Peter Baskerville have commented that 'one would like to know more about the entrepreneurs who promoted industrial development in Upper Canada,' going so far as to speculate that 'It may be that industrialists were primarily drawn form the crafts area.' Graham D. Taylor and Peter A. Baskerville, *A Concise History of Business in Canada* (Toronto: Oxford University Press, 1994), 179. Acheson has suggested that the likelihood of Canada's industrialists boasting artisanal origins increased as one moved west across the country. 'According to this account, manufacturers in the Lake Peninsula of Ontario could claim the most humble origins of any fraction of their class in any region of the country.' See Acheson, 'The Social Origins of the Canadian Industrial Elite, 1880–1885,' in *Canadian Business History*, ed. David Macmillian (Toronto: McClelland & Stewart, 1972), 151. See also Jacob Spelt, *Urban Development in South-Central Ontario* (Ottawa: Carleton Library, 1972), 127–8; John McCallum, *Unequal Beginnings: Agriculture and Economic Development in Quebec and Ontario until 1870* (Toronto: University of Toronto Press, 1980), 91, 101; Douglas McCalla, *Planting the Province: The Economic History of Upper Canada, 1784–1870* (Toronto: University of

Toronto Press, 1993), 115; McCalla, 'Tom Naylor's *A History of Canadian Business: 1867–1914.* A Comment,' Canadian Historical Association, *Historical Papers* (1976); and David Burley, *A Particular Condition in Life: Self-Employment and Social Mobility in Mid-Victorian Brantford, Ontario* (Montreal and Kingston: McGill-Queen's University Press, 1994).

26 Katz, Doucet, and Stern, *Social Organization of Early Industrial Capitalism*, 30–5. Katz and associates base their brief discussion on J.A. Bryce, 'Patterns of Profit and Power: Business, Community and Industrialization in a Nineteenth-Century City,' York University Social History Project, 3rd Report, Working Paper No. 28 (1978). My concerns about Bryce's conclusions regarding the heavy mercantile and commercial interests of the city's industrialists are based on a number of factors surrounding both his questionable assembly of evidence and its interpretation. Bryce's determination of mercantile, commercial, financial, and other involvement was based on a sample derived by cross-linking the 1871 Industrial Census Schedules with the credit ledgers of R.G. Dun and Company. However, this sample is not representative of industrialists as a group since the Dun records are much more likely to record those whose dealings were large (and therefore likely more diversified) or individuals well-ensconced in the trade of the city from the time it was a commercial centre. This sample highly underrepresents such individuals as the artisan-industrialist relying on sweat equity for capital accumulation. Bryce's criterion for involvement in non-industrial enterprise is also somewhat ambiguous. For example, he uses real-estate speculation as one measure of involvement. It is unlikely, however, that industrialists' involvement in real-estate speculation marked them as being of the same 'ilk' as other men of a more decidedly commercial background. Most fundamental, though, is the fact that Bryce, while looking for a 'functional overlap' between industrialists and commercial capitalists, was not asking the crucial question Katz was asking, that is, whether the industrialists of 1871 were the same men, or members of the same families or social community, as the city's traditional commercial elite. In this respect, Katz's assertion about the commercial sponsorship of industrialization cannot by substantiated by Bryce's findings. The more rigorous and balanced methodology offered later on in this chapter will offer a more substantive conclusion on this issue – a conclusion based on something more, for instance, than a 'reasonably careful' reading of only one local newspaper for some years and a 'A casual survey' of it for others. See Bryce, 'Patterns of Profit,' 408n13.

27 T.W. Acheson, 'The Social Origins of Canadian Industrialism: A Study in the Structure of Entrepreneurship' (PhD thesis, University of

Toronto, 1971), 194–99; Acheson, 'Social Origins of the Canadian Industrial Elite,' 154–6.

28 Weaver is also probably singular in the historiography in his speculation that the fact Hamilton foundrymen built their establishments out of their own sweat and handiwork might have had an effect on social relations by fostering a 'spirit of co-operation and craft loyalty' as well as a 'fraternal atmosphere' among the city's enterprising metal artisans. See Weaver, 'The Location of Manufacturing,' 208; Palmer, *Culture in Conflict*, 10.

29 For a discussion of Katz et al.'s particularly troubling and ambiguous treatment of this subject, see Kristofferson, 'Craft Capitalism,' 98–101.

30 Katz, Doucet, and Stern, *Social Organization of Early Industrial Capitalism*, 12, 18, 30–5, 51, 58–61, 161; Katz, *The People of Hamilton,* 143, 196. Burley makes a similar criticism of Katz et al.'s data. See Burley, *A Particular Condition in Life*, 13. In their discussion of sources Katz et al. state that the cost of adding the necessary information to make this distinction was prohibitive, 'especially because the gains would be quite small' (12).

31 These manuscripts have been put into machine-readable form as part of the Canadian Industry in 1871 Project directed by Elizabeth and Gerald Bloomfield at the Department of Geography, University of Guelph. Bloomfield and Bloomfield offer extensive discussions concerning the problems, potential pitfalls, and copious rewards this source offers the historian. For information on this project, see Elizabeth Bloomfield, 'Using the 1871 Census Manuscript Industrial Schedules,' *Histoire sociale/Social History* 19, no. 38 (November 1986): 427–41; Elizabeth and Gerald Bloomfield, 'Mills, Factories and Craftshops of Ontario, 1870: A Machine-Readable Source for Material Historians,' *Material History Bulletin,* 25 (1987), 120–32. For more detailed information, see the numerous research reports generated from this project, available from the Department of Geography, University of Guelph. A separate database was assembled from the 1871 Industrial Manuscripts for Hamilton for his study.

32 The recent multivolume *Dictionary of Hamilton Biography* was especially useful for this purpose, as were some nineteenth-century biographical dictionaries. Also informative were the local history columns popular in local newspapers in the first couple of decades of the twentieth century. Much biographical information was also gleaned from a thorough reading of city newspapers for the period 1840 to 1880. Various city promotionals were also helpful. The census information can be

found in Census of Canada, 1871. Schedule No. 6 'Return of Industrial Establishments.' District No. 24 'Hamilton.' Major sources used for cross-reference include Bailey, ed., *Dictionary of Hamilton Biography* 3 vols., which provide generally well-researched and documented biographies of prominent Hamiltonians in the nineteenth century. See also Geo. MacLean Rose, ed., *A Cyclopedia of Canadian Biography* (Toronto: Rose Publishing, 1886), and G.M. Adam, ed., *Prominent Men of Canada: A Collection of Persons Distinguished in Professional and Political Life, in the Commerce and Industry of Canada* (Toronto, 1892). Turn-of-the-century local history writers include Richard Butler for the Hamilton *Spectator*; see Hamilton Public Library [hereafter HPL], Microfilm #121, Joseph Tinsely (aka 'Jaques'), see HPL, 'Jaques' Scrapbooks and 'Reminiscences of an Old Boy' for the Dundas *Star*, see HPL Archives File, 'W.H. Moss.' Available Hamilton newspapers consulted for the period 1840 to 1880 include the Hamilton *Spectator, Times, Weekly Times, Gazette, Bee, Commercial Advertiser, Argus, Journal and Express, Provincialist, Peoples' Journal,* and *Canadian Illustrated News*. City promotionals consulted include Hamilton *Spectator,* Carnival Edition, (1886); *Industries of Canada, Historical and Commercial Sketches, Hamilton and Environs* (Toronto: M.G. Bixby and Company, 1886); and *Hamilton: The Birmingham of Canada* (Hamilton: Times Printing Company, 1892).

33 This data set should be compared with Gutman's study of Paterson, New Jersey, which was based on the biographical backgrounds of only 'thirty-odd' prominent manufacturers and confined to a study of that city's locomotive, iron, and machinery sectors. It should also be compared with Ross's study of Cincinnati, Ohio, which analysed the backgrounds of only the leading 10% of that city's industrialists in 1850. See Gutman, 'The Reality of the Rags-to-Riches "Myth",' 220 and Ross, *Workers on the Edge*, 79.

34 Given that the historical sources cannot yield conclusive proof of the origins of small masters, this methodology is likely to provide the most accurate prediction.

35 This study was able to identify the origins of 233 out of a total of 328 industrial proprietors from the 1871 Industrial Schedules, roughly two-thirds of the total.

36 It should also be noted that it was not exclusively those 'in between' that could not be identified. There were a number of larger masters, for example, for whom biographical information elucidatory of their origins was not available.

37 Ross, *Workers on the Edge*, 79.

Chapter 3. Craft Mobility and Artisan-Led Industrialization: Continuity in Symbol and Practice

1 Richard Butler, *Saturday Musings*, Hamilton Public Library [HPL] Micro #121, vol. 3: 101.

2 Michael B. Katz, *The People of Hamilton, Canada West* (Cambridge, MA: Harvard University Press, 1975), 138; Michael Doucet and John Weaver, 'Town Fathers and Urban Continuity: The Roots of Community Power and Physical Form in Hamilton, Upper Canada, in the 1830s,' *Urban History Review* 13, no. 2 (October 1984): 75–90; Michael B. Katz, Michael J. Doucet and Mark J. Stern, *The Social Organization of Early Industrial Capitalism* (Cambridge, MA: Harvard University Press, 1982), 160, 18; Bryan D. Palmer, *A Culture in* Conflict (Montreal and Kingston: McGill-Queen's University Press, 1979), xii.

3 See, for example, David Gagan, *Hopeful Travellers: Families, Land, and Social Change in Mid-Victorian Peel County, Canada* (Toronto: University of Toronto Press, 1981); and David Burley, *A Particular Condition in Life: Self-Employment and Social Mobility in Mid-Victorian Brantford, Ontario* (Montreal and Kingston: McGill-Queen's University Press, 1994). This thesis of the limited nature of nineteenth-century social mobility found a powerful early expression in Stephen Thernstrom, *Poverty and Progress: Social Mobility in a Nineteenth-Century City* (Cambridge, MA: Harvard University Press, 1964). For the influence of Thernstrom's thesis on the international literature and some more recent reconsiderations of his findings, see contributions by Edward Pessen, Michael Frisch, Steven A. Reiss, and Stephan Thernstrom in John N. Ingham, ed., 'Comment and Debate, Thernstrom's *Poverty and Progress*: A Retrospective after Twenty Years,' *Social Science History* 10, no. 1 (Spring 1986): 1–44.

4 See: Gordon Darroch and Lee Soltow, *Property and Inequality in Victorian Ontario: Structural Patterns and Cultural Communities in the 1871 Census* (Toronto: University of Toronto Press, 1994), 73; and Darroch, 'Class in Nineteenth-Century Central Ontario: A Reassessment of the Crisis and Demise of Small Producers during Early Industrialization, 1861–1871,' reprinted in *Class, Gender and Region: Essays in Canadian Historical Sociology*, ed. Gregory S. Kealey (St John's: Committee on Canadian Labour History, 1988).

5 The unreliability of the evidence upon which this assertion of craftsworker immobility is based is partly acknowledged in Katz et al., *Social Organization*, 12, 18, 30–5, 51, 58–61, 161; and Katz, *People of Hamilton,* 143, 196. For a fuller discussion see chapter 1 and Burley, *A Particular Condition in Life*, 13.

6 Most particularly, Burley's study of Brantford finds that shrinkage of opportunity in self-employment was especially pronounced for artisans. Burley provides no indication of how widespread this phenomenon was. See Burley, *A Particular Condition in Life*, 17, 51.

7 See Jacob Spelt, *Urban Development in South-Central Ontario* (Ottawa: Carleton Library, 1972), 127–8; John McCallum, *Unequal Beginnings: Agriculture and Economic Development in Quebec and Ontario until 1870* (Toronto: University of Toronto Press, 1980), 91, 101; Douglas McCalla, *Planting the Province: The Economic History of Upper Canada, 1784–1870* (Toronto: University of Toronto Press, 1993), 115; McCalla, 'Tom Naylor's *A History of Canadian Business, 1867–1914*: A Comment,' Canadian Historical Association *Historical Papers* (1976); Darroch and Soltow, *Property and Inequality*, 73; Darroch, 'Class in Nineteenth-Century, Central Ontario'; T.W. Acheson, 'The Social Origins of the Canadian Industrial Elite, 1880–1885,' in *Canadian Business History*, ed. D. McMillian (Toronto: McClelland and Stewart, 1972), 151; Burley, *A Particular Condition in Life*, 186; Ben Forster, 'Finding the Right Size: Markets and Competition in Mid- and Late Nineteenth-Century Ontario,' in *Patterns of the Past: Interpreting Ontario's History*, ed. Roger Hall, William Westfall, and Laurel Sefton MacDowell (Toronto and Oxford: Dundurn Press, 1988), 1; and Ben Forster and Kris Inwood, 'The Diversity of Industrial Experience: Cabinet and Furniture Manufacture in Late Nineteenth-Century Ontario,' *Enterprise and Society* 4, no. 2 (2003): 326–71.

8 This is also partly true of the handful of similar studies in the United States, including Herbert Gutman, 'The Reality of the Rags-to-Riches "Myth": The Case of the Paterson, New Jersey, Locomotive, Iron and Machinery Manufacturers, 1830–1880,' in *Work, Culture, and Society in Industrializing America*, ed. Gutman (New York: Vintage, 1977); Susan E. Hirsch, 'From Artisan to Manufacturer: Industrialization and the Small Producer in Newark, 1830–1860,' in *Small Business in American Life*, ed. Stuart W. Bruchey (New York: Columbia University Press, 1980); and Stephen J. Ross, *Workers on the Edge: Work, Leisure and Politics in Industrializing Cincinnati, 1788–1890* (New York: Columbia University Press, 1985).

9 James Henretta, 'The Study of Social Mobility: Ideological Assumptions and Conceptual Bias,' *Labor History* 18, no. 2 (Spring 1977): 167.

10 See, for example, James R. Farr, *Artisans in Europe, 1300–1914* (Cambridge: Cambridge University Press, 2000).

11 Generally speaking, historians have considered members of the professions, the merchantocracy, or other traditional elite groups as having

constituted the 'middle classes.' The masculinity of the artisan-industrialist awaits study. Works on American middle-class masculinity include Mark C. Carnes and Clyde Griffen, eds., *Meanings for Manhood* (Chicago: University of Chicago Press, 1990); Carnes, *Secret Ritual and Manhood in Victorian America* (New Haven, CT: Yale University Press, 1989); Mary Ann Clawson, *Constructing Brotherhood: Class, Gender and Fraternalism* (Princeton, NJ: Princeton University Press, 1989); E. Anthony Rotundo, *American Manhood* (New York: Basic Books, 1993); and Mary P. Ryan, *Cradle of the Middle Class: The Family in Oneida County, New York, 1790–1865* (New York: Cambridge University Press, 1981). For an expanded discussion of some of the drawbacks of Rotundo's book, see my review of *American Manhood* in *left history* 2, no. 2 (Fall 1994): 133–6.

12 The most notable exception to this is Joy Parr's study of Hanover, Ontario. See Joy Parr, *The Gender of Breadwinners: Women, Men, and Change in Two Industrial Towns 1880–1950* (Toronto: University of Toronto Press, 1990), part 2.

13 Gender historians often present the masculinity of nineteenth-century skilled workers as contextually specific and constructed around such variables as unionization, craft recruitment, skill, technology, gender demographics of the workplace, and the wage-earning experience. Progress through the craft ranks in the construction of skilled worker masculinity is often, at least implicitly, a central feature of much of this work. However, it is usually presented as something that has been disrupted or renegotiated by the jarring impact of industrialization and the hegemony of the wage-earning relationship. For examples, see Cynthia Cockburn, *Brothers: Male Dominance and Technical Change* (London: Pluto Press, 1983); Ava Baron, 'Acquiring Manly Competence: The Demise of Apprenticeship and the Remasculinization of Printers' Work,' in *Meanings for Manhood*, ed. Mark C. Carnes and Clyde Griffen (Chicago: University of Chicago Press, 1990); Baron, 'An "Other" Side to Gender Antagonism at Work: Men, Boys, and the Remasculinization of Printers' Work,' in *Work Engendered: Towards a New History of American Labour*, ed. Baron (Ithaca, NY: Cornell University Press, 1991); Baron, 'Questions of Gender: Deskilling and Demasculinization in the U.S. Printing Industry, 1830–1915,' *Gender and History* 1, no. 1 (Spring 1989): 178–99; Mary H. Blewett, 'Manhood and the Market: The Politics of Gender and Class among the Textile Workers of Fall River, Massachusetts, 1780–1880,' in Baron, *Work Engendered*; Christina Burr, *Spreading the Light: Work and Labour Reform in Late-Nineteenth-Century Toronto* (Toronto: University of Toronto Press, 1999); Burr, 'Defending "The Art Preservative": Class and Gender

Relations in the Printing Trades Unions, 1850–1914,' *Labour/Le Travail* 31 (Spring 1993): 47–74; Patricia Cooper, *Once a Cigar Maker* (Urbana: University of Illinois Press, 1987); Ella Johansson, 'Beautiful Men, Fine Women and Good Work People: Gender and Skill in Northern Sweden, 1850–1950,' *Gender and History* 1, no. 2 (Summer 1989): 200–12; and Keith McClelland, 'Masculinity and the "Representative Artisan" in Britain, 1850–1880,' in *Manful Assertions*, ed. Michael Roper and John Tosh (London: Routledge, 1991).

14 Henretta, 'The Study of Social Mobility,' 167.

15 Charles Stephenson, '"There's Plenty Waitin' at the Gates": Mobility, Opportunity and the American Worker,' in *Life and Labour: Dimensions of American Working-Class History*, ed. Charles Stephenson and Robert Asher (New York: SUNY Press, 1986), 77, 82.

16 Gutman, 'The Reality of the Rags-to-Riches Myth,' 232.

17 See Palmer, *Culture in Conflict*, 13–14; Katz, *People of Hamilton*, 138, 165–71; Katz, Doucet, and Stern, *Social Organization*, 58–61; Katz, *York Social History Project: Third Report – February 1978*, York University, Department of History, Working Paper No. 24, 236.

18 It should be noted that the daily wage rates for selected occupations outlined in table 3.4 could only be compared roughly to the income figures for Hamilton's small artisan-proprietors since the occupational and sectoral categories in each table do not correspond. However, the figures in table 3.4 do allow for a broad comparison of the relative *range* of wage rates that likely existed for skilled workers in the city at this time.

19 For the seasonality of employment in nineteenth-century Ontario, see Elizabeth Bloomfield and G.T. Bloomfield, *Patterns of Canadian Industry in 1871: An Overview Based on the First Census of Canada* (Guelph: University of Guelph, Department of Geography, Canadian Industry in 1871 Project, Research Report 12, 1990), 28–30; Craig Heron, 'Factory Workers,' in *Labouring Lives: Work and Workers in Nineteenth-Century Ontario*, ed. Paul Craven (Toronto: University of Toronto Press, 1995), 494; and Stephenson, '"There's Plenty Waitin' at the Gates."'

20 A total of 95 occupations were reported for the 71 small master's families identified from the census. The 166 skilled worker's families identified contained a total of 271 family members reporting an occupation. The methodology used for this section resembles the one employed in Bettina Bradbury, 'The Family Economy and Work in an Industrializing City: Montreal in the 1870s,' Canadian Historical Association *Historical Papers* (1979): 71–96.

21 For the 71 families headed by small masters, 18 (25.35%) reported

more than one worker. For the 166 families headed by skilled workers, 67 (40.36%) reported more than one worker.

22 In the 18–21 age group 100% of small master's sons reported an occupation (n=11), compared with only 1 out of 16 daughters (6.25%).

23 Stephenson, '"There's Plenty Waitin' at the Gates",' 91.

24 For this study a successful industrialist or large employer is loosely defined by the following characteristics. Many of these men offered employment to considerable numbers of workers. They also ranked highly in their respective industrial sectors or across the city as a whole in terms of annual wages paid, annual value added, or annual product value. These men might also be, if not wildly successful in material terms, still quite well-to-do and heralded in the community as examples of business success. In all, the men discussed here were unanimously recognized by the community for their success in business and most had experienced a very real, if not spectacular, increase in personal wealth over their working lives.

25 *Spectator,* 8 April 1869; 8 September 1870; 2 September, 19 February 1872; 18 April 1873; Butler, *Saturday Musings,* vol. 3.

26 *Spectator,* 14 September 1857, 15 September 1865; *Times,* 5 October 1863, 27 June 1865; Anon., *Industries of Canada*, 48; 1871 Census Index.

27 *The Dictionary of Hamilton Biography*, (hereafter *DHB*), vol. 1, ed. Thomas Melville Bailey (Hamilton, ON: Dictionary of Hamilton Biography, 1981); 'Williams, James M.,' 211–12 and 'Tuckett, George Elias,' 200; *Dictionary of Canadian Biography Online,* 'Tuckett, George Elias'; Canada, vol. 25: 107, R.G. Dun and Co. Collection, Baker Library, Harvard Business School. (hereafter R.G. Dun Records), cited in Katz, *People of Hamilton*, 196; *Times*, 8 December 1863; *Spectator,* 6 March 1920.

28 See Kristofferson, 'Craft Capitalism' (PhD diss., York University, 2003), 139–48 for a detailed portrait accounting of apprenticeship information available for employers across Hamilton's industrial economy.

29 Ontario Agricultural Museum, Lynn Campbell, 'C. McQuesten and Company, 1835–57' (typescript); HPL, Joseph Tinsley (aka 'Jaques'), 'Old Hamiltonians' Scrapbook,' 103–8; *Herald,* 6 April 1907; Laura Edith Brown, *The Boat Builders of Hamilton* (Hamilton: Progressive Printing, 1992), 19; *DHB* 1, 'Smiley, Robert Reid,' 182–3; *DHB* 2, 'Bastien, Henry Louis,' 187–8; HPL, Hamilton Typographical Union, Local 129, Record Box #1, *Constitution of the City of Hamilton Typographical Society with the By-Laws and Scales of Prices,* 1 July 1846 (hereafter cited as HPL, HTU Records); Butler, *Saturday Musings*, 3: 201–2; 4: 172, 201–2.

30 *Dundas True Banner,* 27 November 1884; *Spectator,* 2 December 1915,

26 March 1922, Carnival Edition, 1886; *Times,* 2 January 1909, 9 October 1915; Butler, *Saturday Musings*, vol. 3: 130–4, 171–4; HPL, clipping file, F.H. Armstrong, 'Edward Gurney,' typescript, *DCB* entry; *DHB* 1, 'Gurney, Charles,' 'Gurney, Edward,' 'Burrow, William,' 'Milne, John,' and 'Stewart, Charles,' 89–90, 40–1, 154–5, 187.

31 *DHB* 1, 'Williams, James Miller,' 'Stewart, James,' 'Laidlaw, Adam,' 211–12, 187–8, 117–18; *DHB* 2, 'McCulloch, David,' 103–4; *Spectator,* 22 December 1871, Carnival Edition 1886, 24 December 1890, 22 July 1901; *Times,* 4, 30 September, 8 December 1863; *Ontario Workman,* 8 August 1872; Anon, *Industries of Canada*, 59, 76, and Butler, *Saturday Musings*, vol. 3: 102, 175, 201–2.

32 George Maclean Rose, ed., *A Cyclopedia of Canadian Biography* (Toronto: Rose Publishing Company, 1886), 552; Anon, *Industries of Canada*, 75; *DHB* 1, 'Killey, Joseph H,' 117.

33 *Spectator,* 2 December 1915, 26 March 1922; *DHB* 1, 'Donnelly, Richard Robert,' 'Milne, John,' 62, 154–5; Rose, *Cyclopedia of Canadian Biography*, 63; and Butler, *Saturday Musings*, 4: 172.

34 Whitehern, McQuesten Papers, E. Ladd to — Finch, foreman at the Fisher and McQuesten Foundry, Hamilton, 2 September 1855; HPL, Logie-McQuesten Papers, Bond. Luther Sawyer to Calvin McQuesten, 23 September 1853; Butler, *Saturday Musings*, 3: 171; City Directory 1870–71; *DHB* 1, 'Copp, Anthony,' 'Copp, William,' 53–4.

35 On the tramp, see E.J. Hobsbawn, 'The Tramping Artisan,' *Economic History Review* 3 (1951): 299–320; Patricia Cooper, *Once a Cigar Maker* (Urbana: University of Illinois Press, 1987); R.A. Leeson, *Travelling Brothers* (London: Allen and Unwin, 1979); Eric H. Monkonen, *Walking to Work: Tramps in America, 1790–1935* (Lincoln: University of Nebraska Press, 1984); David Bensman, *The Practice of Solidarity: American Hat Finishers in the Nineteenth Century* (Chicago: University of Illinois Press, 1985); and H.R. Southall, 'The Tramping Artisan Revisited: Labour Mobility and Economic Distress in Early Victorian England,' *Economic History Review* 44 (1991): 272–96.

36 Peter Bischoff, 'Another Perspective on Labour Migrations: The International Iron Molder's Union's Influence on Mobility as Seen through Their Journals, 1860s to 1930s' (unpublished paper). See also Bischoff, 'D'un atelier de moulage à un autre: les migrations des mouldeurs originaires des Forges du Saint-Maurice et segmentation du marché du travail nord-américain, 1851–1884,' *Labour/Le Travail* 40 (Fall 1997): 21–74.

37 Susan Hirsch, for example, has observed that historians tend to consider the dimensions of industrialization as stemming from its most obvious forms, especially large capitalized concerns employing large

numbers of hands. This has been the tendency in much of the Canadian historiography as well. See Susan Hirsch, 'From Artisan to Manufacturer.' In relation to Hamilton, Acheson fell particularly victim to this as a function of his choice to consider industrial growth in the city after the implementation of the National Policy and, therefore, to concentrate on the rise of textile production, the rolling mills, and other large capital industries as representative of the city's industrialization. See Thomas William Acheson, 'The Social Origins of Canadian Industrialism: A Study in the Structure of Entrepreneurship' (PhD diss., University of Toronto, 1971).

38 The transformation of the operations of 'independent small artisans' into 'capitalist production without qualification' was discussed by Marx. Historians have identified this as likely a major component in Ontario's early industrial growth. See Karl Marx, *Capital* vol. 1 (London: Penguin Classics, 1990), 914; McCallum, *Unequal Beginnings*; McCalla, *Planting the Province*, 111; McCalla, 'Tom Naylor's *History of Canadian Business*,' 250. McCalla's thought is informed by Sidney Pollard, 'Fixed Capital in the Industrial Revolution,' *Journal of Economic History* 24 (1964): 299–314. See also Douglas McCalla and Peter George, 'Measurement, Myth and Reality: Reflections on the Economic History of Nineteenth-Century Ontario,' *Journal of Canadian Studies* 21, no. 3 (Fall 1986): 71–86.

39 *Times,* 24 February, 1862, 20 July, 4 September 1863, 7 August 1865, 17 October 1867, 11 July 1871, 13 August 1903; *Spectator,* 16 November 1858, 19 December 1864, 12 April 1865, Carnival Edition 1886, 30 July 1904; *Herald,* 6 April 1907; *DHB* 1, 'Fearman, Frederick William,' 'Lawson, Alexander,' 68–9, 123; *DHB* 2, 'McCulloch, David,' 'Meakins, Charles William,' 103–4, 112; 1871 Database; Butler, *Saturday Musings,* vol. 3, 102, 201–2, 226; HPL cf. Hamilton – Biography – Fearman, F.W.; HPL, Joseph Tinsley, 'Old Hamiltonians' Scrapbooks, n.d., n.p; vol. 1, 103–8, vol. 5, 92; Anon, *Industries of Canada*, 76; Census Index; HPL, Census of Hamilton, 1840–1, microfilm #47.

40 Jeff Merriman, 'Autobiography and Merriman Family History: Horace Owen Merriman, 1888–1972' (1999), typescript in possession of author; John Weaver, 'The Location of Manufacturing Enterprises: The Case of Hamilton's Attraction of Foundries, 1830–1890,' in *Critical Issues in the History of Canadian Science, Technology and* Medicine, ed. R.A. Jarrell and A.E. Roos (Thornhill, ON: HSTC Publications, 1981), 197–217; *Times,* 24 February 1862, 5 October 1863, 27 June 1865; *Spectator,* 14 September 1857; 1871 Database.

41 Times, 6 November 1871, 25 November 1871, 2 January 1909, 9 Octo-

ber 1915; *Spectator*, 2 December 1915, Carnival Edition 1886, Carnival Edition 1903, 26 March 1922; Canada, Royal Commission on the Relations between Labour and Capital, *Report – Evidence, Ontario* (hereafter RCRLC), 834–7; Butler, *Saturday Musings*, vol. 3: 171–4; *DHB* 1, 'Burrow, William,' 'Milne, John,' 'Stewart, Charles,' 40–1, 154–5, 187; Anon, *Hamilton: The Birmingham of Canada* (Hamilton: Times Printing Company, 1892).

42 McCalla, *Planting the Province*, 110–11.

43 *Dundas True Banner,* 27 November 1884; *Times,* 24 February 1862; *Spectator*, 5 September 1870, Carnival Edition 1886; HPL. Gurney file in Hamilton Industries drawer, John D. Burt to ?, 16 September 1876; *DHB* 1, 'Carpenter, Alexander,' 'Gurney, Charles,' 'Gurney, Edward,' 42, 89–90; Butler, *Saturday Musings,* 3: 130–4, 171; HPL, clipping file, F.H. Armstrong, 'Edward Gurney,' typescript *DCB* entry; 1871 Database.

44 Butler, *Saturday Musings*, 3: 181; *Spectator,* 9 June 1869, 24 December 1921; Public Archives of Ontario, McQuesten Papers, Janes to McQuesten, 22 November 1835, Fisher to McQuesten, 20 October 1836, 24 January 1839, 11 March 1839; and Campbell, 'C. McQuesten and Company.'

45 *Dundas True Banner,* 27 November 1884; *Times* 24 February 1862; *Spectator,* 5 September 1870, Carnival Edition 1886.

46 *Times,* 12 December 1863; *Spectator,* 14 September 1857, 24 November 1863; Hamilton City Directory 1853/4, 1870/1; *Times,* 24 February 1862, 5, 9 October 1863, 27 June 1865; *Herald,* 6 April 1907; and Butler, *Saturday Musings,* 3: 95–7.

47 Much of this ground has previously been covered for the metal industry in John Weaver, 'The Location of Manufacturing Enterprises: The Case of Hamilton's Attraction of Foundries, 1830–1890,' in *Critical Issues in the History of Canadian Science, Technology and Medicine*, ed. Richard A. Jarrell and Arnold E. Roos (Thornhill, ON: HSTC, 1983), 208–11.

48 Public Archives of Ontario, McQuesten Papers, Janes to McQuesten, 22 November 1835, Fisher to McQuesten, 20 October 1836, 24 January 1839, 11 March 1839, Sarah Sawyer to Calvin McQuesten, 1844; Whitehern, McQuesten Papers. Fisher to McQuesten, 6 May 1837; HPL, Logie-McQuesten Papers, Bond. Luther Sawyer to Calvin McQuesten; Campbell, 'C. McQuesten and Company'; *Herald,* 7 December 1908; *Spectator,* Carnival Edition, 1886, 24 December 1890; Butler, *Saturday Musings*, 3: 171–4; and *DHB* 1, 'Stewart, James,' 187–8.

49 *Times,* 4, 24 September 1863, 2 January 1909, 9 October 1915; *Spectator*, 2 December 1915, Carnival Edition 1886, Carnival Edition 1903,

26 March 1922; Butler, *Saturday Musings.*, 3: 171–4; *DHB* 1, 'Burrow, William,' 'Jackson, Edward,' 'Moore, Dennis,' 'Stewart, Charles,' 40–1, 108–9, 155–6, 187; *DHB* 2, 'McCulloch, David,' 103–4; HPL, Langsford Robinson, 'The D. Moore Company Ltd. of Hamilton, Ont.: A Historical Outline of the Last Stove Company in Hamilton,' typescript, 1948; Frederick Henry Armstrong, *The Forest City: An Illustrated History of London, Canada* (London, ON: Windsor Publications, 1986); HPL, clipping file, Hamilton – Industries – D. Moore Company.

50 *Times*, 8 December 1863; *DHB* 1, 'Lawson, Alexander,' 'Williams, James Miller,' 123, 211–12; *DHB* 2, 'McCulloch, David,' 103–4; Anon., *Industries of Canada*, 76; HPL, Joseph Tinsley (aka 'Jaques'), 'Old Hamiltonians' Scrapbook, 103–8.

51 *Dundas Star*, 21 October 1909; *True Banner and Wentworth Chronicle,* 19 July 1883; *DHB* 2, 'McKechnie, Robert,' 'Wilson, Thomas,' 106–7, 187; T.W. Acheson, 'The Social Origins of the Canadian Industrial Elite, 1880–1885,' in *Canadian Business History*, ed. D. MacMillian (Toronto: McClelland & Stewart, 1972), 155; *Industrial Canada*, March 1905, *Canadian Manufacturer*, 6 July 1888, RCRLC, *Ontario Evidence*, 856; Acheson, 'Social Origins,' 155; *Canadian Biographical Dictionary,* 1880, 529–30; *DHB* 1, 'Copp, Anthony,' 53; *Times*, 10 December 1869; Anon., *Industries of Canada*, 79; and Acheson, 'Social Origins,' 154.

52 *Times,* 6 November 1871; *Spectator,* 2 December 1915, 26 March 1922; *DHB* 1, 'Milne, John,' 154–5; E.P. Morgan and F.L. Harvey, *Hamilton and Its Industries: Being a Historical Sketch of the City of Hamilton and Its Public and Private Institutions, Manufacturing and Industrial Interests, Public Citizens, etc.* (Hamilton: Spectator Publishing, 1884), 57–8; R.G. Dun Records, vol. 25, 288; Hamilton, *City Directory* (Hamilton, 1871), 351; *Iron Molders' International Journal*, June 1867, 92; Butler, *Saturday Musings*, HPL, Micro #121, 4: 191.

53 Rose, *Cyclopedia of Canadian Biography,* 552; *DHB* 1, 'Killey, Joseph H,' 117; Butler, *Saturday Musings,* 3: 171–4; *Spectator*, Carnival Edition (1886), 22 July 1901.

54 *DHB* 2, 'Allan, Thomas,' 1; *DHB* 2, 'Kidner, Frank,' 'Souter, James Elder,' 'Zingsheim, Jacob,' 84, 145, 191; *Magazine of Industry,* (Hamilton, 1910); Anon., *Industries of Canada,* 42, 47, 76; Hamilton, *City Directory,* 1869–5; *Spectator*, 15 June 1875.

55 *Magazine of Industry*, 6; Hamilton, *City Directory,* 1887–90, 1911–13; *DHB* 2, 'Boggs, Nathan Glass,' 21; *Spectator,* 1 February 1913; Hamilton *Herald*, 28 July 1934; Hamilton, *City Directory,* 1911–13.

56 Elsewhere I argue that this change occurred as part of a prolonged process with roots in the economic depression of the mid-1870s but not

fully dominant in the city until the 1890s or, perhaps, the turn of the twentieth century. See Kristofferson, 'Craft Capitalism,' 449–59.

57 Gutman, 'The Reality of the Rags-to-Riches "Myth",' 233.

58 For a reinterpretation of the Nine Hours Movement of 1872 in Hamilton, see Kristofferson, 'Craft Capitalism,' chap. 8.

59 Ibid., 190.

60 Weaver, 'The Location of Manufacturing Enterprises,' 208.

61 Morgan and Harvey, *Hamilton and Its Industries,* 57–8; R.G. Dun Records, 288; Hamilton, *City Directory* (Hamilton, 1871), 351.

62 *DCB* Online, 'Williams, James Miller'; R.G. Dun Records, 147, 278.

63 *Times,* 8 December 1863; *Spectator,* 6 August 1853, 7 August 1856, Carnival Edition 1886, 10 March 1899, 6 March 1920; Robinson, 'The D. Moore Company'; *DHB* 1, 'Billings, John,' 'Jackson, Edward,' 'Killey, Joseph,' 'Moore, Dennis,' 'Tuckett, George Elias,' 'Williams, James Miller,' 19, 108–9, 117, 155–6, 200, 211–12; Hamilton *City Directory,* 1864–1892; Rose, *Cyclopedia of Canadian Biography*, 552; R.G. Dun Records, 218-A.

64 *Spectator*, 18 February 1873.

65 *Spectator,* 2 September 1872. For an examination of the residual elements of craft culture in Hamilton through this time period, see Kristofferson, 'Craft Capitalism,' chap. 5. For a similar point, see Heron, 'Factory Workers,' 533.

66 Burley, *A Particular Condition in Life.*

67 *Spectator,* 5 September 1870, Carnival Edition 1886, 24 December 1890; *Dundas True Banner,* 27 November 1884; *Times,* 24 February 1862, 8 December 1863; Butler, *Saturday Musings*, 3: 130–4, 170; *Industries of Canada*, 76.

68 In Canada this view has been established for a later period in Craig Heron, *Working in Steel* (Toronto: McClelland & Stewart, 1988).

69 For example, John Taylor, foreman at the Dennis Moore Foundry, remained an active member of the local iron moulder's union while in that position. See Hamilton, *City Directory*, 1869; *Iron Molder's International Journal,* 10 September 1864, September 1868, July 1869, February 1872.

70 *Times*, 28 November 1864.

71 *Hamilton Weekly Times*, 8 February 1872; *Times,* 31 October 1863, 27 June 1865; *Spectator*, 7 August 1856, 3 September 1857; Butler, *Saturday Musings*, 3: 130–4; HPL, D.C. Gunn to Walter Shanley, General Manager, Grand Trunk Railway, 10 November 1858, reprinted in Robert R. Brown, 'The Canadian Locomotive Builders: Part II,' typescript.

72 *Times*, 25 September 1863; *Spectator*, 19 February, 6 April 1872; R.G. Dun Records, vol. 25, 166, 217; H.B. Witton, 'Some Interesting Indus-

trial Figures,' 12 August 1913 on HPL Microfilm #121, vol. 3, 205; *DHB* 1, 'Hoodless, Joseph,' 105.

73 1871 Census Index; Joseph Tinsely (aka 'Jaques'), 'Events in the Early Days of Hamilton,' *Hamilton Herald,* 7 November 1903.

74 Eric Hobsbawm, *Labouring Men: Studies in the History of Labour* (New York: Basic Books, 1965), 297. See also Craig Littler, *The Development of the Labour Process in Capitalist Societies: A Comparative Study of the Transformation of Work Organization in Britain, Japan and the USA* (London: Heinemann Educational, 1982), 64–9; Sidney Pollard, *Genesis of Modern Management: A Study of the Industrial Revolution in Great Britain* (London: E. Arnold, 1965), 38–47; Dan Clawson, *Bureaucracy and the Labor Process: The Transformation of U.S. Industry, 1860–1920* (New York: Monthly Review Press, 1980), 71–125; David Montgomery, *Workers Control in America: Studies in the History of Work, Technology and Labor Struggles* (New York: Cambridge University Press, 1979), 11–12.

75 Paul Craven and Tom Traves, 'Canadian Railways as Manufacturers, 1850–1880,' Canadian Historical Association *Historical Papers* (1983): 254–6; John Weaver, *Hamilton: An Illustrated History* (Toronto: Lorimer, 1982), 49; Palmer, *Culture in Conflict*, 255 n.57.

76 Heron, 'Factory Workers,' 536–8.

77 Paul Craven and Tom Traves, 'Dimensions of Paternalism: Discipline and Culture in Canadian Railway Operations in the 1850s,' in *On the Job: Confronting the Labour Process in Canada*, ed. Craig Heron and Robert Storey (Kingston and Montreal: McGill-Queen's University Press, 1986), 53, 69.

78 Paul Craven and Tom Traves, 'Canadian Railways as Manufacturers,' 254, 280; and Paul Craven, 'Labour and Management on the Great Western Railway,' in his *Labouring Lives*, 341–7.

79 *Spectator,* 25 September 1856, 18 May 1861, 17 February 1873; *Times,* 2 September 1863, 3 September 1863, 4 September 1863; Craven, 'Labour and Management on the Great Western Railway,' 343.

80 Craven and Traves, 'The Dimensions of Paternalism,' 61; Craven, 'Labour and Management on the Great Western,' 344.

81 *DHB* 1, 'Lawson, Alexander,' 'Wingfield, Alexander' 123, 214; *DHB* 2, 'Bastien, Henry Louis,' 'McCulloch, David,' 'Witton, Henry Buckingham,' 11, 103–4, 187–8; Butler, *Saturday Musings*, 3: 102, 201–2; *Times,* 2, 3, 4 September 1863; *Herald*, 22 June 1907; *Spectator*, 4 March 1872; Laura Edith Brown, *The Boat Builders of Hamilton* (Hamilton: Progressive Printing, 1992), 19; Robinson, 'The D. Moore Company.'

82 Especially useful for theorizing Independent Commodity Producers in Canada is Leo Johnson, 'Independent Commodity Production: Mode of

Production or Capitalist Class Formation,' *Studies in Political Economy* 6 (1981): 93–112. Work on the special place of farmers and fisherman in the development of Canadian political economy is too large to cite here.

83 Notable exceptions to this include Joanne Burgess, 'Work, Family and Community: Montreal Leather Artisans, 1790–1831' (PhD diss., University of Quebec, 1986) and William N.T. Wylie, 'The Blacksmith in Upper Canada, 1784–1850: A Study of Technology, Culture and Power,' in *Canadian Papers in Rural History*, vol. 7, ed. Donald H. Akenson (Gananoque, ON: Langdale Press, 1990), 17–193.

84 Here I am thinking specifically of the criticism levelled by Ernesto Laclau at Andre Gunder Frank's assertion that Latin America has been capitalist since colonial conquest. Laclau argues persuasively that Frank's theory is 'indefensible' since many direct producers were not despoiled of their means of production. Laclau essentially argues that Frank has confused accumulation with capitalism. See Laclau, *Politics and Ideology in Marxist Theory: Capitalism-Fascism-Populism* (London: Verso, 1977), especially chap. 1: 'Feudalism and Capitalism in Latin America.' For a Canadian adaptation of this argument, see Allan Greer, 'Wage Labour and the Transition to Capitalism: A Critique of Pentland,' *Labour/Le Travail* 15 (Spring 1985): 7–22, and his empirical study *Peasant, Lord and Merchant: Rural Society in Three Quebec Parishes, 1740–1840* (Toronto: University of Toronto Press, 1985). In the U.S. historiography much of the transition-to-capitalism debate has been concerned more with the relative weightings of use and exchange value or degrees of market integration than with close attention to the mode of production. For an interesting summary of the U.S. debates, see Allan Kulikoff, 'The Transition to Capitalism in Rural America,' *William and Mary Quarterly* 3rd series, 61 (1989): 120–44.

85 Marx, *Capital*, vol. 1 (New York: Penguin, 1976, 1990), 274n.4. My emphasis.

86 Allan Kulikoff, 'The Transition to Capitalism in Rural America,' 120–44.

87 Gary J. Kornblith, 'The Artisanal Response to Capitalist Transformation,' *Journal of the Early Republic* 10 (Fall 1990): 316.

88 Leo Johnson has convincingly argued that the modern bourgeois epoch, which arose after approximately 1400, had characteristics of capitalism, such as production of commodities for exchange. However, this epoch would not truly become capitalist until bourgeois labour relations (i.e., neo-feudalism, modern slavery, or independent commodity production) were dissolved and replaced with truly capitalist labour relations, characterized above all else by the commodification of labour power. In

these terms one can view capitalist production and independent commodity production as two discrete submodes' of production that can coexist *within* the modern bourgeois epoch. The capitalist mode is the ultimate logic of this epoch, but precapitalist modes also exist within the greater context of bourgeois accumulation. See Leo Johnson, 'Precapitalist Economic Formations and the Capitalist Labour Market in Canada,' in *Social Stratification: Canada*, ed. James E. Curtis and William G. Scott (Scarborough, ON: Prentice-Hall 1979), 89–104.

Chapter 4. A Culture in Continuity: Master–Man Mutualism in Hamilton, Ontario, during Early Industrialization

1 Raymond Williams, 'Base and Superstructure in Marxist Cultural Theory,' *New Left Review* 82 (November–December 1973) reprinted in *Problems in Materialism and Culture: Selected Essays* (London: Verso, 1980); Williams, *Marxism and Literature* (London: Oxford University Press, 1977).

2 In addition to a number of article-length studies, the two standard Canadian accounts of working class culture are Gregory S. Kealey, *Toronto Workers Respond to Industrial Capitalism, 1867–1892* (Toronto: University of Toronto Press, 1980) and Bryan D. Palmer, *A Culture in Conflict: Skilled Workers and Industrial Capitalism in Hamilton, Ontario, 1860–1914* (Montreal and Kingston: McGill-Queen's University Press, 1979).

3 See especially David Bercuson, 'Through the Looking Glass of Culture: An Essay on the New Labour History and Working-Class Culture in Recent Canadian Historical Writing,' *Labour/Le Travailleur* 7 (Spring 1981): 94–112, and Kenneth McNaught, 'E.P. Thompson vs. Harold Logan: Writing about Labour and the Left in the 1970s,' *Canadian Historical Review* 62, no. 2 (1981): 141–68.

4 See, in particular, Craig Heron, 'The Crisis of the Craftsman: Hamilton Metal Workers in the Early Twentieth Century,' *Labour/Le Travailleur* 6 (Autumn 1980): 7–48; Ian McKay, 'Capital and Labour in the Halifax Baking and Confectionery Industry during the Last Half of the Nineteenth Century,' *Labour/Le Travailleur* 3 (1978): 63–108; and McKay, 'None But Skilled Workmen,' reprinted in *Canadian Working-Class History: Selected Readings*, ed. Laurel Sefton MacDowell and Ian Radforth (Toronto: Canadian Scholar's Press, 1991), 135–58.

5 The 'consciousness-achieved' advocates include Paul Faler, *Mechanics and Manufacturers in the Early Industrial Revolution: Lynn, Massachusetts, 1780–1860* (Albany: SUNY Press, 1981) and Sean Wilenz, *Chants Democratic: New York City and the Rise of the American Work-*

ing Class, 1788–1830 (New York: Oxford University Press, 1984). Advocates of the 'consciousness-denied' school include Susan E. Hirsch, *Roots of the American Working Class: The Industrialization of Crafts in Newark, 1800–1860* (Philadelphia: University of Pennsylvania Press, 1978) and Bruce Laurie, *Working People of Philadelphia, 1800–1850* (Philadelphia: Temple University Press, 1980).

6 Gary Kornblith refers to this general rubric as the 'declension model.' See his 'The Artisanal Response to Capitalist Transformation,' *Journal of the Early Republic* 10 (Fall 1990): 316.

7 It was Sean Wilenz who popularized this term. See his *Chants Democratic,* 108.

8 The earliest example is British. See Cynthia Cockburn, *Brothers: Male Dominance and Technical Change* (London: Pluto Press, 1983). Another good British example is Keith McClelland, 'Masculinity and the "Representative Artisan" in Britain, 1850–1880,' in *Manful Assertions*, ed. Michael Roper and John Tosh (London: Routledge, 1991). American examples include Ava Baron, 'Acquiring Manly Competence: The Demise of Apprenticeship and the Remasculinization of Printers' Work,' in *Meanings for Manhood*, ed. Mark C. Carnes and Clyde Griffen (Chicago: University of Chicago Press, 1990), 152–63; Baron, 'An "Other" Side to Gender Antagonism at Work: Men, Boys, and the Remasculinization of Printers' Work,' in *Work Engendered: Towards a New History of American Labour*, ed. Baron (Ithaca, NY: Cornell University Press, 1991); Baron, 'Questions of Gender: Deskilling and Demasculinization in the U.S. Printing Industry, 1830–1915,' *Gender and History* 1, no. 1 (spring 1989): 178–99; Mary H. Blewett, 'Manhood and the Market: The Politics of Gender and Class among the Textile Workers of Fall River, Massachusetts, 1780–1880,' in Baron, *Work Engendered*; and Patricia Cooper, *Once a Cigar Maker* (Urbana: University of Illinois Press, 1987). For a Canadian example that follows the dominant paradigm, especially that established by Baron in the United States, see Christina Burr, *Spreading the Light: Work and Labour Reform in Late-Nineteenth-Century Toronto* (Toronto: University of Toronto Press, 1999) and 'Defending "The Art Preservative": Class and Gender Relations in the Printing Trades Unions, 1850–1914,' *Labour/Le Travail* 31 (Spring 1993): 47–74. For a Swedish example, see Ella Johansson, 'Beautiful Men, Fine Women and Good Work People: Gender and Skill in Northern Sweden, 1850–1950,' *Gender and History* 1, no. 2 (Summer 1989): 200–12. Parr's study of the turn-of-the-twentieth-century masculine workplace at the Knetchel Furniture Company in Hanover, Ontario, is one modest exception to this. She has outlined the paternal mutuality practised by

company founder Daniel Knetchel who in his shop thought of himself as a 'craftsman among craftsmen ... drawing authority over his employees from his longer knowledge of the craft they shared.' One of Knetchel's chief pleasures was facilitating the mobility of his own workers to positions of greater independence within the craft. On the whole, though, the continuities of masculine mutuality between masters and men into the industrial era remain open for examination. See Joy Parr, *The Gender of Breadwinners* (Toronto: University of Toronto Press, 1990), 140–42. See also chaps. 6–10. Mary Ann Clawson has made the interesting suggestion that continuities disrupted on the shopfloor by industrial transformation were redirected to and recreated in nineteenth-century fraternal societies. See Mary Ann Clawson, *Constructing Brotherhood: Class, Gender and Fraternalism* (Princeton, NJ: Princeton University Press, 1989), esp. chap. 5.

9 There are modest exceptions to this, but none that ultimately escape the dispossession model. See, for example, David Burley, *A Particular Condition in Life: Self-Employment and Social Mobility in Mid-Victorian Brantford, Ontario* (Montreal and Kingston: McGill-Queen's University Press, 1994); Paul Craven and Tom Traves, 'Dimensions of Paternalism: Discipline and Culture in Canadian Railway Operations in the 1850s,' in *On the Job: Confronting the Labour Process in Canada*, ed. Craig Heron and Robert Storey (Montreal and Kingston: McGill-Queen's University Press, 1986), 47–74; Craven, 'Labour and Management on the Great Western Railway,' in *Labouring Lives, Work and Workers in Nineteenth-Century Ontario*, ed. Craven, 341–74 (Toronto: University of Toronto Press, 1995); and Craig Heron, 'Factory Workers,' in Craven, *Labouring Lives*, 479–594. For a twentieth-century treatment, see Joy Parr, *Gender of Breadwinners*, part 2.

10 Peter Moogk, 'In the Darkness of a Basement: Craftsmen's Associations in Early French Canada,' *Canadian Historical Review* 57, no. 4 (December 1976): 399–439; Joanne Burgess, 'Work, Family and Community: Montreal Leather Craftsmen, 1790–1831' (PhD diss., Université du Québec, 1986), 132.

11 Craig Heron, 'Factory Workers,' 507–9.

12 Examples of this in the Canadian literature include Burr, *Spreading the Light*; Shirley Tillotson, '"We may all soon be first-class men": Gender and Skill in Canada's Early Twentieth-Century Urban Telegraph Industry,' *Labour/Le Travail* 27 (Spring 1991): 97–125; Mercedes Steedman, 'Skill and Gender in the Canadian Clothing Industry, 1890–1940,' in Heron and Storey, *On the Job,* 152–76; and Susan Mann Trofimenkoff, 'One Hundred and Two Muffled Voices: Canada's Industrial Women in the 1880s,' reprinted in MacDowell and Radforth, *Canadian Working*

Class History, 191–204. Selected international examples include Baron, 'Questions of Gender;' Cockburn, *Brothers*; and Cooper, *Once a Cigar Maker.* For an exceptional case, see Nancy A. Hewitt, '"The Voice of Virile Labor": Labor Militancy, Community Solidarity, and Gender Identity among Tampa's Latin Workers, 1880–1921,' in Baron, *Work Engendered,* 142–67.

13 Michael B. Katz, Michael J. Doucet, and Mark J. Stern, *The Social Organization of Early Industrial Capitalism* (Cambridge, MA: Harvard University Press, 1982), 97–101; Michael B. Katz, *The People of Hamilton, Canada West* (Cambridge, MA: Harvard University Press, 1975), 270–73.

14 The manuscripts to the 1871 Industrial Census list only 117 women working outside the clothing industry out of a total workforce of 5743.

15 See Mary H. Blewett, *Men, Women and Work: Class, Gender, and Protest in the New England Shoe Industry, 1780–1910* (Urbana: University of Illinois Press, 1990) and Steedman, 'Skill and Gender in the Canadian Clothing Industry,' 156–60.

16 Robert B. Kristofferson, 'Craft Capitalism: Craftsworkers, Industrialization and Class Formation in Hamilton, Ontario, 1840–1877' (PhD diss., York University, 2003), 80–3.

17 Cooper, *Once a Cigar Maker.*

18 See Burr, *Spreading the Light,* 100 for information on the greater numbers of women employed in the Toronto bindery industry at this time.

19 The ready-made clothing industry and, to an extent, the boot and shoe industry are obvious exceptions to this.

20 Hamilton's rise to a major textile centre, well underway by the 1880s, likely had much to do with this. See Gregory S. Kealey and Bryan D. Palmer, *Dreaming of What Might Be: The Knights of Labor in Ontario, 1880–1900* (Toronto: New Hogtown Press, 1987 [1982]), 42. See also Karen Dubinsky, 'The Modern Chivalry: Women and the Knights of Labor in Ontario, 1880–1891' (MA thesis, Carleton University, 1985). An examination of female employment in the city after 1890 can be found in W. Craig Heron, 'Working Class Hamilton, 1895–1930' (PhD diss., Dalhousie University, 1981).

21 Steven J. Ross, *Workers on the Edge: Work, Leisure, and Politics in Industrializing Cincinnati, 1788–1890* (New York: Columbia University Press, 1985), 82–3.

22 *Times,* 8 December 1863; *The Dictionary of Hamilton Biography* (Hamilton, ON: DHB, 1981) 1, ed. Thomas Melville Bailey; 'Williams, James Miller,' 211–12; 1871 Census Index; *Industries of Canada: Historical and Commercial Sketches, Hamilton* (Toronto: M.G. Bixby and Company, 1886), 76.

23 *Times*, 12 December 1863; *Spectator*, 7 January 1868; 1871 Database.
24 Richard Butler, *Saturday Musings* (Hamilton Public Library), Micro #121, n.d., n.p.
25 *Times*, 11 July 1871; HPL, Logie-McQuesten Papers, Bond. Luther Sawyer to Calvin McQuesten, 23 September 1853, 523–30.
26 *Spectator*, 2 September 1872.
27 E.P. Morgan and F.L. Harvey, *Hamilton and Its Industries* (Hamilton: Spectator Printing Company, 1884), 57.
28 *Spectator*, 2 January 1868.
29 *Times*, 27 June 1865.
30 *Times*, 6 November, 25 November 1871.
31 For the first view, see Palmer, *Culture in Conflict*, especially chap. 2. For the second view, see Burley, *A Particular Condition*, 59–61 and Heron, 'Factory Workers,' 533–5.
32 HPL, Hamilton and Gore Mechanics' Institute, 'Minutebook of the Management Committee,' 16 August 1844, 5 November 1845, and 3 July 1846.
33 *Spectator*, 26 July 1853.
34 *Spectator*, 10 July 1869, 4 July 1872.
35 *Times*, 23 July 1864.
36 *Spectator*, 25 August 1863.
37 *Times*, 1 September 1862.
38 *Spectator*, 24 August 1863, 5 July 1866; *Times*, 26 December 1867.
39 *Spectator*, 18 February 1871.
40 *Spectator*, 12 August 1871.
41 *Spectator*, 17 September 1872.
42 *Spectator*, 17 July 1869, 20 July 1874
43 *Times*, 25 August 1874; *Spectator*, 5 September 1871.
44 *Times*, 14 August 1871.
45 *Spectator*, 12 September 1870, 5 September 1871.
46 *Spectator*, 27 July 1869.
47 *Times*, 30 March, 7 August 1866.
48 By 1885 upwards of 2000 Hamilton unionists attended a picnic held at Dundurn Park in support of striking cigar makers. See *Palladium of Labor*, 30 May, 6 June 1885; *Spectator*, 9 June 1885.
49 Burley, *A Particular Condition*, 57–61.
50 *Spectator*, 6 September 1870, 7 September 1871, 2 September 1872, 27 June, 25 October 1873.
51 *Spectator*, 6 September 1870, 11 March, 2 September 1872, 27 June, 25 October 1873.
52 *Spectator*, 2 January, 27 June 1873.
53 *Spectator*, 6 September 1870, 2 September 1872, 27 June 1873.

54 *Herald*, 7 November 1903; *Spectator*, 1 September 1871, 5 August 1872.
55 *Spectator*, 2 September 1872, 25 October 1873.
56 *Times*, 21 April 1866; *Spectator*, 6 September 1870, September 1871, 2 January 1873.
57 Palmer, *Culture in Conflict*, 56, 58. For a similar account based on the same evidence, see Kealey, *Toronto Workers Respond*, 41.
58 Palmer, *Culture in Conflict*, 56, 57.
59 *Spectator*, 4 July 1867.
60 *Spectator*, 25 June 1867.
61 *Spectator*, 27 June 1867.
62 The fact that the butchers chose an ox to surmount their float on Confederation Day makes some suggestion as to the composition of this group. Samuel Nash ran the city's only large meat-curing establishment, employing twenty-three hands by 1871, but processed only pork. On the other hand, John Campbell, the city's largest beef processor, employed only six men and two boys in his establishment by this date. Most common was still the small butcher shop operated by a master with one or two helpers. *Spectator*, 2 July 1867; 1871 Industrial Census.
63 Kealey, *Toronto Workers Respond*, 41; Palmer, *Culture in Conflict*, 57–60.
64 Palmer, *Culture in Conflict*, 46.
65 The committee is outlined in *Spectator*, 26 June 1867. Cross-referencing members of this group with listings in the 1867–8 and 1868–9 directories for the City of Hamilton determined occupations. Occupation could not be identified for three members of this group.
66 *Spectator*, 26 June 1867, 2 July 1867.
67 Palmer argues that 'workingmen's parades, aside from their significance as moments of exhilaration and craft pride, also possess an inner history of importance. Two brief months after their participation in the Confederation procession, Hamilton's shoemakers would play an important role in the creation of an Ontario-wide boot and shoemaker's organization.' Palmer, *Culture in Conflict*, 60. See also Kealey, *Toronto Workers Respond*, 40.
68 *Spectator*, 2 July 1867.
69 *Hamilton: The Birmingham of Canada* (Hamilton: Times Printing Company, 1892).
70 Ian Davey and Michael Doucet, 'The Social Geography of a Commercial City,' in Michael Katz, *People of Hamilton*, 334, 341–2; John C. Weaver, *Hamilton: An Illustrated History* (Toronto: Lorimer and National Museum of Man, 1982), 64.

71 This was not the only place in the city where the elite were busy developing their particular versions of domestic splendour, but it was the area with by far the highest concentration of well-heeled development.

72 Michael B. Katz, Michael J. Doucet, and Mark J. Stern, *The Social Organization of Early Industrial Capitalism* (Cambridge, MA: Harvard University Press, 1982). While 'masters/manufacturers' are examined in their attempt to show that the 'business class' did not necessarily lead the trend of fathers leaving the home to work (i.e., creating the quintessential 'haven in a heartless world'), Katz and company quantify data into three broad categories: 'home and workplace identical,' 'home and workplace different,' and 'unknown.' As the rest of this paper suggests, the questions posed here require a more detailed methodology that allows assessment of factory owners' embeddedness in their communities surrounding their plants. My study also considers the residential location only of manufacturers with artisan origins, a distinction that Katz and his associates do not bring to their data set. Lastly, Katz looks at *all* masters and manufacturers, whereas the data herein is composed of only large masters (defined as those industrial establishments reporting five or more hands employed).

73 For an introduction to this growing field of research, see Theodore Herschberg, D. Light, H. Cox, and R. Greenfield, 'The "Journey to Work": An Empirical Investigation of Work, Residence and Transportation, Philadelphia, 1850 and 1880,' in *Philadelphia: Work, Space, Family and Group Experience in the Nineteenth Century*, ed. T. Herschberg (New York: Oxford University Press, 1981), 128–73 and A. Victoria Bloomfield and Richard Harris, 'The Journey to Work: A Historical Methodology,' *Historical Methods* 30, no. 2 (Spring 1997): 97–109. For a study of the journey to work in twentieth-century Hamilton, see Richard Harris and Matt Sendbueler, 'The Making of a Working-Class Suburb in Hamilton's East End, 1900–1945,' *Journal of Urban History* 20 (1993): 486–511. The seminal work in this field was K. Liepman, *The Journey to Work* (New York: Oxford University Press, 1944).

74 In Troy, New York, it seems that the character of industrialization whereby manufacturers seemed to have been financially well-off, and not necessary artisans, before they started their factories led to an immediate residential segmentation between industrialists and workers. See Daniel J. Walkowitz, *Worker City, Company Town* (Urbana: University of Illinois Press, 1978), 28.

75 Leonore Davidoff and Catherine Hall have outlined the process whereby Birmingham manufacturers, with some initial ambivalence, separated home from work between 1780 and 1850, removing themselves to villas on the outskirts of the city or to new 'specialized

middle-class enclaves' such as the 'exclusive suburb' of Edgbaston within the city limits. Steven Ross has noted that in mid-nineteenth-century Cincinnati, manufacturers' movement away from mixed residential neighbourhoods near the town centre to more exclusive neighbourhoods or to prominent locations atop hills surrounding the town created an 'increasingly visible contrast between the modest homes of the working class and the ostentatious accommodations of the elite' that helped to further fuel the growing flames of class discontent. Implicit in Joy Parr's study of Paris and Hanover, Ontario, is the interesting suggestion that different paths of industrial growth can lead to much different configurations of social geography: factory bosses in Paris lived in 'separate precincts' from those they employed, whereas the residences of Hanover factory owners were 'intermingled' with those of their workers. See Leonore Davidoff and Catherine Hall, *Family Fortunes: Men, Women and the English Middle Class, 1780–1850* (London: Hutchison, 1987), 364–8; Ross, *Workers on the Edge,* 18, 144, 137–9, 196; and Joy Parr, *Gender of Breadwinners*, 6, 141.

76 Jeff Merriman, 'Autobiography and Merriman Family History: Horace Owen Merriman, 1888–1972,' typescript in possession of author.

77 While journey-to-work methodology often calculates distances as a median straight-line commute, the simpler methodology of number of blocks is as sound and allows for a similar comparative spatial appreciation.

78 *Times,* 11 July 1871.

79 *Spectator,* 24 December 1890.

80 *DHB* 1, 'Carpenter, Alexander,' 42; A.G. McKay, *Victorian Architecture in Hamilton* (Hamilton: Architectural Conservancy of Ontario, 1967), 12.

81 *Spectator*, 2 September 1872.

82 Davidoff and Hall, *Family Fortunes*, 366.

Chapter 5. The 'Self-Made Craftsworker': Transmodalism, Self-Identification, and the Foundations of Emergent Culture

1 *Daily Globe,* 23 March 1872. Reprinted in Michael S. Cross, *The Workingman in Nineteenth-Century Canada* (Toronto: Oxford University Press, 1974), 262.

2 Accounts of the development of self-made manhood and the rise of individualism can be found in explicit form in the recent literature produced by historians of masculinity, but also in implicit form in the works of a number of historians whose primary focus has been issues of class and class relations.

3 The ability of nineteenth-century middle-class men to 'make it' has been shown to have been intimately connected to active support from their families and the masculine support networks embedded in numerous community institutions. As Mary Ryan puts it, 'the vaunted economy and egoism of the nineteenth-century male was not a monument to self-reliance.' See especially Mary P. Ryan, *The Cradle of the Middle Class: The Family in Oneida County, New York, 1790–1865* (New York: Cambridge University Press, 1981); E. Anthony Rotundo, *American Manhood: Transformations in Masculinity from the Revolution to the Modern Era* (New York: Basic Books, 1993); Mark C. Carnes, *Secret Ritual and Manhood in Victorian America* (New Haven, CT: Yale University Press, 1989); Leonore Davidoff and Catherine Hall, *Family Fortunes: Men and Women of the English Middle Class, 1780–1850* (London: Hutchison, 1987); Stuart M. Blumin, *The Emergence of the Middle Class: Social Experience in the American City, 1760–1900* (New York: Cambridge University Press, 1989).

4 Gary Kornblith's study of the early-nineteenth-century Boston printer Joseph T. Buckingham adds an interesting dimension to this debate. He shows how Buckingham's achievement of 'independence' as a master printer 'depended heavily on the material assistance of others.' See Gary J. Kornblith, 'Becoming Joseph T. Buckingham: The Struggle for Artisanal Independence in Early-Nineteenth-Century Boston,' in *American Artisans: Crafting Social Identity, 1750–1850*, ed. Howard B. Rock, Paul A. Gilje and Robert Asher (Baltimore, MD: Johns Hopkins University Press, 1995), 123–34.

5 The seminal work in this field was Mary P. Ryan, *Cradle of the Middle Class*. This position is more fully elaborated in Rotundo, *American Manhood*; Michael Kimmel, *Manhood in America: A Cultural History* (New York: Free Press, 1996); and Carnes, *Secret Ritual and Manhood in Victorian America*.

6 Modest exceptions to this include Mary Ann Clawson, *Constructing Brotherhood: Class, Gender and Fraternalism* (Princeton, NJ: Princeton University Press, 1989); Keith McClelland, 'Some Thoughts on Masculinity and the "Representative Artisan" in Britain, 1850–1880,' *Gender and History* 1, no. 2 (Summer 1989): 164–77; and John Springhall, 'Building Character in the British Boy: The Attempt to Extend Christian Manliness to Working Class Adolescents, 1880–1914,' in *Manliness and Morality: Middle Class Masculinity in Britain and America, 1800–1940*, ed. J.A. Mangan and James Walvin (Manchester: Manchester University Press, 1987). An insightful, singular, and early Canadian example is Allan Smith, 'The Myth of the Self-Made Man in English Canada, 1850–1914,' *Canadian Historical Review* 59, no. 2

(1978): 189–219. Presenting an argument meant to modify the then received historiographical view of 'Canadian conservatism' as being the antithesis of 'United States individualism,' Smith proposes that the self-made man, as a myth at least, had strong social currency in Canada between 1850 and 1914.

7 One has only to look at the two most far-reaching works on middle-class formation in Great Britain and the United States to understand how social historians have largely viewed craftsworkers or other sections of the working class as having little to do with the making of the middle class. See Davidoff and Hall, *Family Fortunes*, and Blumin, *Emergence of the Middle Class*. Recent Canadian examples appear to follow the same paradigm. See especially Andrew C. Holman, *A Sense of Their Duty: Middle-Class Formation in Victorian Ontario Towns* (Montreal and Kingston: McGill-Queen's University Press, 2000).

8 Allan Smith has offered the most direct argument for this view in the Canadian historiography. The Canadian elite's successful detachment of the achievement of 'wealth' from the widely aspired-to model of the self-made man, argues Smith, went a long way towards 'encourag[ing] the formation of a stable workforce.' See Smith, 'Myth of the Self-Made Man,' 207. In recent years simplistic 'top-down' notions of social control or 'bourgeois hegemony' have generally been discarded for theories that offer a much more nuanced appreciation of the ability of subordinate historical actors to act as agents on their own behalf, exerting a real shaping force on the dominant structures of society. Studies of Canadian schooling provide one of the many examples of this new understanding of the dynamic interplay of structure and agency. See Susan Houston and Alison Prentice, *Schooling and Scholars in Nineteenth-Century Ontario* (Toronto: University of Toronto Press, 1988) and Bruce Curtis, *Building the Educational State* (London: Althouse Press, 1988).

9 The large body of historiography surrounding the concept of the 'labour aristocracy' is but one example of this. For useful summaries of this literature, see Gregor McLennan, 'The Theory of the Labour Aristocracy,' in *Marxism and the Methodologies of History*, ed. McLennan (London: Verso, 1981), 206–65; and Eric Hobsbawm, 'Debating the Labour Aristocracy' and 'Artisans and Aristocrats,' in *Worlds of Labour*, ed. Hobsbawm (London: Weidenfeld & Nicolson, 1984), 214–354.

10 For example, Sean Wilenz has shown how craftsworkers in New York City fashioned a vision of individualism distinctive to their class position and subsumed under the general rubric of artisanal republicanism. A similar formulation can be found in Eric Foner's discussions of the

'free labor' ideology. See Sean Wilenz, *Chants Democratic: New York City and the Rise of the American Working Class, 1788–1850* (New York: Oxford University Press, 1984); Eric Foner, *Free Soil, Free Men, Free Labor: The Ideology of the Republican Party before the Civil War* (New York: Oxford University Press, 1970) and 'Free Labor and Nineteenth Century Political Ideology,' in *The Market Revolution in America: Social, Political and Religious Expressions, 1800–1880*, ed. Melvyn Stokes and Stephen Conway (Charlottesville: University of Virginia Press, 1996), 99–127.

11 Of course, Herbert Gutman's preliminary examination of the 'rags-to-riches myth' is one exception to this. See Gutman, 'The Reality of the Rags-to-Riches "Myth": The Case of Paterson, New Jersey, Locomotive, Iron, and Machinery Manufacturers, 1830–1880,' in *Work, Culture and Society in Industrializing America*, ed. Gutman (New York: Vintage, 1977), 211–33. One other interesting exception is the work of Gary J. Kornblith, particularly his 'Self-Made Men: The Development of Middling Class Consciousness in New England,' *Massachusetts Review* 26 (Summer 1985): 461–74. This study of the master mechanic/manufacturer members of the Providence Association of Mechanics and Manufacturers, the Massachusetts Charitable Mechanic Association, and the Salem Charitable Mechanic Association argues that these men's new-found subscription to the concept of the self-made man was built from their material experience. Kornblith also suggests that this formulation likely had some ideological effect on journeymen. But beyond suggesting, rather obliquely, that journeymen may have come to view themselves finding their motivation from 'social mobility, rather than the scale-beam of class justice' (469), however, Kornblith does not elaborate this point.

12 *Spectator*, 4 December 1857.

13 *Spectator,* 25 April 1857.

14 *Spectator*, 24 February 1872.

15 *Spectator*, 1 March 1872.

16 *Gazette*, 29 August 1850; *Spectator* 16 January 1860. See also *Spectator,* 20 November 1855, 12 December, 21 January 1856, 6 February 1857; *Ontario Workman,* 19 December 1872; *Journal of the Board of Arts and Manufactures for Upper Canada*, (1864): 187; *Provincialist,* 5 December 1848.

17 *City Enterprise*, 26 November 1864.

18 *City Enterprise*, 24 September 1864.

19 *City Enterprise,* 23 July 1864.

20 *Spectator,* 25 November 1855.

21 *Spectator*, 25 September 1856.

22 *Spectator*, 3 December 1872.
23 *Spectator*, 23 February 1857.
24 *Gazette*, 10 February 1853.
25 *Spectator*, 27 September 1871.
26 Canada, Royal Commission on the Relations Between Labour and Capital, *Report – Evidence, Ontario*, 834–37.
27 *Spectator*, 2 September 1872.
28 *Ontario Workman*, 19 December 1872.
29 *Ontario Workman*, 3 April 1873.
30 *Spectator*, 24 March 1871.
31 *Spectator*, 9 February 1866.
32 Alexander Wingfield, *Poems and Songs in Scotch and English* (Hamilton: Times Printing Company, 1873), 120.
33 *Spectator*, 22 December 1871.
34 *The Dictionary of Hamilton Biography* (*DHB*) 2, ed. Thomas Melville Bailey (Hamilton, ON: DHB, 1981), 'Tinsely, Joseph,' 172–3; For examples, see Hamilton *Herald*, 21 November 1903 (William and Christopher Lockman), 6 April 1904 (James Foster), 26 February 1904 (Alexander Main), 17 December 1904 (Alexander H. Wingfield), 22 June 1907 (Henry B. Witton), 20 July 1907 (A.T. Freed).
35 *DHB* 3, 'Butler, Richard,' 20.
36 *Herald*, 31 May 1919.
37 Richard Butler, *Saturday Musings, Scrapbooks*, Hamilton Public Library (HPL), Microfilm #121, vol. 3, 171.
38 Documentation of Butler's adherence to this theme is too extensive to cite here, but is presented in voluminous detail in Butler, *Saturday Musings*, vols. 1–4.
39 Ibid., 3: 101.
40 *Ontario Workman*, 5 September 1872.
41 *Workingman's Journal*, 18 June 1864.
42 *City Enterprise*, 23 July 1864.
43 *Spectator*, 27 September 1871.
44 *Garland*, 22 June 1833.
45 *Times*, 16 October 1969.
46 *Times*, 8 December 1863.
47 *Times*, 5 October 1863.
48 *Industries of Canada: Hamilton* (Toronto: M.G. Bixby, 1886), 42, 45.
49 E.P. Morgan and F. L. Harvey, *Hamilton and its Industries* (Hamilton: Spectator Printing Company, 1884), 57.
50 *Ontario Workman*, 6 February 1873.
51 *Ontario Workman*, 5 September 1872.
52 *Ontario Workman*, 4 July 1872.

53 *Spectator,* 12 January 1875.
54 *Spectator*, 27 September 1871.
55 *Ontario Workman*, 3 April 1873.
56 *Spectator*, 24 May 1878.
57 *City Enterprise*, 24 September 1864.
58 *Spectator*, 15 January 1873.
59 *Spectator*, 23 September 1857.
60 *Spectator*, 14 December 1859.
61 *Spectator*, 16 February 1857.
62 Michael Kimmel, *Manhood in America: A Cultural History* (New York: Free Press, 1996), esp. chap. 1.
63 *Hamilton Weekly Times*, 13 October 1870.
64 *Hamilton Herald*, 20 November 1922.
65 *Ontario Workman*, 5 September 1872.
66 *City Enterprise*, 23 July 1864.
67 *Spectator*, 16 August 1872.
68 *Canadian Illustrated News*, 28 March 1863.
69 *Spectator*, 17 February 1873.
70 *Ontario Workman*, 4 July 1872.
71 *Ontario Workman*, 13 June 1872.
72 *Ontario Workman*, 21 November 1872.
73 *Spectator*, 29 January 1866.
74 *Ontario Workman*, 19 December 1872.
75 Butler, *Saturday Musings,* vol. 3, 107.
76 Kimmel, *Manhood in America*, 27.
77 R.W. Connell, *Masculinities* (Berkeley: University of California Press, 1995), 68.
78 *Spectator*, 22 September 1857.
79 *City Enterprise*, 23 July 1864.
80 *Workingman's Journal*, 18 June 1864.

Chapter 6. The 'Self-Improving Craftsworker': Dimensions of Transmodal Culture in Ideology and Practice

1 The demasculinization of craftsworkers has been a central preoccupation of historians of working-class masculinity. Discussions of remasculinization are often presented in this context as a function of craftsworkers' and craft unions' rebuilding of their masculinity within the realities of industrial capitalism. For examples, see Cynthia Cockburn, *Brothers: Male Dominance and Technical Change* (London: Pluto Press, 1983); Patricia Cooper, *Once a Cigar Maker* (Urbana: University of Illinois Press, 1987); Ava Baron, 'Questions of Gender: Deskilling

and Demasculinization in the U.S. Printing Industry, 1830–1915,' *Gender and History* 1, no. 1 (Summer 1989): 178–99; and 'An "Other" Side to Gender Antagonism at Work: Men, Boys and the Remasculinization of Printer's Work, 1830–1920,' in *Work Engendered*, ed. Baron (Ithaca, NY: Cornell University Press, 1991). For a Canadian example, see Christina Burr, *Spreading the Light: Work and Labour Reform in Late-Nineteenth-Century Toronto* (Toronto: University of Toronto Press, 1999).

2 Geoffrey Crossick, *An Artisan Elite in Victorian Society: Kentish London, 1840–1880* (London: Croom Helm, 1978), 21, 134–98.

3 R.Q. Gray, *The Labour Aristocracy in Victorian Edinburgh* (Oxford: Clarendon, 1976), esp. 91–120 and 136–43.

4 Previous to the release of these two works, many historians held the labour aristocracy as a much narrower Leninist conception defined by high and stable earnings and/or authority at work. The seminal work in this line of enquiry was E.J. Hobsbawm, 'The Labour Aristocracy in Nineteenth-Century Britain,' reprinted in his *Labouring Men* (New York: Basic Books, 1964), 272–315. The first to stress authority at work as a key dimension of the labour aristocracy was John Foster, *Class Struggle and the Industrial Revolution: Early Industrial Capitalism in Three English Towns* (London: Weidenfeld & Nicolson, 1974). These historiographic developments are well-summarized in H.F. Moorhouse, 'The Marxist Theory of the Labour Aristocracy,' *Social History* 3, no. 1 (1978): 61–82. See also Alastair Reid, 'Intelligent Artisans and Aristocrats of Labour: The Essays of Thomas Wright,' in *The Working Class in Modern British History: Essays in Honour of Henry Pelling*, ed. Jay Winter (London: Cambridge University Press, 1983), 171–86.

5 Alastair Reid, 'Politics and Economics in the Formation of the British Working Class: A Response to H.F. Moorhouse,' *Social History* (1978): 347.

6 Moorhouse, 'The Marxist Theory of the Labour Aristocracy,' 66. The seminal works in the social control school of the labour aristocracy are Hobsbawm, 'The Labour Aristocracy in Nineteenth-Century Britain,' and Foster, *Class Struggle and the Industrial Revolution.* For the Leninist roots of the labour aristocracy, see V.I. Lenin, *Collected Works*, vol. 22 (Moscow: Progress Publishers, 1964), 93–4 and E. Hobsbawm, 'Lenin and the Aristocracy of Labour,' *Marxism Today* (July 1970).

7 Gregor McLennan, 'The Theory of the Labour Aristocracy,' in *Marxism and the Methodologies of History*, ed. McLennan (London: Verso, 1981), 221. In his explicitly Gramscian argument, Gray concludes that

the 'formation of a labour aristocracy made possible particular forms of ideological hegemony, which set limits on the articulation of working-class consciousness.' See Gray, *Labour Aristocracy in Victorian Edinburgh*, 4–5. For the incorporation of considerations of gender into this debate, see Keith McClelland, 'Some Thoughts on the "Representative Artisan" in Britain, 1850–1880,' *Gender and History* 1 no. 2 (Summer 1989): 164–77.

8 Peter Bailey, '"Will the Real Bill Banks Please Stand Up?" Towards a Role Analysis of Mid-Victorian Working-Class Respectability,' *Journal of Social History* 12, no. 3 (Spring 1979): 336–53.

9 See Reid, 'Intelligent Artisans and Aristocrats of Labour,' for a brief summary of this line of enquiry. See also Henry Pelling, 'The Concept of the Labour Aristocracy, in *Popular Politics and Society in Late Victorian Britain* (London: Macmillan, 1968); Gareth Stedman Jones, *Outcast London: A Study in the Relationship Between Classes in Victorian Society* (Oxford: Clarendon Press, 1971) and his 'Class Struggle and the Industrial Revolution,' *New Left Review* 90 (March–April 1975): 35–69.

10 Palmer conceded that skilled workers did occupy a 'distinct social and cultural place' in their communities and existed in a 'hierarchical arrangement of trades and job classifications.' He also identified aspects of their cultural experience – friendly society, mechanics' institute, or engine house – which drew mechanics into contact with middling elements. However, he argued, 'cultural separation, often expressed in terms of the skilled worker's attachment to respectability, self-help, and social improvement, coupled with preferential wage rates, do not a labour aristocracy make.' In Hamilton, he declared, 'there was no labour aristocracy.' Rather, class position, augmented by such cultural practices such as the baseball diamond and the craft union, worked to create 'a semi-autonomous workingmen's culture, relatively immune to the class manipulation of the city's elite.' See Bryan D. Palmer, *A Culture in Conflict: Skilled Workers and Industrial Capitalism in Hamilton, Ontario, 1860–1914* (Montreal and Kingston: McGill-Queen's University Press, 1979), 239–41. For the solidification of this position in his later work, see Palmer, *Working-Class Experience: Rethinking the History of Canadian Labour, 1800–1991* (Toronto: McClelland & Stewart, 1992), 56–8.

11 Gray, *The Labour Aristocracy in Victorian Edinburgh*, 130, 135. Foster's identification of an elite stratum of subcontracting craftsworkers in Oldham, Northampton, and South Shields can also be seen to partially support this view. See Foster, *Class Struggle and the Industrial Revolution*, 224–38.

12 Palmer, *Culture in Conflict*, 241.

13 This term is borrowed from Asa Briggs, *The Age of Improvement, 1783–1867* (London: Longman, 1959, 1979). For literature positing this idea for the United States in this time period see John S. Gilkeson, *Middle-Class Providence 1820–1940* (Princeton, NJ: Princeton University Press, 1986) and Gary S. Kornblith 'From Artisans to Businessmen: Master Mechanics in New England, 1789–1850' (PhD diss., Princeton University, 1983). The emergent autodidacticism of nineteenth-century workers shines through in various studies of working-class autobiography. See, for example, John Burnett, *Useful Toil* (Harmondsworth, UK: Penguin, 1984) and *Destiny Obscure* (London: Allen Lane, 1982); David Vincent, *Bread, Knowledge and Freedom* (London: Methuen, 1981); Mary Jo Maynes, *Taking the Hard Road* (Chapel Hill: University of North Carolina Press, 1995); and Mark Traugott, *The French Worker* (Berkeley: University of California Press, 1993). For an interesting recent work on worker self-education, see Erin McLaughlin-Jenkins, 'Common Knowledge: The Victorian Working Class and the Low Road to Science, 1870–1900' (PhD diss., York University, 2001). See also Peter Bailey, *Leisure and Class in Victorian England* (London: Routledge and Kegan Paul, 1978) and Richard D. Atlick, *English Common Reader* (Columbus: Ohio State University Press, 1957).

14 *Iron Molders' International Journal*, 19 April 1866.

15 *Ontario Workman,* 4 July 1872.

16 *Journal of the Board of Arts and Manufactures of Ontario* [*JBAM*] (1865), 194.

17 *JBAM* (January 1865), 4.

18 *Ontario Workman*, 27 March 1873.

19 *JBAM* (January 1865), 4.

20 *JBAM* (February 1864), 33–4.

21 *Times,* 16 January 1863.

22 *Spectator*, 6 February 1857.

23 *Canadian Illustrated News*, 20 December 1862. For *Canadian Illustrated News,* see Hamilton Public Library [HPL], Tinsely Scrapbooks, n.d., n.p.; *The Dictionary of Hamilton* Biography, ed. Thomas Melville Bailey (Hamilton: DCB, 1981), *DHB* 1, 'Somerville, Alexander,' 184–5.

24 *Provincialist*, 5 December 1848.

25 *Spectator,* 24 December 1867.

26 *JBAM* (1864), 305.

27 *Ontario Workman,* 27 March 1873.

28 *Spectator*, 21 November 1871.

29 *Spectator,* 12 December 1856.

30 *Spectator*, 21 November 1871.
31 *JBAM* (February 1864), 33–4.
32 *Spectator*, 20 November 1855.
33 *Spectator,* 17 February 1873.
34 *Times*, 5 December 1871.
35 *Spectator*, 12 December 1856.
36 *Ontario Workman*, 27 March 1873.
37 *Times*, 16 January 1863.
38 *Times*, 5 December 1871.
39 *Spectator*, 6 February 1857.
40 *Spectator,* 28 November 1856.
41 This term is borrowed from Briggs, *Age of Improvement*. For literature positing this idea for United States master craftsmen in this time period, see Gilkeson, *Middle-Class Providence* and Kornblith, 'From Artisans to Businessmen.'
42 *Spectator,* 18 May 1961.
43 *Provincialist*, 5 December 1848.
44 *Spectator*, 17 February 1873.
45 *Times*, 5 December 1871.
46 *Spectator,* 23 February 1857.
47 *Spectator*, 12 December 1856.
48 *JBAM* (1865), 201.
49 HPL, Special Collections, Clipping file – Witton, H.B. Henry Buckingham Witton, 'Jottings From the Story of a Life,' n.d. (hereafter, Witton, 'Jottings').
50 *Spectator*, 10 February 1860.
51 Benedict Anderson, *Imagined Communities* (London: Verso, 1983), 6. Building on Homi K. Bhaba's assertion that 'it is the city which provides the space in which emergent identifications … are played out,' Bonnie Huskins has recently asked, given all the recent writing on the 'imagining' of nation and empire, 'what, however, of the imagining of local communities?' Anderson himself has stated that 'all communities larger than primordial villages of face-to-face contact (and perhaps even these) are imagined.' See Homi K. Bhabha, 'DissemiNation: Time, Narrative, and the Margins of the Modern,' in *Nation and Narration*, ed. Bhabha (London: Routledge, 1990), 320; Bonnie Huskins, '"A Tale of Two Cities": Boosterism and the Imagination of Community during the Visit of the Prince of Wales to Saint John and Halifax in 1860,' *Urban History Review* 28, no. 1 (October 1999): 31.
52 *Spectator*, 11 August 1873.
53 *Peoples' Journal*, 2 April 1870.
54 *Spectator,* 10 December 1860.

55 Thomas Connolly, 'A Workman's View of Canada,' originally published in the English publication *The Builder*. Reprinted in *Spectator*, 23, 24 March 1873.
56 *Spectator*, 10 February 1860.
57 *Spectator*, 28 November 1856.
58 *Times*, 27 August 1862.
59 *Spectator*, 16 May 1857.
60 *Spectator*, 7 December 1855.
61 *Spectator*, 23 February 1857.
62 *Spectator*, 7 December 1855.
63 *Canadian Illustrated News*, 20 December 1862.
64 *JBAM* (1865), 4.
65 *JBAM* (1865), 263.
66 *Times*, 5 December 1871.
67 *Times*, 16 January 1863.
68 *Provincialist*, 5 December 1848.
69 *Ontario Workman*, 19 December 1872.
70 *Spectator*, 21 January 1856.
71 *Spectator*, 6 February 1857.
72 *Spectator*, 12 December 1856.
73 *JBAM* (1864), 187.
74 *Spectator*, 20 November 1855.
75 *Provincialist*, 5 December 1848.
76 *Spectator*, 28 November 1856.
77 *JBAM* (1865), 201.
78 *Gazette*, 19 December 1856.
79 *JBAM* (February 1864), 33.
80 *Spectator*, 7 December 1855.
81 *Spectator*, 21 November 1871.
82 Freda F. Walton, 'Early Provision for Libraries in Hamilton,' *Wentworth Bygones* 4 (1963): 22–35; Palmer, *Culture in Conflict*, 49.
83 See, for example, Patrick Keane, 'A Study in Early Problems and Policies in Adult Education: The Halifax Mechanics' Institute,' *Histoire sociale/Social History* 8 (November 1975): 255–74 and Foster Vernon, 'The Development of Adult Education in Ontario' (PhD diss., University of Toronto, 1969).
84 For particularly penetrating analyses of the expansion of mid-nineteenth-century state-run education in Ontario, see Susan Houston and Alison Prentice, *Schooling and Scholars in Nineteenth-Century Ontario* (Toronto: University of Toronto Press, 1988) and Bruce Curtis, *Building the Educational State: Canada West, 1836–1871* (London: Althouse Press, 1988).

85 These assertions range from out-and-out social control models to softer 'contested terrain' interpretations. See Frederick Engels, *The Condition of the Working Classes in England* (Oxford: Basil Blackwell, 1958), esp. 238–9; Edward Royle, 'Mechanics' Institutes and the Working Classes, 1840–1860,' *Historical Journal* 14 (1971): 305–21; Vernon, 'The Development of Adult Education in Ontario'; Keane, 'Study in Early Problems and Policies in Adult Education; and, most recently, Darryl Jean-Guy Newbury, '"No Atheist, Eunuch or Woman": Male Associational Culture and Working-Class Identity in Industrializing Ontario, 1840–1880' (MA thesis, Queens' University, 1992).

86 See Palmer, *Culture in Conflict*, 50. More recently Palmer has proposed that mechanics' institutes 'provided a place where workers could sift the pros and cons of the new industrial-capitalist order through a filter that necessarily took some account of emerging class differentiation.' Palmer, *Working-Class Experience,* 97. For another work that makes some allowance for conscious working-class identifications within mechanics' institutes, see Ellen L. Ramsey, 'Art and Industrial Society: The Role of the Toronto Mechanics' Institute in the Promotion of Art, 1831–1883,' *Labour/Le Travail* 43 (Spring 1999): 71–103.

87 See, for instance Gilkeson, Jr, *Middle-Class Providence,* esp. chaps. 2–4; Gary J. Kornblith, 'Self-Made Men: The Development of Middle-Class Consciousness in New England,' *Massachusetts Review* 26 (Summer 1985): 461–74; and Kornblith, '"Cementing the Mechanic Interest": Origins of the Providence Association of Mechanics and Manufacturers,' *Journal of the Early Republic* 8 (Winter 1988): 355–87.

88 The original executive of the institute, for instance, included such men as lawyer, land speculator, and baronet-to-be Allan MacNab, prominent wholesale and retail merchants Colin Campbell Ferrie, John Young, and Richard Juson, the sheriff E. Cartwright Thomas, and Bank of Montreal 'cashier' Andrew Steven, prompting one historian of the institute to comment, '[h]ardly a real "mechanic" in the lot.' Indeed, a perusal of the membership of the HGMI's board of directors throughout its history shows a continuing heavy involvement by well-known commercial and professional men. Hamilton & Gore Mechanics' Institute, *Minute-book of the Management Committee* [hereafter, HGMI, *Minutebooks*], 5 March 1839; Walton, 'Early Provision for Libraries in Hamilton,' 27.

89 *Spectator*, 20 April 1853.

90 When approached by a deputation from the clerk-dominated Young Men's Association seeking special consideration for attendance of the institute's library, newsroom, and lecture series in 1840, the HGMI board resolved to 'do what they can' within the constitutional parame-

ters of their organization to 'encourage' the young men's access to reading materials and to establish a 'community of privilege in regard to lectures.' The city's clerks did move to form their own Hamilton Mercantile Library Association (HMLA) sometime around 1845. However, the evidence suggests that the city's commercial middling elements did not form this organization in an attempt to distance themselves in any class sense from the 'mechanics'' institute. The reasons for taking this step apparently had rather more to do with the political rivalries of the respective leaderships of the HGMI and the HMLA than with feelings about the unsuitability of a clerk joining a mechanics' institute. While political leanings may have divided these two associations, the broader recognition of their commonality of interest was not lost sight of and was often couched in terms of the largely adult HGMI extending a helping hand to the more youthful members of the HMLA. By the 1850s the HGMI was co-sponsoring the HMLA's popular series of lectures, which were held in the newly constructed and commodious Mechanics' Hall. Members of the HMLA finally acted on the long-recognized 'absence of sufficient scope for the effectual working of both the said Associations' by voting to fold their membership into the general membership of the mechanics' institute in 1859. This was seen as a sensible move by many commercial and professional men whose involvement in the HGMI had long caused them to question the financial wisdom of their younger counterparts attempting to support their own organization when they could just as easily have availed themselves of the 'superior facilities' of the institute. HGMI, *Minutebooks,* 10, 17 December 1840; *Spectator,* 7 March 1855; 8 July 1859; 5, 23, 25 August 1859; 17, 19 November 1859; 25 February 1860. Charles M. Johnson refers to the political division between the two organizations in his *The Head of the Lake: History of Wentworth County* (Hamilton: Wentworth County Council, 1967), 216–17.

91 Indeed, it is interesting to note that at the time of 'union' between the HGMI and the HMLA there was some debate over whether the resultant organization should bear the mechanics' moniker. A number of new names were proposed, but in the end both sides agreed that to save time, money, and paperwork it would most expedient to effect the union 'as speedily as possible under the charter of the H. and G.M. Institute until a new charter shall be obtained under the name of the United Association.' The cost of amending the Act of Incorporation, which a few months before an HMLA committee had estimated at between $120 and $160, may provide part of the explanation for the decision to let the institute's name stand. *Spectator*, 10 February 1858, 26 February, 8 July, 5, 23 August, 19 November 1859, 25 February 1860.

92 After being housed in temporary quarters for its first few years, these arrangements soon proved too small for the growing space requirements of the institute. By 1851 a James Street site across from the city hall was secured and a portion of the funds necessary to initiate the building plan subscribed. On 15 April 1853 the new Mechanics' Hall was opened in a mass community celebration. For Hamilton to gain a building of such a sizable and elaborate character was the source of great civic pride. The grandeur of the new Mechanics' Hall was reported widely across the province. The price paid for this grand display was, however, dear. The total expense of the new building was reported to be about £4000 of which only about £1400 appears to have been raised by subscription beforehand. The mortgage and its accruing interest became a constant source of embarrassment to the institute's directors through the 1850s, '60s, and '70s and hindered substantial initiatives to benefit their membership throughout this period. The few significant 'improvements' that were made were usually undertaken in an effort to increase the hall's rental income to better service its ever-mounting debt. See Walton, 'Early Provision of Libraries in Hamilton,' 28; HGMI, *Minutebooks,* 10 March 1847; *Spectator,* 27 February 1850; *Spectator*, 6 September 1851; HGMI, *Minutebooks,* 1850; *Journal and Express*, 4 March 1853; *Gazette*, 18 April 1853; *Spectator*, 20 April 1853; *Middlesex Prototype*, 20 April 1853; *Spectator,* 2 March 1853; *Gazette*, 3 March 1853; *Times*, 17 October 1866; *Spectator*, 20 September 1871, 4 April 1854, 4, 26 February 1859, 24 February 1866, 5 April 1854, 28 February 1857.

93 *Spectator*, 7 March 1866.

94 *Spectator*, 7 December 1855.

95 *Spectator*, 2 March 1853, 4 February, 3 March 1856.

96 For a similar account of the relationship between the HGMI and GWR management and workers, see Paul Craven and Tom Traves, 'The Dimensions of Paternalism: Discipline and Culture in Canadian Railway Operations in the 1850s,' in *On The Job: Confronting the Labour Process in Canada*, ed. Craig Heron and Robert Storey (Montreal and Kingston: McGill-Queen's University Press, 1986), 65. See also *Spectator*, 3 March 1856, 28 February 1857, 2 March 1863, 6, 9, 23 February, 7 March 1866, 29 February 1868, 23 March 1875, 1 June 1878. It is interesting to note that the classes appear to have been designed solely for 'junior members' (i.e., apprentice members) of the institute. Adult members of the institute seem to have been satisfied with self-directed learning. See *Spectator*, 28 February 1857.

97 *Spectator*, 7 December 1855.

98 *Spectator*, 23 November 1864, 2 April 1867; *Ontario Workman*, 8 August 1872.

99 Paul Craven has shown that the company also established similar rooms at the St Thomas and Harrisburgh stations a few years later. See Paul Craven, 'Labour and Management on the Great Western Railway,' in *Labouring Lives: Work and Women in Nineteenth Century Ontario*, ed. Craven (Toronto: University of Toronto Press, 1995), 352–3.

100 *Provincialist*, 15 March 1849; *Spectator*, 1 March 1848, 27 February 1860, 3 March 1852, 3 March 1853, 5 March 1855, 3 March 1856, 28 February 1857, 1 March 1858, 26 February 1959, 27 February 1860, 23 February 1861, 3 March 1862, 2 March 1863, 27 February 1864, 25 February 1865, 24 February 1866, 23 February 1867, 1 March 1969, 25 February 1871, 24 February 1872, 1 March 1873, 28 February 1874, 27 February 1875; *Times*, 29 February 1868.

101 In Palmer's study of the HGMI he writes, 'in the absence of membership listings we can only speculate as to the degree of working-class involvement in the Hamilton Institute,' a statement rendered doubly strange by Freda Walton's use of these membership listings for an article written sixteen years previous to this and the fact they are still readily available in the research collections of the Hamilton Public Library today. See Palmer, *Culture in Conflict*, 50; Walton, 'Early Provision of Libraries in Hamilton,' 32.

102 HPL, Special Collections, Hamilton & Gore Mechanics' Institute, *Register of Members and Books Loaned, 1862–1864* (hereafter HGMI, *Membership Register*).

103 Of the 668 members listed therein, the occupations of only 395, or 59.13%, could be identified.

104 HGMI, *Act of Incorporation, Rules and Regulations and Catalogue of the Library* (Hamilton: Lawson & Company, 1949, rev. 1867), 10.

105 Kitchener Public Library, 'Diaries of Andrew McIlwraith, 1857–1862 (hereafter McIlwraith, *Diaries*),' Typescript, 20 February 1857; 9 January 1858; 2, 9 March 1858; 14 July 1858; 24 August 1858; 30 November 1858; 1, 8, 28 February 1859; 2 June 1859; 23 February 1861.

106 HGMI, *Act of Incorporation*, 9.

107 *Spectator*, 12 March 1866.

108 HGMI, *Act of Incorporation*, 9. The 1857 Annual Report appears to be the first time the separate category of 'junior members' receives acknowledgment. See *Spectator*, 28 February 1857.

109 *Spectator*, 7 December 1855.

110 *Spectator*, 28 February 1857.

111 *Spectator*, 1 March 1858, 26 February 1859.

112 *Spectator*, 25 February 1860.

113 *Spectator,* 23 February 1861.
114 *Spectator*, 23 February 1867.
115 *Spectator*, 14 December 1868.
116 *Spectator*, 1 March 1869.
117 *Spectator*, 25 February 1871.
118 *Spectator*, 31 January, 8 October 1873.
119 *Spectator*, 26 February 1859.
120 *Spectator*, 4 March 1862, 25 February 1865, 25 February 1871.
121 HGMI, *Act of Incorporation,* Article 5; *Spectator*, 27 February 1875.
112 *Spectator*, 24 December 1870, 25 February 1871.
123 *Spectator*, 14 December 1855, 24 January 1860, 27 November 1868.
124 *Spectator*, 1 March 1854, 28 February 1858.
125 *Provincialist*, 5 December 1848; *Spectator*, 29 January 1848; 15 March 1851; 2 March 1857; 10, 19 December 1860; 23 October 1873.
126 Palmer, *Culture in Conflict*, 51 makes a similar point.
127 *Spectator*, 4 February 1859.
128 *Times,* 5, 9 February 1866; *Gazette*, 15 December 1853; *Spectator,* 20 November 1855, 23 February 1857, 1, 9 January 1858; 10 February 1860; 24 December 1863; 13 January, 18 February, 22 December 1871; 20, 29 January, 1872; 10, 26 February 1872; 29 July 1872; 16 January, 19 April 1873; 30 April 1875.
129 *Western Mercury*, 29 December 1931.
130 *Western Mercury*, 12 September 1833. Walton, 'Early Provision for Libraries in Hamilton,' 22–3; HPL, Special Collections, HGMI Archives – Miscellaneous-I-C-17A-3, Letter, Roy Woodhouse to Freda Walton, 15 March 1947.
131 *Spectator*, 30 July 1851.
132 *Spectator*, 21 April 1947.
133 McIlwraith, *Diaries,* 226.
134 *Spectator*, 16 February 1850, 15 February 1851.
135 *Times*, 5 February 1866.
136 *Spectator,* 11, 25 January, 12 April 1856; 4 October 1857; 12 April, 4 October 1858; 18 March 1859; 20 September 1867. See Thomas Winter, '"A Wise Investment in Growing Manhood": The YMCA and Workingmen, 1872–1929' (PhD diss., University of Cincinnati, 1994) for a brief description of the North American development of this organization.
137 *Spectator*, 11 November 1867.
138 *Spectator*, 4 February, 26 March 1868; 12 February 1969; 12 December 1870; 29 November 1872; 17 October 1873.
139 *Times*, 14 February 1868; *Spectator*, 26 October 1867, 4 February 1868.

140 *Times*, 25 November 1868, 16 October 1869; *Spectator*, 17 June 1869, 30 November 1872.
141 *Spectator*, 4 October 1858, 12 December 1870, 23 November 1872.
142 McIlwraith, 'Diaries,' 31 May, 4 October, 22 November 1858, 4 January, 14 March, 21 March 1859.
143 *Spectator*, 12 December 1870, 23 November 1872, 17 October 1873.
144 *Spectator*, 6 March 1866.
145 Anna Brownell Jameson, *Winter Studies and Summer Rambles in Canada* (Toronto: McClelland and Stewart, orig. 1838, repr. 1986), 229; Johnson, *Head of the Lake*, 216–17; HGMI, 'Minutebooks,' 10, 17 December 1840; *Provincialist*, 5 December 1848; *Gazette*, 19 December 1853.
146 *Spectator*, 4 November 1857; 4 June 1858; 19 January, 24 February, 8 July 1859; 25 November 1871
147 *Times*, 16 January 1863.
148 *Spectator*, 7, 9 February 1863.
149 *Spectator*, 9 March, 4 May, 8 September 1864.
150 *Spectator*, 6 March 1866. A *City Directory* entry for 1872 confirms this society's continued existence.
151 *Spectator*, 1 March 1870, 20 January 1871, 9 April 1872, 8 October 1873, 1 December 1877.
152 *Spectator*, 4 November 1857; 4 June 1858; 19 January, 24 February, 8 July 1859; 25 November 1871; *Mail and Empire*, 5 November 1934; McIlwraith, *Diaries*, 11, 22 June 1858; HPL Archives, Hamilton Association, *Fiftieth Anniversary of the Hamilton Scientific Association* (1907).
153 HPL, Joseph Tinsely aka 'Jaques' Scrapbooks, 'Hamilton Scientific Association Prepares for its Jubilee,' n.d.; *Fiftieth Anniversary*.
154 *Times*, 16 January 1862; Bruce Sinclair, *Philadelphia's Philosopher Mechanics: The History of the Franklin Institute, 1824–1865* (Baltimore: Johns Hopkins University Press, 1974).
155 *Spectator*, 14 April, 6 May, 9 September 1863.
156 *Spectator*, 9 March, 8 September 1864.
157 *Spectator*, 6 March 1866.
158 *Spectator*, 20 January 1871, 9 April 1872, 8 October 1873.
159 *Dundas Star*, 21 October 1909; *True Banner and Wentworth Chronicle*, 19 July 1883: *DHB* 2, 'McKechnie, Robert,' 106–7; T.W. Acheson, 'The Social Origins of the Canadian Industrial Elite, 1880–1885,' in *Canadian Business History*, ed. D. McMillian (Toronto: McClelland & Stewart, 1972), 155; *Industrial Canada,* March 1905; *Canadian Manufacturer*, 6 July 1888; RCRLC *Ontario Evidence*, 856.

160 Wilson is featured in Samuel Smiles, *Self-Help: With Illustrations of Conduct and Perseverance,* intro. Asa Briggs (London: J. Murray, orig. 1858, repr. 1958), a book that the diaries show McIlwraith himself having obtained. Wilson was also featured in the article 'Great Men Who Rose from the Ranks,' published in the *Spectator*, 16 January 1860.

161 McIlwraith took two separate sojourns to work in the Gartshore Foundry, one from 2 March until 19 June 1858 and another from 13 September 1958 until 12 February 1959. Each time he became almost immediately involved with the DMDC and was elected as its secretary on both occasions. McIlwraith, 'Diaries.'

162 Andrew C. Holman, *A Sense of Their Duty: Middle-Class Formation in Victorian Ontario Towns* (Montreal and Kingston: McGill-Queen's University Press, 2000), 123.

Chapter 7. Transmodal Culture in Apogee: 1872 Revisited

1 Hamilton Public Library (HPL), Archive, Hamilton Typographic Union Papers, Book 1 (hereafter HTU Papers); *Hamilton Gazette,* 4 April 1853; 20 February 1854; *Hamilton Spectator,* 6 April 1853, 11, 13 February 1854; 21 December 1863; 24 August 1867; 22 November 1870; 25 January; 23, 28, 29 February 1872; *Hamilton Times,* 9 September 1862, 7 March 1872; *Hamilton Herald,* 7 November 1903; John Weaver, *Hamilton: An Illustrated History* (Toronto: Lorimer, 1982), 70 and Paul Craven, 'Labour and Management on the Great Western Railway,' in *Labouring Lives: Work and Workers in Nineteenth-Century Ontario*, ed. Craven (Toronto: University of Toronto Press, 1995), 373–8.

2 These strikes included house carpenters and joiners (1853), tailors (1854), Great Western Railway mechanics (1856), factory carpenters (1864), moulders (1864), cigarmakers (1865), moulders (1866), bakers (1869), and puddlers (1870). The 'notable exception' was the 1866 moulders' strike, which lasted at two local foundries, on and off and in limited degree, for upwards of eleven months. See *Hamilton Gazette*, 4, 6 April 1853; 13, 16, 20 February 1854; *Times*, 30, 31 May, 1 June, 8 December 1864; *Spectator*, 11 February 1854; 13 December 1864; 11 November 1865; 2 February 1866; 24, 27 April, 7 May 1869; 11 November 1870.

3 *Hamilton Gazette,* 4 April 1853. The results of this meeting or the strike are unknown.

4 Paul Craven and Tom Traves, 'Dimensions of Paternalism: Discipline and Culture in Canadian Railway Operations in the 1850s,' in *On The*

Job: Confronting the Labour Process in Canada, ed. Craig Heron and Robert Storey (Montreal and Kingston: McGill-Queen's University Press, 1986), 66–7; *Spectator*, 6, 7, 8 November 1856.

5 *Hamilton Times*, 30, 31 May, 1 June 1864.

6 *Spectator*, 23 February 1857, 11 March 1872; *Times*, 30 March, 7 August 1866.

7 *Times*, 30 June, 1, 24 July, 12, 27, 28, 29 August, 5, 9, 10, 12, 13, 15, 16, 17 September 1862; *Spectator*, 15 August, 25 July 1862.

8 HTU Papers, Book I; Hamilton Public Library, Microfilm #121, Richard Butler '*Saturday Musings*,' 3: 94, 201–2, 4: 172; *Spectator*, 6 March 1920.

9 Gary J, Kornblith, 'The Artisanal Response to Capitalist Transformation,' *Journal of the Early Republic* 10 (Fall 1990): 318–20.

10 Kitchener Public Library, 'Andrew McIlwraith Diaries, 1857–1862,' typescript, 29 April, 10 December 1857; 6 January, 1 February, 12 April, 7, 28 May, 4, 11 June 1858 (hereafter McIlwraith, 'Diaries').

11 *Spectator*, 20 May 1922.

12 *Spectator*, 25 November 1855.

13 *Spectator*, 16 May 1861.

14 *Journal of the Board of Arts and Manufactures* (hereafter *JBAM*), 1865.

15 *Spectator*, 9 February 1866.

16 *Spectator*, 22 December 1871.

17 Bryan D. Palmer, *A Culture in Conflict: Skilled Workers and Industrial Capitalism in Hamilton, Ontario, 1860–1914* (Montreal and Kingston: McGill-Queen's University Press, 1979), 99–100; Gregory S. Kealey, *Toronto Workers Respond to Industrial Capitalism, 1867–1892* (Toronto: University of Toronto Press, 1980), 43, 130; Christina Burr, *Spreading the Light: Work and Labour Reform in Late-Nineteenth-Century Toronto* (Toronto: University of Toronto Press, 1999), 19.

18 *Ontario Workman*, 5 September 1872.

19 *Spectator*, 16 August 1872.

20 *City Enterprise*, 23 July 1864.

21 *Spectator*, 9 February 1866.

22 *Spectator*, 10 December 1860.

23 *JBAM*, 1865.

24 *Times*, 5 December 1871.

25 *Spectator*, 9 February 1866; *Times*, 9 February 1866.

26 Harold Logan, *Trade Unions in Canada: Their Development and Functioning* (Toronto: Macmillan, 1948), 38–43; F.W. Watt, 'The National Policy, the Workingman, and Proletarian Ideas in Victorian Canada,' *Canadian Historical Review* 40 (1959): 1–26; Bernard Ostry, 'Conservatives, Liberals and Labour in the 1870s,' *Canadian Historical Review*

41, no. 2 (1960): 93–127; Charles Lipton, *The Trade Union Movement of Canada, 1827–1959* (Toronto: New Canadian Publications, 1967), 28–34; John Battye, 'The Nine Hour Pioneers: The Genesis of the Canadian Labour Movement,' *Labour/Le Travailleur* 4 (1979): 25–56; Kealey, *Toronto Workers*, especially chap. 8; Palmer, *Culture in Conflict,* esp. chap. 5; Bryan D. Palmer, *Working-Class Experience: Rethinking the History of Canadian Labour, 1800–1991* (Toronto: McClelland & Stewart, 1992), 106–8; Craig Heron, *The Canadian Labour Movement: A Short History* (Toronto: Lorimer, 1996), 14–17; Heron, 'Factory Workers,' in ed. Paul Craven *Labouring Lives: Work and Workers in Nineteenth-Century Ontario* (Toronto: University of Toronto Press, 1995), 554; and Craven, 'Labour and Management on the Great Western Railway,' in his *Labouring Lives*, 381–4.

27 Kealey, *Toronto Workers Respond*, 128.

28 Palmer, *Culture in Conflict*, 128, 131.

29 *Spectator*, 20, 22, 23, 24, 26, 28 February 1872. It is also interesting to note that at about the same time the firm granted nine hours it changed its style to Wilson, Lockman & Co. The connection of the elevation of Lockman, the firm's practical machinist, within the partnership and the nine-hours movement can only be speculated upon.

30 Craven, 'Labour amnd Management on the Great Western Railway,' 383.

31 *Spectator*, 13 May 1872.

32 *Spectator*, 19 February, 1 March, 20 May, 15 June 1872.

33 This estimate is based on workforce sizes for these establishments reported on the 1871 Industrial Census.

34 *Spectator*, 11, 13 May 1872.

35 The estimates in this paragraph are based on workforce sizes declared in the 1871 industrial census.

36 These figures are calculated for Wilson, Lockman and Gardner based on the 1871 Industrial Census. The Appleton figure was obtained from *Spectator,* 18 April 1873. The Hespeler figure was estimated conservatively as one-half (100) of the workforce the firm's owners estimated would be employed shortly before their opening in 1871.

37 This estimate is based on the following information. The membership of the IMIU No. 26 is estimated at 447, the aggregate number of male employees listed in Hamilton foundries on the 1871 Industrial Census. It is highly unlikely that all these men and boys were molders who would have marched in this contingent. Wanzer's sewing machine works claimed 275 male employees in 1871. The *Spectator* estimated the number of striking marble cutters at 70. See *Spectator*, 15 May 1872. The relative size of this contingent in the overall parade is based

on the *Ontario Workman's* estimate of the parade at 3000 men and boys.

38 This estimate is based on 1871 Industrial Census and the workforce sizes for the Hespeler Sewing Machine Company and Appleton Knitting Machine Company provided in *Spectator,* 17 October 1871, 18 April 1873.

39 *Mail*, 17 May 1872.

40 *Spectator*, 20, 29 May 1872.

41 *Spectator*, 20, 21, 22 29 May, 3 June 1872; *Ontario Workman*, 30 May 1872.

42 *Spectator*, 2 September 1872.

43 *Ontario Workman*, 9 May 1872.

44 *Ontario Workman*, 13 June 1872.

45 *Ontario Workman*, 13 June 1872.

46 *Ontario Workman*, 9 May 1872.

47 Battye has noted that the first Toronto 'mass meeting' of the Nine Hours Movement was in contrast to those held in Hamilton in the fact that it was composed exclusively of 'workingmen.' But even given this fact, he demonstrates, Hewitt's remarks alluding to the irreconcilably differing interests of capital and labour 'were not representative of those made at the meeting.' See Battye, 'The Nine Hour Pioneers,' 32–3.

48 *Spectator*, 29 January, 23 February 1872.

49 *Spectator*, 26 January 1872.

50 *Spectator*, 11, 22 May 1872.

51 *Spectator*, 24 February 1872.

52 *Spectator*, 29 January 1872.

53 Palmer, *Culture in Conflict*, 133.

54 *Spectator*, 29 January 1872; Thomas Melville Bailey, ed., *Dictionary of Hamilton Biography*, vol. 1, 131–2, 214–15.

55 *Spectator*, 29 January 1872.

56 *Spectator*, 26 February 1872.

57 See Bettina Bradbury, 'The Home as Workplace,' in Craven, *Labouring Lives*, 423–6 for a similar discussion.

58 *Spectator*, 28 November 1856.

59 *Spectator,* 29 January 1872; *Ontario Workman*, 18 April 1872.

60 *Spectator*, 29 January 1872.

61 *Ontario Workman*, 9 May 1872.

62 *Spectator*, 29 January 1872.

63 *Spectator*, 28 November 1856.

64 *Times*, 1 July 1862.

65 *Spectator*, 31 January 1872.

66 *Ontario Workman*, 13 June 1872.
67 *Spectator*, 28 November 1856.
68 *Spectator*, 29 January 1872.
69 *Ontario Workman*, 18 April 1872.
70 *Spectator*, 29 January 1872; *Ontario Workman*, 9 May 1872.
71 Cited in *Spectator*, 31 January 1872.
72 *Spectator*, 29 January 1872.
73 *Spectator*, 31 January 1872.
74 *Spectator*, 26 February 1872.
75 *Spectator*, 29 January 1872.
76 *Spectator*, 26 February 1872.
77 *Spectator*, 31 January 1872.
78 *Spectator*, 29 January 1872.
79 *Ontario Workman*, 13 June 1872.
80 *Ontario Workman*, 18 April 1872.
81 *Ontario Workman*, 23 May 1872.
82 *Ontario Workman*, Special Supplement, 15 May 1872.
83 *Spectator*, 29 January 1872.
84 *Spectator*, 26 January 1872.
85 *Spectator*, 29 January 1872.
86 *Spectator*, 20 February 1872. The above evidence can also be well understood as consistent with the paternal guidance expected of them in the pre-existing mutualistic culture of the crafts world.
87 *Times*, 28 August 1871.
88 *Spectator*, 26 January 1872.
89 *Spectator*, 29 January 1872.
90 Ibid.
91 *Ontario Workman*, Special Supplement. 15 May 1872.
92 *Ontario Workman*, 30 May 1872.
93 *Spectator*, 24 February 1872.
94 *Spectator*, 20 February 1872.
95 *Spectator*, 23 February 1872.
96 *Spectator*, 19 February 1872.
97 *Spectator*, 26 February 1872.
98 *Spectator*, 29 January 1872.
99 *Spectator*, 5 February 1871.
100 *Spectator*, 24 February 1872.
101 *Spectator*, 1 March 1872.
102 *Spectator*, 26 March 1872.
103 *Spectator*, 22 February 1872.
104 *Spectator*, 26 February 1872.
105 *Spectator*, 8 June 1872

106 *Ontario Workman,* Special Supplement, 15 May 1872.

107 Ibid.

108 Ben Forster, *A Conjunction of Interests: Business, Politics, and Tariffs, 1825–1879* (Toronto: University of Toronto Press, 1986), esp. chap. 5; Craig Heron, 'Factory Workers,' in *Labouring Lives: Work and Workers in Nineteenth-Century Ontario*, ed. Paul Craven (Toronto: University of Toronto Press, 1995), 496–7; Gregory S. Kealey, *Toronto Workers Respond to Industrial Capitalism, 1867–1892* (Toronto: University of Toronto Press, 1980), 30–1, 49, 53, 58, 153, 154, 156; and P.B. Waite, *Canada, 1874–1896: Arduous Destiny* (Toronto: McClelland & Stewart, 1971), esp. chap. 5.

109 Forster, *Conjunction of Interests*, 103–7 and chap. 6.

110 Heron, 'Factory Workers,' 496–7.

111 Canada, House of Commons, *Journals* (Ottawa), vol. 8 (1874), app. 3 ('Select Committee Appointed to Enquire Into and Report to the House on the Extent and Condition of the Manufacturing Interests of the Dominion'), 2. This source provides some of the most detailed information on the condition of manufacturing enterprise in Canada in the 1870s. For an equally useful source, see Canada, House of Commons, *Journals* (Ottawa), vol. 10 (1876), app. 3 ('Select Committee on the Causes of the Present Depression of the Manufacturing, Mining, Commercial Shipping, Lumber and Fishing Interests. Report').

112 *Spectator,* 2 December 1873; 2 February, 20 December 1874.

113 *Spectator*, 11 November 1874; Paul Craven. 'Labour and Management on the Great Western Railway,' in his *Labouring Lives*, 365, 366, 385; Forster, *Conjunction of Interests*, 95.

114 For an account of this struggle, see Bryan D. Palmer, *A Culture in Conflict: Skilled Workers and Industrial Capitalism in Hamilton, Ontario, 1860–1914* (Montreal and Kingston: McGill-Queen's University Press, 1979), 80–2.

115 *Spectator*, 3 March 1875; Forster, *Conjunction of Interests*, 100.

116 Forster, *Conjunction of Interests*, 102.

117 Thomas William Acheson, 'The Social Origins of Canadian Industrialism: A Study in the Structure of Entrepreneurship' (PhD diss., University of Toronto, 1971), 195–6.

118 Palmer, *Culture in Conflict*, 17. Between 1871 and 1881 capital invested in local enterprise increased from $1 541 264 to $4 825 500. This was the single largest decennial increase after Confederation and before the U.S. branch plant phenomenon of the decade after 1901.

119 John Weaver, *Hamilton: An Illustrated History* (Toronto: James Lorimer and Company, 1982), 85; Acheson, 'Social Origins,' 194.

120 Canada, Royal Commission on the Relations Between Labour and Capital (hereafter RCRLC), *Report – Evidence, Ontario*, 835.
121 *Spectator*, 10 February 1873.
122 Weaver, *Hamilton*, chap. 3.
123 Joy Parr, *The Gender of Breadwinners: Women, Men and Change in Two Industrial Towns, 1880–1950* (Toronto: University of Toronto Press, 1990), chap. 7.
124 RCRLC, 298. Cited in Palmer, *Culture in Conflict*, 29.
125 See the multi-volume *Dictionary of Hamilton Biography* for copious evidence of the growing business interconnections of these elite groups during the late 1870s and early 1880s.
126 See Gregory S. Kealey and Bryan D. Palmer, *Dreaming of What Might Be: The Knights of Labor in Ontario, 1880–1900* (Toronto: Cambridge University Press, 1982) for what has become the standard interpretation of the Knights of Labor.
127 Ben Forster, 'Finding the Right Size: Markets and Competition in Mid- and Late-Nineteenth-Century Ontario,' in *Patterns of the Past: Interpreting Ontario's History*, ed. Roger Hall, William Westfall and Laurel Sefton MacDowell (Toronto and Oxford: Dundurn Press, 1988), 150–73.
128 For an extensive discussion of these issues as they related to Hamilton, see Craig Heron, 'Working-Class Hamilton, 1895–1930' (PhD diss., Dalhousie University, 1981).

Conclusion

1 Herbert G. Gutman, 'The Reality of the Rags-to-Riches "Myth",' in his *Work, Culture and Society in Industrializing America* (New York: Vintage, 1977), 211–34.
2 Harold Innis, *The Fur Trade in Canada* (Toronto: University of Toronto Press, 1962), 385.
3 Karl Marx, *Capital*, vol. 1 (New York: Penguin, 1990), 930–3, 937. See esp. chap. 33, 'The Modern Theory of Colonization.' My thinking was heavily informed on these issues by Leo Johnson, 'Independent Commodity Production: Mode of Production or Capitalist Class Formation,' *Studies in Political Economy* 6 (1981): 93–112. Other related and important discussions include Jacque Chevalier, 'There Is Nothing Simple 'bout Simple Commodity Production,' *Studies in Political Economy* 7 (Winter 1982): 89–124; Johnson, 'Precapitalist Economic Formations and the Capitalist Labour Market in Canada,' in *Social Stratification: Canada*, ed. James Curtis and William G. Scott (Scarborough, ON: Prentice-Hall, 1979), 89–104; Allan Greer, 'Wage Labour

and the Transition to Capitalism: A Critique of Pentland,' *Labour/Le Travail* 15 (Spring 1985): 7–22; Ernesto Laclau, *Politics and Ideology in Marxist Theory* (London: Verso, 1982), esp. chap. 1; Leo Panich, 'Dependency and Class in Canadian Political Economy' *Studies in Political Economy* 6 (1981): 7–33; and Ray Schmidt, 'Canadian Political Economy: A Critique,' *Studies in Political Economy* 6 (1981): 65–93.

Index

THE CANADIAN SOCIAL HISTORY SERIES

Terry Copp,
The Anatomy of Poverty: The Condition of the Working Class in Montreal, 1897–1929, 1974.
ISBN 0-7710-2252-2

Alison Prentice,
The School Promoters: Education and Social Class in Mid-Nineteenth Century Upper Canada, 1977.
ISBN 0-7710-7181-7

John Herd Thompson,
The Harvests of War: The Prairie West, 1914–1918, 1978.
ISBN 0-7710-8560-5

Joy Parr, Editor,
Childhood and Family in Canadian History, 1982.
ISBN 0-7710-6938-3

Alison Prentice and Susan Mann Trofimenkoff, Editors,
The Neglected Majority: Essays in Canadian Women's History, Volume 2, 1985.
ISBN 0-7710-8583-4

Ruth Roach Pierson,
'They're Still Women After All': The Second World War and Canadian Womanhood, 1986.
ISBN 0-7710-6958-8

Bryan D. Palmer,
The Character of Class Struggle: Essays in Canadian Working Class History, 1850–1985, 1986.
ISBN 0-7710-6946-4

Alan Metcalfe,
Canada Learns to Play: The Emergence of Organized Sport, 1807–1914, 1987.
ISBN 0-7710-5870-5

Marta Danylewycz,
Taking the Veil: An Alternative to Marriage, Motherhood, and Spinsterhood in Quebec, 1840–1920, 1987.
ISBN 0-7710-2550-5

Craig Heron,
Working in Steel: The Early Years in Canada, 1883–1935, 1988.
ISBN 0-7710-4086-5

Wendy Mitchinson and Janice Dickin McGinnis, Editors,
Essays in the History of Canadian Medicine, 1988.
ISBN 0-7710-6063-7

Joan Sangster,
Dreams of Equality: Women on the Canadian Left, 1920–1950, 1989.
ISBN 0-7710-7946-X

Angus McLaren,
Our Own Master Race: Eugenics in Canada, 1885–1945, 1990.
ISBN 0-7710-5544-7

Bruno Ramirez,
On the Move: French-Canadian and Italian Migrants in the North Atlantic Economy, 1860–1914, 1991.
ISBN 0-7710-7283-X

Mariana Valverde,
'The Age of Light, Soap and Water': Moral Reform in English Canada, 1885–1925, 1991.
ISBN 0-7710-8689-X

Bettina Bradbury,
Working Families: Age, Gender, and Daily Survival in Industrializing Montreal, 1993.
ISBN 0-19-541211-7

Andrée Lévesque,
Making and Breaking the Rules: Women in Quebec, 1919–1939, 1994.
ISBN 0-7710-5283-9

Cecilia Danysk,
Hired Hands: Labour and the Development of Prairie Agriculture, 1880–1930, 1995.
ISBN 0-7710-2552-1

Kathryn McPherson,
Bedside Matters: The Transformation of Canadian Nursing, 1900–1990, 1996.
ISBN 978-0-8020-8679-2

Edith Burley,
Servants of the Honourable Company: Work, Discipline, and Conflict in the Hudson's Bay Company, 1770–1870, 1997.
ISBN 0-19-541296-6

Mercedes Steedman,
Angels of the Workplace: Women and the Construction of Gender Relations in the Canadian Clothing Industry, 1890–1940, 1997.
ISBN 0-19-54308-3

Angus McLaren and Arlene Tigar McLaren, *The Bedroom and the State: The Changing Practices and Politics of Contraception and Abortion in Canada, 1880–1997*, 1997.
ISBN 0-19-541318-0

Kathryn McPherson, Cecilia Morgan, and Nancy M. Forestell, Editors, *Gendered Pasts: Historical Essays in Feminity and Masculinity in Canada*, 1999.
ISBN 0-978-0-8020-8690-7

Gillian Creese,
Contracting Masculinity: Gender, Class, and Race in a White-Collar Union, 1944–1994, 1999.
ISBN 0-19-541454-3

Geoffrey Reaume,
Remembrance of Patients Past: Patient Life at the Toronto Hospital for the Insane, 1870–1940, 2000.
ISBN 0-19-541538-8

Miriam Wright,
A Fishery for Modern Times: The State and the Industrialization of the Newfoundland Fishery. 1934–1968, 2001.
ISBN 0-19-541620-1

Judy Fudge and Eric Tucker,
Labour Before the Law: The Regulation of Workers' Collective Action in Canada, 1900–1948, 2001.
ISBN 978-0-8020-3793-0

Mark Moss,
Manliness and Militarism: Educating Young Boys in Ontario for War, 2001.
ISBN 0-19-541594-9

Joan Sangster,
Regulating Girls and Women: Sexuality, Family, and the Law in Ontario 1920–1960, 2001.
ISBN 0-19-541663-5

Reinhold Kramer and Tom Mitchell,
Walk Towards the Gallows: The Tragedy of Hilda Blake, Hanged 1899, 2002.
ISBN 978-0-8020-9542-8

Mark Kristmanson,
Plateaus of Freedom: Nationality, Culture, and State Security in Canada, 1940–1960, 2002.
ISBN 0-19-541866-2

Steve Hewitt,
Riding to the Rescue: The Transformation of the RCMP in Alberta and Saskatchewan, 1914–1939, 2006.
ISBN 978-0-8020-9021-8 (cloth)
ISBN 978-0-8020-4895-0 (paper)

Robert B. Kristofferson,
Craft Capitalism: Craftsworkers and Early Industrialization in Hamilton, Ontario, 1840–1872, 2007.
ISBN 978-0-8020-9127-7 (cloth)
ISBN 978-0-8020-9408-7 (paper)

www.ingramcontent.com/pod-product-compliance
Lightning Source LLC
LaVergne TN
LVHW040757070826
844660LV00025B/1172

* 9 7 8 0 8 0 2 0 9 4 0 8 7 *